MAKING
SAMBA

MAKING SAMBA

A NEW HISTORY OF RACE AND MUSIC IN BRAZIL

Marc A. Hertzman

Duke University Press   Durham and London   2013

© 2013 Duke University Press
All rights reserved
Printed in the United States of America on acid-free paper ∞
Designed by Courtney Leigh Baker
Typeset in Minion Pro by Tseng Information Systems, Inc.
Library of Congress Cataloging-in-Publication Data
Hertzman, Marc A.
Making samba : a new history of race and music in Brazil /
Marc A. Hertzman.
p. cm.
Includes bibliographical references and index.
ISBN 978-0-8223-5415-4 (cloth : alk. paper)
ISBN 978-0-8223-5430-7 (pbk. : alk. paper)
1. Sambas—Brazil—History. 2. Sambas—Social aspects—
Brazil—History. 3. Blacks—Brazil—Music—History.
4. Music and race—Brazil—History. 5. Blacks—
Race identity—Brazil. I. Title.
ML3487.B7H478 2013
781.640981—dc23
2012044745

CONTENTS

A NOTE ABOUT BRAZILIAN TERMINOLOGY, CURRENCY, AND ORTHOGRAPHY

Translating racial labels from Portuguese to English is a challenging task. For example, not all of the terms that Brazilians use to denote some form of African ancestry—*negro, pardo, preto, crioulo, mulato,* to name just a few—have clear parallels in English, and racial labels in any language are as messy, clunky, and potentially problematic as racial categories themselves. In the pages below, I frequently use "black" and "Afro-Brazilian," familiar terms to most U.S. readers and ones with accessible Portuguese equivalents, negro or preto, and *afro-brasileiro,* respectively. But neither English term represents a pristine reproduction of the language used by the men and women discussed here. Many studiously avoided assigning themselves racial labels. Others described themselves as preto, negro, pardo (brown), *mulato* (mulatto),[1] or even crioulo, a derogatory term that one particularly bold musician sought to appropriate and make his own. As much as possible, I have preserved these (and other) labels in direct quotations, and in my own prose I have tried to employ terms that I think strike a balance between Brazilian and U.S. convention: in addition to "black" and "Afro-Brazilian," I use "African-descended," "men and women of color," and so on.[2]

As if race did not present enough linguistic and conceptual dilemmas on its own, music complicates matters even more. This book's focus on Afro-Brazilian musicians reflects their central role in creating *samba* and in the development of Brazil's music market. But their centrality should *not* be taken as an assertion that samba, or any other music, may be accurately described as "black," "white," or any other racial label. As Karl Miller writes, "There is no *a priori* separation of musical expression according to racial or ethnic identity. Music practices are not 'white' or 'black,' 'Mexican' or 'Cajun,' until someone says they are, and even such a declaration opens rather than closes the debate."[3] In this book, I frequently place racialized musical labels (e.g., "black music") in quotation marks, a somewhat cumbersome practice, but one that provides an important reminder that for all their power, racially defined musical genres are, like race itself, socially constructed and often misleading.[4]

Currency

During the period covered in this book, Brazil used three units of currency: the *mil-réis* until 1942, the *cruzeiro* until 1967, and then the *new cruzeiro*. (In the 1980s and 1990s, several new units were adopted. Currently the *real* is the national currency.) The mil-réis, composed of one thousand *réis*, is written 1$000. (Six hundred réis is written $600.) One thousand mil-réis was called a *conto* or a *conto de réis*, denoted as 1:000$000. So, for example, the amount 35 contos, 543 mil-réis, and 250 réis would be written as 35:543$250. When the cruzeiro replaced the mil-réis in 1942, one cruzeiro ($1.00) became the equivalent of what had been one mil-réis (1$000), and one thousand cruzeiros ($1,000.00) the equivalent to one conto (1:000$000). In 1967, one new cruzeiro (NC$1.00) became the equivalent of one thousand cruzeiros.[5] In hopes of consistency and clarity, wherever possible and practical I have provided contextual, cost-of-living figures, many of which are summarized in table 6 in chapter 3, and rough U.S. dollar equivalents.[6]

Orthography

Brazilian Portuguese did not have a single set of orthographic standards during the late nineteenth and early twentieth centuries. For the names of individuals I try to use the spelling that most frequently appeared in the contemporaneous documents that I read. This is, admittedly, an imperfect approach. For example, in the case of Benjamin de Oliveira, whom I discuss especially in chapter 3, most of my information comes from a secondary text published in Brazil in 2007 that employs today's spelling. In the primary sources that I consulted about Oliveira, his name appears as "Benjamim" and "Benjamin." When directly quoting those sources, I preserve the original spelling, whether with an "m" or an "n." (I do the same for place names.) But when I write about Oliveira I have used the 2007 text (and today's convention) to break the tie, so to speak, and therefore I use "Benjamin." For facility in finding references that appear in the notes and the bibliography, I have preserved the original spellings for written and published documents and texts. For proper names of places and all other words not quoted in the original, I hew to today's standards.

ABBREVIATIONS

ABCA
Associação Brasileira de Compositores e Autores

AM-BAN
Acervo de Manuscritos, Biblioteca Alberto Nepomuceno da
Escola de Música da Universidade Federal do Rio de Janeiro

AN
Arquivo Nacional

AUBC
Arquivo UBC

CCB
Clube do Compositor Brasileiro

CEST
A Casa Edison e seu tempo

DIP
Departamento de Imprensa e Propaganda

ESXX
Estatísticas do Século XX

GIFI
Grupo de Identificação de Fundos Internos

MIS
Museu da Imagem e do Som

SBACEM
Sociedade Brasileira de Autores, Compositores e
Editores/Escritores de Música

ACKNOWLEDGMENTS

My wife and I used to joke that before-and-after-book photos of either one of us would look grim: two young, happy scholars turned old and jaded. While we have said this tongue-in-cheek, there is no denying the fact that my project evolved over the course of what is now nearly a third of my lifetime, a period filled with painful moments and beautiful ones. It is thanks to many around me that I can look back and smile on the preceding years.

First due goes to my mentors at the University of Wisconsin–Madison, where I learned how to become a historian. Florencia Mallon advised my dissertation and provided peerless critique, support, and insight. The same is true of Steve Stern, who (along with Florencia) also provided the gift of teaching me how to teach. This book's first seeds were planted during an independent study with Francisco Scarano in 2001, and throughout my career he has been an exceptional (and exceptionally caring) adviser and critic. I was also lucky enough to be formulating this project when Jim Sweet came to Madison. It would be hard to quantify the value of his patience, warmth, and intellectual rigor. And I was blessed to have Ron Radano on my dissertation committee. Like the folks mentioned above, he possesses an uncommon combination of intellectual brilliance and personal warmth.

My research would not have been possible without funding, which was provided by three schools (the University of Wisconsin, Wesleyan University, and Columbia University) and Fulbright-Hays, the Doris Quinn Foundation, and the Andrew W. Mellon Foundation. I would also like to express appreciation to the Warner Fund at the University Seminars at Columbia University for their help in publication. Material in this work was presented to the University Seminar on Brazil.

In Madison I was part of a dynamic group of Latin Americanist graduate students that included Gladys McCormick, Solsi del Moral, Andrés Matías-Ortiz, Molly Todd, Ponciano del Pino Huaman, Tamara Feinstein,

Leo Garofalo, Julie Gibbings, Jaymie Heilman, Jess Kirstein, Gabi Kuenzli, Carrie Ryan, Ana Schaposchnik, Ileana Rodríguez-Silva, Cynthia Milton, and Jeff Sanceri. Severino Albuquerque and Kendra Douglas taught me Portuguese, and I simply don't know how I would have begun this project or my career without Severino. Other great friends and colleagues in Wisconsin include Mike Abelson, Scott Burkhardt, Paloma Celis Carbajal, Cindy Cheng, Nan Enstad, Jim Feldman, Sean D. N. Gillen, Mark Goldberg, Will Jones, Jess Krug, Michel Hogue, Neil Kodesh, Mara Loveman, Dan Magaziner, Leigh Payne, Erika Robb, Lou Roberts, Sarah Robinson, Kathryn Sanchez, Ellen Sapega, Stacey Smith, Luis Villar, and, last but certainly not least, Keith Woodhouse. I am indebted to Iver Bernstein, who advised my undergraduate thesis at Washington University and set me on the path to become a scholar. Henry Berger and Richard Walter played a big role in doing the same, and special thanks go to my friends Richard and Mary Harris at the University of New Mexico for helping me generate and analyze a random sample of criminal documents.

Barbara Weinstein and Sueann Caulfield, both of whose work helped draw me to Brazil in the first place, came to Columbia in 2010 to discuss my manuscript. The hours that they spent reading and critiquing the text were a scholar's dream come true. Barbara has also offered an immense amount of intellectual, professional, and personal advice and support. Paulina Alberto is a great friend and an inspiring scholar. Her comments and critiques, for which I am eternally grateful, transformed my project and my understanding of Brazilian history. Amy Chazkel has been an amazing friend for the entire span of this project. She has taught me too many things and helped me in too many ways to enumerate here. I met James Green during my first year in graduate school, just as I was deciding to focus on Brazil. I cannot thank him enough for his time, guidance, and insights at every stage of this process, and I am forever indebted for the fact that he also introduced me to so many wonderful people in Brazil. I extend a huge "thank you" to Bryan McCann for providing a wealth of important and critical ideas and insights, and for writing a book that paved the way for my own. I owe more thanks than I can express here to Bert Barickman, an enormously generous friend and colleague, who, even during the busiest and most stressful times, offers what seems like an endless supply of advice, critique, knowledge, and kindness. And I owe special thanks to Jeff Lesser, another scholar whose work motivated me to study Brazil and who, among other things, introduced me to the best ramen noodles in São Paulo. I have also benefited from the mentorship, friendship, and insights of George Reid Andrews, Peter Beattie, Dain Borges, Alejandra Bronfman, Bruno Carvalho, John Collins, Beth Cooper, Jerry Dávila, Phil Deloria, Christopher Dunn, Marshall Eakin, Brodie Fischer, John French, Sid Greenfield, Marcelo Hazan, Tom Holloway, Scott Ickes, Wiebke Ipsen (in memoriam), Ryan Kashanipour, Hendrik Kraay, Betsy Kuznesof, Hal Langur, Teresa Meade, Pedro Monteiro, Yuko Miki, Vânia Penha-Lopes, Lara Putnam, Laura Randall, Yonatan Reinberg, Ann Schneider, Stuart Schwartz, Tom Skidmore, Steve Topik, Daryle Williams, Joel Wolfe, and Natan Zeichner. Two anonymous reviewers for Duke University Press provided comments and critiques that helped turn my early drafts into a polished book. That transformation would have been for naught without the care and guidance of my editors, Valerie Millholland and Gisela Fosado, who guided me through the process.

Most of my research for this project took place in Brazil, where I met a number of exceptional people, who helped tear down and then build up this book's foundations. It is painful to acknowledge that three of those individuals, Walter Santos Pinto, Jair do Cavaquinho, and Claudio Camanguelo, are no longer here. Marcos Bretas has been a great adviser and friend. Don Pandeiro and Cida Hessel are remarkable in so many ways. I cannot adequately thank them for all their warmth and generosity. The same goes for Conceição Pinto and her wonderful family. I also am indebted to Heitorzinho dos Prazeres, Guaracy das Sete Cordas, Gilberto Gil, Dodô da Portela, Nelson Sargento, Celso Salustiano, Luís Fernando Vieira, Vanissa Santiago, Sérgio Cabral, Flávio Silva, Roberto Moura, José Ramos Tinhorão, Jairo Severiano, Carlos Sandroni, Katia Borges, Maurício Borges and family, Samuel Araújo, Edmea Jafet, Maria (Conceição) Ferreira, Luiz Fernando Nascimento, Flávio Gomes, Maria Clementina Pereira Cunha, Ronaldo Lemos, Martha Abreu, Olívia Maria Gomes da Cunha, Rachel Soihet, Rodrigo Alzuguir, Sidney Chalhoub, Lygia dos Santos, Alcida Ramos, Margareth Rago, Erika Arantes, and Mariza de Carvalho Soares. William Martins, Giovana Xavier, and Álvaro Nascimento are great intellectuals and great friends. I wish that I could see them every day.

Research would have been impossible without the many individuals who make the archives work. I am especially indebted to Satiro Nunes at the Arquivo Nacional, Anna Naldi and Rutonio at the Biblioteca Nacional, Ádua Nesi and Maria Eugênia Cardoso at the Museu da Imagem e do Som, and a number of individuals at the União Brasileira de Compositores.

As a postdoc at Wesleyan I was buoyed by the friendship and intellectual support of my mentor Gina Ulysse and Robyn Autry, Abbie Clouse, Bo Conn, Fernando Degiovanni, Paul Erickson, Demetrius Eudell, Matt Garrett, Patricia Hill, Kēhaulani Kauanui, James McGuire, Claudia Tatinge Nascimento, William Pinch, Claire Potter, Mark Slobin, Margot Weiss, Ann Wightman, and Leah Wright. Since arriving at Columbia, I have been blessed with exceptional department colleagues: Carlos Alonso, Graciela Montaldo, Jesús Rodríguez-Velasco, Alberto Medina, Patricia Grieve, Gustavo Pérez-Firmat, Alessandra Russo, Joaquín Barriendos, Dale Shuger, Wadda Ríos-Font, Orlando Betancour, Ron Briggs, Maja Horn, José Antonio Castellanos-Pazos, and Ana Paula Huback. I also thank Eunice Rodríguez Ferguson, Jonathan Wolfe, Kosmas Pissakos, Hernán Díaz, Pablo Piccato, Nara Milanich, Chris Brown, John Coatsworth, José Moya, Seth Fein, Caterina Pizzigoni, Sean Knowlton, Ana Maria Ochoa, Natasha Lightfoot, Pablo Pinto, Tom Trebat, Esteban Andrade, Maritza Colón, and Eliza Kwon-Ahn for all their kindness and insights. The same goes for my graduate students at Columbia and the members of my "History of 'Black Music'" seminar at Wesleyan, who offered stimulating engagement with earlier versions of this text.

Portions of chapters 5 and 6 appeared in my article "A Brazilian Counterweight: Music, Intellectual Property, and the African Diaspora in Rio de Janeiro (1910s–1930s)" (*Journal of Latin American Studies* 41, no. 4 [2009]). Portions of chapter 3 are taken and adapted from "Making Music and Masculinity in Vagrancy's Shadow: Race, Wealth, and *Malandragem* in Post-Abolition Rio de Janeiro" (*Hispanic American Historical Review* 90, no. 4 [2010]). I am grateful to Cambridge University Press (*Journal of Latin American Studies*) and Duke University Press (*Hispanic American Historical Review*) for their assistance with both publications.

In a sense, my research career began all the way back when I was eight years old and went to Mesa Public Library in Los Alamos, New Mexico, to dig up microfilm accounts of the St. Louis Cardinals' past glory. The following year (1987), St. Louis went to the World Series, only to lose in heartbreaking fashion. With wonderful circularity, the Cardinals won two championships during the time that it took to complete this study, and I enjoyed both of them in person and over the phone with my uncle and cousin, David and Josh Blasingame. My mother, Jeri Berger Hertzman, took me to the library that day in 1986 and has provided an unquantifiable amount of love and guidance. She taught me how to respect, challenge, and investigate. My father has given me so many things for which I am grateful, especially his insistence that I pursue my passions. His technological wizardry also was extremely handy while preparing the photographs for this book. My sister, Rachel, has been a constant source of intellectual inspiration and a model of courage. I never seem able to express just how much she means to me. Yukihiro and Mayumi Asaka, my parents-in-law, welcomed me into their home and into their family and provided, among many other things, indescribably delicious meals.

It is appropriate that I conclude now with a second mention of my wife, Ikuko Asaka; she has been with this project and in my life through its inception, development, and conclusion. In more ways than one it all begins and ends with her.

INTRODUCTION

In November 1916, a young Afro-Brazilian musician named Donga registered sheet music for the song "Pelo telefone" (On the telephone) at the National Library in Rio de Janeiro. Donga's apparently simple act—claiming ownership of a musical composition—set in motion a series of events that would shake Brazil's cultural landscape. "Pelo telefone" became a smashing success and helped thrust the word "samba" into the center of the entertainment world. Within little more than a decade, samba was synonymous with national music and well on its way to becoming a metonym for all things Brazilian. The song's success also embroiled Donga[1] in controversy. A group of musicians claimed that he had stolen their work, and a prominent journalist accused him of selling out his people for profit and fame.

Nearly a century later, another famous Afro-Brazilian musician, Gilberto Gil, set off a controversy that, at least on the surface, has much in common with Donga's. As minister of culture from 2003 to 2008, Gil publicly embraced Creative Commons, the polemical institution that seeks to loosen copyright restrictions and use the Internet to foster "universal access to research, education, and culture."[2] In 2004, Gil became one of the first musicians in the world to make portions of his work available for free via the Internet, an act he previewed several years earlier in his song "Pela internet," a playful reference to Donga's iconic song.[3]

Gil's actions elicited forceful responses. Fernando Brant, the president of the União Brasileira de Compositores (Union of Brazilian Composers, UBC), a powerful organization whose history is detailed below, was especially vicious. In an angry and wide-ranging opinion piece published in 2007 in *O Globo*, one of Brazil's most influential newspapers, Brant called Gil "the barbarian minister," described his approach to intellectual property rights as anathema to modernity and civilization, and likened him to a slave master *and* a slave. On the one hand, Gil was not different from

Thomas Jefferson, who "attacked slavery in his texts, while keeping two-hundred black slaves under his thumb." On the other hand, Brant derided the minister's speeches as *ladainhas*, orations used in *capoeira*, a combination of dance and martial art pioneered largely by slaves and free persons of color.[4] Remarkably, Brant's column seems almost bland compared to the racist caricature and commentary publicly leveled against Gil in 1988, when he ran for mayor of Salvador, Bahia, and then revived during his time as minister of culture.[5] As it was for Donga nearly a hundred years earlier, Gil's success, dark skin, and provocative approach to intellectual property rights became a recipe for public outrage.

If Donga's and Gil's experiences suggest unsettling similarities between the early twentieth and twenty-first centuries, myriad differences caution against overdrawing the comparison. The Internet, Creative Commons, the rise and fall of Napster, and the larger, growing world of "digital culture" are just a few of the late twentieth-century developments that separate Gil's world from Donga's.[6] And though both men's actions prompted similar reactions, the actions themselves were quite different. Donga came under attack for asserting individual ownership. Gil took fire for just the opposite: promoting the kind of open, shared access to creative production that, according to Brant and others, will obliterate the very rights that Donga sought in 1916.

Though the histories narrated below certainly have much to tell us about current debates, I have resisted the urge to draw a straight, uninterrupted line between 1916 and 2013. Instead, I treat the connections between Donga and Gil as an indication that history often moves in circular fashion, with old problems resurfacing in new contexts and forms. The story told here begins decades before Donga's trip to the National Library (Biblioteca Nacional) during Brazil's preparations for the abolition of slavery (1888) and concludes in the 1970s, when a military dictatorship implemented the system for defending intellectual property rights still in place today.

WHEN DONGA REGISTERED "Pelo telefone," he and the nation stood at a historical crossroads. In 1888, Brazil became the last country in the Western Hemisphere to end slavery. The following year, the nation replaced its monarchy with a republic. Less than three decades removed from these seminal events, Donga's property claims became, intentionally or not, a statement about the related meanings of freedom and the republic, and a crucial moment in a larger trajectory that saw Afro-Brazilian musicians collectively transform themselves from property—slaves rented, sold, and passed on to heirs—into professionals who mediated cultural debates and gained limited access to the fruits of their labor.

As "Pelo telefone" became a hit, Donga drew fire from multiple sides. On the application he submitted to the Biblioteca Nacional, then the clearinghouse for registering original musical and literary works, he identified himself as the composer but gave credit for the lyrics to Mauro de Almeida, a white journalist. He also sought out other white reporters to advertise the song in the press, a common strategy at the time. Both actions reflect the continued importance, years after abolition, of white patronage. On one level, then, "Pelo telefone" provides entrée into the racialized, uneven power relations that persisted in Brazil long after slavery's demise. But "Pelo telefone" also offers a window into less obvious and less studied dynamics internal to Rio de Janeiro's black and mixed-race communities. One of Donga's most vocal and persistent critics was Vagalume (Francisco Guimarães), an influential Afro-Brazilian journalist, who accused Donga of stealing the song from other black musicians and community members. The incident therefore invites discussion not only about persistent racial inequalities, but also about the complex inner workings of Rio's black communities and the intricate, often fraught alliances between whites and blacks.[7]

Donga's property claims also raise interesting questions about race and intellectual property that extend beyond Brazil. While intellectual property has received increased attention in recent years, historians remain behind the curve established in other fields. And though scholars of many disciplines have long been fascinated with the construction of authorship, few have addressed the relationship between intellectual property and postcolonial nation building—especially in the Americas—or the intertwined histories of race, intellectual property, and nation.[8] To explore that relationship and those histories, I place at this book's center Rio de Janeiro's twentieth-century black musical pioneers, a group that defies easy categorization.

Rio de Janeiro and the "Missing Middle"

Many of the challenges that Donga and other black musicians faced were inseparable from slavery and its legacies. But slavery declined earlier and more rapidly in Rio than in most of the rest of Brazil, which meant that a significant number of free people of color incorporated themselves into the city's economic and social fabric sooner and in ways different from those of their counterparts elsewhere. This distinct trajectory helped produce overlapping circles of commerce and sociability, in which blacks and whites had extensive interactions and built important, though rarely equal, relationships.

Like most countries in Latin America, abolition in Brazil followed a series of gradual steps, including the end of the Atlantic slave trade in the early 1850s; the Free Womb Law, which conditionally freed slave children born after September 28, 1871; the 1885 Law of the Sexagenarians, which liberated slaves over the age of sixty; and the 1888 Lei Áurea (Golden Law), which fully abolished slavery. In 1849, approximately 40 percent of Rio's inhabitants were slaves. Twenty years later, that proportion had been cut nearly in half. Between 1872 and 1887, the city's total slave population fell by 85 percent, far outpacing the national average of 52 percent during the same period.[9] A number of forces combined to hasten slavery's decline in Rio. Cholera and yellow fever epidemics during the 1850s struck slaves particularly hard. High death rates and low birthrates among slaves further decimated their ranks. Thousands more were sold to coffee planters, many of whom clung to slavery as the larger institution crumbled around them. Manumission was also crucial. Between 1860 and 1869, nearly thirteen thousand slaves secured "letters of liberty" in Rio, about ten times the number who did the same between 1807 and 1831.[10] In 1872, some seventy-three thousand free people of color—more than a quarter of the city's population—lived in Rio (see table 1). Fifteen years later, months before abolition, there were fewer than seventy-five hundred slaves in the city.[11]

Rio's free people of color found varying degrees of prosperity and stability. Some achieved modest wealth, organized small shops, and even purchased their own slaves. A great many more etched out a fragile existence working as day laborers, peddlers, and itinerant street merchants. "What awaited so many freedpersons," Mary Karasch writes, "was not the golden dream of freedom but rather the nightmare of poverty."[12] Afro-Brazilians lived and worked throughout the city, especially in favelas (shantytowns, also known as *morros*, or hills), the first of which were populated around the turn of the twentieth century; in sprawling, generally impoverished suburban areas (*subúrbios*); and in city neighborhoods such as Cidade Nova (New City), an area that became central to the rise of samba and that was known to some as "Little Africa."[13]

TABLE 1. Estimated Population of the City of Rio de Janeiro (Urban Districts)

	1799* (%)	1849** (%)	1872** (%)
Free people of color	8,812 (20)	13,361 (5)	73,311 (27)
Slaves	14,986 (35)	110,622 (41)	48,939 (18)
Whites	19,578 (45)	144,403 (54)	151,799 (55)
Total	43,376 (100)	268,386 (100)	274,049 (100)

* Urban districts.
** Rural and urban districts.

Sources: Florentino, "Alforrias e etnicidade," 10–11; Klein and Luna, Slavery, 183.

The rise of free populations took place during a time of overall population growth. During the late nineteenth and early twentieth centuries, migrants from across Brazil and abroad flooded into Rio, and the city's population ballooned from 275,000 in 1872 to more than 1 million in 1920. Many new arrivals met harsh conditions. The first two decades of the twentieth century were particularly rough as soaring inflation deteriorated living conditions and helped provoke strikes throughout Brazil. Long after abolition, race marked and divided the labor market and access to means of production. In 1940, more than half a million people of color lived in Rio and among them 86,854 had stable jobs, and only 846 employed their own workers. Put another way, even the most fortunate and well-off citizens of color—those who could count on constant income—were more than one hundred times more likely to have a boss than to be a boss.[14] Even in hard times, black workers and intellectuals across Brazil formed a range of racially and ethnically based organizations, most famously in São Paulo—where a fast-growing black population created a highly visible web of political and social organizations—and Salvador, where an older, equally vibrant community fought to maintain political and cultural spaces. In Rio, blacks controlled important dockworker unions and syndicates and played major roles in strikes and labor mobilizations. Neighborhood homes provided places for socializing, musical composition and performance, and communal worship, often under the guidance of the female religious and community leaders known as tias (aunts). These milieus shaped the lives and careers of Donga and others who would transform Brazil's musical and cultural landscape.

Though some of the individuals discussed below are well known in Brazil, together they represent a spatial and conceptual "missing middle."

The artistic, intellectual, and professional cohorts examined here took shape during a period rarely highlighted by scholars of black Rio. Recent works show that a dynamic relationship existed between the city's overlapping turn-of-the-century working-class and black populations.[15] Others have analyzed the city's explicitly racially conscious cultural and political organizations and movements that formed during the second half of the twentieth century.[16] For all their important insights, these studies leave a gap between the 1910s and the 1940s.[17] This temporal gap is matched by a geographic void between Salvador in the north and São Paulo in the south.[18] While Rio generally receives a disproportionate amount of scholarly attention, the same is not true for the city's black communities, especially in English and especially during the interwar period.[19]

If Rio's interwar black communities represent a "missing middle" sandwiched between periods and places that have drawn greater scholarly attention, the city's African-descendant musicians, many of whom functioned as cultural and economic mediators, occupied a set of rarely explored middle grounds and in-between spaces. For much of the early twentieth century, "musician" was a generally irrelevant professional category.[20] While plenty of people wrote, played, and performed music, few considered it a means for making a living or for securing the protections associated with other work. Though music served a number of essential functions at religious ceremonies, festivals, bars, and communal and private gatherings, it rarely provided a primary source of income. But the precarious, unstable nature of musical labor hardly prevented enterprising artists from scrabbling together livelihoods that more closely resembled that of the city's emerging middle sectors than its poorest classes. In Brazil and elsewhere, it is often assumed that all black musicians are poor and that their poverty is both a source and a sign of musical authenticity. Many of Rio's Afro-Brazilian musical pioneers were, indeed, destitute. Others were not. Many saw their economic livelihoods fluctuate over time. As is so often the case, here single, static definitions of class belie a more fluid and complex reality. Though it would be misleading to describe most of the musicians discussed in these pages as middle class, so too would it be incorrect to define them all as poor. Instead, most occupied a station somewhere in between.[21]

On the one hand, opportunities for limited financial ascension were the product of a unique historical moment and an unprecedented combination of events and forces—a burgeoning worker's movement, a reappraisal of Brazilian racial and national identity, and technological and musical innovations that helped create a lucrative music market. On the other hand, black middle and "middling" groups are found throughout Brazilian history, and the upwardly mobile individuals discussed below may be thought of as both predecessors to and part of a larger national middle sector, which began to form after slavery and took definitive shape between the 1920s and 1950s.[22]

Black musicians in Rio cultivated professional and personal relationships with wealthy whites and did not always forefront color in their public actions or expressions. The city's black communities did not produce an independent black press, nor did they publicly refer to themselves as a "class of color" as often as their counterparts in São Paulo did.[23] While many of the individuals discussed here imagined themselves as conveyors and guardians of African culture, a relatively small number embraced or projected identities or labels associated with the well-studied African "nations" in Salvador.[24] Despite these important differences, it would be misleading to segregate Rio, São Paulo, and Salvador into hermetically sealed spheres. As Paulina Alberto shows, black leaders and thinkers in all three cities engaged in larger debates and struggled against shared, if locally differentiated, challenges.[25] And as Maria Clementina Pereira Cunha, Juliana Barreto Farias, and others remind, many of the migrants who arrived in Rio during the late nineteenth and early twentieth centuries came from Salvador and surrounding areas.[26]

While individuals in Rio rarely had the kind of sustained contact (direct and conceptual) with West Africa that some of their counterparts in Salvador had, they nonetheless found ways to embrace, shape, define, and domesticate "Africa" and to negotiate the terrain between their communities and the city's many overlapping circles of intellectuals, artists, and politicians. One important vehicle for doing so was the city's enormous number of newspapers. The fact that Rio did not develop the kind of black press found in São Paulo may be explained, at least in part, by the fact that Rio's black communities had allies—some white, some black—in mainstream and niche newspapers that neither claimed nor were assigned explicit racial identities. The popular press provided a crucial arena in which musicians advertised their work and engaged with, expanded upon, and rejected the ideas advanced by authors, politicians, playwrights, and journalists. In addition to newspapers, Donga and other black artists used voice, instrument, dress, and financial self-empowerment to further engage with individuals working in fields more commonly recognized as "intellectual."[27] In doing so, they expanded their influence but rarely gained the same kind of recognition often afforded to white artists, writers, and dramaturges.

Culture, Commodity, and Professionalization

By studying the "missing middle" and the related, entangled histories of race, professionalization, and intellectual property in Rio, this book provides an alternative to works that are either overly critical or narrowly celebratory of cultural production and the commodification of music. In his influential study of Brazil's *Movimento Negro* (black movement), Michael Hanchard argues that twentieth-century Afro-Brazilian activism was impeded by a partially self-imposed form of "culturalism," which he defines as "the equation of cultural practices with the material, expressive, artifactual elements of cultural production, and the neglect of normative and political aspects of a cultural process." "Within culturalist politics," Hanchard maintains, "cultural practices operate as ends in themselves rather than as a means to a more comprehensive, heterogeneous set of ethico-political activities. In culturalist practices, Afro-Brazilian and Afro-Diasporic symbols and artifacts become reified and commodified; culture becomes a thing, not a deeply political process."[28]

Hanchard's work, which focuses on post-1945 Brazil, has positively shaped a generation of scholarship, but I strongly disagree with the idea that commodified cultural expressions are by definition bereft of deeper political meaning. The history of Brazil's early music market, the struggles and successes of Afro-Brazilian entrepreneurs within it, and the explicit attempts by those entrepreneurs to commodify culture suggest the limits of Hanchard's dismissive treatment of "culturalist" practices. My views here also depart from those of Bryan McCann, whose work has greatly shaped my own. Citing Eric Hobsbawm, McCann emphasizes the fact that most Brazilian musicians "were professionals, or aspired to be professionals." I fully agree, but I do not necessarily share what McCann calls his own "optimistic interpretation of the commercial nature of Brazilian popular music." Nor do I agree that by the mid-1930s "isolation was impossible" for most musicians.[29] The act of turning cultural symbols into palpable property was a deeply meaningful process, albeit one fraught with tension and unevenness. While commodification, commercialization, and professionalization did not necessarily reduce political meaning, those processes did frequently elevate a single individual or group into a position of privilege and power. Doing so helped create new gatekeepers, strengthen the power of old ones, and involve musicians in their own policing.

Between the 1910s and the 1940s, Rio became home to the nation's first organizations dedicated to defending theater artists' and musicians' intellectual property rights, referred to in Brazil as author's rights (Direito Autoral or Direitos Autorais). The new associations were officially designated as *utilidades públicas* (public utilities or entities), a label that situated them awkwardly within Brazil's burgeoning corporatist structure. The state, which had few obligations to the utilidades, successfully enrolled them to take on the onerous, though potentially lucrative, tasks of tracking, collecting, and distributing author's rights payments (royalties). The associations, in turn, presented a series of choices and dilemmas for Rio's black artists. On the one hand, they could provide institutional support, professional visibility, and musicians' best hopes for collecting money for their artistic and intellectual creations. On the other hand, the organizations were dominated by whites and often unable to deliver on promises of equitable distribution and support. Ultimately, the system put in place to defend intellectual property rights favored a small cadre of well-connected, enterprising white individuals. That system also effectively bound musicians to the state and formally combined author's rights defense and censorship within a single legislative and institutional package. While some Afro-Brazilian artists thrived within them, the author's rights associations helped subsume Rio's black musicians within a broader, interracial entertainment sector. And though that larger group often depicted itself as inclusive and egalitarian, persistent internal hierarchies and stereotypes about authorship, creative genius, and race helped marginalize Afro-Brazilian entrepreneurs and composers. Meanwhile, easily consumable, one-dimensional caricatures of authentic, spiritual, emotive black musicians flourished.

hey look more racism oh boy

‖

Scholarly Influences

My understanding of these projects and processes has been influenced by a number of scholars, several of whom deserve short mention here to provide readers with a sense of my conceptual orientation. In 1999, a year before I entered graduate school, *Hispanic American Historical Review* published a seminal forum about Latin America's "new" cultural history. In one essay, Eric Van Young wrote, "Cultural history and economic history, though most often thought separate from each other, or even antithetical, because of epistemological, methodological, or boundary distinctions, may usefully be united to the benefit of each."[30] In that unifying spirit, I attempt to connect in my work subjects that are still often artificially segregated from one another: "hard" history—politics, economics, quantifiable data—and the supposedly "softer" concerns of culture, discourse, and, in this case, music, racial ideology, gender, and the process of turning something abstract (a song) into legal property.

I have also profited from a handful of texts that discuss, in diverse settings, the related issues of power, race, and culture. Michel Foucault's delineation of the ancillary and hidden pathways through which discipline, surveillance, and power often flow has been fundamental, and the works of Peter Wade, Homi Bhabha, and Thomas Abercrombie have helped me apply some of Foucault's insights to the unique realities of postcolonial, postslavery Brazil.[31] In his study of Colombian *costeño* music, Wade applies Bhabha's "ambivalent slide" concept—the process of "ideology sliding ambivalently from one enunciatory position to another"—to illustrate how Colombian elites alternately embraced and rejected popular "black" musical forms during the twentieth century. Like many of their counterparts in Colombia, Brazil's black musicians were tugged and pulled by a public that both adored and scorned them. While Bhabha and Wade provide great insights about elite ideology, they leave less explored the roles and experiences of others situated lower on the social ladder. Rather than counter their works with a history narrated exclusively "from below," I try to connect actors, events, discourses, experiences, and stories from across the social spectrum.

The strategies and identities that Afro-Brazilian musicians deployed were diverse, complex, and sometimes at odds with approaches that they embraced on separate occasions. Despite this complexity and diversity, and despite internal hierarchies among them, those musicians have almost invariably been reduced to one-dimensional symbols. That reduction resembles a parallel process that occurred in a dramatically different context, described by Abercrombie. In Bolivia, rural Aymara people strategically combined Spanish colonial ideals with their own by defining themselves as "civilized sons of Christ" and "their pre-Columbian ancestors as the defeated satanic race of a prehuman age." To remain connected but also superior to those ancestors, they worshiped underworld deities, which functioned as a source of potency now properly domesticated by Christian powers. Over time, the Aymara separation of savage and civilized was itself appropriated and distorted by urban Bolivians, who viewed native rural people "through a sort of cultural pidgin." That pidgin, Abercrombie shows, flattened the temporally and spatially dynamic Aymara worlds into one dimension: "Prevailing urban notions romanticize Indians, stripping them of their complex understandings of history and power relations and projecting them as living fossils . . . thus taking a version of one-half of [their] own ambivalent identity sources for the whole."[32]

Afro-Brazilian musicians also ordered themselves and their history into hierarchical spheres and strategically claimed connection to both a civilized, modern present and a distant primordial past. Their complex renderings were in turn often collapsed and read by others in one-dimensional terms. As both subjects and architects, Rio's black musicians were squeezed into rigid categorical boxes but also found ways to shape and make use of the labels, assumptions, and myths attached to samba, race, gender, authorship, and "Brazilianness" (brasilidade). The full range and results of their actions are fully visible only when stale divisions among economics, politics, and culture are cast aside, and only when viewed through lenses trained simultaneously on the diverse forms of self-policing and racial domination described by Foucault, Bhabha, and Wade and the kind of unexpected and resourceful modes of resistance and self-identification employed by the Aymara.

The Outline of This Book

The various processes and developments considered here created a rich, often conflictual array of images and ideas, evident in the photograph that adorns the paperback cover of this book. Like many bands at the time, the one in the photo incorporated the word "jazz" in its name. Yet, as we will see, on other occasions some of the same musicians adopted a dramatically different style by dressing in rural costumes and exchanging saxophones for stringed instruments. One of the group's leaders, Pixinguinha (standing tall at the center of the frame, with saxophone in hand), would choose neither samba nor jazz to describe his greatest works. The many musical hats that he and others wore are a testament to the fluid nature of musical genres and are indicative of the many complex and even seemingly contradictory components that went into "making samba."[33]

During the nineteenth century, long before Donga registered "Pelo telefone," samba was a somewhat obscure term that referred to a number of different cultural and musical manifestations. The first known printed reference to samba appeared in 1838 in northeastern Brazil, but it was not until 1917, with the success of "Pelo telefone," that the term began to embed itself in the music market and the broader public conscience. According to Flávio Silva's meticulous count, the term appeared in Rio de Janeiro newspapers three times during Carnival in 1916, twenty-two times in 1917 (not counting specific references to "Pelo telefone"), and thirty-seven times in 1918. Between 1917 and 1921, "samba" came to mean almost any "successful Carnival music."[34] As Carlos Sandroni shows, increased use of the word did not perfectly coincide with musical distinctiveness. "Pelo telefone" hewed closely to earlier musical patterns that were popular in Brazil and throughout the Americas during the nineteenth and early twentieth centuries. It was not until the late 1920s and early '30s that musicians in Rio would develop a unique rhythmic paradigm, which came to define the music during its so-called golden age (ca. 1929 to 1945).[35]

Samba's rise overlapped with monumental political changes. During the first four decades after abolition and the declaration of the republic, entrenched powers in the state of Rio de Janeiro, São Paulo, and Minas Gerais dominated national politics. In 1930, Getúlio Vargas seized the presidency, which he held until 1945 and then, after being elected, served again from 1951 to 1954. In 1964, ten years after the end of Vargas's influential reign, the military installed a dictatorship that ruled Brazil for the next two decades.

Considering a longer arc that begins well before samba became a unified, recognizable genre and that stretches across abolition, the age of Vargas, and into the 1970s, provides a unique view of the full life spans of Donga and other influential artists whose careers intersected with and helped shape historic transformations in Brazil. The development of samba, Brazil's twentieth-century music market, and intellectual property law advanced alongside the gradual evolution (and, eventually, the withering critique) of the idea that Brazil was a unique "racial democracy": a place where black, white, and indigenous peoples mixed peacefully. Scholars have long exposed the myths of racial democracy, and in recent years attention has turned to understanding *how* and *why* the idea gained, and in many ways still continues to hold, validity and strength.[36] I provide my own interpretation of the "how" and the "why" through a narrative that unfolds in chronological order but also regularly backtracks and retraces its steps to account for multiple and distinct timelines.

Chapter 1 describes the social and economic worlds inhabited by nineteenth-century musicians, a fundamental starting point for understanding the subsequent trajectory of popular music, the music market, and intellectual property rights. Foreign travelers and Brazilian authorities and elites looked upon black and mixed-race musicians with a mix of fear and fascination. Meanwhile, those musicians carved various niches in Rio's urban landscape. Some played for the royal court and at popular celebrations. Others worked as jack-of-all-trades barber-musicians. Though some slave musicians were able to secure a portion of their earnings, they were, by and large, viewed as fonts—not possessors—of wealth. This paradox of slavery, which made blacks sources but not holders of capital, shaped the bases upon which Afro-Brazilian musicians built careers during the late nineteenth and early twentieth centuries.

Any history of samba inevitably must engage with a well-known but rarely researched origins narrative that I call the "punishment paradigm": the widely accepted idea that samba music was violently suppressed and systematically marginalized before it became a symbol of national identity. To make sense of and ultimately move beyond the punishment paradigm, I place music in a larger framework of policing and social control. After abolition, lawmakers employed anti-vagrancy measures meant to establish and maintain economic and social order. Chapter 2 uses a sample of four hundred vagrancy cases and dozens of individually selected police records to show that Rio's authorities were less concerned with music than they were with more lucrative "vices," especially gambling and prostitution. Chapter 2 also describes the formal and informal markets attached to Carnival and discusses instances in which the police mediated between rival Carnival groups, a role that contrasts with standard depictions of adversarial musician-police relationships. When music is placed more precisely within the larger contexts discussed in chapter 2 it becomes clear that Rio de Janeiro's police had less interest in repressing music than in asserting control through economic means. My reinterpretation of the punishment paradigm and samba's origins also suggests that the paradigm itself helped erase female contributions to the formation and elevation of samba.

Around the same time that police were enforcing anti-vagrancy laws, advances in sonic technology dramatically transformed the consumption and production of music in Brazil. Chapter 3 discusses Rio's early music market, turn-of-the-century Brazilian intellectual property law, and the opportunities and challenges attached to each. After slavery, popular entertainment served as Brazil's most visible and public stage for black men. In pursuing fame, fortune, and musical property rights they were often held under the microscope by audiences and critics struggling to define the contours of post-abolition, republican Brazil. Related struggles surrounded the controversial debut of "Pelo telefone," the entry point for chapter 4, which also explores the rise and success of the Oito Batutas, a band that Donga helped organize. (A later iteration of the group, without Donga, appears on the cover of this book.) The stories of "Pelo telefone" and the Oito Batutas show how palpable legal claims like Donga's were often intimately tied to less formal, symbolic forms of property. As the actions of samba musicians (*sambistas*), audiences, and critics make clear, "owning" Brazil and its music was often as much a discursive project meant to secure a place within the nation as it was a contest to seize legal control of musical commodities.

Struggles over both legal and discursive forms of property helped create and exacerbate divisions and hierarchies within musician cohorts. Chapter 5 describes how Rio's Afro-Brazilian musicians engaged with journalists to promote personal and group interests and to secure a foothold in an expanding entertainment world. As cultural and financial mediators, musicians were able to secure new spaces for themselves and their allies. But success often came at the expense of others, especially female artists of color. In chapter 6, we see how the lives and careers of black musicians were shaped and often circumscribed by competing projects to define Brazil, its music, and its racial order. White writers, scholars, musicians, and critics' attempts to order the past and present often linked up in surprising ways with more formal state-driven projects to control vagrancy, surveil black masculinity, and establish the desired economic order. Meanwhile, Afro-Brazilian musicians and intellectuals put forth their own categories and definitions, some of which lined up in surprising ways with those advanced by their white counterparts.

As Rio's black musicians were forming cohorts and building careers, a larger entertainment class was taking shape, spurred largely by the 1917 creation of Brazil's first author's rights association, the Sociedade Brasileira de Autores Teatrais (Society of Brazilian Theater Authors, SBAT), a group dominated by white playwrights and theater musicians.[37] The little-known story of the SBAT, told in chapter 7, is crucial to understanding intellectual property law, the professionalization of popular music, and the crystallization of internal hierarchies within the entertainment world. The SBAT also provides a unique opportunity to explore the origins of proto-corporatist and corporatist structures that eventually bound musicians and other Brazilian workers awkwardly but firmly to the state. Chapter 8 discusses the rise of the UBC, the institution that Fernando Brant eventually came to lead and Brazil's first and most powerful musician-centered author's rights society. Formed by disaffected members of the SBAT, the UBC helped usher in and control an era of great wealth in the music industry. But as money poured in, the disparity between haves and have-nots within the industry grew. Tied to the state and dominated by record executives, the UBC ultimately could not deliver on all of its promises.

The narrative closes in chapter 9 with a brief discussion of the post–golden age era, when Donga and several other influential black musicians dramatically reinvented themselves and found their way back into the national spotlight, often by embracing identities that hardly resembled those crafted decades earlier. To fully understand and appreciate those transformations and to trace the long, winding path from "Pelo telefone" to "Pela internet," we will begin in the nineteenth century, when slavery ruled and when samba was still an obscure, little-known term.

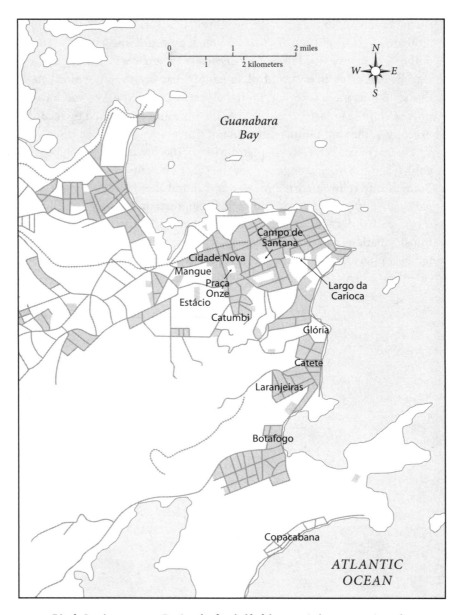

MAP 1. Rio de Janeiro, ca. 1890. During the first half of the twentieth century, Rio underwent dramatic physical transformations—the construction of a new port, the razing of low-rent tenements and entire hills to construct "modern" boulevards, and landfills that changed the city's shorelines. The map depicted here therefore represents only an approximate snapshot of the city at the end of the nineteenth century. Nonetheless, the neighborhoods and landmarks provide a general orientation. I am grateful to Bruno Carvalho and Bert Barickman for their assistance in preparing this map.

1

BETWEEN FASCINATION AND FEAR

Musicians' Worlds in Nineteenth-Century Rio de Janeiro

During the colonial (1500–1822) and imperial (1822–89) eras, myriad sounds filled the streets of Rio, the colonial and national capital from 1763 to 1960. Vendors hawked their wares. People conversed in Yoruba, Kikongo, and Kimbundu and played music on European, African, American, and newly improvised instruments. Passersby could expect to hear the sounds of slaves keeping rhythm on drums and rattles, or clapping and singing as they trudged through the city bearing enormous loads of cargo on their backs, shoulders, and heads. The adventuresome, unimpeded paths traveled by those sounds contrasted with the strict codes of conduct that governed the street as well as the home. Some slaves were required to bow or kneel while kissing their master's hand each morning. Outside, etiquette demanded that they cede the walkway to oncoming whites and forbade them from returning blows leveled against them by whites. The city's social hierarchy was marked by dress, hairstyles, and jewelry. Owners often draped their slaves in fine clothing as a display of their own status. Place of residence and consumption practices also helped define social standing. Private music lessons were among the most obvious signs of privilege.

In 1845, a Christian missionary from the United States commented on what he saw and heard in Brazil. "Music has a powerful effect in exhilarating the spirits of the negro, and certainly no one should deny him the privilege of softening his hard lot by producing the harmony of sounds, which are sweet to him, however uncouth to other ears." "It is said," he continued, "that an attempt was at one time made to secure greater quiet-

that they could

ness in the streets by forbidding the negroes to sing." The attempted prohibition ultimately failed when slaves ceased working in protest. The
sounds of the street remained etched in the missionary's mind. "The
impression made upon the stranger by the mingled sound of a hundred
voices falling upon his ear at once, is not soon forgotten."[1]

Passing through Rio, Thomas Ewbank, a U.S. diplomat, noted how
music shaped the workday. There is a "general use," he wrote, of "a species
of melody, regularly executed, morning, noon, and night," which called
slaves to work and signaled the end of the day.[2] The sounds that filled Rio's
streets often blurred the lines between Europe, Africa, and the Americas.
As slaves learned to play European instruments, they often added their
own interpretation. Some were said to apply "African imagination" to
the seemingly dull task of ringing church bells. Travelers observed slaves
humming or whistling the latest songs from Europe and noted their mas-
tery of religious songs with Latin lyrics and of other intricate vocal pieces.
Musicians performed on Afro-Brazilian feast days, in elite concert halls,
and in the confines of wealthy private residences. An observer estimated
that one-third of the members of the orchestra at Rio's opera house were
of African descent. Well-to-do *cariocas* (people or things from Rio) competed to bring the best black and mixed-race musicians into their homes
for private concerts.

The number of instruments on which music was played matched the
variety of sounds floating through Rio's streets.[3] But no instrument drew
more attention or elicited more fear among travelers and elites than the
drum. Drums of various shapes and sizes were prominent at the massive gatherings that took place every Sunday at the Campo de Santana,
a square where as many as two thousand slaves regularly congregated.[4]
Tolerance for such manifestations fluctuated over time. Before abolition,
authorities regulated and often forbade large slave gatherings, especially
those with music. In 1817, dances held by the Nossa Senhora do Rosário
brotherhood at the Campo de Santana were prohibited. In 1833, a justice
of the peace sought to prohibit slaves from playing drums by arguing that
the noise attracted slaves from neighboring plantations. In 1849, the police
broke up a group of more than two hundred slaves performing *batuque*,
a broad term used to describe drum circles and various drum-based performances. In response to repressive measures, slaves played drums surreptitiously and employed other percussion instruments—scraps of iron,
pottery, seashells, stones, wood—or simply created rhythms by clapping
their hands.[5]   *welp.*

Prohibitions against drum circles and other musical manifestations were tied to fears of slave revolts and marked by confusion about how and where to draw the line between legitimate music and illicit religious devotion. An 1835 uprising of Malê slaves in Bahia stoked fears sparked earlier by the Haitian Revolution, and it sent shocks of panic through Brazil's slave-owning circles.[6] The fact that many African-derived religious rites involved musical accompaniment made it difficult for outsiders to distinguish between entertainment and what elites deemed to be savagery or subversion. As part of larger measures to prevent slave rebellions during the 1830s and 1840s various towns and provinces prohibited slave carnivals and certain religious practices.[7] Popular perceptions that linked blackness, music, and *feitiçaria*, a broad term used to refer to "witchcraft" and "devil worship," endured long after those laws expired or ceased to be enforced.[8]

As did local elites, travelers looked upon slave music and religion with a combination of fascination and fear. Ewbank described a file of furniture-porting slaves. "While looking on, a yell and hurlement burst forth that made me start as if the shrieks were actually from Tartarus. From dark spirits they really came. . . . Chanting only at intervals, they passed the lower part of the Cattete in silence, and then struck up the Angola warble that surprised me."[9] The performance of a band of black musicians produced similar consternation in the French artist and traveler Jean-Baptiste Debret. The combination of instruments (clarinets, a triangle, a horn, and two types of African drums) and a repertoire that included waltzes, marches, and *lundus* created what Debret called a "horrible racket produced by shrill and out-of-tune music." "That unexpressable 'imbroglio' of style and harmony," he continued, "irritates the nervous system with its revolting barbarism [and] imprints a feeling of terror in the heart of man, even a well-disposed one."[10]

The massive gathering he witnessed at the Campo de Santana tantalized Briton J. P. Robertson. "If slavery were not to be seen in any other form than the one in which it was exhibited to me there," he wrote, "I should be forced to conclude that, of the many conditions in the world, that of the African slave is one of the most happy." In the performance he found "a singular spectacle of African hilarity, uproar, and confusion, as is not perhaps to be witnessed, on the same extensive scale, in any other country out of Africa itself." Robertson was particularly intrigued by the elaborate dress worn by many of the participants. Their suits and hats contrasted the "almost naked" black workers he saw elsewhere. Ultimately, it was the performers' bodily displays that most fascinated him. To the furious sounds of rattles and drums, "eight or ten figurantes were moving to and fro, in the midst of the circle, in a way to exhibit the human frame divine under every conceivable variety of contortion and gesticulation." Some participants "seemed wrapped in all the furor of demons." The frenzy continued until nightfall, when participants collapsed in a sweaty, exhausted heap:

> Every looker-on participated in the sibylline spirit which animated the dancers and musicians; the welking rang with the wild enthusiasm of the negro clans; till thousands of voices, accompanied by the whole music on the field, closed in a scene of jubilee which had continued nearly all day, under the burning rays of a tropical sun, and which had been supported by such bodily exertions on the part of the several performers, as bathed their frames in one continual torrent of perspiration.[11]

Robertson's fascination with sounds and bodies is indicative of a larger obsession with the physicality of race, prominently on display in the pages of nineteenth-century Latin American travel writings, which commonly included descriptions of local flora and fauna alongside intricate and sensational illustrations and descriptions of body shape, piercings, and markings of "savage" African and American peoples. His observations also resonated with long-standing tropes linking blackness, Africa, musicality, and rhythm.[12] As was true elsewhere, in Brazil the mix of fear and fascination expressed by travelers like Robertson dovetailed with definitions of race and music already centuries in the making and which would remain in place for many years to come.

The Tangled Roots of Lundu

Brazil's vast area and regional power cleavages hindered full cultural or political cohesion, but that did not prevent observers (domestic and foreign) from treating single musical genres as representatives of the entire colony or nation.[13] One such genre, which in fact can refer to a dance and several styles of music, was lundu. Lundu (also often *lundum, landu, londu,* etc.) is often referred to as Brazil's first black or African national music. The word apparently derives from *calundu,* a Central African healing ritual featuring drums, scrapers, and a circle of adherents surrounding one or two leaders.[14] Many of calundu's characteristic elements — collec-

tive gatherings, spirit possession, curing, percussive music, and dance—
are also found in various Afro-Brazilian religions.[15] The calundu that was
practiced in Brazil through the early eighteenth century closely resembled
rituals performed at the same time in Central Africa, the region of origin for the vast majority of slaves who were brought to Brazil during the
seventeenth century. During the first two decades of the eighteenth century, the influx of slaves from the Bight of Benin brought new rituals,
though few Luso-Brazilian observers distinguished one African practice
from another. By the turn of the nineteenth century, calundu had become
a generic term, at least among Luso-Brazilians, who used it to describe
multiple rituals. Among the various forms of lundu dance (*lundu-dança*)
performed in Portugal and Brazil, several basic characteristics stand out:
a circle of participants and musicians, two individuals dancing in the
middle of the circle, arms raised and moving, feet stamping the ground.
The partners probably began and ended their performances by touching
bellies with *umbigadas*, or belly blows.[16] The first known written mention
of lundu as a dance, penned in 1780, suggests that it was executed at least
on occasion by whites and pardos, and this description distinguishes it
from fully African practices.[17]

Domingos Caldas Barbosa (ca. 1738–1800), the son of a white man
and an Angolan woman, is credited with popularizing lundu salon music
(*lundu-canção*), a genre distinct from both calundu healing rituals and
lundu-dança. Barbosa, who spent the last thirty years of life in Lisbon,
played a crucial role in securing visibility for Brazilian music abroad.
Though long recognized as the creator of lundu-canção, the vast majority
of the works credited to him were labeled lundus only after his death, and
there are some doubts about whether he actually composed music or just
wrote poetry set to music by others.[18] Regardless, Barbosa certainly wrote
about the dance "lundum" and was influenced by what he saw and heard
at popular gatherings in Brazil, where revelers danced lundu. But a distinct musical genre of the same name does not appear to have congealed
until the early 1800s, after Barbosa's death. In Portugal, Barbosa and Portuguese artists developed lyrics and music that either referenced lundu-
dança or was meant to accompany it. By around the middle of the nineteenth century, Brazilians had embraced lundu-canção on a large scale,
but the definition of "lundu" remained elastic, referring to both a circle
dance rooted in a form of calundu and music played in posh salons. By
the turn of the twentieth century, this latter form of lundu-canção was
closely associated with an evolving Brazilian national identity. But refer-

ences to calundu and lundu-dança lived on in the lyrics and music of lundu-canção, as did circle dances, which were still practiced especially in rural areas.

Despite the tangled relationships among calundu the Central African healing ritual, calundu the later generic term for various African ceremonies, and lundu-canção and lundu-dança, twentieth-century observers often used "lundu" as a generic umbrella term to emphasize direct African origins. In 1944, the famous writer and music scholar Mário de Andrade described lundu as "the first Afro-black musical form to be disseminated among all classes of Brazilians and become a 'national' music."[19] A more recent study suggests, "Lundu arose in the early eighteenth century from the music of Bantu slaves."[20] Another states that the music was "probably originally developed by Angolan slaves."[21] Scholars who locate lundu-canção entirely within African and Afro-Brazilian traditions often fail to distinguish between the dance and the music. They also often treat syncopation, an often racialized term, as a sign of lundu's African origins. In the simplest terms, syncopation may be described as a surprising pause or rhythmic dislocation. Though syncopation is found in all kinds of music, it is frequently (and narrowly) associated with "black" or "African" forms.[22]

Carlos Sandroni challenges the simple equation of blackness and syncopation by showing how white, formally trained musicians in nineteenth-century Brazil often sought to infuse their music with what they considered to be African characteristics. They did so somewhat awkwardly, unable to perfectly reproduce the sounds that they associated with Africa and Afro-Brazilians. As a result, parts of their music seem out of place or irregular: in a word, syncopated. The syncopations of most nineteenth-century Brazilian lundus, Sandroni shows, are not the expressions of Africa they are often taken to be and instead are products of a rough collision of European, African, and American influences.[23] Nineteenth-century salon lundus, Sandroni writes, were

> composed by professionals . . . [who] employed syncopations the way that white actors painted themselves black: the musical dialectic of bourgeois lundu [was] "marked," like a country accent . . . syncopations were applied enthusiastically, as a characteristic ingredient and an imitation of what would have been, to white ears of the day, musical "negritude."[24]

"Musical blackface" was complemented in salon lundu with lyrical caricatures of slave life. Black protagonists depicted in song spoke with a lisp, mispronounced words, and were otherwise depicted as hapless, happy-go-lucky stooges. Male characters danced, made jokes, and entertained their white masters. As they did elsewhere in the Atlantic world, white performers in Brazil donned black paint to sing about slave life.[25] Dark-skinned women danced and entertained in the worlds conjured in lundu lyrics, often serving as examples of black lasciviousness or as objects of male desire. While lundu made few direct musical contributions to twentieth-century samba, its legacy was far-reaching in other ways. As we will see, samba, like lundu, was shaped by multiple groups and individuals but is often defined simply as black, its complex history reduced to essentialized, oversimplified terms and origin stories.

State Patronage and the "Civilizing Mission"

In 1808, the Portuguese royal court, fleeing Napoleon, arrived in Brazil and lifted bans on cultural institutions such as the printing press. After the court's arrival, prince regent Dom João, later King Dom João VI, welcomed in "refined" literature, science, and music from Europe. Dom João VI, his son Pedro I, and his grandson Pedro II all nurtured personal interest in the arts and enthusiastically courted experts from abroad to help cultivate a "native" culture, which would be acceptably sophisticated and also uniquely Brazilian. Most funding went to literature, painting, and the sciences, but music was by no means ignored.[26] One author describes Dom João's reign in Brazil (1808–21) as a "musical orgy" and his return to Portugal a "disaster for music in Brazil."[27] Pedro I and Pedro II both studied musical theory and played and wrote music. João VI encouraged musical instruction for slaves, many of whom sang in church choirs. He also built a musical program in the Capela Real (Royal Chapel). An autonomous musical conservatory, the Conservatório de Música, was established in 1841.

Pedro I shared his father's passion for the arts, but lack of money prevented him from extending the kind of patronage that marked João VI's time in Brazil.[28] In 1831, Pedro I returned to Portugal, leaving the kingdom to a regency and his young son, Pedro II. Though state support for music waned in the aftermath of Pedro I's abdication, in 1838 the regency helped found the Instituto Histórico e Geográfico Brasileiro (Institute of

Brazilian History and Geography), a body fashioned after European institutions but meant to foster national intellectual production. The institute became a center of activity and patronage for Brazilian Romantic artists and writers. Even when state patronage ebbed, the circulation of music increased, especially after 1834, when the Frenchman Pierre Laforge arrived in Rio and initiated the process of printing, labeling, and distributing Brazilian musical compositions.[29] Pedro II allotted money to fund prizes for his favorite artists, writers, and composers.[30] Cultural patronage was crucial to both the image of an "enlightened monarchy" and the desire for a unified Brazilian culture.[31] Favored artists enjoyed financial support and symbolic capital.[32] The Crown's approval guaranteed opportunities and respect in elite circles, though political tastes and alliances forced a number of accomplished, formally trained artists to maintain careers without state assistance.

Royal patronage was a crucial piece of what Jeffrey Needell calls the Crown's "civilizing mission," which intended to bring European culture to Brazil's masses.[33] Pedro II was an opera enthusiast, and in 1857 he created the Imperial Academy of Music and the National Opera.[34] In the 1850s and 1860s, Romantic writers received royal support to produce works that combined "European norms with original aspects of Brazilian culture."[35] That process produced, among other things, caricatured depictions of indigenous people, whom writers and artists treated as symbols of Brazil's unique racial character. Images portraying natives as exotic, mysterious, and noble became part of an origins narrative that depicted Brazil as the product of indigenous mystique and Portuguese civility.[36]

The civilizing mission and European-style music flourished beyond the bounds of state patronage. Rio's elite founded private music societies that promoted concerts, catered to Europhile audiences, and provided a stage for original compositions written and played by members who received private musical tutelage.[37] In addition to concerts, clubs held *saraus*, events that combined music, poetry, and theater. Though music was central to these gatherings, the accompanying dinners, teas, cookies, drinks, and late-night balls emphasized their social nature. Some clubs supplemented musical events with fencing, card games, and reading rooms replete with European newspapers. One of the most famous clubs, Fluminense, enjoyed the occasional presence of the imperial family.

Elite composers and performers were mainly but not exclusively white. The famous musician and priest José Maurício Nunes Garcia was one prominent exception. Born in Rio in 1767 to former slaves, Garcia (known popularly as José Maurício) studied religion with his mother and aunt and received training in music from Salvador José, a prominent mixed-race musician and instructor.[38] Eventually, José Maurício opened a school for musical instruction in his own house, for a time received a pension from Dom João VI to train musicians and priests, owned his own slave, and conducted at the Capela Real. José Maurício's prominence shows that European music was not simply or exclusively forced on or spread to dark masses by an all-white elite; the civilizing mission did not flow in just one direction. But the challenges that José Maurício faced throughout his career also indicate that racism affected the careers of even the most respected artists of color.

In 1856, twenty-six years after his death, José Maurício was included on a short list of Brazilian heroes compiled for the Instituto Histórico e Geográfico Brasileiro by Manuel de Araújo Porto Alegre, a well-known painter and writer. Noting that José Maurício was an educated "legitimate son" (born to married parents), Porto Alegre enthusiastically recounted that João VI appointed José Maurício to the Capela Real "without the least reluctance."[39] To Porto Alegre, the appointment was an example of João VI's enlightened appreciation for all Brazilians. In José Maurício, Porto Alegre maintained, João VI saw a unique success story: though the son of former slaves, he was refined and sophisticated. Porto Alegre explained what racism José Maurício encountered as the product of ignorant outsiders such as Marcos Portugal, a musician who moved from Portugal to Brazil and leveled nasty invectives at José Maurício. According to Porto Alegre, the abuse from foreigners like Portugal contrasted with the more enlightened disposition of João VI. Despite his color, Porto Alegre wrote, José Maurício "was tolerated in the court. . . . Senhor D. João VI was the only one who truly never distinguished incidents or accidents in men."[40]

Porto Alegre commented extensively on José Maurício's appearance. He noted that the musician "had a noble physiognomy," despite the fact that "in his lips, in the form of his nose, and in the prominence of his cheek bones he had mixed-race characteristics." European scientists, Porto Alegre insisted, had misinterpreted those characteristics, especially one phrenologist who analyzed a reproduction of José Maurício's skull and concluded that he, like other dark-skinned people, was inferior. To Porto Alegre, the phrenologist was mistaken because "it is the brain, not the skull," that determines one's worth, a point repeatedly missed by the phrenologist, who had analyzed a "great number of Brazilian heads."[41] Porto Alegre's comments anticipated the work of Brazilian eugenicists and intellectuals, who during the late nineteenth and early twentieth centuries countered European race "science" by arguing that racial mixture was not the liability that scholars to the north insisted it to be and was instead a potential means for social and genetic improvement.[42] Porto Alegre's careful valorization of José Maurício's racial identity also tapped into ideological currents already decades in the making. In 1830, a political broadside urged the abdication of Pedro I and enthusiastically encouraged the ascension of his young son, whom the publication referred to as "cabra como nós" (colored like us), a label that belies the young monarch's blond hair and blue eyes but illustrates what was at the time a growing acceptance of the idea that Brazil could define itself through, and gain strength from, racial mixture.[43] Porto Alegre's description of José Maurício also shows how rhetoric about racial mixture and unity was, paradoxically, often inscribed with reaffirmations of racial difference. While José Maurício's skin color was said not to matter to an enlightened ruler like Dom João VI, it did merit comment. The illustrious musician prospered despite "the accident" of his color. Lips, nose, and cheekbones notwithstanding, he had a "noble physiognomy."

Barbers, Bloodletters, and . . . Musicians

José Maurício's life and career were unique in many ways, certainly quite different than those of most African, Afro-Brazilian, and mixed-race musicians, many of whom were enslaved and worked as barbers. Some possessed and performed a dizzying array of skills, including hair cutting, shaving, bloodletting, surgery, dentistry, and entertaining customers by playing any number of musical instruments. Barber-musicians' multiple talents provide a necessary baseline for understanding the long process of musical professionalization. The individuals who created the "warble" and "horrible racket" on the streets of Rio played, performed, and worked in a variety of settings. Some earned extra cash by singing and dancing on the street. Others played for orchestras hired by Rio's elite, including the royal family.[44] Money earned from music was turned over to masters, kept by slaves or *libertos* (freed persons), or used to support church brotherhoods. Music also provided respite and relaxation from brutal workdays. Through at least the 1850s, barber-musicians were fixtures in Rio and Salvador.[45] Debret compared the city's barbershops to stores in Portugal and Spain, with the major difference being that in Rio all of the workers were black, "or at least *mulato*."[46] Debret insisted that this did not "impede habitants of Rio from entering one of those shops with confidence, certain to find in a single person an able barber, a surgeon familiar with the scalpel, and a skillful applier of leeches." These jacks-of-all-trades, he observed, commanded "one-thousand talents" and were "as capable of fixing a stocking" as they were playing violin or clarinet.[47]

When they were not shaving, bleeding, or entertaining their customers, barber-musicians played music at public festivals, auctions, and in the streets.[48] Demand for barber bands was particularly high during the first half of the nineteenth century, when it seemed that hardly a festival took place without them.[49] Theaters hired barber bands to play at premiers, and religious brotherhoods contracted them in the hope of attracting congregants.[50] Debret observed musicians seated near a church door playing music at the bequest of a brotherhood to "stimulate the faith of the faithful, for whom inside the temple awaits an orchestra more adequate for worship."[51] Barber bands played wind instruments—especially trumpets, trombones, and flutes—fiddles, guitars, triangles, and a variety of drums.[52] Most barber-musicians probably learned to play multiple instruments on their own or with the help of friends and colleagues.[53] In a 1904 memoir, the writer and folklorist Mello Moraes Filho recalled a celebration more than fifty years earlier at which some barber-musicians played music by memory while others used sheet music "fastened by pins to the back of the musician in front of him, who served as a lectern."[54] Barber-musicians played any one of a number of genres, including *dobrado*, *quadrilha*, Spanish *fandango*, lundu, waltz, Portuguese *chula*, and French *contredanse*.

One observer commented that the already impressive noise level at a Bahian market was "more noisy, merry, and gay" than any he had seen, and that was before a barber band began to play, raising the sound level even higher.[55] Another described a church festival that was attended by a "noisy public" and punctuated by:

> a shrill music . . . of fados or lundus, that disorderly black tarantela, in which each one performs impudent sleights of hand and movements. The more unbridled and licentious, the louder the applauses . . . until the wee hours of the night rolled on this black bacchanal to celebrate a Catholic church festival.[56]

A Brazilian novelist described a similar scene in which "a musical band of real professors" alternated with an "infernal orchestra, playing gay marches."[57] Moraes Filho wrote of a band that played at the "noisiest functions."[58] Citing a 1908 study that referred to barber bands as "bad orchestras," Mário de Andrade asserts that the term *música de barbeiros* (barber music) was often used to refer to "an orchestra, band, or any sort of instrumental group" that played "awfully."[59] Others commented on what they saw to be blacks' natural ability to make noise and to be happy. Thomas Lindley described the performers he saw in Brazil as "Harmony's dark children" who had been "itinerant musicians since time immemorial."[60]

The sensationalist, often dismissive, accounts of barber-musicians belie their economic significance, highlighted in Zephyr Frank's study of wealth among "middle groups" in nineteenth-century Rio de Janeiro.[61] Band members belonging to Antônio José Dutra, himself a former slave, earned more money for their owner than the combined value of his property holdings and the proceeds from his barbershop.[62] To maximize earnings, Dutra and other owners advertised their slaves' musical abilities. A master in Salvador rented the services of her slaves, who were known for their "large and varied repertoire." A traveler noted that possession of a slave band "bespeaks a certain degree of superiority, consequently the planters pride themselves upon their musicians." An 1847 advertisement published in Rio described "a good black barber, blood-letter, tailor, who plays several instruments, all of which he does with notable perfection." One rural landowner was said to have exchanged an entire farm for a single slave renowned for his abilities with the violin.[63] Barber bands' economic significance is further evident in the wills of slave owners like Dutra, who passed musicians and musical instruments on to heirs.[64]

Despite helping owners amass capital, for most barber-musicians music was less a discrete profession than a hobby, a task, or a means for making extra cash. Though they were valuable commodities to owners like Dutra, barber-musicians themselves were rarely thought of as professional musicians. Even highly skilled and well-trained slaves often performed and practiced on the side rather than for a living.[65] Andrade defined barber music as that "executed by a group of black ex-slaves . . . who added to [*somavam*] the profession of barbering, the practice of being a musician."[66] He also cited nineteenth- and early twentieth-century sources that refer to barber music as a source of "extra income" and as a skill refined during leisure hours. The narrator of an 1875 novel sourly described a group of barber-musicians who "[falsified] symphonies with manifest tarnish to the poor authors and offense to the ears of those nearby." The narrator went on to note that music was simply the barbers' "occupation of the moment" (*mister de ocasião*). Their "permanent state" was practicing "the art of barbering."[67] Another observer placed barber-musicians among a larger class of black jacks-of-all-trades, or *pau para toda obra*: "The African performed, among us, the task of pack-mule. . . . He was the *pau para toda obra*: in domestic service, farming, mechanical arts."[68]

While some individuals earned as much from playing music as they did from barbering, most were bought, sold, rented, and passed to family members in the same manner as musical instruments, mules, silverware, or clothes. Barber-musicians could earn money by performing, but those who were slaves most often had to turn over at least a portion of that income to their owners. They could innovate by combining and adapting strange instruments and sounds with more familiar ones, but they had little recourse to claim exclusive ownership of their artistic handiwork. In short, few barber-musicians could fully access or control the financial fruits of their musical labor. While slave musicians and bands provided significant income to slave owners, hardly any enjoyed professional recognition or institutional support.

DURING THE NINETEENTH CENTURY, lundu's popularity lent credence to the idea that the music created by black and mixed-race groups could become a defining feature of brasilidade. But the embrace of lundu did little to reverse old assumptions about black physicality or to allow Afro-Brazilians access to or control over the fruits of their musical creations. As a result, essentialized depictions of blackness and black music came into greater view through the same pathways that helped marginalize African and Afro-Brazilian musicians. Elites and the Crown provided funds for "civilized" culture, but even a respected, classically trained artist like José Maurício was subject to insults and "scientific" examination. While slave musicians and barber bands provided significant income for their owners, they were rarely if ever thought of as professionals. Instead, their musical prowess was defined as natural, athletic, or savage, their labor as more of a hobby or an "add on" to "real" work.

Porto Alegre was convinced that a man of color could carry the nation's banner and help refute European theories about race. But the attacks that José Maurício suffered during his career and Porto Alegre's enthusiastic description of how João VI appointed José Maurício to the Capela Real "without the least hesitation" show that the embrace of mixed-race and black musicians rarely if ever came without qualification. Like the barber-musicians, José Maurício lived in a society that valued his art and his background, but in specific and limited ways. For him and other musicians of color living in Rio in the nineteenth century, respect, recognition, and lucrative opportunities were elusive if not altogether impossible to find.

2

BEYOND THE PUNISHMENT PARADIGM

Popular Entertainment and Social Control after Abolition

Around Christmas in 1889, far from the bustling streets of Rio de Janeiro, a man was arrested for disturbing the peace in Rio Novo, a small town in the state of São Paulo.[1] The perpetrator, José Antônio Piranha, had been hosting a "noisy fandango" replete with drums and singing. Displeased with the fine imposed on him, Piranha contested the charges. While he acknowledged holding the event at his house, Piranha argued to the town council that he should be absolved of any wrongdoing because other residents, including the well-known captain Antônio Gabriel, had done just the same. In fact, Piranha claimed, others exceeded his own transgressions by playing *jogos de búzio* (probably a religious ceremony involving shells) and *truques, a card game*. In response, the officer who levied the fine claimed that Piranha was mistaken and that in other homes individuals "only played ditties that are Christmas Eve pastimes." At Captain Antônio's house, the officer explained, revelers played nothing more than a "merriment called samba, which does not appear to me to be prohibited by our codes, which specifically refer to fandango."[2] While the officer appears to have been unfamiliar with the "merriment called samba," he had seen or heard enough of it to distinguish it from fandango and illicit religious practices.[3]

The officer's defense of Captain Antônio is remarkable. By suggesting that samba was not just a permissible practice but also grounds for *refuting* charges of wrongdoing, his actions represent a total inversion of the widespread belief that before it became popular, samba was a target of, not a shield from, police abuse. With this enticing incident as a starting point, we may begin to explore the punishment paradigm—the widely held but rarely researched idea that samba was directly and systematically repressed before it ascended to the level of national symbol. In the process, we will fill in economic and social contexts necessary for understanding Brazil's early twentieth-century music market and forge a more precise understanding of the challenges that Rio de Janeiro's black musicians faced as slavery, the monarchy, and the heyday of the barber-musicians faded into the past.

The Punishment Paradigm

Shot in unknown circumstances sometime during the 1930s or 1940s, this photograph depicts a familiar and seemingly straightforward scenario, described in the caption: "João da Baiana paid with prison time for the ugly 'crime' of singing samba and playing *pandeiro*."[4] (See figure 1.) The accompanying newspaper article traces samba's origins and tells the story of João da Baiana, the musician pictured behind bars. No details about the photo are provided, but the article's author uses it as an example of an earlier period when samba was said to have been prohibited, a period that looked archaic from the vantage point of the "new" Brazil, where samba had become a part of national identity and racism was said to be a thing of the past.

In interviews conducted throughout his life, João da Baiana recalled being arrested and harassed by the police, and nearly every time he described how authorities confiscated and destroyed his pandeiro before hauling him off to jail. Considered together with the photograph—where he holds the instrument while standing behind bars—the interviews raise interesting questions. Was the moment captured on film exceptional? Had he been arrested for something unrelated to music, and somehow smuggled the pandeiro into jail? Was the image staged? If it would be misguided to take the disjuncture between image and interview as an indication that João da Baiana was simply lying or misremembering during his interviews, or to suggest that he and other musicians were never harassed or abused by authorities, the contrast does provide a clear invitation to question literal readings of the punishment paradigm and to explore the paradigm's multiple meanings and uses.

While this particular photo and article tell a specifically Brazilian story, the image also speaks to larger American histories. Before samba and

FIGURE 1. Musician João da Baiana, holding his instrument, in jail.
Courtesy Museu da Imagem e do Som.

other forms of "black music" became accepted as national symbols they are known to have been repressed. Samba's rise has been explained in a number of ways, but the starting point is always a period of punishment that is said to have extended through slavery and into the early twentieth century. The punishment paradigm took shape during samba's golden age and became widely accepted in the 1960s and 1970s, thanks in large part to an ambitious project engineered by Rio de Janeiro's Museum of Image and Sound (MIS, Museu da Imagem e do Som). The MIS, which interviewed sambistas who had helped popularize the music decades earlier, launched its project soon after the museum's creation in 1965.[5] Press coverage of the project helped produce a shared knowledge, summarized in the headline of a 1970 newspaper article about João da Baiana, who, the headline declared, came "from the age when samba was prohibited."[6] Similar articles celebrated sambistas as both tragic and heroic: tragic because of the hardship they had faced and heroic because they persevered. The combination of tragedy and heroism often melded together in the figure of the *malandro*—the clever, flashily dressed, womanizing, hustler figure, closely associated with golden age samba.[7] As foils to authority, malandros were often depicted as having both suffered and resisted police violence. Press coverage surrounding the first MIS interviews displayed photos of malandro musicians in their youth, decked out in flashy suits with handkerchiefs tucked in the breast pocket, stylish hats, and shiny shoes (see figure 2). The exploits of clever, handsome malandros who evaded the police lent stories about police repression a heroic, entertaining air.

The idea that samba was once prohibited has been repeated in a seemingly endless stream of scholarly work. One author writes that during the early twentieth century, "black sambistas" fought "police violence and government oppression."[8] Another suggests that "before becoming accepted by the middle class, [popular music] was continuously and hypocritically persecuted . . . by the police because it was associated with Rio's lower classes."[9] Others go as far as to suggest that it was once illegal to play samba. One author insists that samba was "prohibited by the [1890] Penal Code."[10] Another claims that the music was "outlawed by the authorities in the first decades of its existence."[11] Such statements are not just misleading; they are incorrect. As we will see, the 1890 Penal Code did not mention music. Though a handful of local regulations limited the kinds of music and instruments that could be played at specific times or places, samba was never systematically outlawed. An 1889 law banned batuque in Rio, and a similar law was passed in Salvador in 1904. During the early 1910s police in both cities intermittently prohibited pandeiros, samba, and batuque at select public celebrations.[12] While these examples demonstrate how authorities often linked music with disorder, they do not substantiate overarching claims about systematic or coordinated repression. Further, arguments that link pre- and post-abolition regulations lend false historical unity and depth to a musical form that did not consolidate into a single genre until the late 1920s. In the decades following abolition, authorities sought to stamp out vice and divide licit from illicit forms of work. The violent, arbitrary force often used to do so has

FIGURE 2. João da Baiana displaying malandro style.
Courtesy Museu da Imagem e do Som.

been well documented, as have the brutal campaigns meant to "civilize" low-income, mixed-race, and black populations.[13] Because the groups targeted by "civilizing" projects were often the same as those associated with samba, stories about the music's repression fold neatly into the well-documented histories of racist police violence.

Motivations for accepting or deploying the punishment paradigm vary, as do specific interpretations. To some, telling the history of samba's repression is an important way to call attention to and denounce racism. One of the narrative's more appealing and powerful aspects is the assumed continuity between Africa, slavery, and the twentieth century. The fact that the term "samba" did not gain wide use until the mid-1910s and that a distinct musical genre did not congeal until the late 1920s has not deterred commentators from finding in samba an unbroken link between precolonial Africa and twentieth-century Brazil. That perceived link has provided a potent tool with which to critique slavery's long-lasting legacies and to recover and reconstruct histories and connections destroyed by the Middle Passage.[14] Others have employed the punishment paradigm to opposite effect, using it to define inequality and racism as things of the past, left behind by a now enlightened, egalitarian society.

The reality is that João da Baiana and many musicians were, in fact, intimately familiar with multiple kinds of punishment, including but not limited to the kind captured in the iconic photograph. But to him and others, punishment could also mean something subtler, even self-inflicted. It could involve self-censorship or the embrace of greater government oversight of music, both of which often accompanied professional ascension and attempts to secure intellectual property rights. Or it could involve the multiple by-products that came from struggles to perform, domesticate, use, and literally and figuratively own "authentic" or "African" objects, songs, and images. To understand this full range of possibilities, explored at length in the following chapters, it is crucial to first set in place a detailed portrait of turn-of-the-century police practices, social control projects, and the place of music in each.

The Anti-Vagrancy Campaign and Rio's "Machinery of Power"

Some punishment paradigm arguments may be dismissed out of hand. The notion that samba was prohibited by the 1890 Penal Code or that it was outlawed in its first decades is simply untrue. The 1890 Penal Code, in effect until a new code replaced it in 1940, did not refer to samba or any other form of music. While music often carried stigmas, it was not repressed or targeted in the way that it is said to have been. Because the code did not, in fact, mention samba or any other form of music, some scholars assume that authorities used broadly conceived anti-vagrancy laws as legal justification to harass musicians. To test this hypothesis, I analyzed a large collection of police documents, including hand-selected arrest records of musicians and a random sample of four hundred vagrancy cases. The case sample, involving 424 individuals, is drawn from records housed and indexed at the National Archive (Arquivo Nacional) in Rio. The cases span from 1890 to 1940 and are all *processos*—cases for which formal charges were brought—stemming from vagrancy arrests made in the police districts Santana and Santo Antônio, an area that included "Little Africa," Praça Onze (a famous gathering point for musicians, razed in 1942 as part of urban renovations), parts of Rio's port area, and a number of homes and meeting places of individuals who figured prominently in the development of samba and the city's larger Afro-Brazilian religious and cultural milieu.[15]

Legal vestiges of slavery remained intact long after 1888 in Brazil.[16] Less than two months after slavery was abolished, Brazil's politicians debated a bill to repress idleness (*ociosidade*). The bill was meant to address concerns raised by a group of legislators (*deputados*) who feared that the end of slavery would pose a threat to individual property and security and would result in chaos and disaster. The fact that abolition's gradual path in Brazil meant that most people of color were free prior to 1888 did not prevent the deputados from tapping into fears that the Golden Law would somehow unleash a mass of untrained workers. The deputados' bill received widespread support and laid the groundwork for Article 399 of the Penal Code, which defined vagrancy (*vadiagem*) as a failure "to exercise a profession, position, or any kind of occupation." Listed under the code's section of *contravenções* (petty crimes), the law also required all individuals to have a fixed residence and forbade subsistence through any "occupation prohibited by law or manifestly offensive to morals and good customs." Those in violation were subject to fifteen to thirty days in jail.[17] Article 399 inspired a larger anti-vagrancy campaign that was based around two explicit goals: to ensure societal order and to transform libertos and vagrants into workers (*trabalhadores*).[18] To these stated objectives may be added three implied intentions. First, the campaign's architects sought to preserve long-standing hierarchies while simultaneously attempting to leave slavery behind. Second, by outlawing livelihood through any "occupation prohibited by law or manifestly offensive to morals and good customs," lawmakers sought to draw a line between licit and illicit means of making money. In practice, the line was exceptionally blurry and constantly moving, a flexibility that lent the law extra power. Third, through police techniques like fingerprinting, physical examinations, and compulsory identification, authorities sought to identify and monitor dangerous sectors of the population.[19]

Most deputados felt that libertos and the poor in general were prone to vice and ill-prepared for post-abolition society. To ease the transition, former slaves would need education and, the past centuries of forced labor notwithstanding, an appreciation of hard work. Ociosidade was seen as a gateway to more serious crimes; only an upright worker's ethic could be its antidote. Those who were doubtful about the possibilities of turning former slaves into free laborers encouraged the influx of foreign, especially European, workers, who would bring a solid work ethic and help "whiten" the nation.[20] Both the intention to repress vagrancy and the desire to attract foreign workers were rooted in an *ideologia da vadiagem*, a set of ideas and stereotypes that evolved over several centuries. George Reid Andrews defines the most prominent post-abolition version as the "firm and unshakable belief in the innate idleness and irresponsibility of the black and racially mixed Brazilian masses."[21] In 1878, one politician advocated the establishment of special schools to instill a good work ethic among former slaves. These schools, the politician urged, would replace distractions "such as the guitar, gambling, or any other such vice" with honest hard work.[22]

Assumptions about black idleness shaped Brazil's Free Womb Law and the Law of the Sexagenarians.[23] Both pieces of legislation included requirements for libertos to work and to remain under government supervision for at least several years. The monitoring of former slaves and the suppression of vagrants were parts of long-standing projects to count, oversee, and, in theory, protect the population. Vagrants were judged not just for what they did, but also for what they might do. Wandering (*vagando*) and the failure to prove stable employment or a permanent residence were said to be symptoms of more dangerous criminal behavior. Offenders were said to be "parasites" or "professional vagabonds." Fear that such individuals would take advantage of well-meaning but gullible citizens inspired four articles in the Penal Code dedicated to "false beggars."[24]

Vagrancy accusations alone could mark suspects with "stigmas of dishonor."[25] Once arrested, many were subjected to invasive physical examinations, ostensibly conducted to determine whether they were fit to work. Homosexual men who broke no laws but nonetheless violated public mores were frequently subject to vagrancy accusations.[26] As a means to challenge suspects' honor, scrutinize their economic means, probe their

TABLE 2. Vagrancy Cases in Santana and Santo Antônio (1901–40)*

	Total	High Year/#	Low Year/#	Average per Year
1901–5	664	1904/277	1901/13	132.8
1906–10	1,753	1907/815	1909/69	350.6
1911–15	1,258	1912/420	1911/179	251.6
1916–20	1,707	1917/614	1918/93	341.4
1921–25	568	1921/256	1924/8	113.6
1926–30	857	1927/252	1926/49	171.4
1931–35	585	1935/230	1932/34	117.0
1936–40	105	1937/79	1940/1	21.0
Total	7,497	—	—	187.4

*Data from 1901 to 1911 are just from Santana. The remaining years are from Santana and Santo Antônio.
Source: AN, CODES Instrumentos 0R and 6Z.

bodies, and mark them as deviants, Article 399 provided police with a device for maintaining "order" in intimate and intrusive ways.

Though the anti-vagrancy campaign was conceived specifically with African-descendant men in mind, it also entangled poor men and women of all backgrounds, who together constituted an enormous swath of Rio's population. Indexed records from twenty-one police districts at the Arquivo Nacional register more than fourteen thousand processos stemming from violations of Article 399 and Article 400, which applied to repeat offenders. About half of those cases were filed in the districts of Santana and Santo Antônio, where between 1901 and 1940, police filed an average of 187 vagrancy cases per year.[27] Processos fell from about two thousand for the first decade of the twentieth century to below one thousand during the 1930s. But while overall numbers declined, trends varied from year to year. In 1935, 230 cases were filed, far fewer than in 1917, for example, but far more than in 1901, 1909, 1911, 1918, and 1924 (see table 2).[28]

During a typical vagrancy arrest, an officer would apprehend an individual for engaging in a vaguely defined activity, such as "wandering," "perambulating without a destination," being a "known vagabond" or "contumacious vagrant," or for simply being found in a "state of frank idleness." As Amy Chazkel points out, *vadiagem* has a telling etymological link to the word "vague."[29] Police clerks, who paraphrased in their reports the testimonies of the arresting officer(s), witnesses, and those accused of wrongdoing (*acusados*), recorded ambiguous descriptions to seemingly endless repetition. The vague phrases make it difficult to know exactly what most acusados did to provoke imprisonment. Clerks were not just trained in the art of repetition, but also rewarded for creativity. Competitions for clerkships included a test that required applicants to invent and narrate a fictitious crime and arrest. Those who wrote the most exciting, detailed accounts were rewarded. Olívia Maria Gomes da Cunha aptly describes the product of this unseemly combination of fiction and bland repetition as a collective *folha obscura* (obscure page).[30]

Suspected vagrants used multiple strategies to fend off the police. Some acusados changed their names or provided false information. Others rejected charges by seizing the deputados' rhetoric and flipping it on its head. In elaborate defenses, suspects claimed that the police had not transformed vagrants into workers and had instead done just the opposite: mistreated honest trabalhadores and turned them into vagrants. A substantial number of acusados (160 of 424) made these points in lengthy and elaborate written statements authored by lawyers, fellow inmates, and the suspects themselves. For male acusados, the insinuation that they had no home, lacked steady work, and could not provide for their family represented a direct attack on their masculinity.[31] One acusado responded by asserting that he was a "clean man." Another declared that he was "not a vagrant" and that he sustained "his poor old mother, having a fixed domicile." A third claimed to be "a peaceful boy, of good habits; a respectful, obedient, and good child." A fourth suspect's written statement screamed in capital letters "his PROFESSION IS COAL PEDDLER," and it insisted that the acusado was doing his best to help his family, especially his sister, who was "struggling to support herself and her little daughter."[32] Countless others employed titles like *regenerado* (regenerated), trabalhador, and *homem trabalhador* (roughly, "working man").

The defenses proffered by suspects are especially significant considering the fact that guilt and innocence had little effect on time served and that judges acquitted the majority of those individuals processed for vagrancy. In my sample, roughly 70 percent of those charged with violating Article 399 were judged innocent or had their cases thrown out. But the final decision in a case rarely correlated with the amount of time spent behind bars. On average, all suspects remained incarcerated for more than thirty-four days while awaiting judgment. Out of 424 suspects, only 5 had their cases heard within a week of being arrested. Some 232 spent twenty-one days or more in jail before the judge reached a decision, and those who were found innocent or whose cases were dismissed still spent an average of nearly thirty-six days in custody between arrest and release, or six days more than the longest prescribed penalty for those convicted.

Despite the disconnect between judgment and time served, acusados found meaning in claiming to be upstanding trabalhadores and in doing so also defined themselves in the image of the ideal worker envisioned by the anti-vagrancy campaign's architects. In this sense, the campaign may be understood as an example of the "machinery of power" that Foucault identifies as crucial to the exercise of social control.[33] The arguments that suspects offered in defense of their character helped make trabalhador and *vadio* (vagrant) "visible and permanent realit[ies]," twin components of a "principle of classification and intelligibility" that helped order society. The deputados' desire to inculcate a worker's ethic and foster widespread moral "regeneration" demonstrates an intimate link between individual character and larger political and economic structures. In addition to forcing recalcitrant former slaves and vagrants to work, deputados saw the need to remake the whole person. Doing so would not only ease the transition from slavery, but also provide the social and moral conditions for Brazil to become a civilized nation.

Black Laborers

The anti-vagrancy campaign and the ideologia da vadiagem especially affected Rio's Afro-Brazilian workers, many of whom were engaged in increasingly combative labor struggles. Between 1890 and 1919, workers in the city staged more than 250 organized work stoppages.[34] Through organized mobilizations and in less formal arenas, workers used multiple strategies to secure stable work, gain leverage with employers, and distance themselves from demeaning stereotypes associated with the ideologia da vadiagem. Such tasks posed unique challenges for black laborers, who struggled to organize and find work while combating racial stereotypes. The prominent Afro-Brazilian lawyer and labor advocate Evaristo de Moraes commented that port authorities "do not distinguish between a worker . . . and a sea bandit or a vagabond and hooligan. For them they are all scum and niggers."[35]

Workers employed various strategies to combat racism and secure rights. Two Afro-Brazilian-run stevedore unions, both founded in 1903, sought to provide stability and protection for workers in a labor market marked by constant turnover and employer caprice. Two years later, a

group of mainly black and mixed-race dockworkers formed the Sociedade de Resistência dos Trabalhadores em Trapiche e Café (Warehouse
Workers and Coffee Porters' Resistance Society). The organization was
formed not only to give them more power over their working lives but
also to distinguish its members from the urban poor and gain definitive
distance from slavery and the ideologia da vadiagem.

Though its ability to alter societal perceptions about blackness and
vagrancy was somewhat limited, the organization was able to create an
important space for black and mixed-race leadership. Between 1910 and
1929, nonwhites held 83 percent of the administrative positions in the organization and 78 percent of overall membership.[36] Some black laborers
likened unions and worker's rights to a second abolition. In 1918, a Resistência member recalled how black workers were frequently and publicly
beaten, in scenes that differed little from those perpetrated under slavery.
Referring to the date of emancipation, the member said, "The Resistência
gave us a new 13th of May, a new set of rights."[37]

Organizing provided multiple ways for workers to distinguish themselves from vadios and the poor. Regulated wages and "closed shop"
agreements with employers lent a measure of stability amid frequent labor
surpluses. Steady work distinguished those lucky enough to find it from
the masses of individuals without steady jobs. The 1920 census classified
the occupations of approximately half of the city's inhabitants as diversas,
a catchall label that included the unemployed and those whose profession was "undefined" or "undeclared."[38] Even steady work might not be
enough to support a family. The basic cost of living tripled between 1889
and 1897, and the situation did not improve greatly thereafter, despite a
subsequent corrective deflation. In 1903, Brasil Operário reported that the
salary of a typical male textile worker was barely enough to cover the rent
and fees owed to his employer. Even with a wife and young children working daily, the typical working family barely made enough to survive.[39] Between 1887 and 1912, the general cost of living in Rio skyrocketed by as
much as 940 percent.[40]

Rio's black dockworkers were not the only ones trying to eke out a
living under dire conditions or to distance themselves from slaves, "vagabonds," and "hooligans." In 1911, the labor lawyer Raphael Pinheiro gave
a speech at the União dos Empregados do Comércio, an organization
that represented office clerks, shop assistants, and various other middling
laborers in commerce. He referred to his listeners as proletários de casaca,
or "proletarians in suits," a phrase that reflected both their working-class

roots and their desire to leave those roots behind. Aware of the potential gains to be had from aligning with other workers, but also convinced that they performed more dignified tasks than those of factory hands or dock-workers, the proletários de casaca were both part of and distinct from Rio's larger workers' movement.[41] Nonetheless, they, like so many others, were after the same basic goals: a decent wage and a social distance from vadios and other impoverished cariocas.

The Elusive Musician

Musicians occupied an ambiguous place along the worker-vagrant spectrum and within Rio's labor hierarchy. Their craft was not illegal, but neither was it recognized as work. A city publication counted forty-four workers associations functioning in 1912, including groups of barbers, boatmen, and streetcar workers, but nothing related to music.[42] Missing from that list was the Centro Musical do Rio de Janeiro, an organization founded in 1907 by a group of elite, mainly white, music instructors. The organization, which represented just a small number of artists, proclaimed itself as a defender of the "musician class."[43] While not formally associated with other worker organizations, the group hoped to gain the protections outlined in a 1907 decree, which transformed unions into state-controlled syndicates.[44] The many musicians who did not belong to the Centro Musical were not without their own organizations. A large number belonged to dancing and social clubs, Carnival ranchos[45] and cordões,[46] and (beginning in the late 1920s) samba schools (escolas de samba). But despite the important roles they played, those institutions rarely if ever provided access to the kinds of professional rights and recognition sought by the Resistência and other workers organizations or protection against vagrancy accusations—roles often filled by trade associations.

Because few musicians belonged to worker associations *as musicians* and because "musician" was not a prevalent professional category during the early twentieth century, finding musicians within the police archive is a difficult task. In my vagrancy sample, two striking absences suggest that, contrary to foregoing wisdom, the police did not use Article 399 to target musicians. First, hardly any individuals arrested for vagrancy self-identified or were identified by the police or witnesses as musicians. Second, I did not find a single vagrancy case overtly related to music. Each absence has its own significance and explanation, best dealt with in turn.

Disingenuously or not, individuals charged with violating Article 399 claimed to hold any one of a number of different jobs. Vagrancy cases revolved around a set of core biographical details provided by the suspects or assigned by the police. The information was recorded when the acusado was arrested and then again during subsequent interrogations, fingerprinting, and examinations. Suspects often restated or changed their information in defense statements, and basic biographical information often varied within a single report. A representative case might define a suspect as a dockworker in the transcript of the initial questioning, as unemployed in the interrogation, and as a trabalhador in a written statement presented to the judge.

During initial questioning alone, acusados in the sample named eighty-three different types of employment, an indication of the constructed nature of police records and also a reflection of the many arenas in which cariocas sought work. Sidney Chalhoub points out that intense competition for jobs in turn-of-the-century Rio helped produce "thousands of individuals who, not able to or not wanting to become salaried workers, survived . . . as street vendors, numbers runners, professional gamblers, beggars, etc."[47] While a factory worker could often produce a boss's letter to prove gainful employment and refute vagrancy charges, a fruit peddler most likely could not. As a result, the thousands of individuals who fell into the "diversas" category in the census had an especially difficult time providing solid proof that they "exercised a profession, position, or any kind of occupation."

A line—thin, moving, and contested—separated acceptable means of subsistence from those that were illegal or "manifestly offensive to morals and good customs." Of the individuals who refuted vagrancy charges by claiming to be employed, perhaps the most notable were women who declared their work to be prostitution, a trade that was, in theory at least, legally permissible. When one woman whom witnesses called a "lowly prostitute" was arrested for vagrancy and finally received a hearing twenty-five days later, the judge reasoned in her favor. "It is not enough to allege that the defendant has an occupation prohibited by law," he wrote. "Instead, it is necessary to prove in exactly which way said profession is illegal and that its penal censure is provided for and defined by law." In the accused, the judge saw neither a "criminal nor 'contraventional' figure" and insisted that "it is better that the act remain unpunished than for judges to usurp legislative authority."[48]

The arbiter based his call for judicial restraint on the fact that the Penal Code did not explicitly prohibit prostitution. The law targeted pimps and gave police "discretionary powers" in dealing with prostitutes. This did not create an unchallenged, autonomous space for women, but rather a gray area often invaded by the police, who harassed and extorted money from prostitutes. While the judge's decision may have been reassuring to this particular defendant, it undoubtedly provided no solace during the preceding twenty-five days she spent in the Casa de Detenção (House of Detention). Eight other women in the sample presented similar arguments.[49] Though less than the number of suspects claiming to be trabalhadores or cooks, for example, more suspects named prostitution as their profession than they did popular professions such as carpentry, painting, and barbering.

While suspects claimed to hold a wide array of occupations, they almost never mentioned music. In the entire sample, only two acusados named "musician" (músico) as their profession.[50] As proof of employment or residence, acusados often presented written documentation signed by an employer, landlord, or union or trade association official. Such documentation was generally unavailable to musicians, at least as musicians. A dockworker who made extra money by playing guitar on the side had a far better chance of proving employment through his job at the port than through his activities as a musician.[51] While proof of employment may have had little effect on sentencing—and sentencing little effect on time served—suspects who sought to define themselves as workers had a much smaller chance of doing so as a musician than as any one of a number of other occupations.

A final explanation may be given for the fact that almost no suspects defined themselves as músicos. Concern for the maintenance of honor, decency, and traditional family values often made bars and other establishments that featured music and dancing the object of public scorn. Even if music was not illegal, it was often associated with criminal behavior. In one telling incident, residents complained to police about "scandalous" scenes and "cackles and strumming guitars" at an alleged brothel.[52] Most acusados were surely aware of the association between music and the underworld (submundo) and were therefore unlikely to further associate themselves with either to the police.

It is possible that my sample simply missed cases involving self-identified musicians. To check that possibility, I searched police records by name, looking for arrest records of any kind involving musicians.[53] Thirty-six cases turned up, spanning 1902 to 1949 and involving a number of crimes, including vagrancy, physical offenses, and deflowering.[54]

The way that police identified the musicians, and the way that they identified themselves, corroborates the (non)findings from the sample, though
there is indication of an important change over time. The cases fell evenly
on either side of 1929, the beginning of samba's so-called golden age, with
eighteen occurring through the end of 1928 and eighteen occurring after
that. In only one of the pre-1929 cases did a suspect identify himself as a
musician, and he was charged with "physical offenses," a crime for which
occupation theoretically would have no bearing. In the eighteen cases that
occurred between 1929 and 1949, five individuals identified themselves
or were identified by the police as musicians. That more musicians defined themselves as such after 1929 than did before is not surprising. The
advent of commercial radio during the 1930s, the rise of author's rights
associations, the increased production and circulation of records, and the
growing popularity of samba provided more, and more lucrative, opportunities for musicians. However, greater opportunity did not necessarily
mean equal access, and the additional thirty-six cases make clear that
professional and market growth did not magically bring wealth to all. In
three of the post-1928 cases, músico or "composer" (compositor) appeared
multiple times in the same arrest record, an indication that music was the
suspect's primary, perhaps sole, source of income. In two other examples,
musician was a more fluid category. In April 1929, Ismael Silva (Mílton
de Oliveira Ismael Silva), an influential artist discussed in subsequent
chapters, was apprehended for his sixth alleged violation of Article 399.
During prior arrests, he described his profession in a number of ways —
painter, sales clerk, office worker, trabalhador, "employed in commerce"
(empregado no comércio) — but never as a musician. In 1929, he once again
claimed to be empregado no comércio, and on this occasion added that
he was "also a musical composer."[55]

Nineteen years later, Geraldo Pereira, another well-known musician,
was arrested on charges of possessing an illegal firearm and threatening a
café owner with it.[56] Despite commercial success, when prompted to state
his occupation during the various stages of interrogation, he described
himself not as a músico and instead as a motorista profissional (professional driver, chauffeur). The case would have included no indication that
he even played music had an officer not commented in his case summary,
"Being a samba composer, [Pereira] is fairly well known on the airwaves."
The fact that a well-known musician worked as a driver underscores how
supporting oneself entirely from musical work alone was a rare privilege,
even during samba's golden age.

Thirteen of the thirty-six individual cases stemmed from alleged violations of Article 399. The only suspect who refuted the charges by claiming to be a musician was Silva. The other acusados referred to more stable and recognizable professions. Many individuals arrested for vagrancy may have played music and made money doing so, but few considered it their primary occupation, especially in the presence of the police. The fact that so few suspects identified themselves as músicos also indicates how music occupied a vague area between the worker and vagrant poles. Unlike the prostitutes who challenged the notion that their trade should be considered illicit, few individuals who played music chose to emphasize their "musician-ness" when confronted by authorities.

Significantly, none of the thirty-six hand-selected cases had a direct connection to music. Within that selection, most of the vagrancy arrests included only sketchy details about the acusado's alleged offense, while others described links to illegal gambling or prostitution. Witnesses described Baiaco (Oswaldo Caetano Vasques), a famed hustler and occasional composer, as a "contumacious vagrant" who passed his time gambling on street corners. One person swore that Baiaco was homeless and could be "found sleeping in the doorways of bars in the red-light district . . . he does not have a profession." In a separate case, police accused him of assaulting and robbing a former girlfriend. Two men, Sílvio Fernandes and Noel Rosa, faced deflowering charges. Others, including Benedito Lacerda, Hilário Jovino Ferreira, Jamelão (José Bispo Clementino dos Santos), Oswaldo Santiago, and Paulo da Portela (Paulo Benjamin de Oliveira) were arrested for involvement in fistfights or armed confrontations, several of which occurred during or around public festivals.[57] While several cases took place during Carnival, none included a single reference to music. There is, quite simply, no evidence that music played any role in these arrests.

In June 1908, Elói Antero Dias (Mano Elói) was arrested while celebrating Dia de São João (Saint John's day). Mano Elói would soon become a prominent figure in Rio's music scene, both as a composer and cofounder of several samba schools. In 1936, a citywide vote made him Carnival's Cidadão Samba (roughly, Citizen Samba). On 23 June 1908, he was just another celebrant on the streets. At around 7:30 PM, he saluted São João with a revolver, firing several shots into the air, one of which struck a shop owner in the arm, an indiscretion that earned him fifteen days of forced labor.[58] While it would be misleading to artificially segregate Dias's shots from the music associated with public celebrations, it would be equally incorrect to suggest that Dias was arrested or imprisoned because he was a musician. His gun—not a pandeiro or a guitar—caught the police's attention.

The silences regarding music in the criminal records are ascribable in part to the vague nature of the folha obscura. The phrases that police officers and clerks frequently used to describe Article 399 violations— "perambulating without a destination," being found in a "state of frank idleness," and so on—give little indication about the actions that preceded any given arrest. But while the vagrancy records are obscure, they are not entirely opaque. Clerks were rewarded for their creativity, and though often vague, the records themselves are not completely devoid of descriptive material. Suspects were not just vagrants, but also "incorrigible vagabonds," "thieves," "robbers," "gamblers," and "lowly prostitutes." They were accused not only of "wandering," but also of such specific actions as gambling, drunkenness, and prostitution. In one case, an officer described a woman "completely naked, drunk . . . making a scandal . . . uttering obscenities." Another told of a suspect "uttering obscene words" and "throwing rocks." One officer claimed "to know all of the bad elements" in his area of patrol, among them "drunks, disorderlies, thieves, vagrants, and prostitutes." A clerk recounted a policeman's description of a row at a bar, punctuated by "a terrible, tumultuous sound of smashed cups and other glass dishes."[59] The prevalence of descriptive labels like "lowly prostitute" and the vivid if less frequent descriptions of fights and disorders make the absence of similar references to music and musicians all the more significant. If the police repressed music with the same zeal as it did prostitution, a practice that was not forbidden by law, why are the vagrancy records full of biting descriptions of "lowly prostitutes" but not "lowly musicians"? Why were sambistas not named among gamblers as "bad elements"? If officers and clerks mentioned foul language and described the sounds of breaking dishes, why did they not also note offensive drums or noisy guitars?

Beyond the Folha Obscura: Vice, "Witchcraft," and Economic Order

While the findings discussed above clearly indicate the need to rethink the punishment paradigm, the folha obscura should not be read too literally. Because individuals who played music neither described themselves nor were identified by authorities as musicians, it is unsurprising that they are hard to locate in the police archive. While the absolute absence of cases apparently related to music is a strong indication that the police did not file formal vagrancy charges against individuals for playing music in the street, the records do not reflect informal interactions. Police officers could smash guitars, pandeiro players could bribe their way out of sticky situations, and individuals could be detained temporarily, all without leaving behind a paper trail.

In 1932, Wilson Batista, who would soon become a major figure in popular music, celebrated the release of his first record by partying late into the night. Years later, he colorfully described that celebratory evening. "I decided to commemorate the event by drinking in every café on the Praça Tiradentes. I drank a lot. I drank too much. I drank until I had nothing left in my pockets and ended up at the District Police." After being held for several hours, Batista asked to speak with the supervising officer. Upon explaining the situation, Batista was happy to learn that the officer was an amateur composer. "We talked about music for a while, and he ordered another officer to get coffee for the two of us. Later, he sent me away in peace, and on the way out loaned me five mil-réis [about 35 cents]."[60]

Even if embellished, the incident serves as a good example of the kind of interactions that left no paper trail. A reading of a small number of *livros de ocorrência*, the books in which police recorded daily activities and interactions, revealed no detainments related to music, and it is reasonable to believe that when the police did harass individuals carrying musical instruments, they rarely took note of doing so. While documentation for incidents like the one that Batista described is hard to come by, there are enough examples in oral interviews and newspapers to suggest that ad hoc repression did in fact occur. But such incidents do not constitute sufficient evidence to support claims about systematic or widespread repression.

Attempts to distinguish between acceptable and "offensive" forms of work, and between licit and illicit behavior, were closely related to a growing, though rarely straightforward or uniform, tendency of intellectuals and elites to recognize and even embrace certain Afro-Brazilian "symbols and ideas."[61] But while musical forms associated with Brazil's African-descendant peoples were celebrated in some circles, they were criticized in others. The author of a 1915 article published in São Paulo derisively referred to "these *mulatos* of conked hair, guitar, and knife."[62] The limited, often contradictory recognition and valorization of Afro-Brazilian culture coincided with increased attention paid to Rio's so-called submundo, a space invented, in part, by Rio's *cronistas*, writers and journalists who chronicled daily life. Cronistas, Chazkel writes, helped "invent the underworld." As "voyeur[s] and active participant[s]," cronistas described illegal gambling dens, brothels, street corners, shantytowns, clandestine religious gatherings, and bars, and in doing so brought upper- and middle-class readers face-to-face with taboo people and places.[63] But while cronistas provided a way to (mis)understand activities like gambling and prostitution, they left caution in the hands of their readers. The submundo was dangerous and forbidding, and therefore also inviting. Cronista journalism moved in new directions during and after the 1910s, as a new generation of writers wrapped music, crime, religion, and the submundo into a single package for audiences to read and consume. A number of well-known writers began their careers as police reporters and later moved on to music, Carnival, and popular culture.

While chronicling the submundo drew them closer to it, the same act imbued journalists with power and clearly distanced them from the individuals they wrote about. The pioneering writer João do Rio (João Paulo Alberto Coelho Barreto) fancied himself a *flâneur*, a title which made him a "vagrant" but only in the most romantic sense. "To be a flâneur," he wrote, "is to be a vagabond and to reflect, it is to be a vagrant and to make commentary, to have the virus of observation that is connected to that of vagrancy. It is to wander around, in the morning, in the day, at night, to walk around the masses."[64] Like João do Rio, Orestes Barbosa, a prolific poet and writer who also composed music and wrote the lyrics for dozens of recorded songs, saw himself as a privileged observer of the city. In 1933, he published *Samba: Sua história, seus poetas, seus músicos e seus cantores* (Samba: Its history, poets, musicians, and singers). The book was published on the heels of two earlier volumes, *Bambambã!* and *Na prisão: Chronicas* (In prison: Chronicles), both of which detailed his time as a prisoner in Rio's Casa de Detenção.[65] In both, Barbosa weaved descriptions of musicians and dance halls into narratives of a mysterious, alluring, and sometimes frightening collection of prison worlds. To Barbosa and other writers, crime and music were closely related, even symbiotic spheres.

Jogo do bicho (the animal game), a popular form of gambling, was another node at which crime and music met, at least in the popular imagination. Like prostitution, jogo do bicho occupied the gray legal terrain between outright prohibition and tacit tolerance.[66] Police and *bicheiros* (jogo do bicho ticket sellers) shared an irregular relationship, in which authorities alternated between repressing games and allowing gambling to take place by looking the other way. Bicheiros were frequently arrested for vagrancy, even though six articles of the Penal Code specifically addressed gambling.[67] Gambling houses (casas de tavolagem) and impromptu street-corner games such as chapinha or vermelinha received similar treatment. The already fuzzy line between licit and illicit was blurred further by the fact that different forms of gambling were afforded distinct degrees of autonomy. Ritzy casinos in posh neighborhoods like Copacabana generally avoided police attention.

Police postures toward capoeira and religion were also uneven. The 1830 Penal Code did not refer to the practice, but police nonetheless made hundreds of capoeira-related arrests during the nineteenth century. But capoeira gangs also led public processions and parades and were even employed by politicians to enforce favorable results at the polls. Capoeira was made illegal in the same section of the 1890 Penal Code that covered vagrancy: "Of Vagrants and Capoeiras."[68] As was the case for capoeira, the 1830 Penal Code included no mention of feitiçaria, defined by Dain Borges as "the loose, derogatory term for all unorthodox magical and religious practices."[69] The 1890 Penal Code included three articles that prohibited feitiçaria. Because early republican law protected religious freedom, the prohibitions were justified on the grounds that spirit possession and folk healing could harm unknowing individuals who might confuse those practices with "legitimate" forms of medicine or science.

Definitions of feitiçaria and acceptable forms of religion varied by region and changed over time. In northeastern Brazil, "traditional" or "pure" African expressions were tolerated and encouraged more than in Rio, where practices such as umbanda, which combined African-Brazilian and indigenous traditions with spiritism, a set of beliefs inspired by the Frenchman Allan Kardec, flourished. Heterodox religious sects grew across Brazil during the early twentieth century. In 1937, sixty-seven candomblé houses joined to form an association in Salvador, and, between 1904 and 1920, the Brazilian Spiritist Federation claimed to provide between one hundred thousand and three hundred thousand consultations per year in Rio.[70] Raimundo Nina Rodrigues, a criminalist anthropologist, first viewed candomblé with disdain and feared that its survival would cause the entire state of Bahia to "turn black."[71] But he was also fascinated with the religion, which is organized around divination, sacrifice, healing, music, dance, and spirit possession, and he came to advocate for its measured incorporation into society. In Rio, throughout the early twentieth century, rumors that politicians and other well-to-do cariocas frequented clandestine religious gatherings circulated widely.

The portion of the 1890 Penal Code that addressed witchcraft focused on the unlicensed practice of medicine and the manipulation of well-meaning or gullible citizens. The feitiçaria provisions forbade the practice of "any of the branches of medicine, dentistry or pharmacy" without a license and prohibited the use of "spiritism or magic" to "arouse sentiments of hate or love . . . [or] to fascinate and dominate the credulity of the public." The code also made illegal the prescription of "a substance from any of the kingdoms of Nature, thus performing or exercising the profession of folk healer [*curandeiro*]."[72] Separate articles addressed poisonous substances and regulated the circulation and distribution of medications.

Judges often pointed out that no religions—as religions—were prohibited by law. Summarizing a 1915 ruling, a jurist wrote that the law only forbade certain religious practices when they served as a means "to illicit ends . . . that abuse public credulity."[73] An 1895 decision stated that witch doctors (*feiticeiros*) and anyone else exercising medicine without a license could not enjoy the "professional liberty" protected in the constitution. Such individuals forfeited their rights by preying on the "weak spirit" of "ignorant persons" and inspiring among their victims "illusory hopes." A separate case reinforced the language of the Penal Code by finding that folk healing (*curandeirismo*) was "not a profession."[74] João do Rio distinguished between "sincere" and "exploitative" healers, the latter referring to those who took advantage of public "credulity."[75] The difference between well-meaning professionals and exploitative witch doctors resonated with the code's focus on "false" beggars and the larger desire to distinguish between workers and vagrants and between acceptable and unacceptable methods of acquiring wealth. The police used Article 399 to control individuals engaged in any one of a number of illegal or marginal moneymaking schemes. In addition to pimps, prostitutes, thieves, bicheiros, and street-corner gamblers, people circulating false currency were also incarcerated for vagrancy. The importance of delineating acceptable economic practices is seen in the defense statement of an alleged fortune-teller (*cartomante*), arrested in 1917 for vagrancy. Quoting a well-known legal scholar, the statement defined vagrancy as "social parasitism . . . an individual, social, and economic phenomenon," punishable when the act "constitutes a germ . . . or [affects] the interests of the economic order or of social security." The accused, the statement insisted, represented no such threat.[76]

The case illustrates how police actions often focused on reprimanding and controlling informal monetary transactions, a fact that provides important clues about why music did not receive the same treatment as the illicit activities commonly associated with it. Individuals who gathered in public to play pandeiros hardly wielded the economic influence to threaten "public credulity" or "economic order." While the police could extort money from prostitutes, pimps, and individuals who played jogo do bicho (*jogadores*), fewer opportunities existed to do the same to someone who pocketed a bit of cash from playing music on the street or who gathered in private with family and friends. And yet such individuals were not immune to police abuse. In 1900, a man told a reporter from the daily *Jornal do Brasil* that the police confiscated his guitar one day without explanation and later required him to pay a fee to get it back.[77] But if guitar players could be susceptible to police abuse, there is little evidence to suggest that the police saw in musicians the kind of threat to "economic order" that they saw in others.

Carnival and Clubs

While police did not view musicians as threats to economic order, there were arenas in which authorities did exercise direct control over music. The Festa da Penha, a popular celebration held annually in October outside the famous church Santuário de Nossa Senhora da Penha, served as an unofficial commencement to the lucrative Carnival season, which culminated months later during pre-Lenten festivities. Musicians often introduced songs at Penha to position themselves for popularity and success during Carnival. Additional opportunities for financial gain existed in selling Carnival objects such as confetti, streamers, masks, costumes, and *lança-perfumes*—in the nineteenth century, the latter were projectiles that could be filled with perfumed water or less appetizing liquids; in the early twentieth century, they were tiny glass canisters that sprayed a form of ether that gave people a temporary high.

As a lucrative and also raucous festival, Carnival often turned into a site of conflict and contestation. Such was the case in 1912, when officials attempted to delay Carnival after the death of the statesman and man of letters the Baron of Rio Branco (José Maria da Silva Paranhos

Júnior). Rio Branco's passing rocked the city's elite and created a cloud of uncertainty around the impending Carnival festivities. The newspaper *A Noite* declared Rio Branco's death a "national catastrophe" and questioned whether Carnival would be delayed as a sign of respect. Asked if he would impose a delay, the president of the republic, Marechal (Marshal) Hermes de Fonseca, told the paper, "I don't have the ability to do that. It is the *povo's* [people's] celebration, and so it is the povo who may or may not postpone Carnival."[78] For the next seven days, in seeking an authority who would provide more guidance, *A Noite* interviewed the chief of police, the prefect, Carnival clubs, and even merchants who sold Carnival products.

While no elected official was willing to take a definitive stand, authorities publicly asked Carnival clubs to postpone their celebrations and also sought cooperation from bars and bands, hoping that without music, revelers would have no choice but to remain inside. Military bands were forbidden from performing, and the police persuaded bar, club, and theater owners to delay large parties until April.[79] The entertainment magnate Paschoal Segreto agreed to follow suit. A group of factory owners approached the police chief with an offer to prohibit worker bands from participating in parades. In addition to asking Carnival societies and other organizations to delay their celebrations, authorities adopted other measures, including extra patrols and an edict issued by the prefect prohibiting the sale of Carnival objects until April.[80] Despite these measures, downtown was hardly the deserted, quiet place desired by those wishing to honor Rio Branco in solemnity. On the recently renamed Avenida Rio Branco, clowns mingled with revelers armed with lança-perfumes and automobiles filled with guitar players. A journalist was seen fighting his way through the chaos, attempting to distribute a monograph he had written in honor of Rio Branco.[81] Swept up by the "great animation," a theater owner reneged on his promise to remain closed.[82]

The failure to postpone Carnival meant that the city ended up holding two celebrations: the informal, spontaneous one in February, and the rescheduled, official festivities in April. As the city prepared for its second celebration, *A Noite* gauged enthusiasm for the second round by referring to the health of seasonal Carnival markets. "Will the next Carnival be animated?" the paper asked. "There is no doubt that it will be. . . . There is the same enormous enthusiasm of every year in the purchase of [Carnival objects]."[83] The paper marveled that the director of one club paid 800 mil-réis (800$000, approximately US $260) for his costume, nearly the average annual salary of a factory worker.[84] Prices for lança-perfumes were a bit more accessible: 8$000 (US $2.60) for ten grams, 13$500 (US $4.40) for thirty, and 22$000 (US $7.10) for sixty grams of Rodo-brand liquid. Vlan, "a good national product, sold with no alteration," went for 7$000, 12$000, and 18$000.[85]

That *A Noite* used the market for Carnival objects to gauge the festival's health underscores that the celebration, often cast as either a delirious inversion of societal norms or a competition between brute police force and popular resistance, was also an intrinsically economic event.[86] The fact that Carnival and other festivals could dramatically alter consumption patterns and prices was clear to a team of scholars who decades later set out to conduct a "scientific" study of the cost of living in Rio de Janeiro. To obtain a representative sample of household spending, the researchers made sure that the monthlong cost logs they asked respondents to compile did not fall during any large public celebration, when an inordinate amount of money was likely to be spent on costumes, food, and drink.[87]

Entrepreneurs with sufficient resources and connections seized on Carnival markets to promote and sell new products for which they had secured patents. Rubino and Trimas, an Italian and Brazilian, designed a "new system" of "Twentieth-Century Carnival Masks," which boasted unique molding that, the inventors promised, would support a Carnivalgoer's face longer than any other mask. Dr. Otto Raulino, a resident of Rio, registered his "patriotic" confetti and streamers, "made of two- or multi-colored paper, representing the colors of the Earth's principal nations." In 1901, spurred by "great development . . . in the confetti industry," Antonio Alves Pinto Guedes sought to "add one more quality to that industry, making the inoffensive pastime even more perfect and attractive." Rather than scenting confetti with just any liquid or powder, as street vendors would, his "Ideal" brand used "already prepared" substances.[88]

As they did with healing practices, authorities, consumers, and the press divided Carnival products into licit and illicit categories. Registered vendors sold lança-perfumes and advertised their wares in newspapers, while unaffiliated merchants sold what *A Noite* called "falsified" products.[89] Replacing perfumed water with urine, sewer water, and other foul-smelling liquids in Carnival projectiles was an old trick, long described by social critics as an example of "degeneracy."[90] During the 1880s, several writers criticized the police for persecuting "poor young ladies" who earned "scant profits" from selling objects on the street while taking no action against the advertisement and sale of similar wares in high-society magazines.[91]

Attempts to regulate commerce and root out the production and sale of illicit Carnival objects were not the only strategies police used to control festivals. Violence and mass arrests were common, but police authority was also contested and flouted. To circumvent a prohibition against instruments at the Festa da Penha in 1908, individuals beat pieces of wood against glass bottles and clapped their hands in time.[92] But Carnival groups and participants did not simply resist the police; they also looked to authorities for assistance in disputes against neighbors and rival clubs. Authorities often mediated between groups who vied for popularity, bragging rights, and the financial prizes attached to both. Carnival groups raised money by charging membership fees and holding dances. The more popular the group, the more money it stood to earn. Their members' standing in the community, the quality of the events that they held, and their Carnival parties, floats, musical processions, and parades also shaped clubs' reputations. Competition among the clubs frequently led to clashes that required police intervention. On 9 November 1902, the Carnival club Grupo Carnavalesco Flor da Lyra met for a special assembly meeting at its headquarters in Bangu, a working-class neighborhood. At roughly 8:50 PM, the meeting was interrupted when members from a rival club, the Grupo Flor da União, invaded the headquarters of Flor da Lyra and attacked its members, who filed a criminal complaint against Flor da União.[93] It is unclear what provoked the attack, but the incident emphasizes how the police's role in Carnival extended beyond brute repression.[94]

In addition to mediating disputes, the police also exerted economic control, often at the city's numerous recreational societies (*clubes* or *sociedades recreativos*). The societies, though immensely popular, were generally held in much lower esteem than the city's *grandes sociedades*, which were founded in the middle of the nineteenth century, attracted the city's elite, and received government funding for their Carnival displays. Located mainly in working-class neighborhoods, the clubs offered their members a place to congregate for family occasions, dances (*bailes*), and parties. Clubs were required to petition the police annually for licenses to function and to hold Carnival parades. Most petitions were granted, but the police did not hesitate to close clubs, especially those that they considered to be magnets for "bad elements." Newspapers frequently ran stories about fights and even murders at the clubs. A police official rejected one club's petition and denounced its members as "disorderlies and vagabonds." A week later, a different official approved the petition, lauding the same members as "upright men of work with permanent domiciles." The police official who read the petition of a different club accused its members of participating in illicit gambling and questioned whether the club, which permitted nonmembers to pay a small fee to gain entrance, could reasonably control the quality of individuals who frequented the premises. By letting in nonmembers, the official wrote in denying the license, the club would forfeit "scruples or choice" over who attended its gatherings.[95]

Clubs went to great lengths to portray their members (*sócios*) as honest workers, using language and terms that closely resembled the defenses presented by and for vagrancy suspects. Club statutes, which were reviewed by the police, required members to always display "good behavior," carry themselves as upstanding citizens, and maintain a steady job and a permanent home. New members were admitted only with recommendations from existing sócios. A criminal conviction, and sometimes even an acquittal, could disqualify a candidate. One club's statutes required "morality and an honest occupation" from any would-be member and prohibited persons involved in "any criminal case."[96]

In addition to requiring members to hold steady work and maintain a clean slate with the police, many recreational societies prohibited specific behaviors and went out of their way to portray themselves as dignified and moral. A number of the clubs were racially integrated. One included statutes that promised to accept individuals regardless of "color, nationality, or profession." But the same club was not open to all comers. Like many others, it required references of "good conduct" from any would-be member. Another club threatened to expel any member who "became publicly known as an immoral or shameful person."[97] Club Carnavalesco Caprichosos de Jacarepaguá prohibited its members from "smoking, causing uproars, disturbances, illicit discussions that could result in disharmony, drunkenness . . . [using] obscene words . . . [and] dancing continuously with only one woman." The club also denied the admittance of guests who were not party to "legitimate matrimony." Another society listed "family gatherings" and "diversions permitted by law" as its primary activities. Even the Enemies of Work (Inimigos do Trabalho) forbade the presence of unknown guests and provided for the expulsion of any member who "made himself into a nuisance" or disturbed the functioning of the club's general assembly.[98]

On one level, these examples of self-policing may be read as posturing in the face of authorities. But in many cases the strict codes of behavior were more than just window dressing. Club statutes were often lengthy and complex, with detailed descriptions of intricate power structures and a rigorous schedule of meetings and functions. These were not meaningless documents thrown together simply for the sake of the police, but rather serious codes of conduct and organizational structure, indicative of club members' desire to disassociate dances, Carnival, and, above all, themselves, from violence, crime, and anything else that could result in a stigma.

The process by which the police approved or denied petitions was subjective, informed by a club's track record, the perceived quality of its application and statutes, and the personal knowledge and whim of the police inspector. Requirements listed on the standardized form that police issued when granting licenses indicate how social and economic control merged in the petitioning process. Clubs were required to prohibit illegal gambling and to conclude rehearsals by 10 PM and dances by 2 AM. Carnival rehearsals could be held only on particular days in January and February. In addition, clubs were expected to function with "doors open" and provide unlimited access to police. Most important to the clubs: they could charge admission only after securing police approval.

Free admission to dances did not mean that anyone could attend; it was just the opposite: entrance was limited to members and their guests. Opening an event to anyone who could pay a small entrance fee might give the impression that the club had no "scruples or choice" over who attended its events. Clubs caught attempting to raise money through paid admission were shut down. Without the opportunity to raise revenue through ticket sales, clubs sustained themselves—officially, at least—by collecting monthly dues. To the police, making club events private was a way to monitor attendance. But the strategy worked only if societies themselves were vigilant. The clubs' strict codes of conduct suggest that many groups complied, though others surely charged admission on the sly. The only direct control over musicians was levied by the clubs themselves, which often forbade their artists to play for the competition. The defection of a top performer would mean the loss of prestige and profits. Prohibiting musicians from "double dipping" also portended a strategy adopted later by record labels and intellectual property associations, which limited the affiliations of their members for similar reasons. The clubs' responsibilities—to control the mobility of its musicians and to select and reprimand its members—meant that they played an integral role in their own surveillance. Within the clubs, it was not musicians or music that most concerned the police, but rather the flow of money and the violent and disorderly behavior often associated with large gatherings.

Informal Patronage and the Musical Geography of Tia Ciata's House

Struggles to control popular music extended beyond the bounds of Carnival and the clubs. One of the most famous stories about musicians and the police involves João da Baiana (João Machado Guedes), the individual pictured in figure 1 holding a pandeiro while behind bars. In 1908, Pinheiro Machado, a well-known senator, held a party at his house in Rio de Janeiro. He contracted Guedes and several other musicians to provide musical entertainment. Guedes never arrived, having been stopped by the police, who confiscated his pandeiro. Without it, he had little reason to attend the party. Upon hearing the news, Machado ordered a new instrument made, bearing the inscription, "With admiration, João da Baiana.— Senator Pinheiro Machado."[99]

This encounter was probably not the only one between Machado and Guedes, who would later recall the presence of the senator and other well-known public figures at the musical gatherings organized by his mother, Tia Perciliana (Perciliana Maria Constança). The pandeiro that Machado ordered for Guedes was more than just a prized gift. According to Guedes, the senator's signature also served as a form of identification that he could flash to authorities wishing to imprison or harass him. During the 1930s and '40s, official paper documents, including worker identification cards, marriage and birth certificates, property titles, formal rental agreements, and national identity cards, gained increasing importance in determining status and affecting the outcomes of trials and criminal proceedings.[100] Decades before that, João da Baiana secured his own less formal "document" in the form of a musical instrument. His story suggests that while most musicians did not have access—at least as musicians—to the formal patronage relationships often available to workers through their bosses or unions, a select few enjoyed informal protection.

João da Baiana was well connected through his mother and Tia Ciata (Hilária Batista de Almeida), one of the most influential and well-known

Afro-Brazilian women in Rio. João da Baiana and a number of other talented musicians met regularly at Tia Ciata's house to play music, socialize, and engage in religious devotion. Because the gatherings, believed to be the place of genesis for Donga's "Pelo telefone," involved a combination of music, religion, and merriment, they also attracted politicians and elite cariocas regularly. Tia Ciata's husband, João Batista da Silva, worked as a typesetter for the *Jornal do Commercio* and later as a customs official. Before moving to Rio, he attended medical school in Bahia. The couple's grandson Bucy Moreira recalled that Silva earned protection and powerful friends by providing medical care for Wenceslau Braz, president of the republic from 1914 to 1918. In return for his services, Silva secured a low-level job working for the chief of police.[101]

It is easy to imagine that gatherings like those that took place at Tia Ciata's house—where men and women, many of them dark skinned, drummed, danced, and sang—could attract unwanted attention. And there is no indication that the police would care to, or even could, distinguish music from illicit religious practices. Like conked hair, guitars, and knives, "samba" implied any one of a number of labels—"black," "poor," and "criminal" among them—even before the term came to signify a single coherent musical form. But as we saw in the case of Captain Antônio Gabriel in Rio Novo, samba could also represent something more than crime or disorder. On occasion it might even insulate against police persecution. João da Baiana and others who attended the famous parties at Tia Ciata's house were well aware of the fact that some musical forms were "safer" than others, and they organized their gatherings accordingly. Based on conversations with Tia Ciata's relatives, the writer Roberto Moura reconstructed a basic blueprint of her house, which was partitioned into several sections and included a small area and shack around back. The sections allowed for a graduated division of music, worship, and festivities. In the front room, facing the street, the most refined musicians performed while others danced. Walking toward the back of the house, one would encounter younger, less accomplished musicians in drum circles, and outside, near the shack, religious devotion.[102] Pixinguinha, a friend of João da Baiana's and Donga's, recalled how the musical geography of Tia Ciata's house placed the most presentable and acceptable performances and performers in public view. "Samba," Pixinguinha told interviewers in the late 1960s, was "João da Baiana's thing. I wasn't part of samba. They would play their sambas out back and I would play my *choros* in the front room.[103] The division between samba and choro, a fast-paced music featuring guitar, *cavaquinho*, and flute, suggests how hierarchies and distinctions drawn by musicians informed and were informed by outside perceptions. Gatherings of any kind could attract the police, though for those who knew someone like João Batista da Silva, personal connections might hold the authorities at bay. In any case, it never hurt to hide "witchcraft" and the rawer beats behind a polished parlor facade.

Gendered Silences

The punishment paradigm is misleading not only because it distorts the nature of post-abolition social control but also because it encourages marginalization and silence. In 1992, journalists asked Acelino dos Santos—known in his prime as the Carnival dancer Bicho Novo (New Critter)—about a period during which he had disappeared from public view. "It was during the war," he said, "1941 or '42." While attending a party at his samba school, a fight broke out, and he fled. Within hours, the police caught and arrested him, before temporarily releasing him. "The police invaded my house and threw me in [jail], accused of murder. I was there without knowing what I had done." Eventually, the police informed him that a man had died during the fight and that Bicho Novo, "practically the school's president," should have done something about it. "I refused to accept the blame," he said, "and they sent me to [jail] for three months, at which point the judge absolved me for lack of proof and let me go."[104]

Police records tell a dramatically different story. According to documents housed at the Arquivo Nacional, Bicho Novo was imprisoned in July 1941, but for a crime that apparently had nothing to do with music. Four years earlier, he had attacked his girlfriend Arlinda Maria da Conceição with a knife, stabbing her first in the face and then in the right arm. After examining Conceição, a doctor reported that an eleven-centimeter facial wound and a twenty-seven-centimeter gash in Conceição's arm would probably result in permanent "deformity."[105] Two individuals testified that Bicho Novo attacked Conceição when she failed to promptly deliver a meal that she had prepared for him. After the alleged assault, Bicho Novo evaded the police for four years. After being apprehended in 1941, he received a three-year prison sentence, later reduced to twenty-one months.

Even when taking into account the multiple absences and distortions common to police documents, it is hard to believe that these charges were false. The police were hardly above inventing evidence or making arrests without providing clear justification. But in this case there appears to have been little motivation for the police to lie. Bicho Novo, by contrast, had every reason to sculpt his own version of the truth. For an elderly artist (he was eighty-three years old at the time of the interview), the police-repression story was surely a more attractive option than confessing to having committed a brutal crime.

Bicho Novo's use of the punishment paradigm and his erasure of Conceição are indicative of a larger set of processes through which women have been marginalized and silenced. The silencing of women within the historiography (popular and scholarly) of samba took place on multiple levels. Women like Tia Ciata and Tia Perciliana exercised great influence but rarely had the same opportunities to establish careers or make property claims as those available to the men who gathered at their houses. But both women expertly managed and marketed their cultural knowledge and expertise. Tia Ciata made and sold Bahian culinary specialties and also created Bahian clothes and costumes, which she sold to theater companies and Carnival groups. Eventually, her business grew to the point where she had to hire employees outside of her family. Tia Perciliana opened a small shop where she sold religious objects.[106]

Attacks like the one perpetrated against Conceição appear regularly in police records and have long been described in popular song. Between 1926 and 1934, the police arrested the musician Brancura (Sílvio Fernandes) at least eight times—on five occasions for vagrancy and once each for *defloramento* (deflowering), light physical offenses, and possession of an illegal firearm.[107] Fernandes belongs to a long list of individuals who helped pioneer samba but have received little public or scholarly attention. Born around the turn of the century, Fernandes had a brief career, dying in 1935, six years after he recorded his first song.[108] It is unclear who gave him the moniker *brancura* (whiteness), but the label was undoubtedly made tongue-in-cheek. According to one source, "He earned the nickname from his friends . . . on account of his brilliant black skin."[109] While biographical details of Brancura are rare, his rough treatment of women is well known. According to the *Dicionário Cravo Albin*, "He is remembered for his bravado and, in keeping with 1920s . . . *malandragem* [the art or practice of being a malandro], for never going out without his knife. . . . He would even stab the girls he dated."[110] In 1926, the mother of a fourteen-year-old girl initiated a defloramento case in which she accused Brancura of forcing her daughter, Angela, to have sex at knife-point. The case concluded with the two getting married.[111] It is unclear how Angela and her mother felt about the decision. Marriage was seen as an "honorable" resolution and may have provided some solace to the mother, who told the police that her daughter had been *deshonestada* (dishonored, or robbed of her innocence). But the case's violent nature, which distinguishes it from most others on record, must have given both women pause about the prospect of Angela marrying her assailant.

Race and class marked this and many other defloramento cases. Angela's mother attested that the family lived in a "state of miserableness" (*estado de miserabilidade*), and Angela's birth certificate identified her skin color as parda (brown). The fact that Brancura faced no criminal punishment even though the judge found the charges to be accurate reflects how victims' racial and socioeconomic background often determined the outcome of defloramento cases. Sueann Caulfield writes, "As the victim's color got darker, the likelihood of indictment as well as conviction decreased."[112] Of course, race also often worked against dark-skinned defendants, but in this case it was Angela's skin color, more than Brancura's, that influenced the outcome.

A separate defloramento case involving Noel Rosa—white, middle class, and one of the great samba musicians of all time—ended in similar fashion. In 1934, the mother of a young white woman named Lindaura Martins filed a defloramento complaint against the popular musician.[113] The case, which includes no mention of violence or force, concluded with Rosa and Martins marrying in December of the same year. As with Brancura, Rosa's record with women is legendary. Rosa's cousin and biographer, who makes no mention of the defloramento charges, suggests that Noel entered into the marriage conveniently, without disturbing his fast lifestyle:

> He had plenty of opportunities to marry women from established families. He . . . had plenty of young admirers in high society. He didn't want any of them. Out of his good nature, he married Lindaura, the daughter of a laborer. Linda was not ugly or evil, and Noel was satisfied. . . . The marriage was of little consequence. . . . Noel would continue his life in bohemia, writing sambas and dedicating poems to other women.[114]

Two other authors emphasize Rosa's carefree lifestyle. Before meeting Martins, his life had been carefree: "no hard work, only samba, bohemia, and liberty to do whatever he wanted." Somewhat ironically, given the fact that he chose matrimony over a possible prison sentence, they write, "Marriage? He would rather go to prison."[115]

NO,
REALLY

The cases of Rosa, Brancura, and Bicho Novo reflect how female voices have often been silenced or marginalized by biographies and music histories that celebrate male sexual exploits and conquest. When Bicho Novo spoke with journalists in 1992, he situated himself within a familiar history, one that was equal parts tragic and heroic. In the past, he and other musical pioneers suffered, but ultimately they persevered. That narrative, which helped him shape his own legacy, clearly had a different effect on Conceição, who was effectively erased.

The three cases also emphasize a point made throughout this chapter: when musicians came into contact with the police, their interactions rarely resembled those canonized in the punishment paradigm. To officers patrolling the streets of Rio de Janeiro during the early twentieth century, music was rarely a major preoccupation. Popular musicians—who were not yet accepted as professionals, but also not necessarily guilty of practicing an "offensive" trade—occupied a particularly murky space in Rio's shadowy legal landscape. Police harassed guitar- and pandeiro-toting individuals and prohibited the playing of certain instruments at public festivals but did not systematically target musicians. Some musicians perpetrated illegal or violent acts, and others suffered arbitrary abuse. But individuals who played or composed music were rarely if ever arrested because they were musicians. False and vague accounts of how samba was "prohibited" fail to reflect the fact that the anti-vagrancy campaign entangled Rio's poor in a system of social and economic control organized around the vagrant-worker poles and dependent on self-surveillance. Early twentieth-century policing techniques were significant and successful not only because they targeted destitute populations, but also because they enrolled those populations in monitoring and shaping their own behavior and identities.

To some musicians, the punishment paradigm represented an opportunity to turn "alienation into self-actualizing performance," a phrase that Daphne Brooks uses to describe the creative and resourceful ways that nineteenth-century black performers on both sides of the Atlantic transformed marginalization into a source of power.[116] To Brazilian artists, recounting police abuse could function as a denunciation of racism or serve as a stamp of authenticity—indication that an artist had paid his dues and assurance that his music was soulful because it had been shaped by pain and oppression. As the case of Bicho Novo makes clear, similar stories could also be put to use toward very different ends.

In 1948, a journalist for a Bahian newspaper journeyed to Rio where he conducted an interview with João Mina, a nonagenarian favela resident said to be one of the last living former slaves in the city.[117] João Mina described to the journalist animated religious gatherings that took place decades earlier. By the end of the night, he recalled, the gatherings would often devolve into disputes and physical confrontations among male participants. Sometimes those confrontations attracted the police. When that happened João Mina and his friends had a proven go-to strategy. They would tell the women to dance and, when the police arrived, explain that there was really nothing to see: just a harmless little samba party among friends.

3

MUSICIANS OUTSIDE THE CIRCLE
Race, Wealth, and Property in Fred Figner's Music Market

While politicians and officers of the law were designing and implementing the anti-vagrancy campaign, musicians, inventors, and entrepreneurs were transforming the way that Brazilians played, purchased, and listened to music. By the early twentieth century, rituals and musical forms that placed musicians in large circular formations, shoulder-to-shoulder with dancers, singers, and revelers—calundu and certain forms of lundu, for example—ceded space to genres that situated instrumentalists away from dancers. Spatial transformations placed new focus and attention on individual musicians, whose work was reproduced and redistributed on a new scale. Phonographs became regularly available to wealthy Brazilians around 1897, and the ability to record music in Brazil arrived in 1902. In 1927, electromagnetic recording opened up a whole new world of Brazilian sound that could be recorded and reproduced. By the late 1930s, radios were affordable to a significant portion of the population. These changes helped move musicians literally and figuratively "outside the circle" and into the public spotlight, where they found new opportunities and new challenges.[1]

On the Run: From Slavery to the Circus and Beyond

Benjamin de Oliveira, a multitalented performer and entrepreneur, was among the most visible and successful artists to launch his career amid these changes. He was born in 1870 to two Brazilian-born slaves in rural Minas Gerais. Both parents held relatively privileged positions in the slave hierarchy. Benjamin's mother was an "escrava de estimação," a designation that made her children free at birth. Her husband, Malaquias, was famous for his imposing physical presence. Benjamin recalled his father as a "black Hercules"; Malaquias was frequently deployed to catch runaway slaves, many of whom returned dead. At the age of twelve, partially in fear of his father, Benjamin ran away with a traveling circus and later gave himself the last name de Oliveira.[2]

Over the better part of six decades, until his death in 1954, Oliveira transformed Brazilian entertainment as a clown, mime, acrobat, musician, playwright, and stage director in the circuses and popular theaters of Rio and São Paulo. Before achieving stardom, he bounced from circus to circus. During a retrospective interview, he told a journalist, "My destiny was to flee. [It's] black people's destiny."[3] He recalled being apprehended by a white man who assumed he was a runaway slave. Oliveira insisted that he was free and that he worked in the circus. He performed a tumbling routine on the spot, satisfying the planter, who let him go. Even if Oliveira embellished the story, its larger point is clear: proof of a trade or employment was sometimes the only way for men of color to claim their freedom in the face of skeptical authority figures.

Oliveira played guitar, sang, and made several records, but he was better known as a clown, actor, and mime. His career took off in the late 1880s, and over the next three decades he starred in the circus and the *teatro de revista* (a combination of vaudeville and "light" comedic theater), arenas with substantial overlap and cross-fertilization.[4] Between the 1890s and 1920s, traveling circuses were among Brazil's most important entertainment institutions and conduits, bringing music and theater performances from Rio and São Paulo to distant locations. Most of Rio's early recording stars spent time playing at or performing in the circus. Between 1919 and 1922, the city had at least thirty-five circus venues, with an average capacity of seventeen hundred people.[5]

Oliveira was a gifted and dedicated entrepreneur, who carefully and painstakingly built a career and popular following. Like other circus performers and theater artists, he took to the streets to distribute pamphlets and advertise his skills and repertoires to passersby. He also visited newspaper offices and provided journalists with press releases and interviews. In 1910, he directed and starred in an elaborate production for Rio's famous Spinelli Circus of the *Viúva alegre*, a Brazilian version of *The Merry Widow*, replete with acrobats, clowns, trapezists, and moving images from past productions projected onto screens mounted around the theater.[6]

During one performance, an audience member shouted that Oliveira should take lessons from the Portuguese actor Grijó. "With the greatest ease," a journalist wrote, "Benjamim responded immediately, 'Grijó is a foreigner and I am in my land.' Prolonged applause and *bravos* echoed through the circus."[7] The anonymous heckler was not the only one who considered Oliveira to be out of place. Early in his career he ate alone, away from the tables shared by white performers. He ran away from one circus company after its owner tried to trade him for a horse.[8] Eventually he secured a delicate celebrity. In a 1907 article about "the most picturesque manifestation of the povo," the author and playwright Artur Azevedo described Oliveira as "one of the most popular artists in the Spinelli circus. He is a negro, but an Apollonian negro, toned; a negro who, clothed in his baggy 'clown' pants, gives the impression that Othello jumped straight from the pages of Shakespeare into a circus in Cidade Nova." The same journalist who recounted the Grijó exchange described Oliveira as the "preferred actor of Mangue [the city's red-light district] and surroundings; [he speaks] in mutilated Portuguese, which is natural." Azevedo was impressed with Oliveira's dazzling array of identities, which included a number of white characters, which he portrayed by donning powdered wigs and white makeup. In addition to being "an admirable acrobat and celebrated guitar player," Azevedo wrote, Oliveira was "an artist who can create any face that he desires, here as a blond European . . . now [a] red Indian." "He is," the playwright concluded, "our Tabarin," the famous seventeenth-century French performer.[9]

In one of the first plays that he wrote, *O negro do frade* (The friar's black son), Oliveira cast himself as Arlipe, the poor black protagonist who falls in love with the white daughter of a nobleman, who wishes her betrothed to the son of a rich white acquaintance. The daughter is passionately in love with Arlipe, whose mother is a washerwoman and whose absentee father is rumored to be a local friar. At the end of the play, the friar recognizes Arlipe as his son and bequeaths him an enormous inheritance, just as the daughter's white suitor falls into financial ruin, all of which clears the way for Arlipe and his lover to build a life together. The play, advertised as a *farsa-fantástica*, became a staple of circus-theater into the 1920s.[10] It at once reaffirmed expectations about wealth and color (black = poor, white = rich) and also tweaked them. The play's romantic ending emphasized the potential for transformation but was only possible thanks to a set of unlikely events: the demise of a young white nobleman and the ascension of a poor young black man who magically acquires social standing and wealth. It played to growing enthusiasm for controlled racial mixture while safely depicting Arlipe's transformation as the stuff of fairy tales.

Fred Figner and the Record Industry

While the circus provided artists like Oliveira an extensive, traveling arena in which to perform, it could not match the cachet or reach of recorded sound. In the late nineteenth and early twentieth centuries, songs were delivered to audiences through new devices and technology, a great number of which were imported, marketed, and sold by one man: Frederico (Fred) Figner, an entrepreneurial European immigrant who pioneered the production and sale of records in Brazil. Figner was born in 1866 in what is today the Czech Republic. He gained U.S. citizenship in 1891 and Brazilian citizenship in 1921.[11] In 1891, he bought several phonographs in San Francisco; traveled to New York to purchase cylinders, batteries, and additional equipment; and then boarded a ship for Belém, Pará, in northern Brazil. The following April he arrived in Rio, where he eventually settled down. He arrived in Rio little more than a decade after the 1878 debut of Thomas Edison's "talking machine" before an enraptured audience at a weekly lecture series frequented by the royal family. Figner tirelessly promoted his wares and held countless exhibitions to raise money and build popular interest.

In 1902, Figner solidified his place in the music industry by orchestrating the first Brazilian sound recording. Casa Edison, his store and record label, soon issued a catalog offering records and cylinders made by musicians who squeezed themselves, up to twelve at a time, into the tiny studio behind Figner's store on the bustling Rua do Ouvidor in downtown Rio. Figner was in step with the very latest global advances in sonic technology. It was the same year that Columbia and Victor pooled their recording patents, a move that helped usher to a close the use of cylinders in favor of discs and what *Grove Music* describes as "the beginning of recorded sound as a serious medium."[12] In addition to cylinders and records, Casa Edison's catalogs offered a variety of phonographs, graphophones, gramophones, zonophones, telephones, moving-picture machines, stylish lamps, fancy pens, cameras, and firearms.[13]

To build his empire, Figner combined business acumen with creativity, access to capital, and relationships with executives in Europe and North America. Fluent in five languages, and having lived and traveled throughout Europe, the United States, and Latin America, he was uniquely prepared to prosper in a Brazilian market dominated by foreign interests. Even after he brought recording technology to Brazil, the production of records involved key stages that took place in Europe. The wax discs used to record songs in Brazil had to be sent to Germany, where they were finished, transformed into copper negatives, plated in silver, and finally turned into the matrices that were used to create the records, which were then shipped back to Brazil and sold by Figner and other vendors.[14] It was not until 1912 that Brazil would manufacture a disc forged, produced, and recorded entirely on its own soil. In 1913 Figner opened Brazil's first record factory, which had eleven departments and employed 150 workers. Thirty manual presses provided the capacity to turn out 125,000 78 RPM records per month.[15]

Figner hoped to exploit markets for both Brazilian and European music. He secured the patent rights to the two-sided record, which he used to appeal to consumers' national loyalties and European affinities, selling discs with a Brazilian artist on one side and a European recording on the other.[16] He was a tireless advertiser and an enthusiastic producer, working late into the night preparing cylinders only to wake up a few hours later to hawk his merchandise. Figner made his services known through newspaper advertisements, direct mailing, and word of mouth. By 1903 he was filling orders from customers in dozens of cities across Brazil.

The power and influence of European and North American corporations and executives served as both a tool and an obstacle to Figner. In 1893, he visited Milan, where he participated in private recording sessions with artists from La Scala opera house. Fifteen years later, he became Brazil's exclusive distributor of records made by Società Italiana di Fonotipia, the prestigious label associated with La Scala.[17] His relationships with Europeans and North Americans cemented his control over the Brazilian market, even while often leaving him at the mercy of others. In 1900, Figner wrote to a British supplier for whom he was Brazil's top record vendor and requested that a technician be sent who could help him make his own recordings. He received no reply. He was only able to record in Brazil when the music magnate Frederick M. Prescott approached Figner with a golden opportunity: securing a Brazilian patent for two-sided records.[18]

Prescott, who represented Napoleon Petit, the inventor of the two-sided record, saw Petit's invention as an opportunity to corner the Brazilian market. By using a single impression to create one disc with two distinct sides, Prescott could double production without increasing costs. Doing so would allow Prescott and Figner to "give to the public the equivalent of two records for the former price of one." Prescott assured Figner that if he would secure a Brazilian patent for the new technology, then Petit, Prescott, and Figner could gain "absolute" control over the Brazilian market.[19] In return, Figner was obligated to secure the patent and make regular purchases from Prescott.[20] In 1902, Prescott sent a German mechanic to help Figner orchestrate the first recording session conducted on Brazilian soil.[21] Nearly eight hundred tracks were recorded, shipped to Germany, transferred onto two-sided records, and then sent back to Brazil for resale.[22]

Figner competed with entrepreneurs, inventors, and businessmen, all of whom battled to control the fast-evolving field of sound reproduction. Harnessing the latest innovation not only required an inventor, but also a patent, a distribution plan, and a marketing strategy. Constant improvements in sound technology led to patent wars, lawsuits, and corporate mergers and dissolutions. In such an environment, Figner was both dependent and benefactor. The British supplier's decision to ignore his request for recording assistance illustrates his reliance on foreign firms. But Prescott's subsequent offer shows that Figner also wielded his own power as gatekeeper to the Brazilian market.

While Figner relied on patent law to control rights to the double-sided record and to secure a relationship with Prescott, on other occasions he flouted the legal system. An 1878 decree granted Thomas Edison the exclusive right "to introduce in the [Brazilian] Empire the phonograph of his invention," but it was Figner who displayed, marketed, and profited most from the machine.[23] Because the process of granting patents could drag on for years, and because enforcement was often lax, Figner went around patent law as often as he relied on it. But despite often ignoring the law, he was well aware of and often capitalized on the cultural capital attached to patents. One Casa Edison catalog proudly described the store as "the only one that, guaranteed by patent N. 3,465, can sell double-sided records in Brazil."[24] Figner also aggressively registered trademarks and signed exclusive contracts with foreign manufacturers. Between 1904 and 1908, he minted deals with Zonophone, Odeon, Columbia, and Fonotipia. To powerful individuals like Figner, paper property was an invaluable, if selectively respected, resource. Foreign magnates would not distribute their wares through Figner if they doubted his ability to secure patents and fend off intellectual piracy. By both capitalizing on and skirting legal regulations, Figner was able to fortify his domain and shape the creation and consumption of music.

In 1911, Figner used his wealth and connections to secure rights to vast music collections. Upon learning of plans by Columbia Records to obtain rights to Brazilian repertoires through local *editoras de música*, the companies and recording houses that published and often owned the rights to popular songs, Figner sprang into action. In an unpublished memoir, he recounted his strategy:

> I grabbed about a hundred *contos* and went . . . to all the editoras and acquired all of their Author's Rights and any that they would command during the next twenty years. . . . The authors, grasping the situation, from then on, with rare exceptions, sold the printing rights to the publishing houses and the recording rights to myself and others.[25]

The incident emphasizes how events in Brazil were often closely tied to those abroad and also underscores Figner's ability to use his wherewithal and personal fortune to deflect foreign advances. Columbia's planned incursion came during a crucial moment in the global development of intellectual property law. In 1908, European nations met in Berlin, where they revised the 1886 Berne Convention for the Protection of Literary and Artistic Works. The new European agreement explicitly extended composers' rights to the realm of mechanical reproduction.[26] The U.S. Copyright Act of 1909 provided legal protection for composers against unlicensed mechanical reproductions. In 1911, Great Britain codified its intellectual property laws, a transformative event in the global history of intellectual property rights.[27] Meanwhile, Brazil's music market remained governed by few official rules or regulations. Law 496, the nation's first comprehensive intellectual property legislation, was signed on 1 August 1898. The law provided basic guidelines for reproducing and selling works of literature, art, and music, but it was vague and did little to accommodate the sea changes in recording that took place in the following years and decades.[28] The uneven, evolving terrain created by Law 496 is evident in a 1911 recording contract, which granted Figner the right to record music "for talking machines" and other technologies "already or yet to be invented."[29]

Law 496 defined and guaranteed the rights of authors, broadly defined to include literature, science, and art, a category that included musical and "dramatic-musical" compositions. The law gave any author born or residing in Brazil the sole privilege "to reproduce or authorize the reproduction of his work for publication, translation, representation, execution or any other form." (Those rights were extended to foreigners in 1912.) Article 4 made "the author's rights . . . movable, transferable, and transmittable in whole or by part" and allowed them to be passed on to heirs. More than a decade after the passage of Law 496, the transfer of author's rights was far from a uniform or well-regulated practice. The law provided no guidelines to help determine the price or rules for transactions. The ad hoc nature of those transactions is evident in the hundreds of typed and handwritten contracts issued by Figner, many of which hewed to a standard template and many others that did not. Law 496 also failed to distinguish between a composer and a lyricist, a significant omission given the frequency with which the two collaborated or overlapped.

A lack of archival material makes it difficult to gauge the full effect of Law 496. But 196 Casa Edison contracts signed by 82 musicians in 1911 (and one from 1910) provide a small critical mass from which to draw at least tentative insights about the financial arrangements between Figner and his employees.[30] A composer doing business with Figner in 1911 could typically expect to receive about 20$000 (US $6.50) per song, with a range of 10$000 (US $3.25) for the least-accomplished musicians all the way up to 100$000 (US $32.50), which one man, Casemiro Gonçalves da Rocha, received for rights to his 1904 Carnival hit "Rato! Rato!" (Rat! Rat!). Most artists signed only one or two contracts with Figner, and most contracts referred to only one or two songs. For the entire year, individual artists earned between 10$000 and 480$000 (US $155), for an average of just over 87$000 (US $28), but with earnings clustered among low earners (less than 40$000) and a smaller group of high earners (180$000 and above) (see tables 3–5).

Thirteen of Figner's eighty-two composers made 180$000 (US $58) or more, and forty-five made less than 50$000 (US $16). Three composers earned only 10$000 in 1911, a tenth of the amount paid to Rocha for "Rato! Rato!" and the equivalent of the pay for about three days' work in a factory. Rocha earned 430$000 (US $139) in 1911, which put him in elite company near the top of Figner's payroll. Meanwhile, Figner himself sold 840,000 records and netted a whopping 700 contos (700:000$000, US $227,000) between 1911 and 1912.[31] Most artists earned between 10$000 and 100$000, a significant amount of money but not enough to subsist on for more than a short period of time (see table 6). In 1913, a prominent

TABLE 3. Individual Total Earnings
(Casa Edison, 1911)

Composers (n = 82)	Earnings (mil-réis)
14	< 20
27	20–39
5	40–59
3	60–79
7	80–99
4	100–119
7	120–139
2	140–159
0	160–179
13	$\geq$ 180

Source: CEST Documentos, Direito Autoral.

TABLE 4. Contracts per Composer
(Casa Edison, 1911)

Contracts (n = 191)	Composers (n = 82)
1	47
2	14
3	4
4	8
5	0
6	4
7	0
8	2
9	1
$\geq$ 10	2

Source: CEST Documentos, Direito Autoral.

TABLE 5. Contract Value (Casa Edison, 1911)

Contracts (n = 191)	Contract Value (mil-réis)
71	< 20
65	20–29
16	30–39
2	40–49
9	50–59
4	60–69
2	70–79
3	80–89
1	90–99
18	$\geq$ 100

Source: CEST Documentos, Direito Autoral.

TABLE 6. Price and Salary Comparison for Rio de Janeiro (Casa Edison data in gray)

Activity/Provision	Year	Salary/Price (mil-réis)
Annual earnings of Fred Figner	1911–12	700:000$000
Value of Neves-Cearense-Quaresma contract	1911	5:000$000
Highest single contract value (excluding Neves-Cearense-Quaresma contract)	1911	300$000
Estimated cost of living: family of four (per month)	1913	210$000
Bookkeeper/cashier salary (per month)	1910–13	200$000–600$000
Baiano's salary with Casa Edison (per month)	ca. 1905	150$000
Police salary (per month)	1911–13	120$000–200$000
Estimated cost of living: single male (per month)	1913	110$000
Monthly room and board at a pension described by Briton J. C. Oakenfull as "unsuitable for better class people."	1910–13	100$000–300$000
Clerk salary (per month)	1910–13	100$000–200$000
Eduardo das Neves's salary with Casa Edison (per month)	ca. 1905	100$000
Contract value for Casemiro da Rocha's "Rato! Rato!"	1911	100$000
Day laborer/factory worker salary (per month)	1910–13	50$000–104$000
Male servant salary (per month)	1910–13	40$000–150$000
Highest individual total earnings (calculated per month) (excluding Neves-Cearense-Quaresma contract)	1911	40$000
Average single contract value (excluding Neves-Cearense-Quaresma contract)	1911	37$513
Cook salary (per month)	1910–13	30$000–200$000
Average price per song per artist	1911	19$810
Lowest single contract value	1911	10$000
Lowest individual total earnings (calculated per month)	1911	8$333
Average individual total earnings (calculated per month)	1911	7$250
Lança-perfumes, 10–60 grams	1912	7$000–22$000
Price of beef (per kilogram)	1910–14	$400–1$525
Price of bread (per kilogram)	1910–13	$400–$500
Price of salt (per kilogram)	1911–13	$400–$500
Price of milk (per liter)	1910–14	$400–$500
Price of rice (per kilogram)	1910–14	$300–$747
Streetcar fare	1910–12	$100–$400

Sources: A Noite; Affonseca Jr., O custo da vida na cidade do Rio de Janeiro, 14–16; CEST Documentos, Direito Autoral; Damazio, Retrato social, 48; Hahner, Poverty and Politics; McPhee, "'Standing at the Altar,'" 183; Oakenfull, Brazil in 1910, 251–56; Oakenfull, Brazil in 1911, 355–62; Oakenfull, Brazil in 1912, 436–38; Oakenfull, Brazil (1913), 564–71.

textile union estimated that average expenses for a single carioca male worker totaled 110$000 (US $35.50) per month. Providing for a family with two children cost about 210$000 (US $68) per month. Wages for even the highest-earning textile factory workers rarely exceed 90$000 (US $29) a month, not enough to purchase even basic foodstuffs.[32]

While average earnings for a Casa Edison composer were not enough to provide long-term subsistence, it seems that few of Figner's musicians lived in poverty. Some came from privileged backgrounds and probably viewed composing as a hobby or as supplemental income. Anecdotal data are available for instrumentalists and vocalists, some of whom were also composers, and other kinds of Figner employees. During the first decade of the twentieth century, the popular entertainer Baiano earned 150$000 (US $48 in 1905) per month. Eduardo das Neves, a transcendent Afro-Brazilian artist, received a monthly salary of 100$000, about the same amount that it cost a single male to support himself in 1913.[33] Technicians and administrators earned as much as 400$000 per month, nearly double the cost of living for a family of four.[34] In 1906, Mário Pinheiro signed a contract with Figner that paid him 40$000 (US $13.15) a month, plus an additional 40$000 for each recording. While base salaries for most were relatively modest, a single successful song could have a transformative effect. The three instrumentalists who recorded "Rato! Rato!" in 1904 each earned 5$000 (US $1.25), but Rocha, the song's composer, saw a much larger payday.[35] In addition to the 100$000 he received in 1911, he came to command 50$000 per composition, five times more than what was typically paid to lesser-known musicians and more than double the average that Figner paid to all composers in 1911.[36]

Fewer than two dozen of the eighty-two individuals who signed contracts in 1911 went on to have notable careers. Little information is available for the remaining sixty-odd artists, and biographical details for even some of the more accomplished stars are hard to find. Nonetheless, it is possible to sketch broad outlines about those who worked with Figner in 1911. Most, but not all, were white. Among the eighty-two who signed contracts, only three were women, one of whom signed on behalf of her son-in-law and another for her deceased husband, who had bequeathed to her the rights to his song. A number of Figner's artists came from families that provided material support for musical careers. José Pedro de Alcântara, born in Copacabana in 1866, studied flute as a child and at the age of fifteen performed at a Mass attended by Emperor Dom Pedro II.[37]

Even the wealthiest of Figner's artists sought work in other musical arenas—playing for symphonies, orchestras, bands, theaters, circuses, rival record labels, and private parties—and often held jobs outside of music. Agenor Benz worked as a public health official, Basilio de Assis Andrade as a typesetter, and Alcântara as a postal clerk. Many worked as public functionaries. Sophonias Dornellas worked his way up from private to second lieutenant in the military. Together, Benz, Andrade, Alcântara, and Dornellas earned a total of 245$000 (US $79) in contracts with Figner in 1911, little more than what it cost to support a family of four for one month.

The sketch that emerges from the Casa Edison data, compiled less than a decade after the first Brazilian sound recording, suggests that the music industry offered significant income to a handful of elite musicians and much smaller amounts to less established ones. For most, Law 496 and the opportunities made available by new sonic technology provided important but limited advances. In theory, turn-of-the-century artists had far greater legal protections for their creative work than did nineteenth-century barber-musicians, but the music market functioned with little oversight, and a mogul like Figner could both use the law and sidestep it to his benefit.

Race, Authorship, and Success

The contrast between Figner, a white, worldly immigrant with ready access to capital, and Benjamin de Oliveira, the son of slaves, could hardly be more absolute. While the music industry allowed for a limited degree of fluidity and flexibility, an artist's success and visibility were always tied to skin color, audience taste, the actions of power brokers like Figner, and disparate values assigned to performers and composers.

Casa Edison's early repertoire mainly featured polkas and waltzes, labels that are as much an indication of Figner's Europhile clientele as a description of specific rhythmic or melodic style (see table 7). A few decades later, those same songs might well have been called sambas. Casa Edison's first catalogs were dominated by the works of three men: Baiano (Manoel Pedro dos Santos), Cadete (Manoel Evêncio da Costa Moreira), and Anacleto de Medeiros. Baiano and Cadete were the faces of the first catalog. Portraits of each were prominently displayed above their vast repertoires, which, including six duets, comprised 288 songs in the 1902 collection. Dressed in dark suits, with high-collared white shirts and neckties, the two artists are pictured gazing earnestly into the distance.

TABLE 7. Songs by Genre (Casa Edison, 1911)

Genre	Number (%) n = 367
Polka	117 (31.9)
Waltz	97 (26.4)
Tango	41 (11.2)
Dobrado	39 (10.6)
Schottische	29 (7.9)
Mazurka	12 (3.2)
Miscellaneous*	9 (2.5)
Marcha	8 (2.2)
Choro	8 (2.2)
Quadrille	7 (1.9)

*Miscellaneous = Batuque (1), Cançoneta (1), Maxixe (1),
Pas de Quatre (1), Peça Característica (1), Salsa (1), n/t (3).
Source: CEST Documentos, Direito Autoral.

In addition to the six duets he performed with Cadete, Baiano sang 157 lundus, *modinhas,* and *cançonetas* (short, often humorous, songs or ditties). Born in Bahia in 1870, Baiano began his career in the circus and the theater, where his popularity helped secure connections that eventually led to lucrative contracts with Figner and to several film roles. Cadete was also born in the northeast. In 1887, at the age of thirteen, he came to Rio and enrolled in the Escola Militar, a preparatory school for the prestigious Military Academy. He was well known among *seresteiros,* the roving guitar players and vocalists who filled Rio's nights with songs and serenades. In 1895, he met Catulo da Paixão Cearense, one of Brazil's most prolific and well-known lyricists. Cearense was the godfather of Cadete's son and a close acquaintance of Figner's, an indication of the intimate, almost incestuous world of elite artists.[38]

Anacleto de Medeiros joined Cadete and Baiano as Casa Edison's top draws. A versatile and talented musician, Medeiros was born in Paquetá, an island just off the shores of Rio in the Bay of Guanabara. His mother was a freed slave, and he began his early musical training at the Companhia de Menores do Arsenal de Guerra, one of Brazil's military apprenticeship schools, which served as boarding schools, shelters, and "proto-penal institutions" for young orphans, vagrants, capoeiras, and criminals.[39] While there he learned to play flute. In 1884, he entered the Conservatório de Música (which later became the Instituto Nacional de Música and then the Escola Nacional de Música), where he studied clarinet until 1886. In 1896, he became director of the Banda do Corpo de Bombeiros, a popular band connected to the local fire brigade, beating out several prominent white musicians for the coveted spot.[40] He also organized a number of smaller musical groups at factories and in neighborhoods, and he frequented informal musical gatherings at houses around Rio and Paquetá.

While Cadete and Baiano's faces adorned the catalog, Medeiros's did not, despite the fact that he and his band recorded seventy-eight tracks. His relatively dark skin may have led Figner to conclude that he was less marketable than Baiano and Cadete, though two surviving photos of Medeiros show that makeup, hair wax, and photography could "whiten" him. In one portrait, his skin looks significantly lighter than it does in the second, and in the first image his mustache and hair appear to have been manicured.[41] But it was not just skin color that helped make Baiano and Cadete, and not Medeiros, the faces of Casa Edison's 1902 catalog. A master of composition and arrangement, and a highly skilled, versatile instrumentalist, Medeiros was accomplished in many of the less celebrated and visible aspects of early music production. In addition to writing, arranging, and conducting, he also helped engineer Figner's earliest recording sessions, which were executed with rudimentary technology in the tiny studio behind his shop. By contrast, Cadete and Baiano were known primarily as singers, a role that helped them maintain a presence and a visible connection to their work that Medeiros, as a composer, did not. While the 1902 catalog describes Medeiros as the director of his band, it does not recognize his authorship of any song. In fact, few songs in the entire catalog are attributed to a composer and are instead linked exclusively with the recording artist(s). Only the names of well-known European composers (e.g., Massenet and Puccini) appear alongside their works. It is difficult to know Figner's intentions in putting together the catalog the way he did, but the results are clear: a compendium that prominently featured the images of two fair-skinned musicians and the works—but not the portrait—of Medeiros, the faceless African-descendant maestro. In Figner's music market, race was important but not immutable. It could be altered with hair wax and photography or, intentionally or not, hidden through the recording process.

With Anacleto, Baiano, and Cadete as his main draws, Figner's enterprise flourished. A number of other stars soon became affiliated with Casa Edison, including Eduardo das Neves, an Afro-Brazilian poet, musician, clown, composer, singer, instrumentalist, and entrepreneur extraordinaire. Neves went by a host of nicknames, including Dudu (short for Eduardo), Black Diamond, and Black Clown. He was probably born in 1874 in the outskirts of Rio, though details about his origins are sparse.[42] He served in the National Guard and also worked for a time as a firefighter and as a brakeman on trains. In "O crioulo," an autobiographical poem written in 1900, he recalled that his boss at Rio's Central Station "did not like my *ginga* [strut or sway]." According to Neves, his flamboyant style led to his dismissal, under the false accusation of participating in a strike.[43] Neves's ginga was part of his larger character, and he is generally recognized as the first malandro, the flashy hustler figures which became staples of samba and contested symbols of national identity during samba's golden age. He described his malandragem in published collections of poetry and verse and recorded two of the earliest songs to reference malandros.[44]

With the possible exception of Benjamin de Oliveira, Neves was Rio's most visible and successful turn-of-the-century black performer. In 1895, he dedicated himself exclusively to entertainment as a singer and clown in Rio's web of circuses and small theaters. In 1900, he published the first of four collections of poetry and song lyrics with the popular publisher Editora Quaresma.[45] Neves's description of how he met Figner and broke into the record industry reveals an aggressive business style and an acute sense that others profited unfairly from his work. After hearing one of his own songs played "in such a way, with so many errors, so adulterated that it was impossible to understand," he marched into Figner's store and began to sing, impressing Figner "so much that he signed a contract with [him] on the spot."[46]

Neves published his second collection of lyrics and verses, *Trovador da malandragem*, sometime between 1902 and 1905. The volume, reissued in 1926, combined love songs with satirical pieces, humor, political statements, and patriotic declarations. The collection includes "A conquista do ar" (Conquest of the air), which Neves wrote in honor of Alberto Santos Dumont, the Brazilian pioneer of aviation. "Europe bowed before Brazil [*a Europa curvou-se ante o Brasil*]," Neves proudly proclaimed. "Powerful old Europe" sought to be first in flight, "but the winner in the end was our Brazil instead!"[47] In other pieces, Neves commented on taxes, food shortages, and public hygiene, but explicit political commentary made up only a portion of the collection; love and humor dominated.

Dark-skinned and from a poor part of town, and dressed alternately in fine suits, clown outfits, and elaborate Carnival costumes, Neves traversed and referenced multiple worlds. His vast musical repertoire, equally diverse, included more than 320 songs as an *intérprete* (performer) and dozens more as a composer. In addition to lundus, he wrote and performed marches, military hymns, modinhas, and cançonetas. The reissue of *Trovador da malandragem* and some fifteen reprints of another collection, *Trovador popular moderno*, are clear indications of his popularity. He traveled and performed throughout Brazil and, together with Oliveira, owned a popular circus troupe, for which both men wrote and performed sketches and musical numbers.[48] He also worked and performed for Paschoal Segreto, an Italian immigrant and Rio's unofficial entertainment czar.[49] In addition to the monthly salary he earned at Casa Edison, in 1911 Neves signed a lucrative contract with Figner, Catulo da Paixão Cearense, and the proprietor of Editora Quaresma. The contract, worth 5:000$000 (US $1,615), officially transferred Cearense's and Neves's works and any that they would produce during the next twenty years to Figner.[50] Neves carried stationery that described him as the "Official Singer of Casa Edison" and offered his services at "theaters, parks, cinemas, *cafés-concertos*, bars, etc." The stationery also alerted customers that he possessed a large wardrobe and could dress *a caráter*, in any role that his customers requested.[51] As an actor, clown, poet, and musician, he could wear any number of hats and could literally and figuratively perform whatever part he or his audience desired.

Despite and because of his business acumen, Neves struggled against racialized assumptions about wealth, ownership, and authorship. In *Trovador da malandragem*, he addressed "all those in whose heads resides the smallest doubt" about the authorship of his work. His songs, Neves wrote, had been "memorized, repeated, and sung by everybody, everywhere, from noble salons to street corners, until the wee hours of the night." "For what reason do you doubt," he asked his readers, "that [these works] are mine, exclusively mine?!"[52] The influential cronista João do Rio provided one answer. He counted Neves among a handful of important "street muses," and while praising Neves's patriotism he also mocked his authorship claims. The writer linked what he described as Neves's obsession with money with the ills of the record industry, which he disdainfully referred to as "the industry, the profit, the lucre, the lucre, that mirage." Neves, the cronista pointed out, had been a firefighter "before becoming notable." When Neves "became a music-hall number, he lost his bearing and walked around in a blue suit-jacket and a silk hat. His fantasy went even further: he published a book titled *Trovador da malandragem*, with a preface full of fury against those who doubt the authorship of his works." João do Rio dismissed Neves's claims as evidence of conceit. "No one has heard the songs of *Senhor* Eduardo in noble salons, but he has a definitive conviction about this and many other things."[53] João do Rio was not the only one who found Neves to be out of place. The prominent Afro-Brazilian journalist Vagalume recalled that in Rio's affluent white neighborhoods, "Eduardo . . . was considered to be a *foreigner*."[54]

Works on Neves often highlight his marginalization and his malandragem, the latter often cast as a strategy born of necessity in the forbidding economic atmosphere that followed abolition. Others depict malandragem as a form of subaltern resistance and a rejection of capitalism. Two authors write that "malandragem requires the constant rejection of being inserted into [a capitalist system of] production."[55] Martha Abreu writes that Neves perfectly "represented and disseminated [the malandro] character," which she defines as "the symbolic antithesis of the disciplined worker and the well-behaved citizen: idle, disrespectful of the law and of good habits."[56] Abreu also shows that Neves disregarded taboos attached to interracial relationships. Both his "antithetical" malandro and his pursuit of white women were crucial pieces of Neves's identity. But he also had a third, rarely recognized, ensemble in his wardrobe: that of the audacious entrepreneur, who embraced wealth, capitalism, and the promises of inclusion within the republic.

The full significance of this third, often overlooked, piece is seen clearly through an exploration of why Neves's actions so offended João do Rio. Born in the city reflected in his nickname, João do Rio gained entry to the Brazilian Academy of Letters at the age of twenty-nine. His mother was of African descent, but his skin was significantly lighter than Neves's, which, along with makeup, allowed him to hide his origins, at least in most circumstances.[57] Fastidious in his appearance, he presented himself in much the same way that Neves did, dressing "meticulously in elegant attire, complete with a hat, monocle, and a walking cane."[58] Whatever linked the two men on the surface faded at a deeper level. Afro-Brazilians were subjects of João do Rio's chronicles, not members of his ilk. He fancied himself a gatekeeper of the circles in which he socialized. If he had his way, Neves—black and once poor—would not enter those circles.

Like the Penal Code's architects, João do Rio was urgently concerned with methods for accumulating wealth. In an article about "Músicos ambulantes" (Street musicians), he described individuals who unscrupulously used music to earn money.[59] "Almost all of these street musicians and adventurers earn rivers of money," he wrote, likening them to "the most avaricious businessm[e]n." Of special concern were the portable organs, which he called *realengos solteiros malandros* (bachelor malandro organs) and which were used by street musicians to woo unwitting society ladies.

Neves would have bristled to be called an ambulante, but João do Rio might well have had him in mind on the seventeenth anniversary of abolition, when he published an article titled "Negros ricos" (Rich blacks).[60] The satirical piece recounts a conversation with "the wise, old *alufá* Julio Ganam."[61] Much to the journalist's surprise, Ganam, whose name could be a play on the verb *ganhar* (to earn), says that emancipation lacked significance for "black Africans." Most slaves, he explained, purchased their freedom long before the end of slavery, a revelation that stuns João do Rio almost as much as the assertion that many freedmen had, by 1905, become "rich." "But it's not possible, it's just not! . . . Old blacks, ex-slaves! No! It's unthinkable!" Eventually, he processes the shocking news. "So, you don't know?" Ganam asks him. "Everybody wants money!" The conversation causes the journalist to reflect. "Why judge blacks by their skin . . . as different than us? There's just a difference in process, and white millionaires are sometimes more malandro than blacks." Like much of João do Rio's work, this article is full of exaggeration and satire. The writer's feigned shock nonetheless reveals the kind of assumptions that he expected his readers to harbor. Blacks were malandros, whites were not; the idea that a former slave could make himself rich was, if not truly "unthinkable," still unexpected. To individuals who imagined all Afro-Brazilians to be poor, Neves's transformation into a confident celebrity was unsettling. João do Rio attacked him not because he was the "antithesis" of the ideal worker but because he brazenly pursued and displayed his wealth, which he acquired through a combination of business acumen and the successful branding and selling of his creative production. Neves was dangerous not because he rejected capitalism, but because he crashed society's gates and embraced wealth. Other prominent Afro-Brazilian men faced similar challenges. His sense of "foreignness" was shared by upwardly mobile Afro-Brazilians elsewhere.[62] The politician Monteiro Lopes was lampooned in the press for the elaborate clothes that he wore and was often depicted as a pedantic, bumbling orator. João do Rio targeted him in a satirical 1906 play. In printed cartoons and on-stage caricatures, Lopes and other well-dressed black men were depicted as comical and out of place in their fancy clothes.[63]

It was not only Neves's unbefitting clothes, but also his audacity, particularly regarding his own sexuality, that offended critics like João do Rio. The journalist took particular issue with a passage in Neves's autobiographical poem "O crioulo" in which the musician described his own devastating effect on women. While João do Rio criticized Neves's brazen sexuality, others capitalized on it. *Mysterios do violão* (1905), another collection of Neves's work, included an advertisement for a *Sweethearts' Handbook* (Manual de namorados), which revealed to readers the best ways to "please ladies, make declarations of love, dress elegantly, etc., etc."[64] His unabashed masculinity did not simply attract criticism, but also bolstered his popularity and marketability. He drew attention to his skin color and his masculinity by calling himself a crioulo, a controversial label brazenly splashed across the pages of *Trovador da malandragem*. "Crioulo" has several meanings in Brazilian Portuguese. During the late nineteenth century, it was used to refer to blacks born in Brazil, often in a disparaging way. A dictionary published in 1878 defined the word as "(from *criar* [to raise]) black slave, born in the house of his master; animal, born and raised in our care."[65] After abolition, the word suggested particularly dark skin and conjured the slave past. Despite the negative connotations that the word could carry, a little more than a decade after abolition Neves proclaimed himself the "Crioulo Dudu." Throughout "O crioulo," which ends at a wedding, Neves links the word to what he describes as his own irrepressible charm. Upon hearing him play guitar, a bride becomes smitten, commenting to the maid of honor (*madrinha*), "This crioulo will be my perdition." Already set to be married, the bride settles for a small consolation, begging the madrinha "to at least tell me his name." But her wish has already been filled; Neves is at her side, introducing himself and leaving the rest to the imagination. "I am," the piece concludes, "the crioulo Dudu Neves." Neves's appropriation and use of "crioulo" angered João do Rio, who expressed his shock and dismay that Neves would "complacently" use the term to refer to himself.[66] In a society that viewed "rich blacks" as anomalies, Neves's self-proclaimed crioulo-ness, and his transformation from a humble firefighter to a well-known, well-dressed star was surprising and threatening.

Neves also used his work to convey pain. In "Nasci para sofrer" (I was born to suffer), Neves's narrator asks God to take pity on him by ending his life. The source of his troubles is apparently a "crime of love," committed "in the flower of youth," but the song's imagery clearly references slavery. "I live scorned in the world, gathering [*carpindo*] my pains, the horrors of bondage [*cativeiro*]! / I cannot forget my lamentation because it is also my mantle." Neves's word choice is telling. Both carpindo (from the verb *carpir*) and cativeiro hold special significance in relation to slavery. "Carpir" means to gather or lament, and in southern Brazil also refers to clearing a plot of land and preparing it for cultivation. "Cativeiro" is nearly interchangeable with *escravidão*, slavery. "Without a homeland or a home," the agonized troubadour sets off for the isolation of the forest. "I'm going to live in isolation / . . . / in the woods / . . . / where I won't even see the moonlight." [67] "Nasci para sofrer" resonates with Benjamin de Oliveira's comment about Afro-Brazilians' destiny "to flee" and provides a dramatic counter to the buoyant spirit displayed in "O crioulo" and much of Neves's other work. Like "O crioulo," "Nasci para sofrer" was published and sold, but neither piece may be understood simply as a commodity produced for consumption. Both compositions represent the kind of disarming openness that confounded observers like João do Rio, who expected "crioulos" to act a certain part. Malandragem was expected of Neves, but he also marketed himself and embraced the promises of postslavery Brazil. As a clown, actor, troubadour, entertainer, and author he challenged boundaries demarcated by class, race, and sexuality, each intimately linked together, and each of which made his identities and performances all the more threatening to a self-styled gatekeeper like João do Rio.

The Pitfalls of Democracia do Preto no Branco

Neves forged his career during an era when many embraced the idea that Brazil could "whiten" itself through controlled racial mixing. Like João do Rio, prominent intellectuals such as the abolitionist André Rebouças and the author Machado de Assis downplayed their African heritage, at least in public. [68] Despite a pervasive white ideal and the bitter criticisms launched against him, Neves secured a place, though not an entirely stable one, in the upper echelons of the music industry. Not all musicians reached such lofty heights. But obscurity did not necessarily insulate against the kind of scrutiny directed toward Neves.

A dramatic illustration of how brutal life could be for Brazilian entertainers of color is found in the aftermath of an apparent murder-suicide perpetrated in 1911 by Octavio Icarahyense Dias. Dias went by the nickname Moreno, a racial label that denotes black-white mixture but falls much closer to white than to crioulo. Moreno performed in Rio's circuit of small bars and cafés, where he met Dora Henriqueta dos Santos, a singer from Portugal. According to the press, the couple's demise was rooted in Moreno's jealousy and his dependence on Santos for money. The popular weekly *O Malho* suggested, "He had been out of work and she became obligated to cover every expense. . . . And so . . . the crioulo's jealousy grew."[69] Calling Moreno a crioulo reflected the press's desire to portray him as dark-skinned and dangerous. While Neves embraced the word to flip a racial epithet on its head, journalists used it to transport Moreno back to the days of slavery. The fine clothes that he wore were said to hide a savage killer inside. His nickname provided a similar disguise. "Dias," the daily *O Paiz* wrote, "was twenty-seven years old and a crioulo. He was generally known by his nickname 'Moreno,' because when people called him negro, he retorted, 'Not negro, moreno!'" "No one," the paper suggested, "wanted to believe in that union, of a crioulo and [Dora]."[70] In a letter he purportedly left behind, Moreno explained why he "committed this crazy act": "I'm full of brio and am well known throughout Rio. This woman is known by everybody, and everybody knows of the disgrace she has brought me."

To the press, Moreno was a savage beast hidden behind a well-dressed facade. In a portrait published in *O Malho*, Moreno clutches a brass-handled cane and gazes upward, his lips pursed and eyebrows slightly raised (figure 3). Dressed in a striped suit, dark vest, high-collared white shirt, and dark bowtie, his appearance is almost dainty. *O Malho* reported that he requested to be buried "in the best clothes that I have," and noted that he was "always properly dressed, never dispensing the monocle secured with a black cord that stood out noticeably against his white vest." The magazine also called him a "pretentious, elegant crioulo" and repeatedly referred to his financial dependence on Dora. "He learned to sing a few little songs and to tell jokes on the stages of small clubs. It was in this way that he made a living." His occupations were described as ranging from less than serious to illegal. *O Paiz* noted that he was once arrested

FIGURE 3. Portrait of Dora and Moreno, ca. 1911. Courtesy Casa Rui Barbosa.

with false banknotes and eventually "became a singer in cheap clubs." He was, in a word, a malandro.

Lacking a serious occupation, financially dependent on Dora, and shamed by her improprieties, Moreno hardly cut a figure of masculine strength. *O Malho* questioned whether he was even strong enough to

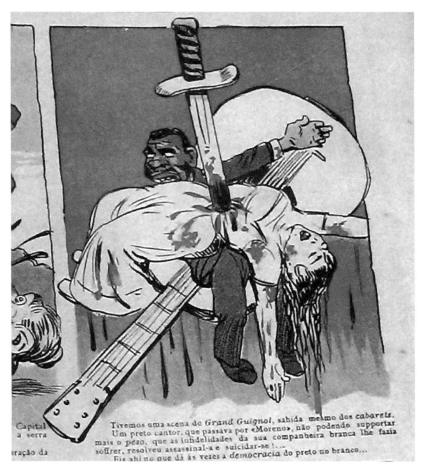

FIGURE 4. Cartoon of Dora and Moreno, 1911. Courtesy Casa Rui Barbosa.

have overpowered Dora, whom *O Paiz* described as "robust." In the portrait published in *O Malho*, she appears large and stocky next to Moreno, whose slender build is accentuated by the tight shirt and high, rigid collar. A lurid *O Malho* cartoon depicts a giant sword pinning a bloody Moreno and Dora to an oversized guitar (figure 4). The caption reads, "A *preto* singer, who used to pass as 'moreno,' was unable to bear any longer the weight of this white *companheira*'s infidelities. And, so he assassinated her and killed himself!" "Sometimes," the paper concluded, "black into white democracy (*a democracia do preto no branco*) ends up in scenes like this one." "Preto no branco" ("black into white") is a direct reference to "whitening," the belief that Brazil could "bleach" out its dark populations through gradual and controlled social engineering.[71] "Democracia" may be an early iteration of "racial democracy," the theory that Brazil was home to a uniquely benevolent form of racial mixture. The word may also have been meant to refer to Brazil's burgeoning democratic republic and its theoretically color-blind 1891 constitution.

Whether *O Malho*'s "democracia" was a reference to "racial democracy" or to republican inclusiveness, the caption's not-so-subtle message about the danger of interracial courtship is crystal clear, emphasized further in the cartoon, which depicts Moreno with bright red lips, fang-like teeth, and wild, pupil-less eyes. Dora lays prone on his lap, covered in blood, and cloaked in white. Her skin is light, almost comically so when held up against the photographic portrait, in which her complexion appears much darker. The giant, blood-covered sword protrudes from Dora's stomach and, farther down, from Moreno's groin, an apparent allusion to his sexual potency and his demise: a dangerous phallus and an instrument for self-castration.

The press treated Moreno and Dora as a cautionary tale: an extreme example of what could happen when a black man "dressed up" or thought of himself to be lighter than he "really" was. Dora's light skin in the cartoon emphasizes the darkness of Moreno's. Her physical malleability—in one image, dark and broad; in another, lily white—helped set the coordinates of Brazilian female normativity in two ways. While depicted as a white maiden in the cartoon, in other instances the press emphasized the fact that she was Portuguese and insisted that good Brazilian girls would never have placed themselves in such a dangerous situation in the first place. Her career as an entertainer surely linked her, at least in the minds of some readers, to prostitution. Both *O Malho* and *O Paiz* frequently referred to her as *rapariga*, a term that roughly translates as "lass" but is often associated with prostitutes. Dora's friends, *O Malho* reported, "upbraided her eccentric taste" and pleaded with her to leave the relationship. *O Malho* and *O Paiz* made Moreno not just a sexual predator but also a cuckold, and therefore simultaneously exaggerated and diminished his masculine potency. Two men, or one with two identities, emerged from the press coverage: the dainty, frail moreno, and the violent, deranged crioulo/preto/negro. While it was the latter portrayal that *O Malho* chose for its cartoon, the former was no less significant. Aside from committing murder, Moreno's crime was his inability to provide for Dora. The fake bills, the "few little songs" and jokes told to earn money, and the dependence on his female companion were all proof that he was unfit to produce and contribute in modern Brazil. Like Neves, Moreno constructed his identity in dialogue with the ideologia da vadiagem. Both men shared a desire to claim the prizes and privileges theoretically available in postabolition Brazil. For Moreno, that meant dating Dora, wearing nice clothes, and climbing racial and social ladders. Neves staked his place in society by building a career, courting white women in song, honoring Santos Dumont as a national hero, and brazenly displaying his wealth. Both performers were sharply and publicly reprimanded for their aspirations and their transgressions.

The press coverage of Moreno's crime was clearly a product of the couple's violent end. But the murder-suicide reveals larger apprehensions about race, equality, and wealth, all laid bare on the pages of two highly influential publications.[72] During the 1910s and 1920s, social commentators viewed crimes like Moreno's as evidence of a rise in "authentic savagery," "masculine cowardliness," and the "retrocession of civilization."[73] Though legal protection for crimes of passion had long since been abolished, male defendants continued to be exonerated through arguments that "grave affronts" to their honor had made them act violently.[74] Lawmakers sought to reverse de facto tolerance for passion crimes less to protect women than "to successfully transform [Brazil's] 'anarchistic' society into a modern, prosperous, orderly bourgeois nation."[75] That impulse resonated closely with the anti-vagrancy campaign. Vadiagem and passion crimes were not mutually exclusive concerns, a point made clear in a 1928 newspaper article about a young baker who killed his estranged lover before taking his own life. The paper described both individuals as pardo and grimly noted that the young woman had left her companion because he was "no friend of work."[76] While lawmakers sought to curb legal protections for passion crimes, misogyny was celebrated in song. João da Baiana's "Pedindo vingança" (Asking for revenge, 1925) depicts an ex-lover "crying, on your knees and at my feet."[77] "Dá nela" (Smack her) was awarded first prize in a 1930 Carnival contest sponsored by Casa Edison.[78] "Deixa essa mulher chorar" (Let that woman cry) was a Carnival hit in 1931.[79]

While relationships between white women and dark-skinned malandros like Moreno were publicly discouraged, other forms of interracial sexual encounter were tacitly, if unevenly, embraced. During the nineteenth century, white performers sang lundus about slave life and portrayed black male characters who spoke with lisps, danced, and joked to entertain their white masters. Afro-Brazilian women were depicted as lascivious sexual objects.[80] Similar tropes persisted in *maxixe*, a lyric-less dance music that became the rage in Rio and beyond during the late nineteenth and early twentieth centuries.[81] If lundu was seen as a window into rural slave life, maxixe was viewed as a "modern" urban form offering a close encounter with the submundo.[82] The sensuous hip movements associated with maxixe and the music's association with Mangue, the city's red-light district, made the music an ideal vehicle for delivering long-standing stereotypes about race and sexuality.[83] Carnival hits such as "Vem cá, *mulata*" (Come 'ere, mulatta), provided additional vehicles for advancing the idea, soon to become a hallmark of national identity, that Brazil was the unique product of amorous relationships between white men and slave women. But when the roles were reversed, and a dark-skinned man was pursuing a light-skinned woman, reactions were quite different. Racial mixing could be acceptable, but only in certain forms. Celebrations of interracial sexual encounters—sung or shouted during Carnival, hummed on the street, or played on a record—left miscegenation at the safe and evocative level of fantasy. The actions of Moreno and Neves made those fantasies, and the fears attached to them, threatening and real.

CONSIDERED IN A LARGER postabolition context, the public images cultivated by Neves and Moreno—sharp dress, confidence, unchecked sexuality—may be understood as more than just exuberant marketing ploys. The anti-vagrancy campaign divided economic haves from have-nots and honorable family men from dishonorable vagabonds. While neither Neves nor Moreno was forced to respond directly to vagrancy charges, both challenged expectations about who they were supposed to be and how they were supposed to act. Their actions were responses, even if indirect, to the ideologia da vadiagem and Article 399 of the Penal Code. In different ways, both claimed the rights, privileges, and pleasures theoretically available to any Brazilian man.

Entertainers broke no laws by plying their trade, but neither did they contribute to society in the ways imagined by the nineteenth-century politicians who hoped to transform slaves and itinerant workers into a stable and productive industrial workforce. In that sense, musicians and the music industry itself represented something of a threat, or at least an alternative, to the established or desired order. At the same time, cronistas and their readers viewed individuals like Moreno—and the songs and dances they performed—as points of access into alluring, forbidden worlds. Moreno and Neves did not simply challenge stereotypes or the expected order of things. Both men also helped construct and shape those stereotypes and orders. By packaging their music and their masculinity for paying audiences, they turned themselves and their work into consumable objects open to applause, critique, and derision. In a society hungry for intimate accounts of taboo places and people, the fact that both men transgressed established boundaries made them exciting figures. Neves was proud, flamboyant, and sexual. Moreno was a cautionary tale, or the proverbial train wreck: shocking, frightening, sickening, and therefore all the more fascinating.

Both men helped make Rio's turn-of-the-century music market into one of the first and most public arenas in which black men were judged as free members of the nation. As they moved outside the circle and into the spotlight, musicians became more than just entertainers. They also served as windows into the nation's past and future, litmus tests for its racial fears and fantasies, and gauges for the viability and shape of its postslavery economy as their financial means, like those of accused vagrants, were scrutinized and criticized. The ridicule of upwardly mobile Afro-Brazilians and the delineation between acceptable and unacceptable forms of making money reflects a double standard inherent in the ideologia da vadiagem and the anti-vagrancy campaign. While Afro-Brazilians were expected to mold themselves into upright citizens and workers or suffer the consequences, they had to do so within narrow legal strictures and even narrower social norms. Market yourself too aggressively and risk being ravaged in the press. Make too little money and disappear within an impoverished mass. Skin color was mutable, and it could be altered with makeup, artists' renderings, and nicknames. But that hardly made it insignificant.

The ability to prosper in Rio's early twentieth-century music market was also clearly tied to authorship and ownership. Trademarks, patents, and contracts were tools that Fred Figner used to build his empire. By creating Casa Edison, he made himself into what Keith Aoki calls a "quasi-author": someone who exercises author-like ownership over products through branding and trademarking.[84] Neves may also be considered a "quasi-" or "almost" author, but for dramatically different reasons. Authorship and intellectual property were crucial components of his entrepreneurship—things he held dear and flaunted (like his wealth) but which, like other hard-earned gains, could be questioned or taken away.

The imbalances and gaps that marked Figner's music market and Brazil's early intellectual property regime presaged future battles. As samba began to consolidate into a single, recognizable music form during the 1910s and 1920s, new laws and regulations would help stabilize the production and sale of music. Meanwhile, the shape and contours of Brazil and brasilidade remained open and fiercely contested, as new rising stars would grapple with challenges all too familiar to Neves, Moreno, and Benjamin de Oliveira.

4

In 1902, the same year that Fred Figner produced the first Brazilian record, the writer and folklorist Mello Moraes Filho published a multivolume collection of "traditional songs." The collection, he wrote unabashedly, was "almost entirely the product . . . of the popular, anonymous muse."[1] While established white writers like Moraes Filho earned money and reputation by publishing stories and songs mined from supposedly anonymous sources, their "popular muses" remained unnamed and unremunerated.

Fifteen years after the publication of Moraes Filho's volume and the first Brazilian sound recording, the unchecked use of popular works was no more exceptional than it had been in 1902. Unspoken rules and assumptions still determined whose authorship and ownership would be accepted without question and whose would be scrutinized. Donga, the ascendant Afro-Brazilian musician who registered "Pelo telefone" at the National Library in 1916, found out that not all appropriations would pass without comment. This chapter focuses on the intertwined histories of "Pelo telefone," the ascension of samba, and the Oito Batutas (Eight Batons, or Aces), a band that Donga helped form in the late 1910s. The popularity of "Pelo telefone" and the Oito Batutas' success in Brazil and abroad helped give rise to "our music" (*nossa música*), a phrase uttered with increasing frequency by musicians and journalists. It was not always clear what that music was, or who exactly owned it. To some, "our music" was something Afro-Brazilian, long marginalized and now finally given a turn on stage. To others, it was a uniquely Brazilian product, with ties to a vaguely defined nonwhite mass but also representative of a larger mixed-race nation.

Struggles surrounding "our music" involved two distinct but inter-twined issues related to authorship and property. Ownership could be something concrete and of monetary value: formal ownership of a song and access to companion royalties. Or it could be something less palpable but no less important: the right to shape and stake claim to an evolving national identity. As the Oito Batutas toured at home and abroad, commentators and the musicians themselves debated the significance of a mixed-race band playing what was defined as national music. By claiming both palpable and less concrete forms of ownership, Donga and his band-mates asserted ownership over "our music" and, by extension, greater Brazil.

The "Pelo telefone" Controversy

During the nineteenth and early twentieth centuries, when "samba" still referred to various religious and musical practices, a number of more well-known genres across the Americas were based in *tresillo*, a musical paradigm organized around eight pulses divided into three unequal articulations (3 + 3 + 2), with emphasis on the fourth pulse.[2] The accented fourth note creates two larger divisions (3 + 5) and distinguishes tresillo from many nineteenth-century European rhythms, which divided cycles into two equal groups (4 + 4) with an accented fifth pulse. Lundu, maxixe, and tango (not to be confused with the Argentine version), each of which was at one point called "typically Brazilian" music, all followed the tresillo form. So did "Pelo telefone" and most songs that were labeled as sambas during the 1910s and 1920s.

Around 1928, the Estácio Sound (or Estácio Samba), a rhythmic pattern named for the Rio de Janeiro neighborhood in which it was pioneered, nudged tresillo aside. Estácio Samba was based in new forms of syncopation that transformed earlier rhythmic stylings and became characteristic of samba as it became Brazil's undisputed national music. In a famous interview, Ismael Silva, one of Estácio's pioneers, famously described the difference between "Pelo telefone" samba and the form that followed it. During the first period, Silva said, "Samba was like this: *tan tantan tan tantan*. That didn't work. . . . So, we began to do it like this: *bum bum paticumbum-prugurun-dum*."[3] Silva's rendering illustrates why

"Pelo telefone" is a samba in name only. During a 1966 interview, Donga conceded as much, saying, "In order to achieve the easiest penetration of the music, [I suggested that] we not stray very far from the characteristics of maxixe."[4]

"Pelo telefone" is often recognized as Brazil's "first samba" or "first recorded samba," but both designations are misleading. In fact, Casa Edison recorded and sold several songs labeled as sambas before the 1917 release of "Pelo telefone." From a musical perspective, the song differs significantly from the genre Silva helped popularize during the late 1920s and early 1930s, and which characterized samba's subsequent golden age. While samba and "Pelo telefone" have become indelibly tied to one another, a broad range of terms were originally used to describe the song, including samba, samba carnavalesco, tango, tango-samba carnavalesco, modinha, and canção. It is unclear exactly why samba, and not the other terms, stuck. In the two most far-reaching mediums at the time, sheet music and records, the song was labeled a samba carnavalesco. The carnavalesco modifier is clearly a product of the song's success during Carnival and of the creators' desire to capitalize on that success. But why samba—rather than tango, for example—lasted is not altogether clear. Whatever the reason, "Pelo telefone" played an undeniably crucial role in popularizing the word "samba." Flávio Silva (no relation to Ismael) writes that the song's "great contribution to the history of 'urban samba'" is found not in its musical structure, but instead in the way that it "spread . . . the term 'samba' among middle-class Carnival-goers." By 1921, the word was applied to almost any popular Carnival hit.[5]

The controversy surrounding "Pelo telefone" began on 6 November 1916, when Donga deposited his petition to secure ownership of the song at the National Library. Nearly three months later, the cronista Arlequim (Paulo Cabrita) wrote a glowing piece in A Notícia about Mauro de Almeida (João Mauro de Almeida), the police reporter and Carnival enthusiast whom Donga identified as the lyricist. Arlequim described Almeida as "slender, kind, and (why not say it?) almost pretty." Almeida, Arlequim cheerfully noted, was an "incorrigible bohemian," able and willing to corrupt "good husbands" with nights of debauchery. Arlequim also congratulated Almeida on "the beautiful verses that he wrote for Dragão's samba."[6] The samba was "Pelo telefone," and Dragão (Dragon) was Donga. In February, three weeks after Arlequim's column appeared in A Notícia, Beléo, another cronista, wrote similar praise of Almeida in

O Paiz and congratulated him on "Pelo telefone," which, he noted, "everybody is singing today!"[7]

Arlequim and Beléo's columns are indicative of the crucial role that newspapers and journalists played in the spread of popular music. A musician's success was often dependent on the tastes of cronistas and editors, who chose which songs to praise and which to pan or ignore. As cronistas ventured to underworld hotspots, they often forged bonds with musicians. Carousing at bars in or near Mangue, for example, was understood to be a part of life for journalists like Almeida, a respected writer and bohemian. During Carnival, papers frequently published song lyrics, a boon to artists, even in a city where around half the population was illiterate.[8] The positive publicity afforded to "Pelo telefone" undoubtedly contributed to the song's success.

While he appreciated the positive comments made by his fellow cronistas, Almeida was not pleased to be publicly associated with "Pelo telefone." In two published letters, he expressed gratitude to both Arlequim and Beléo but also forcefully distanced himself from the song that "everybody was singing." In his letter to Arlequim, he confessed that the song's lyrics were not really his:

> I should tell you, my dear Arlequim, as a way to honor the truth, that the verses of friendly (*simpático*) Donga's samba carnavalesco "Pelo telephone," are not original. Or, better yet, they are not mine. I took them from popular ballads and did what numerous playwrights running around today do: I put them in order, arranging them into music. Nothing more.[9]

He made a similar point in responding to Beléo. "I am not so much the author, but really just the 'arranger' (*arreglador*). Some of those verses were already floating around in popular song; I arranged them so that they could be sung with the music offered to me and Morcego. Only this."[10] Morcego (Norberto Amaral Junior), also a cronista, was a friend of Almeida's. The sheet music that Donga deposited at the National Library was inscribed with a dedication to both men.

Given the song's success, it may seem surprising that Almeida would write a letter, much less two, renouncing his authorship. Given the precedent set by Mello Moraes Filho, who openly admitted taking and selling works by the "popular muse," Almeida's insistence is even more surprising. His hesitancy becomes comprehensible only when understood alongside the complex history of "Pelo telefone," multiple versions of which had, indeed, been "floating around" the city for some time.

By the time that Baiano recorded it in Casa Edison's studio in January 1917, the song was already the year's top hit. But the recorded version was just one of many. In October 1916, a month before Donga filed his petition at the National Library, the prominent Afro-Brazilian journalist Vagalume wrote an article in the *Jornal do Brasil* about a Carnival group called Macaco É Outro (Monkey Is the Other One), which congregated near Tia Ciata's food stand at the Festa da Penha. Amid the smell of "a succulent Bahian *angu* [manioc boiled with salt] with all the requisites from the land of *vatapá* [manioc mixed with oil, pepper, and meat or fish]," Germano, one of the group's leaders, cheerfully sang that despite rumors to the contrary, the chief of police had authorized festivalgoers to dance and play samba: "The chief of police / Told them to call me / Just to say / That we can *sambar*." [11] This is one of the first known versions of "Pelo telefone."

The lines sung by Germano resemble the first verse of what is often called the song's "anonymous" version: "The chief of police / On the telephone / Called to say / That in the Carioca / There's a gambling wheel / For playing around." These lyrics may date to as early as 1913, when reporters set up a gambling wheel on the Largo da Carioca, a major thoroughfare in downtown Rio, to call attention to corruption and double standards in the police's public campaign against gambling. [12] It is also possible that the anonymous version had a different meaning. In late October 1916, a memo written by the chief of police appeared in local papers, encouraging a crackdown against chic gambling establishments. The memo suggested that officers should announce raids ahead of time "on the official telephone" but was worded in such a way so that the instructions could be interpreted either to mean that police officials should call headquarters before making a bust or that they should call the clubs to warn them. The anonymous version leaves similar room for play. Does the police chief call because he is angry about the gambling wheel or because he himself put it there? There is no evidence to definitively date the anonymous version to 1913 or even 1916, but there is general agreement that it predated the recorded version. [13]

The lyrics and music of the 1917 Casa Edison recording unite several lyrical traditions, further muddling any attempt to attribute definitive origins to the song. The eclectic mixture is best seen through the rhyme schemes of the three versions:

Festa da Penha Version (1916)	Anonymous Version (Date Unknown) (Verse 1)	Recorded Version (1917) (Verse 1)	
1 O Dr. Chefe da Polícia *The chief of police*	(A) O chefe da polícia *The chief of police*	(A) O chefe da folia *The party chief*	(A)
2 Mandou me chamar *Told them to call me*	(B) Pelo telefone *On the telephone*	(B) Pelo telefone *On the telephone*	(B)
3 Só pra me dizer *Just to say*	(C) Manda me avisar *Calls to advise me*	(C) Manda me avisar *Calls to advise me*	(C)
4 Que já se pode sambar *That we can samba*	(B) Que na Carioca *That in the [Largo da] Carioca*	(D) Que com alegria *That staying calm*	(A)
5	Tem uma roleta *There's a gambling wheel*	(E) Não se questione *and not making trouble*	(B)
6	Para se jogar *For playing*	(C) Para se brincar *is the way to celebrate*	(C)

Line five of the recorded version—*Não se questione*—is, in Sandroni's words, "a true syntactical wonder."[14] *Questionar*, "to question," is shoe-horned into the subjunctive, *questione*, to make it rhyme with *telefone*. As a result, the meaning of the song's first verse is not readily obvious, but Sandroni provides a useful "translation" into more conventional Portuguese, rendered above in English in the third column.

That Almeida, Donga, or anyone else responsible for the lyrics went to such lengths to construct an *abc abc* pattern suggests that the song went through significant editing as it was transformed in the studio from "folklore" to record. The less symmetrical structures of the anonymous (*abc dec*) and Festa da Penha (*abcb*) versions are characteristic of Brazilian popular rhymes and of *desafio* and *partido alto*, two rarely recorded, dialogic, partially improvised forms.[15] While the rest of the recorded version is dominated by catchy and uniform (read: more marketable) rhymes, two of the ten verses are in *abcb*. In other words, while the recorded version favors *abc abc*, it also retains examples of folkloric structures, thus combining, in Sandroni's words, "two poetic dictions."[16]

Evidence that earlier versions were at least partially "cleaned up" in the studio is also found in the lyrics themselves. The recorded version replaces *chefe da polícia* (police chief) with *chefe da folia* (party chief). Some have interpreted this as an attempt to avoid problems with the police, though, as Sandroni points out, the switch could just as easily have been a parody.[17] Either way, at least on the surface, the last three lines of the recorded version's first verse—"That staying calm / and not making trouble / is the way to celebrate"—poke less fun at the police chief (or at least poke fun less directly) than the other two versions do. It is unclear how listeners interpreted the recorded version, but the lyrics suggest that there was an attempt to at least make the song *seem* innocent. The number of individuals linked in one way or another to the recorded version—Almeida, Donga, Morcego, Baiano, and Casa Edison employees involved in the recording—makes it all but impossible to know who was responsible for the alterations. While the recorded version altered and combined previous incarnations of the song, the controversy surrounding "Pelo telefone"—and Almeida's decision to distance himself from it—was less about whether Donga and Almeida had faithfully represented the "popular muse" than about perceptions that Donga had profited from and claimed something that belonged to others.

Details about Donga's actual role in the song's composition remain a matter of debate, but it is clear that he was the main party responsible for registering, marketing, and turning the song into a success. To do so, he needed at least three things: awareness that a musical composition could be transformed into property, knowledge and wherewithal to do so, and a helping hand or two along the way. His petition to register "Pelo telefone" was approved on 27 November 1916, three weeks after he submitted it. Exactly what took place between 6 and 27 November is unclear. The petition included a copy of the sheet music, dated 1 November 1916, and a sworn statement (*atestado*) signed on 16 November by Arlequim and another man, Júlio de Suckow. In the atestado, Arlequim asserts that the song's first public performance had occurred on 25 October at the Cine Teatro Velo. It is unclear what kind of relationship Donga and Arlequim shared, and it is also uncertain what transpired between 6 November, when Donga turned the petition in, and 16 November, when he delivered the atestado. Flávio Silva surmises that upon turning in the petition, Donga was informed that he was missing a key ingredient, required to register any work at the Biblioteca Nacional: documentation of the song's first public performance. The original petition asserts that the song was played at an "audition to the press" on 3 November. Such auditions were common, but in his exhaustive research, Silva found no reference to one for "Pelo telefone." If the clerks at the National Library doubted the validity of the performance, they could have required Donga to provide proof that it had, in fact, occurred. It is reasonable to think that Arlequim would be unwilling to vouch for a performance that never happened. Turned away initially, Donga may have then devised a new strategy. A note, written and signed by Donga, added to the original petition, and dated 20 November, states that the song was played on 25 October at the Cine Teatro Velo. In scouring local newspapers, Silva once again came up empty, an intriguing but inconclusive nonfinding, given the fact that the Cine Teatro Velo was a small, obscure venue. If Arlequim wanted to vouch for Donga, but feared that referring to a press audition that never took place would be too risky, he may have either taken Donga's word about the Cine Teatro Velo show or perhaps suggested using the small venue as a safe cover. Complicating matters further, the handwriting for the original petition does not match that on the note attached on 20 November by Donga. Who penned the original document? A clerk at the National Library, Arlequim, Almeida, another knowledgeable ally? Hard to say. But we do know that on 27 November the National Library accepted Donga's revised application and made him the song's official author.

In early 1917, as the city prepared for Carnival, different versions of the song were played in multiple settings. Military bands played instrumental versions, revelers sang parodied versions, and Carnival societies feted guests and members to seemingly endless repetitions of the catchy tune. On 21 January, the *Jornal do Brasil* reported that at one club, "Mr. Ernesto Santos's samba (with lyrics by Mr. Mauro de Almeida) was the success of the night, with five performances on stage, each one followed by an encore."[18] On 23 January, *A Notícia* ran Arlequim's column about Almeida, and *Jornal do Brasil* published lyrics for the recorded version. As the song's popularity grew, so did the number of variations. Individuals shaped the music and lyrics into an array of new forms, ranging from satire (of a failed police campaign against prostitution, for example) to advertising (for Fidalga Beer).

Almeida's decision to distance himself from the song appears to have been inspired largely by the fallout that followed the song's registration and success. On 4 February the *Jornal do Brasil* published lyrics for an adapted version of the song, pointedly directed at Donga. The *Jornal do Brasil* version, published by Vagalume, accused Donga of theft. Vagalume attributed the lyrics to Grêmio Fala Gente, a little-known group said to include Tia Ciata, Sinhô (a member of Tia Ciata's circle and soon to be known as "the King of Samba"), Hilário Jovino Ferreira (also part of the circle, and an influential individual among turn-of-the-century Carnival groups), Didi da Gracinda (another famous tia), and Germano.[19] While its members were well known, the Grêmio itself was so obscure that Flávio Silva questions whether it actually existed. Perhaps Vagalume published the words in the role of a whistle-blower and invented a collective name for the song's neglected authors.[20]

Vagalume printed the new lyrics along with a note that he claimed was written by the Grêmio. The note announced that the "true tango 'Pelo Telefone'" would be performed the next Sunday on the Avenida Rio Branco by Germano, Tia Ciata, Hilário, and João da Mata, yet another musician tangled in the song's web. The note claimed that the song was arranged "exclusively" by Sinhô and dedicated to "Mauro" on 6 August 1916, before the Festa da Penha and before the publication of Donga's sheet music. One stanza, clearly directed at Donga, reads, "How shameless / to tell in all the rodas [circles] / that this song is yours!" And another: "We wish you'd take it back / hadn't gone and done this. / Writing down what belongs to others, / your priorities are amiss."[21]

Coming ten days after Almeida had publicly disassociated himself from the song, Vagalume's article reflected rather than precipitated Almeida's uneasiness. But the fact that a group of individuals from "Little Africa" may have exerted enough pressure to cause Almeida to publicly reverse course suggests the kind of influence that Vagalume and other black leaders could wield. At the same time, the controversy itself reflects the uneven nature of author's rights. The Vagalume/Grêmio Fala Gente lyrics asked Donga not only to give credit where credit was due, but also to keep his "priorities" straight. He was resented not only for taking something that was not his but also for betraying a larger community. In 1933, more than fifteen years removed from the initial controversy, Vagalume once again took aim at Donga. "Samba dies," he wrote, "in the forgetting, the abandonment to which respected sambistas are condemned when they pass from the mouths of our people to the gramophone disc: when [samba] becomes an *industrial article* to satisfy the greed of editors and *authors of the productions of others*." Donga's "assimilation called 'Pelo Telefone,'" he bitterly remarked, was a "precursor of the samba industry."[22]

Vagalume printed these harsh words in his book *Na roda do samba*, which he dedicated to Eduardo das Neves, whom he called "that dear, departed black artist, who honored in so many ways the race to which I proudly belong."[23] Writing in 1933, Vagalume equated Neves, by then fourteen years deceased, with a distant era when money and individual interests did not pollute music. In a short span of time, Rio's crioulo malandro had undergone a dramatic transformation. He was no longer a symbol of avarice and instead was a pure, authentic artist, uninterested in money, and a foil to Donga, the latest greedy black public enemy.

The Oito Batutas: Formation and Early Success

Despite the controversy, Donga soon launched a successful career. He and the cofounder of the Oito Batutas, his friend Pixinguinha (Alfredo da Rocha Viana Júnior), turned it into one of the era's most popular and influential bands. Both men grew up in rich musical environments with close ties to multiple Carnival groups. Pixinguinha was born in 1897 on the outskirts of Rio. He wrote his first composition, "Lata de leite" (Can of milk) at the age of eleven, when he was already adept at playing a number of instruments.[24] Over the next half century he wrote, arranged, or recorded more than three hundred songs. Pixinguinha's parents, particularly his father, took great interest in developing his musical talents, providing him with material support and exposing him to a great number of accomplished musicians.

Donga, born in Rio in 1889, received less guidance from his father, who worked in construction and played tuba "in his free time." Like Pixinguinha, he traveled through Rio's many musical worlds. Though he did not have as many resources as Pixinguinha, he was by no means deprived. His mother provided a strong musical presence. Thanks to frequent tia gatherings and occasional sessions held by his father, he could proficiently play several instruments at an early age, including guitar and cavaquinho.[25] As a young man, he attended parties with some of the city's most prominent artists. Donga described the ambience in which he grew up as one in which "writers appreciated music and musicians appreciated poetry."[26]

Donga and Pixinguinha used their talents and connections to earn positions with popular Carnival groups. In 1911, Pixinguinha performed with the Grupo Carnavalesco Filhas da Jardineira as a member of the orchestra. His music instructor, Irineu de Almeida, was one of the group's directors. In 1912, Pixinguinha directed the Rancho Paladinos Japoneses and in 1914 made his first sound recording, with Casa Editora Carlos

Wehrs.[27] Donga also participated in multiple Carnival groups, including the Filhas da Jardineira and Dois de Ouro, considered by many to be Rio's first rancho. His mother was among the group's founders.[28]

Like many others, Pixinguinha benefited from personal connections. His older brother China (Otávio Littleton da Rocha Viana) helped him secure a gig at a bar, where he played the flute from 8 PM until midnight for 5 to 6 mil-réis per night, about the same amount his family had paid for an entire month of private schooling before he dropped out.[29] His friend Tute (Artur de Souza Nascimento) took him to several shows at the upscale Teatro Rio Branco, where he played in the orchestra.[30] Eventually, Tute convinced the theater owner and the orchestra director to allow Pixinguinha to fill in for an absent flautist. Pixinguinha capitalized on the opportunity, and his time at the Teatro Rio Branco helped catapult him to further successes.[31]

In 1919, the president of the Tenentes do Diabo, one of Rio's original grande sociedade Carnival associations, invited the Grupo Caxangá, a band with some twenty members, including Donga and Pixinguinha, to perform at the society's Carnival functions. Though the Grupo's members all had experience playing at Carnival, the engagement with the Tenentes represented a major breakthrough and helped them secure engagements at the Cinema Palais, an upscale theater located downtown.[32] Catching on at the Palais, a venue that normally featured white, formally trained musicians, brought opportunity and some difficult decisions. To begin, Donga, Pixinguinha, China, and another musician, Raul Palmieri, were required to pare down the group to eight members. Those eight—Donga (guitar), Pixinguinha (flute), China (guitar and vocals), Nelson Alves (cavaquinho), Palmieri (guitar), Jacó Palmieri (mandolin and *reco-reco*), José Alves de Lima (mandolin and *ganzá*), and Luís de Oliveira (mandolin and reco-reco)—became known as the Oito Batutas.[33] Four were white, and four were black, but the band's racial composition would fluctuate in the coming years as individuals departed and were added.

While Pixinguinha's superior talents made him the group's musical leader, Donga served as the de facto manager. "It was an improvised deal," he recalled years later. "I was always the group's adviser [*orientador*]. I don't know why, but it was always me who took care of the commercial aspects, the services. They started to call me the boss. I always directed the group, but with respect to the 'spalla' of the group, that was always Pixinguinha."[34] Donga's stewardship of the band and his personal successes are preserved in his photo and newspaper album, given by Donga's daughter to the journalist Sérgio Cabral years ago and now resting in Cabral's personal archive. The album itself is a treasure, full of old photos and scores of newspaper articles and programs. At some point, the clippings and photos exceeded the number of pages in the book, so Donga (or maybe someone close to him) recycled old ledgers, previously used to record the Batutas' earnings. The figures not obscured by memorabilia reveal that, on many nights, the group did quite well. The small sample shows single-show earnings ranging from 100 mil-réis, about the cost of a month's rent at a rundown pension in 1913, to more than one and a half contos. On several of the ledger-turned-scrapbook pages, newspaper articles about Donga obscure the group's earnings. One headline from 1932 reads, "Donga, the general of samba, wrote 'samba is ours,'" a vivid representation of both Donga the entrepreneur and Donga the spokesperson for a larger "we." In this case, "we" referred not to Afro-Brazilians alone but a larger national collective. "It's ours," the article declares of samba, "totally ours, and very Brazilian."[35]

Catching on at the Palais during Carnival led to shows at the Assírio, a chic café in the basement of the Teatro Municipal (Municipal Theater), and then to tours in Brazil, France, and Argentina. As they traveled from Carnival to the Cinema Palais and then through Brazil and beyond, the Oito Batutas helped shape the meaning of "our music." The same year that they started at the Palais, they recorded six songs with Odeon, and Pixinguinha and Donga were invited to write the music for a show at a local theater.[36] Thereafter, band members maintained high profiles, performed at private engagements, appeared in and wrote for theatrical productions, and received frequent attention in the press. Among the carioca elite who invited them to perform at private parties was Arnoldo Guinle, who was a wealthy white patron of the arts, the president of the Fluminense Football Club, and a founding member of the Rio Yacht Club. He paid for a number of the Batutas' trips. In October 1919, after a sendoff at the Brazilian Press Association, the group departed for São Paulo and Minas Gerais. Two years later, they traveled through Bahia and Pernambuco in the northeast.

Guinle treated the trips as research missions, charging the musicians with the task of gathering musical material. As researchers and not just performers, the Batutas helped chart a musical map of Brazil, a project already set in motion by individuals like Moraes Filho that gained greater impetus during the late 1920s through 1940s as prominent musicians and scholars sought to trace the origins of national rhythms. The tours also helped popularize Rio's music, which in fact had already been shaped and influenced by migrants from the areas the Batutas visited. The band's research assignments in the southeast and northeast make clear that individuals like Guinle looked upon Brazil's large rural areas as untapped resources, much as Moraes Filho viewed "the popular, anonymous muse" whose work he copied and sold. The mixed-race Batutas adeptly negotiated the worlds they were charged to research and those in which they played, fluidly channeling audience desires for folklore and cosmopolitan, urban, modern music. During Carnival, they paraded as *sertanejos*, rural folk dressed in rustic clothing. Early photos depict the Batutas in similar dress. Its members also frequently donned sharp dark suits, reminiscent of countless Jazz Age ensembles across the globe.

As they played for diverse audiences in various settings, the Batutas represented different things to different people: here a window into a distant, pastoral world, there a symbol of urban cosmopolitanism and modernity. Their repertoire was accordingly diverse. Pixinguinha recalled, "What we played commercially—as professionals, in our group— came from everywhere. We'd go to dance, to play what was ours. But we'd sprinkle in a little fox-trot to vary things. Commercially, we had to play a little bit of everything. And we survived like that, varying the program."[37] The band played its mixed repertoire with a diverse set of instruments, including those common to jazz and marching bands (trombone, flute, trumpet, tuba, piano) and others more often associated with rural music (cavaquinho, guitar, *chocalho*, and *cabaça*).[38]

When the Batutas left for France in 1922, the stated intentions were different from those for their domestic trips. Absent from discussions surrounding the group's transatlantic voyage was the notion that they would be traveling to Europe to do research. While the hottest band in Brazil had license to explore the nation's interior, no such privilege was assumed in France. In Europe, the Batutas' mission was to represent Brazil to the "civilized" world, not to gather musical knowledge. But the band's members did not put their own musical curiosity on hold while in Paris. In later interviews, both Donga and Pixinguinha recalled absorbing and learning, just as they had while traveling through Brazil. To both artists, the research mission did not necessarily stop or start where Guinle and others said that it should.[39]

A "Loving Flower"

The Batutas traveled to São Paulo and Minas Gerais in 1919 and 1920, to Bahia and Pernambuco in 1921, and then to Paris in early 1922. Soon after recrossing the Atlantic, they packed up again and headed to Argentina.[40] Traveling inside and outside Brazil, the group was often treated as a symbol of national identity. Some observers objected to the Batutas taking that role. Others applauded it. It is in the apparently laudatory descriptions of the Batutas, as much as in attacks against them, that we may glimpse the full meaning of evolving early twentieth-century racial definitions and ideologies. The group's members changed various times, but it always retained a racial mix. Despite (or perhaps because of) this, the group was often referred to collectively as *pretos*. As the Batutas departed for France, social commentators were divided in their appraisal of such a group representing Brazil abroad. A number of journalists hailed the trip, but others were less sanguine. A writer in Pernambuco did not know whether "to laugh or cry" at the fact that this musical mission did not represent "sophisticated Brazil, elite Brazil," and instead "pedantic Brazil, negroid and ridiculous."[41]

To many audiences, the Batutas represented Brazil's *sertão*, the Northeast's vast interior, a region often associated with drought, bloody revolution, and backward, mixed-race people. Twenty years before the Batutas' Paris voyage, Euclides da Cunha immortalized the region and its peoples in *Os sertões* (*Rebellion in the Backlands*). He described the area's landscape as rough and its inhabitants as "unbalanced" and dangerous.[42] In contrast to the harsh images popularized by Cunha, the Batutas' sertão was idyllic and calm. In the Bahian capital of Salvador, the group was hailed as "genuinely national." Of a show at the "elegant Moderno Casino" in Recife, one journalist wrote that their "primitive and admirable poetry" gave the "sensation of being in the sertão."[43] On the eve of its departure for France, writer Benjamin Costallat denounced the band's critics. "The Oito Batutas will not demoralize Brazil in Europe. To the contrary . . . they will carry the perfume of our crowded woods, the pride of our forests, the greatness of our land, [and] the melancholy of our people . . . sung through simple verse . . . of the *alma popular* [popular soul]."[44]

To Brazilians who viewed the band positively, its members displayed just the right combination of big-city sophistication and sertanejo simplicity, charm, and modesty. Before and after Paris, labels applied to the

Batutas alternated between sertanejo and "jazz band." Whatever pretensions the band had of being defined as modern and urban—and despite the fact that some Brazilian supporters thought that the trip to Paris added civility to the band—the humble sertanejo label often stuck with them, even after returning from France and despite donning jazz-band suits. But both before and after the trip, the group defied singular definitions. It was rarely just a rural *conjunto regional* (regional group) or a *conjunto sertanejo*, but also a "troupe" and an "orchestra." Lines were made especially fuzzy in a short 1923 article that described the Batutas as a "Jazz-Band sertanejo."[45] The Batutas often performed in, or played on the same bill as, rural-themed musicals and plays, such as the "sertaneja operetta" *Flor Tapuia*.[46] In "A Night in the Sertão," presented at Rio's upscale Teatro Lyrico in 1920, the Batutas played against a backdrop of "picturesque photography of individuals and customs from the patrician interior."[47] An article about the group's Paris trip defined samba as "our favorite dish, the quintessence of indigenous choreography [and] the 'juice' of regional hip-wiggles." A Niterói publication described the Batutas as "truly sertanejo musicians" and saw in their work "visions of the countryside [*roça*]."[48]

Repeating a phrase coined several years earlier by the poet Olavo Bilac, a writer for *Vanguarda* called the Batutas' music the "loving flower of three sad races."[49] In the Batutas, the writer saw Brazil's racial soul:

Brazilian music, an enchanting tropical blossoming of our race of
strong enthusiasms and smooth sentimentalisms is a suggestive
individualization of our people, who already united themselves
and their desires into that subjective organism that Gustavo [*sic*] Le
Bon calls the "Racial Soul," the secret of the uncontrollable force of
patriotism which defines mature nationalities.

Written in September 1922, the comments appeared on the heels of the Batutas' Paris trip and amid two watershed events: the hundred-year anniversary of independence and São Paulo's Modern Art Week, a gathering of literati who spawned the modernist movement in Brazil. The centennial celebrations in Rio featured a performance by the Batutas and Brazil's first radio broadcast.[50] The modernists who met in São Paulo were determined to flip a number of long-held beliefs on their head, including the notion that racial mixing necessarily led to degeneration. Music figured significantly in the new ideas.[51]

In the hands of some Latin American intellectuals, the French racial theorist Gustave Le Bon's ideas about black inferiority, the danger of racial mixing, and degeneration in tropical climes provided justification for programs to control reproduction, improve hygiene, bolster education, and "whiten" dark and mixed-race populations. Some Latin Americans rejected Le Bon's theories, while others tweaked them by embracing a neo-Lamarckian vision of genetics, which saw power in nurture as well as nature and therefore fit well with the idea that mixed-race populations could "improve" themselves.[52] In the same spirit, the *Vanguarda* writer rejected Le Bon's pessimistic understanding of racial mixing in favor of the idea that each nation had a particular "racial soul," which, in the case of Brazil, was embodied by the Batutas.

What was it about the Batutas that made them the nation's soul? Everywhere the band played, audiences adored them. Newspapers praised the Batutas' talents and often described them as *artistas* or "patrician" (*patrício*), though the second term often seemed to veer closer to "noble savage" than to imply sincere respect.[53] The thin line between earnest appreciation and exoticization or patronizing wonderment is evident in the widespread fascination with Pixinguinha's ability to mimic a bird's chirp with his flute. Brazilian and Argentine audiences took the display as a sign both of Pixinguinha's musical genius and of his apparent connection to nature. A newspaper in La Plata praised Pixinguinha's "admirable imitation of the warble of birds characteristic of Brazil."[54] A São Paulo paper noted his "always happy physiognomy."[55]

Because the Batutas were said to balance savagery with modesty and even sophistication, its members could also be "patriotic" and "genuinely national," labels frequently used to describe them. It was safe to define the Batutas as national symbols because they were also exotic, modest, spontaneous, and happy, traits that hardly challenged long-held racial stereotypes. The cronista Jethro saw in the Batutas an authentic expression of the Brazilian countryside. "I admire the hick [*caipira*]," he wrote, because of his distance from the tedious day-to-day of "cultured man, who has every activity linked to all the impulses of progress." The caipira was

> happy, always happy, never made angry by terrible luck, no matter how bitter. . . . In this sweet contemplation, the caipira is much more content than the man who knows and travels through the pages of history in search of more knowledge, drowning in an ocean of uncertainty. . . . Not the caipira; he does not involve him-

self in the evolutions of eras, and only reads the book of his own existence. . . . Life for the caipira is a richness with no limits. . . . This singular type, resigned and happy, pointing his guitar towards the song of his ministers . . . today will be present with the 8 Batutas, who will . . . offer to our spirit a living tradition, in whose simplicity, speaks to us of a civilization better than the one we have now: the civilization of peace and of indifference to the world's glories.[56]

A journalist in Minas Gerais wrote that in the "breast" of the band's "hopping, wiggling" music "beats the passionate soul" of the *caboclo*, an individual of European and Indian descent commonly associated with rural areas.[57] Another article referred to the band's members as "authentic representatives of the sertão and the subúrbios," two spheres not often linked together, and described the Batutas' music as "rudimentary manifestations of the popular sentiment."[58] The Niterói magazine that saw in the Batutas "visions of the roça" also enjoyed Pixinguinha's "magical flute" and the group's "sentimental verses." In that flute and in those verses, the magazine writer said, "One does not find the work of the great maestros of metrification, but instead the truth of the Brazilian poetic soul, expressed by rhyme and the pungent choro of guitars, cavaquinhoos [*sic*], and pandeiros."[59]

Across Brazil, the Batutas were hailed as expressions of the sertão and described as a "truly national" band that possessed an innocent, soulful, and sensual kind of savagery. The group frequently performed alongside comedians, variety acts, and shows parodying caipira speech and customs. Zé Filarmônica, a novelty performer who participated in many of the Batutas' shows, could "perfectly reproduce" with his mouth sounds made by musical instruments and animals.[60] The Batutas themselves often seemed content to nurture their backcountry identity, though in their lyrics and in the musicals and shows in which they participated, modesty often slipped into parody, as did a song about "João Boeiro," a hapless, aw-shucks country bumpkin.[61] The meaning of such parodies was in the eye of the beholder. To most audiences, the musicians were "authentic sertanejos" and living embodiments of the people and places they sang about. To the band's members, their own relationship with the roça must have been more complex. A number of the Batutas were either born in rural areas or had family or friends who were. But the band also made money by parodying those places and gained distance from demeaning stereotypes by performing them and thus casting themselves as cultured, refined mediators.

Journalists balanced "passion," "authenticity," and "spontaneity" with frequent references to the musicians' humble nature. Renan, a cronista "transported" to the "hinterland" during a Batutas show, described this combination. Unlike other groups, which "have a sort of licentiousness," Renan wrote, the Batutas are "modest, simple, and exciting, creating the best of impressions."[62] Even white elites in São Paulo, many of whom were at the time transfixed with the idea that they represented a privileged island of whiteness and civilization in a mixed-race Brazilian sea, found something distinctly national in the Batutas' performance.[63] One show, described by a São Paulo reporter as a "true success," made "city-people nerves vibrate." The Batutas, whom he called "authentic sertanejos," played music "born in the heart, without work," with "an enchanting spontaneity of the simple and passionate soul of our sertanejo, crude and brave, smoothly sad and deliciously ingenious."[64] A week earlier, another reporter wrote, "I am going to fall once again, in soul and body, into an orgy and festival of lundus and modinhas, feeling in the magic of those ballads, the smell of Brazilian earth, the semi-barbarous shout of noisy warrior samba, and the sweet pain of *saudade* [longing] . . . inherited from Lusitanian guitars."[65]

Benjamin Costallat, who defended the group as it departed for France, called the Batutas "modest," "spontaneous," and "heroic" and differentiated the group from North American bands. To those who protested the Batutas' trip by crying "they're black!" Costallat replied, "Who cares?! They're Brazilian!" He was not so accepting of dark-skinned musicians from the United States, whom he saw as the Batutas' foil. A few months earlier, he had witnessed a show by

"The Syncopated Band," a big black American orchestra that plays Beethoven and all of the classics to the accompaniment of automobile horns, train whistles, bells, old cans, and the most infernal and prosaic noises that the jazz band's morbid imagination can invent. . . . The Americans take noise [to Paris]. Ours [the Batutas] take sentiment. What was played with cans, now will be played with hearts. The difference is great. . . . No more Beethoven with rattles for the French. This is music from a land and a soul of a distant people. A land of moonlight, the cabocla [woman of Portuguese and Indian lineage], and the guitar.

That combination, Costallat was sure, would win over the French. "Hearing our modinhas, and hearing sung our moonlit nights, our sertão, the eyes of our morenas, our love, and our saudades, many Frenchmen will be moved."[66] The Batutas were simple, authentic, and even "exciting," but they were also reserved enough not to exceed their bounds, modest enough not to place themselves alongside "the great maestros of metrification," and wise enough not to slaughter Beethoven with crude instruments. A Brazilian living in Paris in 1922 expressed a similar view. The Batutas, he cheerfully reported, "are not presenting themselves here as representatives of Brazilian art music (which would be ridiculous) and instead as specialists and introducers of our samba, which is gaining enormous acceptance."[67] This comment, made five years after "Pelo telefone" was first recorded and six years before the consolidation of Estácio Samba, serves as a clear indication of the length and depth of the multiple processes that "making samba" entailed. In 1922, it was "samba" the word, not yet the distinct, fully formed musical style, that had "gained acceptance."

Pixinguinha's feelings about how he and the Batutas were depicted in the press are accessible only in limited and filtered snapshots, which stop short of providing a full picture but clearly show his ability to cater to public taste. In an interview with *A Notícia*, conducted soon after he returned from Paris, he described his time there with words that closely matched those of the expatriate. "It's good to know," Pixinguinha told the paper,

> that when we left here for Paris—celebrated by some, ridiculed by others—we did not have the foolish pretension of going to represent Brazilian art music abroad. What we were going to present in Paris, and what we did, with decency, thank God!, was simply play a few features of our music, the essentially popular and characteristic kind. . . . We were simply a group of modest but profoundly sincere artists, making heard the easy, unpretentious music of our popular songs.[68]

"Art music," mentioned by both Pixinguinha and the Brazilian living in France, refers to a loosely unified genre, written mainly for orchestras and chamber performances. Many of the musicians associated with art music—Heitor Villa-Lobos, Camargo Guarnieri, and Francisco Mignone, in Brazil; Carlos Chávez (Mexico); and Amadeo Roldán (Cuba)—were heavily influenced by "primitive" indigenous and African American traditions. But art music is almost always held above, or at least separate from, the music of "popular" groups.[69] Though the article purports to capture three voices—Pixinguinha's, the journalist's, and Donga's—the language remains strikingly similar throughout the "transcript." It is certainly possible that the journalist or editor modified or embellished the musician's words. And, yet, as we will see, throughout his career Pixinguinha deftly defined and redefined himself. In this instance, his statement appears to have been a calculated maneuver meant to tap into the public's desire for appropriately exotic and modest displays.

Who Owns the Sertão? Who Owns Folklore?

At least one person did not agree that the Batutas were the purest and most authentic representatives of Brazil or the sertão. Catulo da Paixão Cearense, the famous white lyricist and a close acquaintance of Fred Figner's, complained publicly about the Batutas' use of his "Luar do sertão" (Sertão moonlight). The piece, which *A Noite* called "Catulo's beautiful savage poem," was a staple of the Batutas' repertoire and had achieved great commercial success.[70] It was first recorded in the early 1910s by Eduardo das Neves and later by other well-known artists. Like "Pelo telefone," it inspired a number of alternative versions.

Cearense portrayed the sertão as the heart of Brazil, full of mesmerizing vistas and innocent, crude people. He felt that the Batutas had corrupted the song's spirit, an opinion he expressed publicly in 1920, when the king and queen of Belgium visited Rio.[71] Upon learning that the group would be performing two of his works, including "Luar do sertão," for the visitors, Catulo openly complained in a letter to the *Gazeta de Notícias*:

> I lament that Their Majesties will hear those poems mixed with the nonsense that is going to be an integral part of our folklore. "Luar do sertão" is a poem known throughout Brazil and appreciated by intelligent people and by the popular soul. Even illustrious foreigners have enjoyed it. I am certain that Their Majesties, learned as they are, would not disdain it if they heard it from educated lips and artistic souls. It would not be difficult, before singing it, to provide a quick translation, a brief synthesis. I, myself, singing could do this. . . . Is there a man in Brazil who could more fittingly represent this genre? In terms of music, I agree that those "batutas" can provide an idea . . . but [not] for poetry.[72]

Upon being asked to give a separate performance for the king and queen, Cearense replied, "The invitation is highly honorable, but I do not accept it. In a more adequate environment, I would not hesitate to embrace the idea. It would be an honor for me to be heard by Their Majesties, who, without vanity I understand would take with them a more acceptable impression of our music and popular poetry."

On one level, Cearense's frustrations resonate with those of Eduardo das Neves, who also saw his work represented and disseminated in ways that he felt corrupted it. On another level, Cearense's disgust with the Batutas and the way that he positioned himself as a "translator" between the unpolished Brazilian interior and "learned" European royalty reveals a racial disparity that informed samba's rise and the evolution of author's rights protection. Privileged white mediators like Cearense and Moraes Filho could enjoy unfettered access to popular themes, songs, and traditions, while those associated with the "popular, anonymous muse" were deemed unable to represent traditions that were supposedly their own. To Cearense and others, the Batutas, talented as they were, had no grasp of poetry and no real claim to respectable authorship.

AS DONGA, PIXINGUINHA, and the Oito Batutas helped shape "our music," two kinds of prizes were in dispute. First, there were intellectual property rights and performance earnings. Second, journalists, audiences, and the Batutas grappled over a less palpable but no less meaningful form of ownership: the right to define and shape the meaning of Brazil and Brazilian-ness. These apparently separate arenas of contestation — one tangible and economic, the other symbolic and sociopsychological — often merged.

Moraes Filho's presumptive use of the "popular, anonymous muse" implied that while poor nonwhite masses could produce folklore and culture, only certain members of society could be trusted to polish and represent that material to larger audiences. Similar presumptions undergirded the Batutas' research missions and Cearense's public declaration that he alone could translate Brazilian music and poetry for European royalty. As the Batutas' success and travel make clear, color was not the only factor that determined who could mediate. But if the Batutas could own and represent a piece of Brazil, it was only one small piece.

The rise of authorship as a right and a concept is often traced to the European Enlightenment and treated as a moment of rupture between individual and society. Foucault writes, "The coming into being of the notion of 'author' constitutes the privileged moment of *individualization* in the history of ideas, knowledge, literature, philosophy, and the sciences."[73] This kind of "individualization" marked the "Pelo telefone" controversy, particularly when Vagalume and the Grêmio Fala Gente accused Donga of "writing down something that belonged to others."[74] But in Brazil there were other variables at play that have generally escaped the view of scholars who study authorship and property rights in Europe and the United States. To Donga, Pixinguinha, Catulo, the *Vanguarda* writer, and Eduardo das Neves, authorship and ownership of legal property rights was often inseparable from discursive projects to shape larger identities and to "individualize" *the nation* in a way that would make it acceptably authentic, unique, sophisticated, and respectable all at once.

5

MEDIATORS AND COMPETITORS
Musicians, Journalists, and the Roda do Samba

Donga and Pixinguinha were able to lay claim to palpable and less concrete forms of ownership thanks in part to their relatively privileged upbringings. Those upbringings stand in stark contrast to the terms that commentators have used, almost without exception, to describe even the most successful Afro-Brazilian musicians. Hermano Vianna treats Donga and Pixinguinha as examples of "musicians of black and mixed race, belonging to the poorest class of Rio society." Micol Seigel, who provides a welcome departure from works that deny agency to black musicians, still lumps Pixinguinha and other Afro-Brazilian entertainers into a "non-elite, poor, [and] marginal" mass.[1] Depicted as members of the urban poor, Pixinguinha and Donga fit neatly into three common narratives. The first paints black artists as victims of whitening projects or of state and elite appropriation. Disney's 1943 film *Saludos Amigos* is a good example of the kind of whitening that occurred through commercialization and marketing. In one scene, stiff white dancers and musicians dance samba in what looks like an office. A scene from Carnival includes nary a brown or black face.[2] But whitening and exploitation were only parts of a larger story, a point made clear in a second important narrative, exemplified by Vianna's book *The Mystery of Samba*.[3] To Vianna, interactions between Pixinguinha and Donga and accomplished white musicians and intellectuals are an indication that samba was forged through collaboration engineered by white "cultural mediators." Those mediators, Vianna suggests, "[sought] out and cultivate[d] relationships with sambistas."[4] In both narratives, agency rests almost exclusively with white interlocutors, who either corrupt or embrace the work of impoverished black artists. A third stream of literature emphasizes musician agency, often to the point of romanticization.[5] In this chapter, I provide a different approach, one that pays close attention to agency but also sheds light on rarely examined examples of mediation, competition, and contestation waged to secure both the tangible and intangible rewards attached to "our music."

The "Pelo Telefone" Generation

Donga and Pixinguinha's formative childhood and adult years point to the shortcoming of all three narratives. Neither musician was rich by the standards of wealth amassed by Fred Figner, but neither was penniless. Pixinguinha's father (Alfredo da Rocha Viana) was a civil servant with shrewd business sense, and his mother, Raimunda, provided extensive educational and musical opportunities for her fourteen children. At the age of eight, Pixinguinha enrolled briefly in private school, a privilege that distinguished him from all but the most privileged cariocas.[6] Convinced that his son was a prodigy, Viana bought him a flute, reportedly paying 600 mil-réis (approximately US $140) for the instrument, enough to support a four-person family for about three months.[7] Aside from strong material support, Pixinguinha and his brothers and sisters (many of whom also played music) benefited from frequent contact with the network of tias and the institution-trained musicians who stayed at or visited the Viana residence. Because it provided a roof for so many, the house, which held eight bedrooms split between two floors, earned the nickname Pensão Viana. João da Baiana, Pixinguinha's friend and collaborator, recalled that the Vianas also owned and rented rooms throughout the neighborhood.

Irineu de Almeida (Pixinguinha's music instructor), Bonfíglio de Oliveira, and Heitor Villa-Lobos were among the famous musicians who either boarded with the Vianas or frequented their large gatherings, at which guests would consume in excess of two hundred bottles of beer.[8] Contact with so many musicians meant exposure to a variety of musical forms. With Almeida, Pixinguinha explored multiple genres, eventually becoming drawn to choro, the music he recalled playing in the front room of Tia Ciata's house while João da Baiana and others played samba out back. Choro flourished in Rio between the 1870s and 1920s and enjoyed a revival decades later. After establishing a name for himself, Pixinguinha studied theory and *solfeggio*, an Italian and French pedagogy for learning scales, at Rio's prestigious Instituto Nacional de Música.

Despite their good fortune, both Pixinguinha and Donga still found themselves below many of the more celebrated white mediators in material wealth and social prestige. Yet such disadvantages hardly precluded agency. While Donga leaned on journalists like Mauro de Almeida and Arlequim, the larger project to register and record "Pelo telefone" was undeniably his own. The Pensão Viana, Pixinguinha's expensive flute, and the private music lessons indicate that his family was part of a burgeoning middle-class sector, distinct if not altogether removed from Rio's most impoverished classes. Within that sector, he and other Afro-Brazilian musicians functioned as both mediators who assisted others and doled out patronage and as competitors who sought the financial prizes and cultural capital that came with successful careers.

Between the recording of "Pelo telefone" in 1917 and the rise of Estácio Samba in the late 1920s, an all-star cast of Afro-Brazilian composers, instrumentalists, vocalists, entertainers, and cultural and community leaders—referred to here as the "Pelo Telefone Generation"—began or consolidated careers in Rio. Some made names for themselves through recording, performance, or composition. Others helped organize community and Carnival groups. Many artists cultivated relationships with journalists to great effect. Some of the city's most prominent black reporters wrote or played music or caroused and socialized with those who did. The overlap of religion, music, and journalism also brought Afro-Brazilian musicians, writers, and spiritual leaders into frequent contact with white artists. The Pelo Telefone Generation was a diverse group, and even the musical range between "tan tantan tan tantan" and "bum bum paticumbum-prugurun-dum" covers only a small sample of the musical forms it helped shape. Aracy de Almeida (Aracy Teles de Almeida), a transcendent female singer and theater performer, was a devoted fan of classical music. Bonfíglio de Oliveira studied at Rio's Conservatório de Música and was recognized in Brazil and Europe as one the era's premier trumpet players. Mano Décio da Viola (Décio Antônio Carlos) is thought to have written some five hundred songs and also helped pioneer the drum-heavy music featured in Carnival parades. In the recording studio, he adapted waltzes by Strauss and songs by European artists whose music he heard at local cinemas. Mano Elói and Amor (Getúlio Marinho da Silva) made commercial recordings of *pontos cantados*, percussive and vocal divinations used to conjure deities and spirits.[9] Bide (Alcebíades Maia Barcelos) helped introduce the surdo and the tamborim into Carnival samba and fashioned percussion instruments from cans and other materials.

A large number of musicians lived in the adjoining neighborhoods Ca-
tumbi, Estácio, and Cidade Nova, each home to diverse collections of
Brazilian migrants, foreign immigrants, and native-born cariocas. Others
were born in the subúrbios or hillside shantytowns. Some grew up in relative comfort, but not all were so fortunate. Alvaiade (Oswaldo dos Santos), who became a prominent member of Portela, one of Rio's first samba
schools, was orphaned at the age of five. He was born and grew up in
Oswaldo Cruz, some twenty kilometers from downtown Rio. In the 1930s
in nearby Madureira, less than 3 percent of streets were paved, fewer than
one-third of buildings had running water, and only one-fifth had electricity.[10] At the age of thirteen, Alvaiade found work at a local printer's
office. Bide began work at an early age in a shoe factory. As a child, Heitor
dos Prazeres was arrested multiple times for vagrancy. In Mangueira, the
favela that gave rise to the famous samba school of the same name, Carlos
Cachaça (Carlos Moreira de Castro) left home at an early age. After his
father disappeared, his mother entrusted him to the care of an illiterate
Portuguese landlord, who raised the future musician and relied on him
to keep track of receipts and written records for his properties. Cartola
(Angenor, or Agenor de Oliveira), another famous Mangueira musician,
was born in Catete and spent several years living in Laranjeiras, generally affluent neighborhoods. In 1919, when he was eleven years old, his
family hit hard times and moved to Mangueira, where he met and became
friends with Carlos Cachaça. As early as the age of nine, João da Baiana
did menial work for the military. He also worked as a carpenter, and in his
early twenties he began a career at the port, where he maintained steady
work and advanced through the ranks until he retired in 1949. He claimed
to have missed the Oito Batutas' Paris trip in order to keep his job on the
docks.[11] Mano Décio da Viola sold newspapers as a young teenager on
the Largo da Carioca. The environments and social strata occupied by
the Pelo Telefone Generation suggest that familiar narratives that emphasize poverty are based in a certain reality; many of the era's most famous
musicians did, in fact, grow up poor and remained so for their entire lives.
But the generation's diversity and the distance that separated Pixinguinha
and Bonfíglio de Oliveira, for example, from Alvaiade and Carlos Cachaça
makes clear that Rio's Afro-Brazilian musicians were hardly the monolithic, impoverished mass they are so frequently depicted to be.

Like Pixinguinha, many musicians received support from their families. Before moving to Rio from Minas Gerais, Ataulfo Alves learned to
play multiple instruments under his father's instruction. Eduardo das

Neves's son Cândido took up the guitar when he was five years old but was reportedly prohibited from playing it by his own father, who felt that the violin and piano would bring his child more respect and better career prospects. Bonfíglio de Oliveira received instruction from members of his father's band in Guaratinguetá, São Paulo, before the family moved to Rio. Mano Décio da Viola's family organized its own rancho. Zé da Zilda (José Gonçalves), also known as Zé Com Fome (Hungry Zé) for his habit of stashing food in his guitar case, learned to play cavaquinho and guitar from his father, an accomplished musician. Extended social networks provided additional support and opportunities, and artists were exposed to new music and met potential collaborators at choro circles, through workplace bands, and at private gatherings and parties.

Musical collaboration and exchange fostered community but also engendered divisions and rivalries. As we have already seen, early twentieth-century Carnival groups often turned to the police for protection against rival clubs and organizations. Acrimonious disputes were also waged over musical authorship and religious differences. In the neighborhoods adjacent to Rio's ports, the famous *babalorixá* (Afro-Brazilian priest) João Alabá competed with other prominent religious leaders, including Cipriano Abedé, Mãe Aninha de Xangô, and Benzinho Bambochê, for followers and influence.[12] Musicians were intimately tied to these struggles, and many members of the Pelo Telefone Generation crisscrossed the overlapping worlds of religion and music. Tio Faustino (Faustino Pedro da Conceição) was not only a religious leader but also a musical entrepreneur. Tancredo da Silva Pinto, who spent years living in Estácio, composed a handful of recorded songs but is better known for his role in developing, maintaining, and writing about religion.[13] Hilário Jovino Ferreira was an *ogã*, an official or honorific titleholder, in Alabá's *terreiro* (place of worship, also often a center for gathering and living). A number of musicians' mothers were influential tias. Vagalume dedicated *Na roda do samba* to, among others, Oxunã da Praça Onze (Henrique Assumano Mina do Brasil), a *pai-de-santo* whom Sinhô, a member of Vagalume's Grêmio Fala Gente, was known to petition for protection and guidance before releasing a new song.[14]

The relationship between music and religion shifted during the 1920s and 1930s. Tia Ciata died in 1924, Alabá in 1926, and Mãe Aninha and Benzinho Bambochê in 1938. Their passing signaled the beginning of a transition that, during the 1940s, saw the city's main Afro-Brazilian religious centers move to outlying neighborhoods.[15] Some migrants in Rio socialized primarily with others from the same state or town, but others did not. While the exact number of immigrants who came to Rio from Bahia during the late nineteenth and early twentieth centuries remains a matter of dispute, Maria Clementina Pereira Cunha shows that the association between popular music and the *idea* of Bahia marked and divided the music world. During the 1910s and 1920s, musicians divided themselves into groups "'for' and 'against' [the] association between Bahia and samba."[16] Like religion and living conditions, birth origins and regional affiliation served as markers that identified and divided members of the Pelo Telefone Generation.

"The King of My Sambas"

Few issues created more division or animosity than musical authorship. Sinhô (José Barbosa da Silva), known widely as the King of Samba, was at the center of multiple disputes. A light-skinned *mulato* born and raised in Rio, he became a master pianist and recorded about 150 songs before dying in 1930 at the age of forty-one. His biographer, Edigar de Alencar, suggests that it is nearly impossible to trace how many times his musical stylings were appropriated by others.[17] Sinhô also did his fair share of appropriating, famously commenting, "Samba is like a little bird: it belongs to whoever grabs it." Some musicians forcefully objected to the privileges he took with their music. Hilário Jovino Ferreira, like Sinhô a member of the so-called Grêmio Fala Gente and fellow complainant against Donga, took special exception to Sinhô's smashing 1920 success, "Fala meu louro" (Speak, my parrot), which satirized the Bahian politician Rui Barbosa.[18] As he did with "Pelo telefone," Vagalume gave public airing to the alleged impropriety, publishing a column in which he quoted Hilário calling the song "one of the most audacious plagiarisms" in "the history of sambistas." Hilário felt that Sinhô "plagiarized" in two senses: by stealing music and by asserting his authenticity as a samba musician. In "Entregue o samba aos seus donos" (Give samba back to its owners), a bitter musical reply full of allusions to Bahia's distinctive, African-influenced cuisine, Hilário challenged Sinhô's connection to real samba and authentic Brazilian culture. To Hilário, Sinhô had crossed a line not only by appropriating his music but also by staking claim to a Bahian culture of which he saw himself as guardian.[19]

Hilário was not the only one who felt wronged by Sinhô. Heitor dos Prazeres claimed that the chorus for Sinhô's "Dor de cabeça" (Headache) belonged to him.[20] According to Alencar, Prazeres recanted the claim on his deathbed.[21] Whether or not that is true, "Dor de cabeça" was not the only song that Prazeres and Sinhô disputed. Prazeres claimed partial or full authorship of two of Sinhô's most famous hits, "Ora vejam só" (Hey, just look at that) and "Gosto que me enrosco" (I like how you tie me in knots).[22] Prazeres threatened to take legal action over the disputes and apparently secured a series of payments from Sinhô. Prazeres also attacked Sinhô in "Olha ele, cuidado" (Careful, keep an eye on him) and "Rei dos meus sambas" (King of my sambas). In the second song, he called Sinhô an "intelligent malandro."[23] That was a tame attack compared to "O pé de anjo" (The angel's foot), a song that Sinhô directed at Pixinguinha's brother, China. In one stanza, Sinhô describes a "little blade that cuts gold and marble. I also keep it handy to cut / the tongues of those who talk behind my back."[24] On another occasion, Sinhô derisively referred to Donga, Pixinguinha, and China, all dark-skinned and all with relatives from Bahia, as Os Três Macacos (The Three Monkeys), a racially tinged reference to Tia Ciata's Carnival group Macaco É Outro.[25]

In cases of contested authorship, neither law nor convention made it easy to identify the real composer or to distinguish plagiarism from creative appropriation. Mano Décio da Viola's adaptations of the songs he heard at the cinema exemplify the difficulty of clearly distinguishing between theft and creation. Sinhô's "O pé de anjo" raises similar issues. He reportedly wrote the song when a customer at a popular music store requested the Brazilian version of a popular French waltz. After the house pianist played the song, Sinhô took a turn at the bench, riffing off what he just heard and in the process creating what became a Carnival hit and the inspiration for a popular theater act.[26]

While Vagalume and others were highly critical of Donga's actions in 1917, Sinhô emerged from the various accusations directed at him relatively unscathed. Regarding a disputed case of plagiarism involving Sinhô, the poet Manuel Bandeira commented, "This all made me reflect about how difficult it is to identify at the end of the day the authorship of these carioca sambas that spring up from no one knows where."[27] (There has been significantly less reflection on the sources and origins of Bandeira's work and that of other practitioners of "high" art.) Alencar wrote that Sinhô might have committed "sins" (pecados), but "sins that did not compromise his fame."[28] Almirante (Henrique Foréis Domingues) claims that the appropriations were typical of the era. But he and others found Donga's "pecados" more objectionable. It is difficult to know exactly why

Sinhô escaped the kind of criticism launched at Donga, but the difference is striking. The contrast must be due in part to the fact that Sinhô died young, whereas Donga lived into old age and remained subject to inquiry and criticism. Sinhô's prodigious musical talents also probably helped deflect criticisms, but it is hard to imagine that skin color did not also play a role. While Sinhô's actions are invariably contextualized within a larger era of ad hoc, catch-as-catch-can ownership norms, Donga's blackness is frequently placed front and center in discussions of his authorship.

"Pelo telefone" was not the only proprietary dispute involving Donga. After returning from France, the Oito Batutas split up and reconstituted several times. In one incarnation, on a tour through southern Brazil, Aristides Júlio de Oliveira played drums for the group. In 1931, Oliveira gathered his own musicians to perform at a party sponsored by the Ministry of Foreign Relations and called the band the Batutas. In response, Donga and Pixinguinha wrote a letter, published in O Globo:

> Illustrious Sr. Publisher of O Globo. Warm greetings.—We present ourselves before you with the intention of publishing the following lines in your highly regarded publication, for which we gratefully thank you in advance. In order to avoid any confusion or damage to third parties, the undersigned, directors of the orchestra "Os Batutas," duly registered in the M. Junta Commercial, declare that the only individuals authorized to execute any kind of business referring to the band in question are its directors, and that Sr. Aristides (drums), absolutely does not possess power or authorization to contract engagements for the orchestra in question. All transactions made by [him] for the services of the well-known, aforementioned orchestra are null and void. We also declare that if the same Sr. Aristides continues with his illicit behavior, he will be called to answer, with the intention of avoiding further damages to third parties and the undersigned.—(a) Pixinguinha and Donga.[29]

Two years later, Donga sought to trademark the name and logo of another band, the Guarda Velha (Old Guard). As he described on a trademark petition, the logo was positioned

> horizontally, in capital letters, black in color, over a white background, having below, to the left, the silhouette of six musicians, in action, with the following instruments, from the left to the right: agogô, cabaça or afoxé [sic] (African instrument), horn, drums,

banjo (with the player seated at the piano), and piano, having, further below, to the right, the following wording: "Director Ernesto dos Santos Donga. Rua Maria Romana, 17, casa IV. Telefone 8–1519."[30]

As was the case when Donga registered "Pelo telefone," securing trademarks for "Oito Batutas" and "Guarda Velha" required wherewithal and resources. He had to submit his petition to the Junta Commercial (Board of Trade) along with three copies of the image and a fee. While Donga's small collection of trademarks was paltry compared to Fred Figner's massive arsenal, it distinguished him from the vast majority of Brazilians and most of his professional competitors.

Claiming ownership was difficult for performers, especially women of color. Deo Costa, an Afro-Brazilian actress and dancer, performed (sometimes with Pixinguinha) in several theater troupes organized and run by the Afro-Brazilian impresario, playwright, and actor De Chocolat (João Cândido Ferreira). In one show she played the character Venus de Jambo, an erotic, racialized reference to the fruit of the jambeiro tree. In 1926, De Chocolat replaced her with another actress. A published statement, ostensibly written by De Chocolat, noted that the name Venus de Jambo had simply been "loaned to Costa for use on stage" and that the new Venus de Jambo "inherited her nickname on account of her physique." Costa published a biting reply in a paper in São Paulo, where the troupe was performing:

> If tomorrow, of her free and spontaneous desire, the "heiress" of
> the name "Venus de Jambo" has to quit the company and in order
> to substitute her a proper artist cannot be found . . . will the title
> that was "lent" to me and the other "heiress" simply be applied to
> porter number "twelve" at the Central Station?[31]

Costa's talents and propriety of her artistic production, she made clear, had been unjustly usurped as she was absorbed into a seemingly endless line of interchangeable black female bodies.

In general, female artists found few opportunities during the early twentieth century beyond singing or dancing. Some black and mixed-race women found work on stage, especially after the creation of De Chocolat's Companhia Negra de Revistas (Black Theater Company) in the mid-1920s.[32] But for the most part, women who starred in theater and the record industry were white and hardly ever made names for themselves as composers. Authorship and the music industry were gendered and racialized in ways that placed severe limits on women, especially Afro-Brazilians. Nonetheless, innovative female singers found ways to place their own stamp of ownership on performances. A 1936 article in *Carioca* noted that talented *cantoras* (female singers) "know how to vary samba" and infuse it with their own "particularity." Music, the article's author maintained, "turns into something different on the lips and in the voice of each one."[33]

Clementina de Jesus (Clementina de Jesus da Silva) became a famous singer and composer, but only late in her life. An Afro-Brazilian born in 1901, she worked for most of her life as a domestic servant before launching a successful, celebrated career, which did not take off until the 1960s. The presence and prominent role of women like Tia Ciata at musical gatherings and within musician circles suggests that black women played crucial roles not only as community and religious leaders, but also as musical innovators and instructors. Journalists once asked Donga about his father's influence on his career. "He didn't like choro much," Donga said, "but sometimes got together [and played] with friends." When asked whether his father played any instruments other than tuba, he replied, "No. He cared much more about his profession." "But did he at least sing a few modinhas?" No, again. "It was my mother who sang."[34] As in the case of Deo Costa and Tia Ciata, the musical contributions of Donga's mother are hard to trace, buried beneath the histories of samba kings.

Vagalume and Rio's Black Journalists

In seeking out the press to voice concerns and complaints, Deo Costa and Donga drew on a long tradition. The turn-of-the-century performers Benjamin de Oliveira and Eduardo das Neves visited newspaper offices and provided journalists with press releases, letters, and interviews. Sinhô was known to call journalists every time he came up with a new song.[35] In 1899, Hilário feted writers at *O Paiz* with an elaborate meal in hopes of securing publicity for his Carnival group.[36] The close relationship between journalists and Carnival groups goes back perhaps even farther, to the middle of the nineteenth century, when Rio's grandes sociedades, founded and maintained by wealthy white cariocas, came into being.[37] In deciding which musicians and songs to feature in their papers, journalists and editors shaped the lucrative Carnival season. A number of prominent writers also composed, played, and wrote lyrics, often collaborating with established musicians.[38]

Musicians collaborated and sought favor with all kinds of journalists in Rio, including a small but influential cadre of black journalists, especially Vagalume, also an advocate for the ranchos, cordões, and other small Carnival groups, whose members were generally much poorer and darker than those who belonged to the grandes sociedades. In 1916, the rancho Ameno Resedá published a short biographical piece about Vagalume, whom it had made an honorary member. His parents, the article explained, were "poor, but hardworking and honorable." He distinguished himself in school and was "discovered" by a journalist writing an article about a rail line where Vagalume worked. In 1893, he volunteered for the army, fighting for President Floriano Peixoto against an armed group of Navy officers in the Revolta da Armada. In 1896, he began his career in journalism, which came to include work as a police reporter, multiple running columns, and stints with approximately fifty publications.[39] He took the nickname Vagalume (Firefly) while writing a column for *A Tribuna* titled "Ecos noturnos: Reportagem da madrugada" (Nocturnal echoes: Dispatches from daybreak). He dabbled in playwriting and composed lyrics for a handful of sambistas, including Sinhô. Around 1903, a group of musicians and Carnival revelers founded the Clube Carnavalesco dos Vagalumes and named him honorary president.[40]

Other Afro-Brazilian journalists, including Luís Correia de Barros, who went by the nickname "Brown" (*Marrom*), and K. Peta (Primitivo Rimus Rodrigues Prazeres), wrote for popular daily and weekly papers and often specialized in Carnival and music coverage.[41] Jota Efegê (João Ferreira Gomes), whose skin was at least as light as João do Rio's—a contrast to Vagalume, Barros, and K. Peta's, all of whom had dark skin— became perhaps the most influential Carnival cronista of the twentieth century. He described his father as "an educated *mulato*, who spent time in Paris and spoke French well," and was raised by his father's mother, an Afro-Brazilian from Bahia. Vagalume, Marrom, and K. Peta all spent time at the *Diário Carioca*, a paper founded in 1928 that, after several transformations, came to cast itself as a voice piece for Brazil's poor and working class. In its first years, circulation was small—around five thousand readers—but by the early 1950s it had grown to forty-five thousand for weekday editions and seventy thousand on Sundays.[42]

In Vagalume and other Afro-Brazilian cronistas, Rio's black residents had influential connections but not a black press per se. Ameno Resedá used a community newsletter to publish its short biographical sketch of

Vagalume, and there is no reason to believe that other Carnival groups did not publish similar papers. In 1935, Marrom helped found *A Voz do Morro* (The Voice of the Hill), the "official organ" of Mangueira's famous samba school. The paper, which had a short run, distinguished itself from "luxury magazines and papers that shout and dominate." *A Voz do Morro*, its founders proudly declared, was "born from samba, for samba, and by samba."[43]

Na roda do samba

The book *Na roda do samba* (In the samba circle) provides a rich example of how Vagalume used his position and connections to represent, redefine, and mediate between the different worlds he inhabited. The text, which has received little scholarly attention, also offers an opportunity to consider how black leaders in Rio conceptualized and shaped emerging definitions of race and nation. *Na roda* is divided into two parts. Part 1, "Samba," is dedicated exclusively to samba, its origins, current condition, and future. In part 2, "Life in the Morros," Vagalume describes his visits to a number of the city's favelas. While the book's stated goal is to trace the roots of samba, part 2 addresses the related project of challenging widespread notions about favela life and the culture and people associated with samba, referred to collectively by Vagalume as *gente da roda* (people of the circle). Throughout the text, Vagalume studiously avoids labeling the gente da roda as black, and at times includes whites in the circle. But he also makes clear his desire to counter pervasive racial stereotypes by presenting his readers with a new, more positive depiction of poor, black, and mixed-race cariocas.

Vagalume asserts his authority and his role as mediator in multiple ways. He prefaces the book by emphasizing its "extremely modest" (*modestíssimo*) nature, and he suggests that what the text lacks in "rhetorical flourish" it makes up for with firsthand knowledge. His reporting, he assures readers, came from information gleaned from authorized and trustworthy sources. But Vagalume was no slum-dweller, a point he repeatedly emphasizes. He did not live in the morros. He journeyed to them, always by car. While he peppers the text with slang, he also frequently uses phrases in Latin, Italian, English, and French. He was not a faceless member of the roda, but rather a guide leading his readers through worlds at once distant and close to their own. Vagalume also clearly saw himself as a guardian of the past and gatekeeper of the present, responsible for determining who belonged in the roda. In publishing his book, he wrote, "I had no other objective than to separate the wheat from the chaff."[44]

In this case, the "chaff" referred to those who exploited "modest men" (*homens modestos*) for personal gain and turned meaningful cultural and spiritual traditions into watered-down commodities. Chapter 1 delineates the relationship among samba, money, and race in no uncertain terms. Here Vagalume explains the origins of the word "samba." Long ago an "African slave" in Bahia saved a considerable sum of money after years of hard work and "with much sacrifice." As his health flagged, he revealed to his youngest son the hiding place of the money, which was to be used to purchase the family's freedom. But the greedy son stole the money and fled. Out on his own, a fugitive, he avoided authorities and turned his father's money into a fortune. Years later, beset with guilt, he returned to Bahia intending to return the money. But when he arrived he found that, thanks to years of hard work, the family was already free, and his father was still alive. Despite his own wealth, the son was still an outlaw, obliged to appear before an "African chief" to gain his freedom and publicly ask his father for forgiveness. During the ceremony, the people there exhorted him to repay the money by shouting "Sam!," an "African word," Vagalume explains, meaning "pay." The son produced a package containing the stolen money. The chief and his councilors urged the father to "receive" the money: "Ba." The two men embraced as the crowd and the court continued to voice their instructions: Sam! . . . Ba! Sam! . . . Ba! A party ensued. A music was born.[45]

The story's principal lesson—that community will trump individuality and greed—is told with clear implications for the music industry. It is, after all, in this same text that Vagalume attacks Donga and describes samba's death as "the forgetting, the abandonment to which respected sambistas are condemned when they pass from the mouths of our people to the gramophone disc." Throughout parts 1 and 2, Vagalume repeatedly describes the power and beauty of a bygone era when music was played free of monetary influences.

Of all the problems he associated with the music industry—simple rhythms, inequality, no respect for the past—the most pressing, by far, was the theft of music and lyrics. "We find ourselves," he declares, living under an "Empire of Plagiarism."[46] If Sinhô was the King of Samba, the Emperor of Plagiarism was, at least to Vagalume, Francisco Alves, also known as Chico Alves, Chico Viola, and the Rei da Voz (King of Voice).

Alves's family was white but occupied social strata similar to the ones inhabited by many of the upwardly mobile black members of the Pelo Telefone Generation. As a young teenager, he polished shoes on the street before finding work in a factory and then as a chauffeur. Like so many other performers, his career began in the circus and the teatro de revista. By 1933, when Vagalume published *Na roda*, Alves was firmly ensconced at the top of the music world, thanks largely to his recordings of songs written by Ismael Silva and other Estácio musicians.

The nature of the relationship between Alves and Silva has been subject to much speculation. Some suggest that Alves stole from Silva or bought his songs for a pittance. Others see a more symbiotic relationship, one controlled and even initiated by Silva. According to one account, the relationship was born in the late 1920s when Bide persuaded Silva, laid up in a hospital bed and in failing health, to sell his songs and secure a more comfortable life. In one interview, Silva depicted his relationship with Alves as one of mutual understanding.[47] Whether or not Silva glossed over inequalities (perhaps to protect Alves or to avoid the appearance of having been duped), it is beyond doubt that Alves profited immensely from the relationship. A public inventory executed after he died in a car crash in 1952 revealed enormous earnings. Between 1947 and 1951, his salary at Rádio Nacional and a constant stream of royalties provided income ranging from Cr\$ 158,000 (US \$8,320) to Cr\$ 305,000 (US \$16,060) per year, sums that dwarfed the incomes of all but the richest cariocas.[48]

The vast distance between Silva and Alves is indicative of several larger trends. As was the case for Anacleto de Medeiros, whose skin color and work as a composer combined to place him in the background of the early Casa Edison catalogs, for Silva race and the division between composers and performers combined to hinder his earning potential. That Alves, a popular recording artist, would earn more than Silva, a composer, is no more surprising today than it was at the time. Performers almost always earn more acclaim and fortune than composers. But race was also a determining factor. Silva stood little chance of starring in radio (in which shows were often recorded live before audiences), a medium dominated by white singers, and Alves simply did not have to go to the trouble of writing songs. For Silva, an emerging system of author's rights protection was his best, perhaps *only*, chance to secure income, but the way the system evolved meant that he would not benefit from it as much as some of his white counterparts.

Vagalume made no bones about his dislike for Alves:

[He] does not belong to the circle, nor does he know the rhythm of samba. But he does know the makers of samba (*os fazedores de samba*), the *musicistas*—the little guys—with whom he does business, buying their works and hiding their names. And anyone with a good song, whatever the genre, who wants to record with Casa Edison, has to sell it to Chico Viola, because any other way simply won't work! They say, almost everyone does, that Chico is a magnificent performer and nothing more. They say that he is incapable of producing a single thing because, well, anything that's good isn't his, and anything that's his isn't worth a lick.[49]

Vagalume also mocked Alves's impeccable appearance and immaculate teeth, which, someone told him, cost the singer "an arm and a leg" (*custou os tubos*).[50] Alves, Vagalume wrote, is "a stepfather, the adoptive dad of an infinite number of sambas" from the morro. "We do not mean to say that everything Chico Viola records is from the Morro do Salgueiro. No. Many are also from São Carlos and Mangueira."[51]

In a column published soon after the book's release, Jota Efegê praised Vagalume's work but also pointed out that any book written "in pieces, at tables in cafés . . . without careful revisions, without citations, is prone to include omissions, lapses, errors, and embellishments."[52] This carelessness, Jota Efegê explained, accounted for Vagalume's misguided attacks on Alves and the fact that the book made no mention of Almirante or Noel Rosa, two enormously popular white musicians. The idea that the knowledgeable and fastidious Vagalume casually misinterpreted Alves's actions, or that he carelessly forgot about Almirante or Rosa is not believable. Vagalume meant for his text to define who belonged to the roda and who did not. The individuals whom Vagalume excluded from the roda are as significant as those whom he defended. While the book makes multiple references to Estácio, there is no mention of Ismael Silva or of the other musicians who lived there. For Vagalume, *real* samba was a thing of the past, something to be preserved, defended, and protected, not meddled with or inserted further into an already corrupt music industry. Lamartine Babo and Ary Barroso, two successful white artists, appear in the book, closer to the circle than Alves, but still not full members. Babo, Vagalume wrote, "is undeniably a talented young guy and a good element who entered into the world of sambistas without, however, belonging to the roda do samba." Barroso, meanwhile, "is a great musicista. . . . But he is not a sambista in the [real] expression of the word. He would not be

capable of creating sheet music for a samba with the same ease and precision as a Pixinguinha. . . . He is a marquee name, but in the roda do
samba, his name is profane."[53]

Vagalume did not use race alone to separate the "wheat from the
chaff." Indeed, his book is full of favorable references to white men, and
he pulled no punches in criticizing black artists like Donga. He dedicated
Na roda to a number of individuals, including Eduardo das Neves, Sinhô,
Hilário Jovino Ferreira, and the influential pai-de-santo Henrique Assumano Mina do Brasil. He also gave special thanks to a number of white
men, including Pedro Ernesto (Pedro Ernesto Baptista), who, as prefect,
pushed forward important initiatives to link favela dwellers to the city
government, including the subsidizing of samba schools and Carnival.[54]
Vagalume prefaced *Na roda* with a "Sign of Friendship and Recognition of
Great Friends," a list of 114 names, including the prominent white theater
men Abadie Farias Rosas and Alvarenga Fonseca, and Lourival Fontes,
the director of several government censor offices during the 1930s and
1940s.

If Vagalume did not simply condemn whites—instead carefully select-
ing which ones were allies and friends and which were not—neither did
he blindly celebrate all Afro-Brazilians. Aside from positive references
to several tias, women of color are described as objects, almost always
through racy or misogynist song lyrics. While Vagalume gave some black
men unqualified praise—Neves, for example—he treated others with
ambiguity or outright disdain. He called João da Baiana a "hero" but also
criticized him for recording an old song that did not belong to him:

> *He almost always confuses* what he heard and learned as a boy with
> the originalities [*sic*] that he tries to record on victrola records. It
> is possible that João da Baiana's imagination, his thick head [*bes-
> tunto*], will still provide us a decent work, but never like [the one]
> . . . sung in Carnival of 1882, and which the young sambista, edu-
> cated in the old school, came to record as if it were his . . . fifty-one
> years later![55]

Vagalume harbored similar doubts about Heitor dos Prazeres. While Prazeres knew "samba and belongs to the roda," Vagalume found his recent
work to be of poor quality and in need of "rehabilitation." "*Off-side* as
[Prazeres is], he needs to hit the *penalty* and score a *goal* so as not be
eliminated from the *team*."[56]

Donga's place in the roda was similarly in doubt. Considering his repeated critiques of Donga, the fact that Vagalume wrote anything positive about him is itself surprising. But Donga's past and his connection to Rio's black religious and cultural circles gave the journalist hope. "He was born in the roda do samba," Vagalume pointed out. "Precious few know as he does the secrets of a partido alto samba. . . . Since he was a little kid, Donga watched, listened, and learned." Nonetheless, Vagalume felt that Donga "rested on his laurels." Conjuring perhaps the worst insult he could imagine, Vagalume linked Donga to Alves, calling "Pelo telefone" a "precursor" to an industry that, in Vagalume's estimation, now belonged to the King of Voice.[57]

In tracing samba's origins and drawing a line around the roda, Vagalume clearly had a racial project in mind, and yet, in separating the wheat from the chaff, he maintained a degree of racial flexibility and ambiguity. Vagalume's treatment of white musicians like Babo and Barroso, neither of whom belonged in the circle nor in the same category as Alves, suggests that the roda was mainly but not exclusively a black space. Meanwhile, Vagalume positioned himself in relation to his audience and his subjects by occupying multiple overlapping social and racial spheres. On the one hand, he placed himself within the roda, and on the other hand, he clearly signaled to readers that he was comfortable elsewhere. A chapter titled "Samba and Grammar" expresses his desire that samba remain true to its roots, connected to its origins, and capable of expressing the thoughts and feelings of "a primitive man." "We want samba without grammar, the kind that says what it feels and which makes us feel what it says."[58] Like the white observers who valorized the Oito Batutas for their unassuming, pastoral style, Vagalume saw in Rio's black musicians something authentic, romantic, and satisfyingly simple.

If sections of *Na Roda* resonate with idealized depictions of "pure" black musicians, in part 2, "Life in the Morros," Vagalume clearly distinguishes himself from other writers by presenting a radical critique of societal inequality. Where João do Rio's portrayals of the submundo and of "Rich Blacks" were laced with sarcasm and a mocking tone, Vagalume sought to dignify and humanize morro residents, though to do so he often fell back on essentialist tropes. While traveling between city and morro, Vagalume drew a direct parallel between musical theft and the forms of exploitation that created hellish living conditions in Rio's favelas. Just as Francisco Alves exploited homens modestos in part 1, unnamed villains in part 2 rob land and generally make life miserable for favela residents. "The great desire of the poor," Vagalume writes, "is to live in what is theirs." Illegal land grabs and the lack of public services made doing so nearly impossible, as did the actions of city planners and landowners described by one of Vagalume's informants as "pirates and exploiters of our sweat."[59]

The presence of crooks, unsavory businessmen, and politicians who preyed on *favelados* (favela residents) ties the second part of the book to the first. Throughout, privileged power brokers are seen stealing property—music or land—and turning it into their own profit, all at the expense of the poor. The residents of São Carlos, Vagalume writes, "live their lives dedicated to honest work. Laborers of various occupations, men with diverse specialties at the ports, all dedicated to some kind of service, from which they earn enough to sustain an honorable family." The residents there "work and preserve samba."[60] While each hill had its own distinctive feature—abject poverty in Querosene, discipline in Mangueira, an upright workers code in São Carlos—all were tied together by shared histories of exploitation and their residents' universal desire to earn honest wages, play a little samba, and own a small piece of Brazil.

These depictions both challenged and reinforced prevailing wisdoms. On the question of hygiene, Vagalume critically appropriated the language used by city planners. In 1930, the French urban planner Alfred Agache synthesized plans for Rio in a sprawling 320-page tome.[61] Throughout the second part of *Na roda do samba*, Vagalume directly uses Agache's vocabulary, especially "embelezamento" (beautification) and "progress." But in no uncertain terms, Vagalume declares, it is city planners and exploitative landlords who are the real "enemies of progress" and who should be held responsible for providing basic services.[62]

In an era when journalists and politicians roundly criticized favelas as centers of vice and disease, Vagalume's work stands out, though it was not entirely unprecedented. As Brodwyn Fischer shows, the 1927 hit song "A favela vai abaixo" (The favela's coming down), written by Sinhô and sung by none other than Francisco Alves, presented a romantic, positive view of favelas, much like the ones put forth in *Na roda*. The contrast between the visions of planners like Agache and the scenes described by Sinhô and Alves make the song, to Fischer, a "radical manifesto."[63] Of course, the fact that Alves was the intérprete made it anything but that to Vagalume. *Na roda do samba* was, among other things, Vagalume's response to Alves's (and Agache's and others') depiction of favela life. In putting forth his own definition of the morros, while also mercilessly attacking Alves, he cast himself as the single, authoritative representative of Rio's gente da roda.

Seu Paulo and the Press

Vagalume was hardly the only one to claim that title. During the 1920s and 1930s, Paulo da Portela (Paulo Benjamin de Oliveira) became one of Rio's most vocal and influential musicians and community leaders. He was born in 1901, just as Eduardo das Neves and Benjamin de Oliveira were making names for themselves, and he moved to Oswaldo Cruz, a neighborhood on Rio's outskirts, in the 1920s.[64] Like their contemporaries throughout the city, residents of Oswaldo Cruz congregated and socialized at gatherings that combined music and religious devotion, often under the direction of female leaders. A white woman named Esther Maria Rodrigues and her husband, an Afro-Brazilian, hosted one of the most popular gatherings, which frequently attracted dignitaries and musicians from miles away.[65] Paulo participated in the festivities at the Rodrigueses' house, and in 1926, along with several friends, founded a Carnival bloco that would become the samba school Portela.

In Portela, Paulo and his cofounders envisioned an organization that would give voice to the poor, serve as a community center, and provide a stage from which to launch Carnival productions and parades. He required Portela's musicians to wear ties and polished shoes. After his death in 1949, a local councilman remembered him as "Preto, tall, dignified, with a certain air he carried himself as a real king of those people, all of whom followed him with great discipline." *O Radical* described him as "a disinherited black" (*preto desherdado*) who became a "poet of the race, feeling in his flesh the sting of social inequality."[66]

Paulo, Antônio da Silva Caetano, and Antônio Rufino dos Reis formed Portela's organizational and administrative core. The three had frequent contact with musicians from other parts of town, most notably Estácio, and projected themselves as community leaders. They wore matching suits, ties, and straw hats and commissioned a friend to make them silver rings engraved with their own initials. According to his biographers, when people called to Paulo on the street, he told them to address him with the honorific "Seu Paulo."

Like other musicians, Seu Paulo carefully cultivated relationships with journalists and politicians. In 1935, *A Nação* held a contest to decide the best samba composer from Rio's morros, which would provide "the final triumph of humble people, of people who live in conditions that are more or less inferior," the paper declared. "Never before today have the morro malandro and sambista, who live their whole life up above . . . had a king's crown from a great triumph. And that is what *A Nação* is doing now."[67] Thanks to a coordinated campaign that stretched from March until June, Paulo won the contest. (That he did not actually live in a favela was less important than the fact that his black skin made him a believable symbol of the impoverished communities.) Readers submitted votes by cutting ballots from the paper and mailing them to *A Nação*. In addition to publicly asking readers for their help, Seu Paulo depended on a cadre of supporters who diligently bought papers and mailed in votes. Antônio Caetano secured a loan from a wealthy merchant to purchase thousands of papers and ballots. By the time voting ended in June, Seu Paulo had amassed more than forty-four thousand votes, outdistancing his nearest competitor by more than ten thousand votes. In 1936, he won a similar contest sponsored by *Diário da Noite*, which named him Cidadão Momo, the King of Carnival. The next year, *A Rua* made him Cidadão Samba, a contest that required each contestant to be "associated with the morro" (*do convívio do morro*) and "to prove with qualified documents his [upstanding] conduct." Commenting on his appearance at the Carnival parade, *A Pátria* described Seu Paulo as "extremely elegant in his white jacket, adorned with silver embroidery." With cane in hand, he led the parade, "greeting the povo carioca and claiming a space for his people!"[68] After winning the Cidadão Momo title, Paulo gushed to reporters, "I owe all of my victories—and I say this without shame or exaggeration—to the press, that unmistakable power that honors and dignifies our nationality."[69]

Paulo projected a sharp, distinguished appearance but also capitalized on his perceived association with Rio's favelas. Like Eduardo das Neves, he expressed his nationalism through public displays that could be at once patriotic and subversive. He called Brazil the "land of liberty" and extolled its beautiful landscape. After being elected Cidadão Samba in 1937, he issued eight "decrees," including one that directed "all the aristocrats of this extremely democratic Republic" to "adhere to my government and realize that Samba is made from pieces of the soul, scintillations of the brain, much love, and big dose of patriotic love."[70] In 1946, a reporter at the *Diário Trabalhista* asked him about his political leanings. "I never belonged to any political organization. My politics have always been in samba. I have helped many politicians and have their promises amounted to anything? . . . Our Samba Schools, our houses still have nothing." He then laid out a "Program of Action." The seven-point plan called for the creation of "efficient services and social assistance" that would be provided by the government and run through the escolas, standard schooling, and protection for abandoned infants and incapacitated elderly residents. He hoped the Partido Trabalhista Nacional (National Labor Party, PTN), a party formed in 1945 by a coalition of Vargas loyalists and São Paulo regionalists, would adopt his plan. How had he come to think of the PTN as a potential ally, the paper asked. "My [journalist] friends," he replied.[71]

Mediations

While musicians' relationships with journalists were crucial, they were prone to shifting political winds, turnover at press offices, and individual caprice. For all the doors they could open, reporters were unequipped to deal with the many imbalances and vagaries of the record industry. Nor could they offer the kind of institutional support or financial stability provided by workers' syndicates or patronage relationships. The record industry fostered uneven relationships, even between so-called *parceiros* (partners) who collaborated to create the music, lyrics, and recording for a given song. As samba rose in prominence, the term *comprositor*, a hybrid of *comprar* (to buy) and *compositor* (composer), came into popular use. By purchasing music from destitute or enterprising composers, Francisco Alves and other musicians—Afro-Brazilians among them—legally became authors. The line between purchasing and stealing was not always clear. At Café Nice, a famous gathering point for musicians, one writer quipped, "Even the walls have ears."[72]

Power within such an environment rested in the hands of a few. But though they did not wield the same power and control as Fred Figner, black impresarios and artists such as Eduardo das Neves, Benjamin de Oliveira, and De Chocolat also held keys to the industry and the ability to grant or deny opportunities to aspiring artists. In creating the Oito Batutas, Donga and Pixinguinha cut more than ten members from the Grupo Caxangá. For private parties and special events, wealthy cariocas often sought out accomplished and well-known black musicians, who in turn selected who would play with them and who would stay home. In 1940, the British composer and conductor Leopold Stokowski traveled to Brazil in search of "the most legitimate popular Brazilian music." His quest produced the album *Native Brazilian Music*, released in small number by Columbia Records in 1942.[73] Before traveling to Brazil, Stokowski contacted the famous musician Heitor Villa-Lobos, asking him to organize a group of musicians who could play the "legitimate" music that he sought. Villa-Lobos wrote Stokowski and asked for $500 to organize the musicians. Villa-Lobos then asked Donga to help him contact individuals who could record for Stokowski. Donga agreed and sent a letter to Villa-Lobos that enumerated a list of expenses totaling 1 conto, 700 milréis (1:700$000, US $103). The $500 in U.S. money that Villa-Lobos requested from Stokowski was worth more than 8 contos, or nearly five times Donga's asking price.[74] It is unclear what Villa-Lobos did with the money, or how much, if any of it, Donga and his musicians received. The story nonetheless suggests that the relationship between the powerful and the nameless had multiple links and flowed in more than one direction. Stokowski sought out Villa-Lobos, who turned to Donga. Donga responded with his own demands and was responsible for providing musicians, a task that most likely entailed an additional set of negotiations and exchanges. While Villa-Lobos clearly was a mediator, so too was Donga.[75]

Pixinguinha functioned as a different kind of financial arbiter in 1939, when he wrote a letter on behalf of Ismael Silva to Mozart de Araújo, a respected scholar and musician. During a distinguished career, Araújo served as the vice president of the Brazilian Symphonic Orchestra and had helped to build and direct the MIS. In his letter, Pixinguinha described how Silva had fallen on hard times, despite having been "partners" with Francisco Alves, whom Silva had helped "with a series of successes that made him the name he has today."[76] "Ismael," Pixinguinha wrote, "finds himself unemployed, in a bad situation, and with numerous family members to support." Pixinguinha then asked Araújo to collect money "for the popular sambista who has fought through a difficult life. . . . I hope that you will do this for Ismael as if it were for me." Pixinguinha's letter suggests a gap not only between poor musicians like Silva and luminaries like Araújo, but also between Pixinguinha and Silva. If Araújo would not help Silva, perhaps he would assist a more "respectable" artist like Pixinguinha.[77]

As financial go-betweens, Donga and Pixinguinha followed in the footsteps of their predecessors. Eduardo das Neves and Benjamin de Oliveira co-owned a circus troupe, and Oliveira is credited with discovering the white circus star-cum-impresario Antolim Garcia, a stark inversion of the more popular white-elite-finds-impoverished-black-star narrative.[78] China helped his younger brother Pixinguinha secure his first gig, and Alvaiade's career took off after Paulo da Portela brought him into his circle. Seu Paulo then went on to help a number of other musicians, including Candeia (Antônio Candeia Filho), launch their careers. In a seemingly endless set of combinations and in multiple roles—partners, advocates, talent scouts, and so on—Rio's black musicians mediated and shaped the city's music and entertainment industry.

Musicians also used clothing, music, instruments, lyrics, and performance to shape samba and larger definitions of brasilidade and blackness. In January 1933, an interview with Tio Faustino appeared in the *Diário Carioca*. The paper credited him with "introducing" three "African style" musical instruments into samba music: the *omelê* (a friction drum), the agogô (a U-shaped instrument with bells at the end of both legs, struck with a wooden or metal stick), and the *afoxê* (a rattle often adorned with beads or shells). Each instrument has central or western African origins. Tio Faustino sought to claim the instruments as his own and insert them into Brazil's growing music market. He told the paper, "I want to lodge a protest against those who are illegally using the instruments that I introduced." They "are officially registered . . . [and] I want to advise my colleagues not to use them, because, well, otherwise, I will be obligated to act judicially against infractors and guarantee my rights to these exotic instruments." In *Na roda*, Vagalume described how Tio Faustino's omelê improved upon existing friction drums, which tended to lose their tune on rainy or especially humid days, to create a better model.[79]

Like Donga and Deo Costa, Tio Faustino sought out the press to state his case and defend his property claims, which he had also taken legal actions to protect. While relatively few musicians appear to have pursued legal patent and trademark rights as Donga and Tio Faustino did, others claimed informal monopolies on specific aesthetics and styles. Ataulfo Alves, named to one columnist's "Ten Most Elegant" list, was known for his white scarf, described by one author as his "trademark." João da Baiana distinguished himself by wearing a distinctive red cravat. Musicians also defined themselves on stage, in the recording studio, and on the radio. Alfredo (Alfredo José de Alcântara) was "discovered" in Estácio by Caninha (José Luiz de Morais) and was soon dubbed the *Pandeirista Infernal* for the hellish fervor with which he played the pandeiro. In Argentina he performed as the Black Brazilian Pandeirista.

Performers like Alfredo could exercise great power over a song. Edward Said once likened pianists to gatekeepers, who in reducing orchestral works down to a single instrument performed an act comparable to "forcing an army to walk single-file through a single turnstile."[80] Popular intérpretes could wield similar authority. Noel Rosa called Aracy de Almeida "the person who plays with [the most] precision that which I produce." Cartola is said to have been shocked when he heard his work played for the first time on the radio, so different was the recorded version from the original. The significance of musical interpretation is seen clearly in the case of "A favela vai abaixo," which Sinhô may have conceived as a dramatic political statement, but which in the hands of Francisco Alves and the Casa Edison recording team sounded more like a saccharine romanticization of favela life. A similar dynamic is seen in two separate recordings of "Rei vagabundo" (Vagabond king). Ataulfo Alves and Roberto Martins composed one version, recorded in 1936 by Carlos Galhardo (Catello Carlos Guagliardi), who provided vocals for the bouncy, upbeat tribute to Mangueira's "happy" lifestyle. In one refrain, Galhardo, the son of Italian immigrants, sings, "In Mangueira there is a castle / older than any other in the world / There's a goddess who is my queen / And I'm the Vagabond King." Another line declares, "On the hill, everything is beautiful."[81] In 1968, Nelson Cavaquinho produced a more melancholy and critical version of the song, in which a tearful Vagabond King rules a kingdom "full of illusion," and Mangueira's shacks are "castles" only in the "imagination."[82]

Musicians adapted multiple strategies to distance themselves from demeaning stereotypes of favelados and lingering assumptions about blackness and vadiagem. Some musicians flipped racist assumptions on their head through displays that built from Eduardo das Neves's outsized, turn-of-the-century malandro masculinity. In "Lenço no pescoço" (Handkerchief around the neck), Wilson Batista, the musician who found his way out of an arrest thanks to a musically inclined police officer, declared himself "proud to be such a vagrant," a clear rejoinder to the sickly, emasculated vadio figure demonized by reformers.[83] The song, which became something of a malandro's anthem, touched off an acrimonious, now-celebrated musical exchange with Noel Rosa.

In "Lenço no pescoço," Batista described a hat worn tilted on his head, wooden clogs on his feet, a handkerchief around his neck, and a knife in his pocket. His malandro exuded a confident manliness and posed a direct challenge to authority. "I strut around (*passo gingando*) . . . I provoke and challenge . . . I'm proud to be such a vagrant."[84] Rosa grew up in Vila Isabel, a middle-class neighborhood, and briefly attended medical school before becoming one of Brazil's all-time great musicians. Despite his early death, he produced hundreds of works in an exceptionally productive career. In "Rapaz folgado" (Idle boy), he urged Batista to replace his clogs with shoes, exchange his handkerchief for a tie, and discard his knife. "Malandro," he insisted, "is a defeatist word / That only takes away / all of the sambista's value. / I propose to the civilized world / not to call you a malandro / and instead a *rapaz folgado*." As McCann points out, this was a rare statement by Rosa, who otherwise celebrated the malandro's bohemian lifestyle. But to Rosa, Batista's embrace of "being such a vagrant" represented a debilitating step backward. Batista's malandro "is self-satisfied and untroubled. He rejects work, but glibly. There is no tension in his boastful proclamation of independence."[85] While Rosa was no João do Rio, the musician's rejoinder clearly intended to put Batista in his place. Rosa did not really want to rid samba of malandragem, but he objected to Batista's confident display.

In "Mocinho da Vila" (Little boy from the Vila), Batista taunted Rosa for his middle-class origins and called him an *otário* (nerd, or square). In "Frankstein" (Frankenstein) he ridiculed Rosa's face, which was deformed at birth by a doctor's forceps and which, Batista remarked, earned him a spot at "the front of the ugly line." With "João Ninguém" (Joe Nobody), Rosa squarely linked the exchange to evolving meanings of vadiagem. The song's title could have been lifted directly from police and court reports. In 1927, a Rio de Janeiro judge described the seemingly endless line of individuals paraded before him as: "the persecuted, those abandoned by fortune, retarded ones, handicapped, sick, prostitutes, this whole anonymous cast of Joãos Ninguém and half-men."[86] Like that "anonymous cast," Rosa's João Ninguém did not work, had no defining characteristics, and possessed no "ideals" or "opinions." Instead of referencing slavery, as journalists did in 1911 when they called Moreno a "crioulo," Rosa gestured toward a more accessible contemporary sphere populated by vagrants and vagabonds.

Many musicians avoided the malandro stylings embraced by Batista in favor of a more button-down aesthetic, projecting professionalism and work ethic in a way that resonated with Vagalume's industrious homens modestos. Pixinguinha carried himself in a decidedly understated manner, especially when compared to Batista's malandro. During his debut as a young teenager, he wore knee-length knickers, part of a modest, youthful appearance. "I didn't obey the sheet music," he confessed late in life, but otherwise "was very obedient."[87] Even after leaving behind the short pants of his childhood, he never embraced Neves's or Moreno's more garish style. Neither did Donga, who, like his friend and collaborator, sported sharp, understated suits. Like Neves, the Oito Batutas could perform multiple roles for multiple audiences. But even their tuxedos contrast with Neves's blue suit jacket and silk hat, Moreno's elaborate outfits, or the flashy white linen suits, panama hats, and matching red tie and pocket kerchief that malandro musicians like Moreira da Silva (Antônio Moreira da Silva) made famous during the 1930s and 1940s. Perhaps Pixinguinha's flashiest outfit was the white suit, black bowtie, and straw boater that he wore during the 1950s. But that ensemble was meant, above all else, to recollect an older, more innocent age.[88] Generally, Donga and Pixinguinha preferred small bowties, crisp suits, and straw hats.

Embracing a more modest look did not mean abandoning masculinity altogether. To the contrary, the "professional" look represented a retooled, toned-down version of flashier displays. Paulo da Portela wore elaborate, glittery costumes during Carnival, but otherwise preferred more understated attire. The sleek look that he and other malandro musicians cultivated during the 1920s and 1940s may be thought of as a compromise that both built and departed from earlier displays (see figure 5). Compared to Pixinguinha and Donga's conservative look, linen suits and panama hats were sexy and daring. But they were a far cry from Moreno's monocle and cane or Neves's blue suit jacket and silk hat. While Donga, Pixinguinha, and others distanced themselves from louder displays, their general intentions may not have been so different from Neves's and Moreno's. Though modest when compared with their predecessors' wardrobes, the suits and ties that Seu Paulo and his cohort wore clearly distinguished them from the urban poor.

Musicians made similar stylistic choices in the studio. Pixinguinha, a brilliant, versatile composer and arranger, was best known for his brass-infused choros. In 1926, he helped record "Seduções de um beijo" (Seductions of a kiss), a love ballad with soaring, operatic vocals.[89] A decade later, the white crooner Orlando Silva recorded "Carinhoso," one of Pixinguinha's masterpieces. The song begins with these famous lines: "My heart, I don't know why / Beats happily when it sees you."[90] Played to Pixinguinha's soft, fluttering flute, the song is widely regarded as Brazil's greatest love song. Pixinguinha's instrumental "Vagando," recorded in 1950, presents a carefree interpretation of what it means to "wander."[91] Police and journalists frequently used the same word (from the verb *vagar*) to describe the "offenses" perpetrated by homeless, jobless vagrants who roamed the streets. The piece clearly refers to a different kind of "wander-

FIGURE 5. The malandro-musician look (date unknown). From left to right: Paulo da Portela, Heitor dos Prazeres, unidentified, Bide, and Armando Marçal. Courtesy Acervo da Família Heitor dos Prazeres (the Heitor dos Prazeres Family Archive).

ing," something of a musical parallel to the flâneur–cronista journalism pioneered by João do Rio, who distinguished himself from poor vagrants by assuming the role of a privileged wanderer. Pixinguinha's musical interpretation of vagando gave him similar access and control.

In his 1936 book *O choro: Reminiscênscias dos chorões antigos* (Choro: Memories of old choro players), Alexandre Gonçalves Pinto emphasized the hardworking and respectable character of a number of musicians, black and white.[92] To Pinto, the musician Gustavo was "an excellent friend with the finest manners." Agenor Benz was "an excellent family man, who placed high value in his good name." Joaquim Luiz de Sousa was a "productive worker and knower of the marvelous secrets of genuinely Brazilian hymns." Candinho Silva, a "talented, intelligent *mulato* [*mulato de genio*]," was also "a very rigorous man, conservative and reserved. He would wake up every day between 4:30 and 5:00, bathe in cold water, and then take a long walk. He was always very well put together." His compositions, Pinto gushed, were "beaut[ies] in art and in taste."[93]

De Chocolat projected an image of his performers that resonated with the disciplined portraits sketched in *O choro*. "You cannot imagine how satisfied I am," he said. "The black kids (*os pretinhos*) in my company are, in their totality, docile, intelligent, polite, and disciplined."[94] Paulo de Magalhães, who served as president of the SBAT, the theater association dedicated to defending its members' author's rights (see chapter 7), marveled at the company's "clean blacks," who worked "honestly."[95] Building careers and identities in opposition to the ideologia da vadiagem did not necessarily mean becoming an upright trabalhador or family man. Paulo da Portela, who openly associated with workers' struggles, used his silver ring and suit to identify himself as a leader, but he and others knew that sex and malandragem sold. Both Donga and Pixinguinha wrote and played songs about chasing women and partaking in other malandro pastimes.[96]

Many black musicians carefully made mixed-race or black—but rarely white—women the objects of their desire. In 1928, Patrício Teixeira, one of the few black artists to receive substantial radio play during the 1930s, recorded Pixinguinha's "Pé de *mulata*" (*Mulata*'s foot). The song illustrates a brand of masculinity that allowed black musicians to avoid the kind of criticism leveled at Neves and Moreno. The song's subject is a *mulata*, the dark-skinned (though theoretically mixed-race) female figure often used to symbolize Brazilian racial mixture. Teixeira's narrator marvels at the *mulata*'s ability to make men fall at her feet, helpless against her charms. She walks all over them and, Teixeira laments, breaks his heart. Other depictions made the *mulata* little more than an object created by the narrator. The white singer Pepa Delgado played a *mulata* in the Carnival hit "Vem cá, *mulata*!" and a similar role in "O vendeiro e a mulata" (The salesman and the *mulata*). But in "Um samba na Penha" (A samba in Penha) she and a male performer sing together: "Come 'ere my black girl, we're going to samba!" (*Vem cá minha nega, nós vamos sambar!*).[97] By performing the role of a sexualized woman of color in some songs and singing *about* black women in others, Delgado wielded special power.[98]

Black male musicians who made *mulatas* the object of romantic or sexual affection projected a form of masculinity that was accepted in ways that Neves and Moreno's displays were not. In the mid-1910s, Arlequim cheerfully described the magnetlike way in which Donga attracted female suitors: "[He] is an animal! Lover of and loved by the *crioulas* of our city, our man drags behind him a real rosary of women, both pretty and ugly."[99] While Neves and Moreno's masculine expressions elicited fear and disgust, just a few years later Donga was hailed for his sexual exploits. The difference may be explained in part by Donga's carefully cultivated public image, but it is also significant that in celebrating his manhood,

Arlequim made Donga's lovers crioulas. The spectacle of a black "animal" musician whom black women found irresistible was more palatable to a wider audience than was Moreno's scandalous relationship with Dora or Neves's lyrics about white women.

In years to come, the celebration of sexually potent musicians of color would become more common. At the time that they were uttered, Arlequim's words signaled that ascendant black musicians were gaining acceptance, though they had to toe certain lines to do so. By making *mulatas* the object of their songs and their affections, musicians like Pixinguinha and Teixeira helped nudge Afro-Brazilian men into circles from which they were previously excluded. Embracing *mulatas* in song was hardly something new. Plenty of musicians, including and also preceding Neves and Benjamin de Oliveira, did the same, but the understated aesthetics and personas of the Pelo Telefone Generation contrasted the bold expressions of Neves and Moreno. To recruit female dancers for Portela's Carnival performances, Paulo da Portela visited parents' homes and personally promised to take care of their daughters and return them home after the parade.[100] If protective paternalism could score Seu Paulo points with community members, it hardly conflicted with a more brazen, sexually potent image. The writer Lúcio Rangel fondly recalled days and nights in the company of Seu Paulo and the line of *cabrochas* (a rawer version of the word *mulata*) who chased the musician "like gambler[s] after a deck of cards."[101]

IN 1949, PAULO DA PORTELA died suddenly, leaving behind as many as thirty-six godchildren and many more fans and admirers.[102] A newspaper proclaimed that samba had died with him, and one report held that fifteen thousand people attended his funeral. Neighborhood businesses closed their doors to observe his passing, and mourners gathered with friends and family throughout the city.[103] Despite a celebrated, successful career, there were some obstacles that Seu Paulo could not overcome. In an interview in 1933 he complained that, like most of his peers, he was obligated to sell the rights to his songs because he had been unable to break into the exclusive recording world and perform them himself.[104] Even during samba's golden age, Rio's Afro-Brazilian musicians lacked a recognized institution to provide support. The press played a fundamental role in launching careers and as a vehicle for advertising, voicing a complaint, or asserting ownership over a song or an instrument. Portela and other samba schools helped, but they could offer little in the way of stable financial backing. Despite increased visibility, securing musical property rights was not much easier for black artists of the 1920s and 1930s than it had been for Donga in 1917, or for Eduardo das Neves even earlier. Though they significantly altered Rio's cultural landscape, Seu Paulo and other musicians of color knew well that professional security, financial stability, and recognized authorship could be as elusive as a bird in flight.

6

Mapping Africa and Brazil during the Golden Age

What

In 1943, an article titled "Scientific Chronicle" appeared in the Rio de Janeiro daily *Correio da Manhã*. The author sought to use "science" to pinpoint samba's origins in Africa and to suggest how a modern society like Brazil might harness and civilize a wild and savage part of its past.[1] The article was hardly the first or last inquiry into samba's genealogy. Ten years earlier, Vagalume had presented his own account in *Na roda*, and during the 1920s, 1930s, and 1940s, as samba became a fixture in the cultural landscape, intellectuals and artists in diverse fields—ethnomusicology (or at least what would later become known as ethnomusicology), literature, music, and journalism—addressed collective concerns and questions related to music, Brazil, and the origins of both: Where did Brazil (and samba) come from? How could the nation's diverse racial and ethnic heritage be harnessed and presented in such a way that would project a unique, authentic identity that was also acceptably white, civilized, and modern?

In 1941, Heitor Villa-Lobos printed a map that addressed these very questions. Villa-Lobos, one of Latin America's most accomplished and celebrated musicians, is credited with more than one hundred major works. Known for his technical excellence and creative combination of popular and classical traditions, Villa-Lobos mounted massive state-sponsored music education programs that brought together tens of thousands of children whose voices praised in unison the nation's glory.[2] He channeled his fascination with Brazil's national and musical origins into

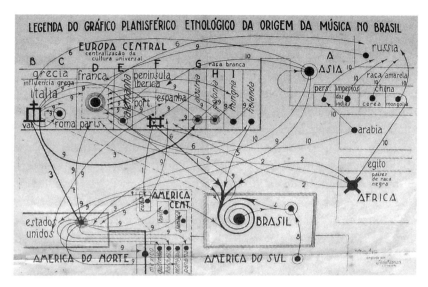

FIGURE 6. Villa-Lobos's "Explication of the Planispheric Ethnological Diagram of the Origin of Brazilian Music" (1941). Courtesy Biblioteca Nacional.

a map that he created with the assistance of a cartographer. I came upon this remarkable document only by chance and thanks to the wonderful staff at the Biblioteca Nacional. Shelved next to a speech in which he described his lifelong quest to chart the "physiognomy" of Brazilian music and declared his respect for the "value of every popular musical manifestation," the map reflects Villa-Lobos's interest in uncovering and studying Brazil's roots and demarcating both its internal hierarchies and its external boundaries.

He titled the map, which has a dizzying collection of arrows, swirling lines, coded letters, numbers, and symbols, the "Explication of the Planispheric Ethnological Diagram of the Origin of Brazilian Music" (figure 6). While the map's focus is Brazil, the tangle of arrows and lines sketches a global picture, tying together Europe, Asia, North America, South America, and Africa. Within that schema, Europe holds a special place, defined by Villa-Lobos as the center of "universal culture." The majority of the map's arrows lead to or from the continent, which is divided into multiple nations, regions, and cities. By contrast, Africa is marked with a single label, "countries of the black race," and appears as an isolated, nearly monolithic block. While multiple "religious" and "cultural" influences flow from, into, and within Europe, the links between Africa and the rest of the world are limited almost exclusively to "rhythm." Arrows flow only away from Africa. Just as Villa-Lobos describes Africa as home to the "black race," Asia is home to the "yellow race," and Europe the "white race," but he neglects to place a racial label on Brazil or any other place in the Western Hemisphere. The "autochthonous" music of South America and of "Brazilian aborigines" is, like Africa, isolated from a dynamic international matrix.

Villa-Lobos's map embodies several important intellectual currents. The separation of Brazil from the rest of Latin America reflects a larger desire to distinguish the nation from other postcolonial American countries. Villa-Lobos draws no connections between Africa and Cuba, Haiti, or Jamaica. This elision makes sense only in the particular context of the map, which elevates Brazil while marginalizing Central, South, and North America. (The Caribbean is conveniently included as part of Central America.) Brazil's African lineage does not link it to a larger diaspora, and instead distinguishes it from other American nations. Villa-Lobos shows Brazil to be distant from Africa but in control of an American monopoly of one caricatured "African" trait—rhythm—represented by the number 2.

Villa-Lobos's map also has characteristics common to larger projects to study Afro-Brazilian culture and history. Beginning in the late nineteenth century, criminalist anthropologists including Raimundo Nina Rodrigues, who sought to "uncover" Brazil's deep history and African roots, and cronistas who ventured into Rio's underworld of vice and exotic pleasure, sought to map and order the nation's far-flung regions, diverse inhabitants, and menagerie of cultures.[3] Literary, anthropological, and pseudo-scientific explorations of Brazil complemented official projects to distinguish the hardworking trabalhador from the lazy vagabundo. In the introduction to *As raças humanas e a responsabilidade penal no Brazil* (Human races and criminal accountability in Brazil), Afranio Peixoto referred to Rodrigues, his mentor and the book's author, as a "discoverer" of Brazil.[4] To Peixoto, Rodrigues's works on race, degeneracy, crime, and disease were invaluable to a "young" nation "without a past."[5] By probing what Peixoto referred to as Brazil's "unexplored territories" and pondering the roots of the nation's social problems, Rodrigues sought to chart his own map of the nation's past, present, and future. Of particular note, he suggested that Article 399 (the Penal Code's anti-vagrancy provision), was hardly enough to fight the "legacy" of idleness among "our mestiços," who could be reformed only through education and large-scale rehabilitation.[6]

Rodrigues's work and Villa-Lobos's map were, in part, responses to the legacy of slavery, which rendered most Afro-Brazilians invisible in the eyes of the law. In 1894, the jurist Clóvis Bevilácqua wrote, "The Negro race contributed to the formation of the Brazilian people as a slave, that is, without personhood, without legal attributes besides those that might be associated with a shipment of merchandise." As a result, "In studying the laws of slavery . . . we find the African element, but incontestably it appears without any peculiar attribute."[7] Gilberto Freyre forcefully countered the related idea that Afro-Brazilians were a people without a history in his classic *Casa grande e senzala* (1933). Freyre argued that the nation had been forged from a unique combination of Portuguese, African, and native Brazilian peoples. In highly gendered terms, Freyre maintained that Brazil had been nurtured since infancy at the bosom of black female slaves. While Freyre was not the first to present this view, his call for the recognition and "valorization" of African-Brazilian culture helped consolidate and canonize earlier ideas.[8] As Villa-Lobos's map makes clear, recognition and valorization often came with strict limits and could imply narrow definitions and rigid hierarchies.

The Origins of Brazil

Mário de Andrade was among the foremost intellectuals to study the intertwined questions of national and music history. In addition to pioneering Brazilian modernist literature, Andrade helped initiate the field of study we now know as ethnomusicology. His long, illustrious career included piano study at São Paulo's Conservatório Dramático e Musical, the publication of his first novel in 1917, participation at the famed Modern Art Week in 1922, several government posts, and a university teaching position in Rio. In 1937, he founded the São Paulo Society of Ethnography and Folklore, which launched a number of ambitious research missions. In 1938, he secured state funding for a project in the Brazilian North and Northeast, where the society collected some three hundred sound recordings.[9]

In *Pequena história da música* (A short history of music), Andrade traced sound from the birth of humanity to the present day, placing Brazil along the way.[10] The book traces a racial teleology that shows "primitive" peoples — Amerindians and Africans — preceding progressively "civilized" cultures: ancient Greeks, then Christians, then modern Europeans. An evolution from rudimentary sound to sophisticated rhythm and harmony follows suit. Like Villa-Lobos, Andrade observed influences in Brazilian music from all corners of the globe, including Africa and the Americas. And like Villa-Lobos's map, *Pequena história* makes clear how internal hierarchies were often created and solidified in dialogue with external ones.

"Our race is strongly impregnated with *guarani* blood," Andrade wrote, and "the African also took part in the vast formation of popular Brazilian song."[11] As they are in Villa-Lobos's diagram, nonwhite musical traditions are defined in narrow terms, with a particular emphasis on rhythm. To Andrade, the predominance of rhythm over melody made "primitive" traditions more natural and physical than musical. "Primitive peoples," he explained, "develop in a 'natural state' . . . in which every manifestation of logical intelligence is less important than the general psychic-physiological manifestation. . . . The body is, for primitives, a kind of first consciousness, a physical intelligence of marvelous perceptiveness."[12] Indigenous influences were limited to dance steps created by Indians and Jesuit missionaries, but "the very lascivious African style of dance remained in our national temperament."[13] Andrade saw "physical-racial-social-cultural differentiations" as barriers between the body and the mind, metaphorically referenced as drums and voice, respectively.[14] While visiting Recife in the Northeast, he witnessed a Carnival *maracatu* that exemplified that differentiation. One music primer describes maracatu as a "slow, heavy Afro-Brazilian processional music," but the rendition that Andrade heard left quite a different impression.[15] He described it as "the most violent thing that one can imagine." The singers' voices were "completely canceled out by the *fortíssimo* beats of twelve *bombos* [large bass drums], nine *gongûes* [iron bells], and four ganzás [shakers]. The rhythm was so violent that I could not stand it, and I was obligated to take a rest from time to time . . . and put in order my breathing and my pulse."[16]

Andrade found in the drums' effect an indication of the difference between intelligent music and natural, unordered sound. Africans and Indians did not think about their music; they created it naturally, or under the guidance of deities or human rulers. Primitive music, he wrote, "never liberated itself from religious, magical, and social function." It was impossible, he reasoned, to know whether those societies were even conscious of the music they made. "Black slaves and *mulatos*" created music not of free will, but instead from a basic need to order their daily tasks or from necessity because they were forced to "specialize" in music by masters who rented their services. "The discovery of music," he continued, distinguished civilized societies from primitive ones:

> If it is true that certain songs of Africans and Amerindians sometimes achieve a degree of musical legitimacy, the concept of Musical Art is not itself consciously felt among these peoples. One may affirm this by noting that music is the only artistic manifestation for which it is not possible to find, among primitives, a normalized technique.[17]

Andrade's observations held clear implications for author's rights. "Primitive" people's supposed lack of musical consciousness contrasts with the genius that Andrade saw among "modern" white artists such as Villa-Lobos and Catulo da Paixão Cearense.[18] Villa-Lobos and Cearense created and shaped; dark-skinned artists did little more than spew forth raw material. Brazil, Andrade maintained, was being held back by a lack of creativity and invention. To make this point, he referred to a nineteenth-century German observer, who, Andrade said, "lament[ed] our ignorance and frivolity, which prevents us from completing serious musical studies and makes us create music 'almost like canaries.'"[19] To overcome that past, it would be necessary to appropriate African-derived (and to a lesser extent, native-derived) music, but only under the watchful gaze of trained individuals.

Andrade saw the early twentieth century as a turning point in international history with serious implications for music and politics. In Brazil, he wrote, "we remained musically colonial" until World War I. After the war, "new governments, renovated sciences," and "new arts" emerged throughout the world. As a result, "the Portuguese musician wants to be Portuguese; the Brazilian wants to be Brazilian; the Polish, Polish; and the African, African."[20] Andrade saw Brazil's diverse origins as a potential source for forging a unique, postcolonial identity. But while Afro-Brazilian culture could provide sources for that identity, "Africa" could never be fully civilized or assimilated.[21] This reasoning suggests how the idea of Brazilian racial democracy was marked not only by the desire to assimilate and mix, but also the seemingly contradictory impulse to map, delineate, and even preserve difference. Africa, and to a lesser extent Native America, could contribute to a new identity, but only in specific ways. Afro-Brazilian artists could produce raw material, but ownership, authorship, and creative genius would remain the domain of cultured white intellectuals. It was through this sort of reduction, and only with the musical tools of "civilized" culture, that Andrade and others found it acceptable to sift through the sonic archives of Brazil's dark masses to retrieve, map, and refine rhythm and other magical devices.

Andrade's background shaped his complex views on race.[22] Like João do Rio, he was a light-skinned *mulato*. His interest in Afro-Brazilian culture and music was sincere, even well intentioned, but he, like João do Rio, approached it from the self-assigned position of an enlightened outsider. Though he often embraced essentialized definitions of African and Indigenous peoples, he was also sensitive to racial discrimination, especially when it occurred outside of Brazil. He turned down multiple opportunities to travel to the United States, perhaps in protest of Jim Crow policies there and perhaps because he feared that North Americans would consider him to be black. In "Canção de Dixie" (Dixieland song), he declared (in English), "No, I'll never be / In Colour Line Land."[23]

In 1928, the same year that he published his most well-known work on music, *Ensaio sobre a música brasileira* (Essay on Brazilian music), Andrade released his famous novel *Macunaíma: O herói sem nenhum caráter* (*Macunaíma: The hero with no character*).[24] The book's seventh chapter depicts a religious ceremony in Mangue. Macunaíma, the main character, attends the gathering to exact revenge on a rival. The "priestess" who leads the ceremony is named Tia Ciata, a clear reference to the well-known community leader.[25] It is widely believed that Andrade drew on conversations with Pixinguinha to write the chapter and used him as a model for the character Olelê Rui Barbosa.[26] Pixinguinha described how Andrade and other "illustrious" figures were "always around [*viviam com a gente*]. Wherever we would go, they'd go, too, always asking, always wanting to know, always discussing, always taking notes."[27]

The ceremony at Tia Ciata's house is replete with spirit possession and a goat-blood-smeared "Polish whore." Olelê "spanks" his drum to make "a song in a free style full of scurrying notes with tricky syncopation; a crazy ecstasy, a low-pitched throbbing working up to a frenzy."[28] Seemingly every occupation and social category in Rio is represented at the gathering, all having come to seek the favor of Exú, a powerful deity. Macunaíma's quest for vengeance yields quick results. Moments after contacting Exú, his rival, miles away in São Paulo, howls in pain with a gaping stomach wound and a fractured skull. The ceremony in Rio then quickly turns into a "party," with the guests "eating some excellent ham and dancing samba to a loud and lively measure on the guitar, which everyone enjoyed with a good deal of freeness and revelry."[29] *Macunaíma* is a complex text, full of satire and magic. But there is no indication that Andrade crafted the chapter as complete fantasy. His conversations and relationship with Pixinguinha suggest instead that he hoped for the scene to reflect a certain reality.

In a little-known article titled "Força biológica da música" (The biological force of music), Andrade provided a straightforward interpretation of what he understood to be music's magical qualities. When music and feitiçaria mixed, Andrade explained, the results could have "extraordinary power over individual action and over the masses." "My apologies to the doctors," he wrote, "but those treatments work: shiny amulets, little stones from Africa, sacrificed black roosters, or jars of *pinga* [strong alcohol] left on the beach all make sores, arthritis, and nephritis disappear." Music, he continued,

> has been the cause of legitimate epidemics, exercising the effect
> of a vibrant swarm of microbes, proliferating all of a sudden. . . .
> Now, would it not be reasonable, even instinctive, that it would
> not occur to use this extremely strong biological power of music in
> medicine?[30]

To Andrade, "black music" had powerful potential, good and bad. It could disorient and destabilize breathing and heartbeats, but it was also capable of aiding catharsis.

Rio's Afro-Brazilian musicians had their own views about the power of music and the relationship between Africa, Brazil, and samba. Some of those ideas challenged the views of Villa-Lobos and Andrade. Others came closer to lining up with them, though rarely in simple or straightforward ways. In 1925, Pixinguinha's brother China gave a remarkable interview, worth quoting here at length, with the newspaper *O Jornal*:

> Everyone knows that samba was born in Africa. . . . Just as the
> building of Brazil is attributed to the negro slave-hand . . . one
> cannot deny the infiltration of his customs. . . . [The writer] José
> Joaquim de Campos da Costa de Medeiros e Albuquerque wrote,
> and I read, that the black race never contributed to our arts and
> letters. But no one has said anything about the *mulato* . . . [who]
> has been everything, in every form of human production imagin-

able, in this land: artist, priest, laborer, general, soldier, poet, everything. . . . The *mulato*, when he has good hair and clean skin, insists on denying his African blood. But blood runs deep, and all of far-off Africa appears in him, when he least expects it. In order to counter the illusion of whiteness that is so cherished today, allow me to refer to many *mulatos*, talented musicians. Who brought samba into society? It was the *mulato*. . . . People say that the pure-blooded negro is dimwitted . . . and maybe that is true. [But] we must agree that he provided elements for the creation of the *mulata*. . . . The negro should be credited with this work of art . . . at least half of it. . . . As for the *mulato*, people say, and I confirm, that he is always intelligent and wise."[31]

In his extraordinary and complex statement, China remained vague about his own identity. He referred to *negros* and *mulatos* in the third person but also clearly challenged those who bought into "the illusion of whiteness." By confronting a white ideal and making a positive link between samba and Africa—while still denigrating *negros* in favor of *mulatos*—China charted an interesting alternative to the pessimistic and racist pronouncements made by Medeiros e Albuquerque and others. Though he challenged whiteness as an ideal, he stopped short of valorizing blackness without qualification. Samba came from Africa, but it was only through *mulato* mediation that music or "African blood" could be appropriately incorporated into Brazil. It also bears mentioning that China described "the *mulata*" as the "dimwitted" *negro*'s contribution to society. While *mulato* men could be cultured mediators, their female counterparts were objects—"works of art"—shaped, transformed, and delivered across the Atlantic through the same processes that brought samba to Brazil.

By simultaneously harnessing and distancing himself from Africa, China put his own spin on a growing concern among black intellectuals, many of whom had become increasingly wary of pan-African political movements and any association with Africa. One particularly vocal black writer in São Paulo declared, "We are not Africans, we are Brazilians!"[32] But China's comments did not perfectly match those expressed by others. In fact, in some ways they more closely resembled the ideas of João Batista de Lacerda, the white director of Rio de Janeiro's National Museum and one of the main proponents of "whitening." Though Lacerda infamously projected the disappearance of blacks, he also touted the contributions made by mixed-race men (whom he referred to as *mulatos* and *metis*, a

French word for people of mixed racial backgrounds). In a paper lauded by W. E. B. DuBois for its recognition of the contribution of mixed-race peoples, Lacerda noted:

> The metis of Brazil have given birth down to our time to poets of no mean inspiration, painters, sculptors, distinguished musicians, magistrates, lawyers, eloquent orators, remarkable writers, medical men and engineers, who have been unrivaled in the technical skill and professional ability. The co-operation of the metis in the advance of Brazil is notorious and far from inconsiderable.[33]

China roundly rejected the white ideal that undergirded Lacerda's philosophy, but the similarities between the men's statements suggest a profound and perhaps surprising overlap between two otherwise distinct ideologies. Lacerda clearly believed the "illusion of whiteness" that China challenged, but both men recognized the contributions and importance of "refined" mixed-race men.

Like Lacerda, Andrade, Villa-Lobos, and others, China saw himself as a mediator fit to determine the shape and extent of Africa's presence in Brazil. His acceptance of racial mixture was, like Villa-Lobos's and Andrade's, predicated on the identification and isolation of specific, caricatured racial traits. And yet his ideas do not square entirely with others'. His emphasis on the difference and distance between *mulatos* and *negros* is particularly noteworthy in light of Andrade's lumping together of *mulatos* and "black slaves." To China, the two were not the same. Rather, he saw the *mulato* as a messenger who delivered polished samba from far-off, uncivilized Africa.

Tio Faustino, the musician and religious leader who claimed legal ownership over the omelê, the agogô, and the afoxê, had his own slightly different take on the relationship between Africa and Brazil. During his interview with *Diário Carioca*, he explained that those instruments were new to samba and worthy of legal protection. Both ideas implicitly disaggregated a musical form that was widely assumed to be an ancient African relic from instruments thought to be equally timeless. In doing so, he did not simply discard popular notions about Africa but instead selectively used them to his advantage. On the surface, Tio Faustino's attempt to register and control the instruments appears to have been inspired by his own economic interests. Indeed, warning other musicians that he would be "obligated to act judicially" if they did not respect his property rights leaves no doubt that he saw the instruments as an opportunity to secure his own place in a competitive market environment.[34] He came to Rio from Bahia in 1911, traveling in the company of Julio Viveiros Brandão, a powerful politician.[35] In Rio, he eventually became part of Pixinguinha and Donga's popular Grupo da Guarda Velha (Group of the Old Guard) and circulated among the web of religious and musical gatherings in Little Africa.[36]

Tio Faustino told the *Diário Carioca* reporter that he would soon publish a "manual of African terms" and, during the interview, he also made a point to distinguish macumba from candomblé. The latter, he told the paper, had been "adulterated" by white cariocas, who had turned it into macumba. In the early 1930s, Brazilian and North American researchers used the word "macumba" to refer to a wide range of practices, so wide, in fact, that, according to one scholar, the term "lacks any clearly established referent."[37] Like Tio Faustino, the anthropologists Artur Ramos and Roger Bastide associated macumba with the degradation of authentic African practices.[38] Donald Pierson contrasted "the genuinely wholesome character of the Bahian Africanos" with "the Rio de Janeiro Negro, whose candomblé (known locally as the macumba) is now in such a state of disintegration that many unwholesome and even vicious practices have crept into its ritual."[39]

Tio Faustino's designs to publish a manual and his desire to explain to readers the difference between authentic and corrupted culture suggest how he saw himself as an arbiter of Afro-Brazilianness. His manual could be published and marketed, but it would also inform and educate. While some preferred to divide authentic Africa from modern, capitalist Brazil, he found it more logical and productive to mold them together. His ability to mix these two supposedly disparate worlds is seen further in an incident that occurred at some point during the early 1930s. While recording with the Grupo da Guarda Velha, he was forbidden by an RCA Victor executive from using his omelê, whose low, groaning sound, similar to that of the *cuíca*, is a staple of Carnival music. The instrument, the executive felt, produced a "very strong sound [that] ruined the recordings." Members of the band defended Tio Faustino, but the executive relented only after overhearing Tio Faustino say, "Well, well. If my omelê isn't recorded, I'll leave, kill a rooster and offer it to Exú. We'll see whose god is stronger: mine or this American's."[40]

By claiming personal ownership over the musical instruments and seeking to turn them into commodities, Tio Faustino placed them squarely in

Foucault's age of "individualization." In doing so he sought to preserve and display connections to Africa, but he was also after the prizes theoretically made available in a new and evolving legal and political system. To Tio Faustino, mapping Brazil and its African origins was not just a practice in history or nation building. It was also a means of defending his personal interests, maintaining his own livelihood, and asserting his role as a mediator on the border between authentic and corrupted African culture.

"A Black Pan"

Observers often reduced the kind of complex ideas and expressions advanced by Tio Faustino and China into much smaller, simpler terms. In a 1923 article, Orestes Barbosa praised the sensual, mystical genius of Pixinguinha.[41] After paying homage to his fellow writers, Olavo Bilac and João do Rio, Barbosa described Eduardo das Neves as a "crude, but sincere singer" and Pixinguinha, as a "crazy harmonizer and . . . peerless player." Pixinguinha's "magical" flute, Barbosa wrote, "darts like a snake. . . . [He is] a black Pan [playing] among frightened Nymphs." Barbosa's choice to liken Pixinguinha to Pan, the Greek god of wild mountain terrain and rustic hunting music, rather than emphasizing, for example, Pixinguinha's professionalism or his economic success, is significant, especially when compared to comments Pixinguinha made to O Jornal two days before the paper printed its interview with China.[42] In its piece on Pixinguinha, O Jornal quoted a local musical instructor, who called him "the most serious [flautist] I know." In speaking with the paper, Pixinguinha described that seriousness with terms that diverged significantly from the 1922 interview in which he emphasized the humble, innocent intentions of the Oito Batutas. "Do you want to evaluate with certainty [the Oito Batutas'] success [in France]?" he asked O Jornal. "Before our debut, the highest daily earnings [for one club] was 6,000 francs. After we started playing there, it rose to 16,000 and sometimes 20,000 per day." Then he contrasted his "serious" work with samba:

Today's musician should, for the love of art, condemn samba because it restricts musical thinking. Samba is to music what four-syllable verses are to poetry. . . . It is primitive music that does not reflect the amplitude of musical thinking. . . . It is an easy melody that even a spoiled girl with six months of practice can play . . . I

did [wrote] a few sambas but only because, as a well-known composer of all genres, I did not want to appear incapable or inept.

As he would decades later, while discussing the musical geography of Tia
Ciata's house, here Pixinguinha left no doubt about his own relationship with samba: it simply did not interest him. The music market, he
explained, was "infected" with samba, which someday would "return to
the breast of macumba and candomblé and no longer undermine good
music and good taste." To Pixinguinha, it was not the music industry that
corrupted African-derived music, as Vagalume, for example, suggested,
but instead just the opposite. The "primitive music" associated with macumba and candomblé had been reproduced by seemingly everyone, de-
grading a profession that Pixinguinha took seriously and considered to
be a privileged art.

Like his brother, Pixinguinha saw himself as a mediator, capable of
subjugating and still remaining connected to something considered to be
savage and unsophisticated. Just as China disassociated himself from the
"dimwitted *negro*" but still acknowledged that common blood ran deep,
Pixinguinha disavowed samba but also made sure to point out that he
could play it if he had to. Like Tio Faustino, both brothers were able to
selectively access their "wild" side because they also tamed, controlled,
and established distance from it. By domesticating their internal other,
they could also strategically access, harness, and deploy it.[43]

"Separating the Wheat from the Chaff" Revisited:
Luciano Gallet's Reagir! *Campaign*

Pixinguinha, China, Tio Faustino, Andrade, and Villa-Lobos each charted
his own definition of Brazil and its music. So did the renowned musician
Luciano Gallet, who in 1930 spearheaded a project to rescue Brazilian
music and culture. In an article that first appeared in *O Globo* and in *Weco*,
a musical journal that he edited, Gallet issued a call to *reagir*—to react,
or fight back—against the decadence and indifference that he saw around
him. Within weeks, the article had been reprinted or referred to in seemingly every paper in Rio.[44]

Born in Rio in 1893 to a French mother and a first-generation French-
Brazilian father, Gallet displayed prodigious musical talent early in life.
In 1916, he was awarded the prestigious Gold Medal for piano at the Insti-
tuto Nacional de Música. In addition to composing, teaching, and study-

ing music, he worked in radio and journalism and also served as director of the institute.[45] To Gallet and his supporters in 1930, music was in crisis. "Pianos are no longer sold; the creation of serious music is extremely weak, and so people are throwing themselves to records and dance music. . . . One gets the impression that music will soon cease to exist . . . going the way of the mule-drawn cart." Gallet blamed radio executives and record producers, whom he accused of sacrificing quality for quantity. High-volume production had made the market a "game of chance" that favored "'popular artists': whistle composers, performers who play by ear, and ignorant singers." As a result, "good music" had become an elusive "luxury item."[46]

It was not that samba or any other kind of music was inherently bad, just that sophisticated works were rarely distinguished from popular ones. Radio stations "play awful music, without the least selection criteria. In every kind of music, from samba by whistling maestros [*maestros de asso-bio*] to the most elevated form, there can be good and terrible. But it is necessary to select, and that is not happening." The crisis, Gallet hoped, was an indication of nothing more than a lack of direction. Fault lay not in consumers, who knew no better. Rather, it was producers and the nation's leaders who were to blame. Because Brazil suffered a "lack of orientation," it was "absurd to hope that all of these people appreciate chamber music, Beethoven's symphonies, and modern music when they have never been taught what these things represent or how to understand them." Public taste should be "directed, supported, and developed as one would do with any animal, plant, or child."[47]

Gallet made his case not only through published articles but also with letters mailed directly to individuals across Brazil. Almost everyone who published an opinion or corresponded privately with Gallet agreed that money threatened good music and proper musical instruction. In a letter to Gallet, a German-trained composer and instructor criticized the "wicked" influence of the record industry. Well-known music scholar and journalist Luiz Heitor Corrêa de Azevedo (Luiz Heitor) decried "decadence" and Brazil's "musical ruin." Renato Almeida blamed the putative decline on ever-expanding financial opportunity. "Symphonic groups and chamber music can fail, but popular orchestras [and] popular singers with guitars, pandeiros, réco-récos, and cavaquinhos are, today, excellent business. . . . This economic success is the base of this whole lamentable state of things."[48]

At its core, the *Reagir!* campaign was about distinguishing good culture from bad, or, as priest and dedicated musician Pedro Sinzig put it, "separating the wheat from the chaff," the same phrase used by Vagalume in *Na roda do samba*.[49] If Vagalume and Gallet each sought to distinguish good elements from bad and agreed that the music industry was a destructive force, the two did not necessarily see eye to eye about what (or whom) constituted the wheat and the chaff. Though Gallet accepted the idea that "every kind of music" had potential, he also saw a great difference between samba and a well-executed symphony. He saw popular music as raw material, not the product of individual creative genius. Gallet channeled that vision in "Nhó Chico" (Old Frank), a piece that Mário de Andrade lauded for transforming "into *música erudita* the psychological and linear characteristics of the caipira's musicality."[50] Like Andrade and Villa-Lobos, Gallet wrote extensively about Brazilian folklore and incorporated native and Afro-Brazilian forms into his own music. The dances and music of black and native peoples, he said, "constitute a vast wealth which should be exploited."[51] The "mission" of contemporary Brazilian musicians was to "give to that primitive material a new and independent life, and use it to form work of significance and racial character."[52] This, he explained, was why he "collected" and "harmonized" popular songs.[53] His attempts to do so were encouraged and admired by others, and he received numerous requests from authors, composers, and politicians in Brazil and abroad for material.[54] Much like the German observer quoted by Andrade, who complained of Brazilian musicians' canary-like imitations, individuals both aligned with and independent of the *Reagir!* movement lamented the "aping" (*macaqueação*) of European classics.[55] By continuing to reproduce the work of European masters, a writer for *Weco* inveighed, "we will be condemned to [keep] making uninteresting, useless works of imitation."[56]

Gallet's perception about Brazil's lack of original music resonated with Andrade's discussion of musical colonialism and companion ideas about musical classification and property. In 1930, *Weco* ran an article about Sinhô, who had recently passed away. Sinhô's music, the journal reported,

cannot be classified as work of art because it is genuinely popular and created for the masses, who have only rudimentary musical cultivation. . . . But it is also true that his work should not be lumped together with all the rubbish that exists under the rubric of "music for the povo" and is marked by an absolute lack of inspiration and a purely mercantile motivation.[57]

One of Sinhô's "characteristic traits," *Weco* pointed out, was "immodesty," evident in the way that he embraced the spotlight and aggressively pursued property rights. But the magazine also made a point of siding with him against "whistling maestros" who tried to steal his work. Ultimately, *Weco* supported the principle behind Sinhô's pursuit of author's rights, even if it disliked his individualism and style.

No such tensions marked a two-article series on author's rights and the record industry.[58] In *Weco*'s estimation, composers needed to exert the same control over the recording process as record executives and the performers and recording directors they hired. "The author as well as the director should be a guide [during recording] because there is always a bit of inspiration that fails to make it onto the page."[59] In calling for the preservation of artistic creation, *Weco* did not have the "genuinely popular" Sinhô in mind, but rather cultured artists like Gallet. The industry, bent on production and profit, could not be trusted to represent the subtleties of genius. To *Weco*, the difference between Sinhô and Gallet was evident in the two artists' relationship with the povo. While the King of Samba composed pieces meant to be consumed by unrefined, uneducated masses, Gallet shaped popular tradition into polished, serious music, fit for elite audiences and also capable of educating individuals with "rudimentary cultivation."

Gallet and *Weco* also defined musical excellence and authorship in racial and gendered terms. In a 1931 letter to Rio's prefect, Gallet asked for financial assistance that would allow "luxury cafés" to support daily musical performances. Such support, Gallet argued, "will make for a happier physiognomy in the city and provide cash for numerous heads of families."[60] An advertisement for Telefunken radios, which frequently appeared on the back cover of *Weco*, depicted a white family with the father dutifully operating the radio as daughter and wife looked on (figure 7). *Reagir!* proponents also frequently contrasted the licentious nature of popular music with more dignified works. Only by protecting pure music, Gallet wrote, "will we fulfill our obligations as Brazilian men."[61]

In his letter to the prefect, Gallet argued that a burgeoning class of respectable musicians deserved financial support from the city. A journalist who agreed asserted that many musicians had become "unemployed due to the popularity of the gramophone and the talking movie." Another lamented that Brazilian musicians did not "earn enough even to eat!"[62] While serious musicians starved, untalented whistling maestros earned mountains of money. In an editorial, *Weco* called for police repression

FIGURE 7. Telefunken advertisement in *Weco* (1930). Courtesy Biblioteca Nacional.

against a "cast" that "infests our well-heeled capital." Individuals known to crash elite parties "think that a nice suit, a pair of fashionable shoes, and a fancy hat are credentials that will get anyone access to civilized environs." A separate piece described popular music as a lamentable fad, fueled by "purely economic motives."[63]

In separating the wheat from the chaff, Gallet traced a familiar map of music, race, and religion. In a speech honoring the modernist writer José Pereira da Graça Aranha, Gallet quoted a passage from *A viagem maravilhosa* (The marvelous voyage), in which Aranha describes a macumba ceremony: "The gang of Negroes (*a negragada*) accompanied the Pai de Santo, singing a monotonous, somber tune. The women's loud, shrill voices raised above the low, raspy voices of the men. They danced to the frenetic shouts."[64] To Gallet, the passage gave "life and reality" to Aranha's larger work. In 1930, the poet Manuel Bandeira framed macumba's authenticity in a slightly different way. "In Rio," he declared, "the only thing genuine that one hears are sambas by malandros in Estácio and the gloomy melodies of the macumbas."[65] Bandeira's pronouncement suggests the kind of twisted logic often used to link race and authenticity. Residents of Estácio, a place he equated with timeless purity, were at that very moment producing the *new* and innovative rhythms that would shape samba for years to come. To Tio Faustino, the suggestion that macumba was "authentic" would have seemed equally absurd.

Descriptions that defined Afro-Brazilian music and religion as timeless and pure are indicative of larger definitions of race and society embraced by proponents of the *Reagir!* campaign. *Weco* looked hopefully to formally trained "professional" musicians to lead Brazil into the future. The journal described how Villa-Lobos "transformed" popular music "into strong works, full of Brazilian vitality."[66] The composer Oscar Lorenzo Fernandez compared Brazil in 1930 to a man coming of age. "Today's Brazil has consciousness of his existence. He is a young man, leaving behind the challenges of puberty. Already a made man, he begins to feel the virile pride of being . . . *himself.*"[67] That process, which Fernandez also called a "profound racial phenomenon," was part of a larger evolution, which would synthesize disparate musical, national, and racial characteristics into a single evolved Brazilian people.

Of course, a unified race could be attained only if internal differences and hierarchies were mapped and preserved. Gallet made this point forcefully in *Estudos de folklore* (Folklore studies), a collection of pieces prepared in part for a League of Nations conference on global popular culture.[68] The work, organized and edited by Mário de Andrade, left no doubt about the place of nonwhites in Brazil. In a section titled "O negro," Gallet analyzed African musical contributions and referenced works by Rodrigues and Silvio Romero and Gustavo Barroso, two prominent Brazilian writers who studied folklore and embraced various brands of "whitening" philosophy.[69] Their collected works, Gallet wrote, supported his own. Ultimately, he was convinced, the "black race" would become "diluted, absorbed by the white race."[70] While African rhythms were quickly disappearing from popular view, and while he found those rhythms primitive, Gallet still felt that it was important to understand and record them. "How will we talk about the fetishists' songs and instruments without explaining macumba, candomblé, Xangô, etc.? If we here do not know the most about these subjects, what will Europeans say?"[71]

Gallet took a somewhat different stance toward Brazil's native peoples, exemplified in the blunt opening line to the section of *Estudos* dedicated to indigenous people. "The Indian," Gallet wrote, "did not contribute to the formation of our current music."[72] Brazil might have been forged from three races, but its music, he argued, came from just two.[73] But whatever the source material to be found in Afro-Brazilian music, Gallet felt that blacks had collectively sold out to the music industry by attempting to turn themselves into something they could never be. After slavery, he wrote, "The free black, master now of himself, sought to elevate himself to the level of the white man . . . [and] imitated him."[74]

Mapping Bodies and Minds

Gallet's conviction that Brazil was still struggling to develop its own music and his suggestion that nonwhite peoples possessed no independent musical creativity resonated with views from abroad. A pamphlet published by the Pan American Union in 1938, titled "Latin American Composers and Their Problems," suggested, "For content, Latin American composers may draw on that veritable storehouse of melodic and harmonic inspiration—the folk music of the various countries." "The negroid music in Brazil," the pamphlet's author wrote, "offers the Brazilian composer a limitless source of materials."[75] The notion that Afro-Brazilian musicians represented a collective "storehouse" of material and the companion idea that those same musicians were physical and spiritual beings, lacking any serious intellectual capacity, posed obvious challenges for artists like

Donga, Pixinguinha, and Tio Faustino, who sought recognition as intellectual laborers. But if influential writers and musicians discursively separated Afro-Brazilian artists from the fruits of their labor, other projects marginalized them in even more concrete and forceful ways.

Ismael Silva, the artist perhaps most responsible for developing the Estácio Sound, also helped found Rio's first samba schools. He had a long musical career, beginning with his first composition in 1919 and then continuing off-and-on until the end of his life. Silva's collaborations with Francisco Alves and with Mário Reis, another white artist, produced popular hits. Silva reportedly spent several years in prison during the late 1930s for shooting and injuring a man who insulted his sister. It is believed that this time in prison sent Silva on a tailspin from which he never fully recovered.[76] If that is indeed true, the case's documents have gone missing. But records for seven other arrests, each for vagrancy, and each made between 1927 and 1930, are found in the Arquivo Nacional.[77] In addition to providing unique insights about Silva's life, the vagrancy records also vividly demonstrate how projects such as Gallet's *Reagir!* campaign could link up with more formal surveillance projects.

Silva's arrest records bear trademarks of most vagrancy cases. In seven arrests, he was convicted only once, and that conviction was eventually overturned. But he still spent an average of almost thirty-nine days in jail on each count, longer than he theoretically would have had he been found guilty. Silva was forced to undergo physical examinations twice, ostensibly to determine whether he was fit to work. During the first, the doctor found "acute urethritis, venereal cankers and bi-lateral, inguinal adenitis." He concluded that Silva was "a sick person who needs treatment," which could be "ambulatory" and would not "impede his work." Before the second exam, Silva complained of blennorrhea, but "the direct exam did not reveal any sort of illness which would prevent the patient from working."[78]

Like others arrested for vagrancy, Silva sometimes rejected charges by portraying himself in the mold of an upright masculine laborer and provider. On one occasion, his lawyer wrote, "The accused is not a vagrant. He has a home and a family and never committed an undignified or illicit act. He presented himself in a decent manner to the judge, demonstrating that he has means of subsistence and is a worker employed in an office."[79] Other times, Silva resorted to a less common strategy, calling attention to his own frailty. In a separate case, the same lawyer wrote, "This case, against a weakly boy, is a cruelty without name. He is almost tuberculosed and plagued with a sickness that forced him to seek out the Santa Casa da Misericórdia, where he was headed when arrested!"[80]

In addition to the back-and-forth over occupation, residence, and family life that marked nearly every vagrancy case, literacy took center stage during the recorded exchanges among Silva, his advocates, and the authorities. As they often did with vagrancy suspects, the police included illiteracy among the descriptors used to prove Silva's guilt, a charge that he roundly rejected. In four separate statements, Silva insisted that he knew how to read and write. One statement pointed out that he "even has good handwriting."[81] To Silva and his advocates, the false accusations epitomized how vagrancy cases were often made à revelia, or by default and based on assumptions. One letter held, "To understand the false, default assumptions behind this case, it is enough to simply note the proven fact that the acusado knows how to read and write but was described as illiterate." The police's insistence on applying "default" descriptions to Silva almost appears to have been intentional. A record of the testimony that Silva gave after one arrest went beyond the shorthand normally transcribed—"single, twenty-nine years old, homeless, illiterate"—and noted that Silva "declared himself to be illiterate."[82]

Signed court documents and handwritten song lyrics leave no doubt that Silva knew how to read and write.[83] As noted in chapter 2, during his arrests Silva named various professional titles to the police, including "painter," "sales clerk," "office worker," "trabalhador," and "employed in commerce." Only once did he mention his music career and on that occasion stated that he was employed in commerce and "also a musical composer."[84] Composing music (and lyrics) would seem to be an obvious sign of literacy, but neither the police nor the judges nor the advocates who defended Silva saw "musician" as a category that could effectively counter popular definitions of vagrants and vagabundos.

There is reason to believe that, privately at least, Silva felt differently. Between arrests during the late 1920s, Silva helped found Deixa Falar, Rio's first samba school. Documentation about the origins of Deixa Falar and other schools is frustratingly hard to come by, but it seems clear that Silva and others called their new organizations "schools" to make a point about the seriousness of their music. Paulo da Portela handed out "diplomas" to school members in Portela's Carnival parade, a performative act meant to entertain but also linked to his larger project of uplift.[85] On the one hand, Silva clearly felt that it was important to assert his literacy to the police. This was perhaps just a legal strategy, but his repeated insistence about being able to read and write also functioned as a way to assert his intellect and manhood. On the other hand, he knew that his work as a musician was not the best way to differentiate himself from other supposed vagrants. In public, it was his malandragem, much more than his book smarts or literacy, that Silva embraced and deployed and that ultimately came to define him.

Like Silva, his friend and fellow Estácio musician Brancura was arrested multiple times for vagrancy and underwent intense and humiliating police examinations. Brancura several times languished in jail while awaiting trial or otherwise slipped between the cracks of the penal system. In 1930, police arrived at his house to serve a warrant, only to find that he was already at the Casa de Detenção, where he had been for the last month awaiting formal charges for the same incident. By the time he was convicted of vagrancy he had already been imprisoned nearly two weeks longer than the time stipulated in his eventual sentence. In 1933, he suffered a similar fate, held for sixty days after his arrest in a case that the judge eventually dismissed on a technicality.[86] During a separate arrest, a police medical examiner reported, "He is physically robust and in excellent general condition. His upper right limb is slightly shorter than the left, but the musculature is well developed and he is able to move with reasonable efficiency. His penis has developed a venereal sore now almost completely scarred over."[87] In two separate exams (performed during arrests in 1933), doctors reported similar deficiencies, none of which, they concluded, were serious enough to prevent him from working.[88]

SILVA'S AND BRANCURA'S experiences as vagrancy suspects demonstrate how Afro-Brazilian men became entangled in multiple mapping projects. Both men were able to benefit from society's guarded fascination with the submundo, malandragem, and "authentic" music, but both also knew firsthand how stereotypes and the police could circumscribe the acceptance of samba and other Afro-Brazilian "symbols and ideas." It is also worth noting two ways that Silva's and Brancura's police records run counter to the punishment paradigm. First, both men drew the attention of police for reasons unrelated to music. Second, in direct contrast to more triumphant narratives, which suggest that police repression diminished as samba became more accepted, Silva and Brancura were arrested during a time when samba was widely popular. As some opportunities expanded for black musicians, other obstacles remained firmly in place. In fact, it seems that Estácio musicians—not their forebears—suffered the most violent abuse at the hands of the police, even as samba entered its so-called golden age.[89] As Afro-Brazilian musicians asserted themselves as economic and social actors, there were often powerful authorities standing by to put them back in their place.

In the ongoing search for samba's origins, certain discourses and characteristics were repeatedly favored over others. Despite Pixinguinha's emphasis on hard work and economic success and despite Ismael Silva's preoccupation with literacy, commentators and scholars repeatedly associated blackness and samba with malandragem, rhythm, sexuality, and caricatured depictions of Africa. Even decades after abolition, claiming the rights and promises of an inclusive, egalitarian Brazil was rarely a straightforward or easily attainable task for Silva, Pixinguinha, or any other black musician who confronted categories and assumptions that, like the lines on Villa-Lobos's map, were twisted, convoluted, and at the same time also extremely rigid.

The Batutas, ca. 1923. Courtesy Acervo Instituto Moreira Salles, Coleção Pixinguinha.

Donga (second from left), Pixinguinha (second from right), and friends at the port. Courtesy Acervo Instituto Moreira Salles, Coleção Pixinguinha.

Alfredo José de Alcântara. Courtesy Acervo Instituto Moreira Salles, Coleção Pixinguinha.

Pixinguinha (center) and Ismael Silva (second from right), ca. 1956.
Courtesy Acervo Instituto Moreira Salles, Coleção Pixinguinha.

Pixinguinha (second from right) with friends. Courtesy Acervo
Instituto Moreira Salles, Coleção Pixinguinha.

Grupo Caxangá: Pixinguinha is standing with a flute at the far left; Donga is seated with a guitar to the far right. Courtesy Acervo Instituto Moreira Salles, Coleção Pixinguinha.

Anacleto de Medeiros. Courtesy Acervo Instituto Moreira Salles, Coleção Pixinguinha.

7

ALLIANCES AND LIMITS

The SBAT and the Rise of the Entertainment Class

In *Na roda do samba*, Vagalume made two predictions—one apocryphal, the other right on the money. The first had to do with instruments. "There is no doubt," the journalist wrote, that Tio Faustino's omelê "will soon be an obligatory instrument in every center where samba is cultivated." By contrast, the cuíca would soon fall into disuse, he said. He could not have been more wrong with this prediction. The cuíca became (and remains) a ubiquitous presence in samba and at Carnival, whereas the omelê fell into obscurity. But Vagalume's second pronouncement was more prescient. "Very soon," he suggested, "*the authors of other people's works* will come around . . . earning rivers of gold." In Rio, he continued, "Wise guys there are a-plenty, and suckers, too. What's missing are police."[1] Indeed, as cash flowed—and as musicians gained greater visibility but few means with which to protect their authorship or collective financial interests—artists turned to an unlikely source for help: the police. This chapter explains how and why this surprising turn came to pass.

In 1930, a month after seizing control of the country in a bloodless coup, Getúlio Vargas was greeted at the presidential palace by a large gathering of musicians. Shouts of "Viva Vargas!" punctuated the national anthem, played by several military bands. The musicians marched from downtown, winding their way through the adjacent neighborhood of Catete and eventually to the presidential residence. Vargas and his wife, Darcy, appeared on their balcony to greet the procession. After the anthem was played, Brazil's new leader moved inside to receive a seven-person commission that included Donga and Pixinguinha. Face-to-face with the president, the group handed over a memorial that lauded Vargas, elucidated their concerns, and laid out a three-point plan to improve their "precarious" and "distressed" state.

The *marche aux flambeaux*, or torchlight march, as the nighttime procession was called, represented the hope for state support in hard times. In looking to Vargas for assistance, the musicians were by no means alone. A week earlier, a group of unemployed workers had gathered in front of the palace to ask the new president for help.[2] During his two stints as head of state (1930–45, 1951–54), Vargas came to be known by some as "Father of the Poor."[3] Throughout Latin America, the worldwide economic depression helped usher in an era in which states were made increasingly responsible, at least in theory, for the well-being of their citizens. Spurred by Mexico's 1910 revolution and then by the fall of export-oriented economies that plunged along with international prices, nations throughout the region sought new paths to wealth and stability. A wave of populist leaders, Vargas included, initiated state-led projects of industrialization and embraced rhetoric suggesting that the exclusion of vast sectors of the population would be reversed.

The musicians who gathered in Catete had special reason to think that Vargas would be sympathetic to their cause. Two years earlier, as a representative from Rio Grande do Sul he sponsored what became known as the Lei (Law) Getúlio Vargas, a piece of legislation meant to protect author's rights. In 1930, he again played the part of advocate, assuring Donga, Pixinguinha, and the others that he "would carefully study" their concerns "in good faith" and with the hope of satisfying their wishes.[4] The marchers presented themselves and were depicted as a unified class, one that crossed racial and socioeconomic lines. The *Diário da Noite*, which with *O Jornal* sponsored the march, wrote that the "collective manifestation" brought together a "near totality" of "all of the elements of this great and useful class." Musicians from São Paulo and Minas Gerais sent letters in support of their colleagues.[5]

The organized, united front on display at the march was both a harbinger of the real gains that musicians—black and white—won between the turn of the century and the 1930s and a facade that hid underlying divides and simmering tensions. The procession, which included composers, performers, and thespians, brought together a large array of individuals with all kinds of backgrounds. Conceived and executed more than a decade after the release of "Pelo telefone," nearly ten years after the Oito Batutas Paris trip, and just as musicians from Estácio were helping to launch samba into its golden age, the march is also a reflection of musicians' growing public presence. Nonetheless, as the letter that Donga and Pixinguinha handed to the president suggests, all was not well for musicians.

"Our Precarious and Distressed State": Feast and Famine in a Growing Market

The station of musicians had palpably changed during the two decades preceding the marche aux flambeaux. In 1911, the contracts that Fred Figner signed with his musicians were worth a total of 12:165$000 (US $3,925 in 1911). Two decades later, his Casa Edison paid out 103:389$250 (US $11,077 in 1930) in the first half of 1930 alone.[6] The astounding increase between 1911 and 1930 was due, in part, to the fact that Casa Edison made payments not only to individual musicians, as it mainly did in 1911, but also to rival record labels, bars, casinos, Carnival associations, and the SBAT (Society of Brazilian Theater Authors), the first organization in Brazil dedicated to defending author's rights in theater and music. The SBAT distributed money from Casa Edison and other labels to its members in Brazil and to affiliated associations in foreign countries. While the music market grew, and while select entrepreneurs and artists were flush with cash in 1930, others were not so fortunate. Less than two years after the marche aux flambeaux, Villa-Lobos estimated in a letter to Vargas that Brazil was home to thirty-two thousand musicians, a great portion of whom found themselves without work and in need of the president's assistance.[7] Gross disparities divided even those who found employment. During the first half of 1930, Casa Edison paid Francisco Alves 11 contos de réis (US $1,178), while little-known Luis Areda took home only 7 milréis (less than US $1).

Market growth was partially fueled by new advances in sound technology, which helped bring the new music to a rapidly expanding audience. In 1927, electromagnetic recording became available in Rio for the first time, providing recordings that were of higher fidelity and enabling the reproduction of subtler and more complex sounds, especially those made by drums. When Vargas took power in 1930, nineteen radio stations existed across the country. The lucrative but still underdeveloped technology presented Vargas with a dilemma: follow Great Britain and Germany and use the state to exclude commercial interests, or adapt the model favored by the United States and embrace private sponsorship. With funds short, and with Argentine radio threatening to expand into Brazil, Vargas chose the latter option, approving a law in 1932 that defined the radio as a "national interest" and launched the medium into its commercial phase.[8] By 1945, more than one hundred stations existed around the country, and by 1950 the number had grown to three hundred. Radios themselves became increasingly affordable over time. The polling organization IBOPE estimated in 1945 that 85 percent of households in Rio and São Paulo owned radios, and in 1950, 95 percent. In addition to educational segments, comedy routines, and government programs and speeches, stations filled the airwaves with music performed by live bands or played on records. While radio opened new opportunities for all kinds of musicians, in the middle of the twentieth century it remained a hierarchical and elitist sphere. Though black musicians found work in radio, most played backup roles to white stars.[9]

As radio grew during the 1930s, multinational corporations came to dominate record production. By 1932, Figner's once massive enterprise was fading, but the market hardly skipped a beat. Local entrepreneurs continued to do well for themselves and helped make the Brazilian record industry, in McCann's words, "one of the most successful Latin American cases of import-substituting industrialization in the 1930s." Though a portion of sales profits went north, the production of other lucrative activities (radio shows, public performances, etc.) remained under local control.[10] How money was distributed within Brazil was another matter.

If technological advances helped the music market grow, they also posed new challenges. Silent films, which employed live bands and orchestras to provide background music, declined after 1929, closing off an important area of employment.[11] In support of the marche aux flambeaux, musicians from Juiz de Fora, Minas Gerais, wrote a letter to Vargas that suggested that "governmental indifference" had caused Brazil to fall behind nations of "less intense civilization." The "ominous, absorbing empire of the gramophone" and new talking movies had dealt a "death blow" to "good national music," plunging "our poor class" into a "lamentable crisis." "Little by little," the musicians concluded, "traditional Brazilian music is disappearing."[12] The letter from Juiz de Fora captured two related concerns: the precarious financial state in which a number of musicians found themselves and the perceived disappearance of "traditional" music. While the musicians represented at the marche aux flambeaux were urgently focused on the present, their concerns also had deeper histories, each attached to the rise of the SBAT.

In its coverage of the marche aux flambeaux, the *Diário da Noite* highlighted a public pronouncement of support made by the SBAT president, Abadie Farias Rosa, who attended the march.[13] The press attention given to Rosa is indicative of the SBAT's high profile at the time. Composers, playwrights, and journalists founded the organization in 1917, the same year that "Pelo telefone" exploded on the Carnival scene. Between 1917 and the end of 1930, the society distributed more than 2,500 contos de réis (2,500:000$000, worth nearly US $270,000 in 1930) of author's rights payments to its members and affiliates.[14] During its first two decades of existence, the SBAT not only played a crucial role in regulating the distribution of author's rights payments, but also in delineating boundaries and internal hierarchies of a burgeoning entertainment class and in articulating a new relationship between entertainers and the state. While the SBAT ostensibly served all Brazilian artists, its interests clearly lay with the playwrights and composers—the vast majority of whom were white men—who formed the society's majority. Its first president was none other than João do Rio.[15] Mauro de Almeida, the journalist who helped Donga register "Pelo telefone," was also a charter member.

Vargas blunted hopes that many held for his administration through increasingly authoritarian tendencies that crystallized with the 1937 declaration of the Estado Novo (New State).[16] The promise of a more inclusive and freer society was circumscribed by, among other things, Vargas's desire to make the state present everywhere and at all times. After returning from Germany in 1934, a cabinet member, Luiz Simões Lopes, marveled, "What impressed me most in Berlin was the systematic propaganda. . . . There is not in all of Germany a single person who does not experience on a daily basis contact with Hitler's 'Nazism.'"[17] During the 1930s, local and national governments in Brazil took an increasingly active approach toward culture, arts, and mass media, distributing money and exercising control over programming. In 1939, Vargas transformed the Office of National Propaganda (Departamento Nacional de Propaganda) into the Office of Press and Propaganda (Departamento de Imprensa e Propaganda, DIP). The new agency was wider in scope than its predecessor and fell under Vargas's direct control.[18]

Lopes and Vargas were not alone in their admiration of totalitarian states. In December 1933, SBAT President Rosa wrote glowingly about laws recently passed in Hitler's Germany and Mussolini's Italy.[19] Four years later, Vargas made Rosa head of the newly created Serviço Nacional de Teatro (National Theater Bureau). Rosa and others particularly admired German and Italian regulations that required prior registration and approval for all public music performances. In 1932, the playwright and SBAT member Oduvaldo Vianna delivered a speech lamenting the lack of institutional support for Brazilian theater. Mussolini was among the examples of heads of state who he felt gave adequate backing to the arts.[20] In 1931, Ary Barroso, an extremely popular composer and SBAT member, echoed Vianna's sentiments, suggesting that Brazil adapt the Italian leader's strict regulation of scheduling for sporting events, cinema, and theater events.[21]

The SBAT's origins, borne out of a larger impetus for the defense of national artistic production, are often traced to a legendary story involving Chiquinha Gonzaga (Francisca Hedwiges de Lima Neves Gonzaga), the most accomplished Brazilian female musician of her time and one of the organization's architects. Just after the turn of the century, she traveled to Berlin, where she entered a music store and stumbled upon unauthorized copies of her work for sale. Over the next decade and a half, she and others grew increasingly vocal in protesting the illicit trafficking of music.[22] The Gonzaga origins story is indicative of how intellectual property defense came to be framed as a national concern. But while composers and playwrights presented their cause in patriotic terms, they also often struggled against an unresponsive state. Their designs were further complicated by Brazil's (and their own) enduring obsession with European culture. Together, these challenges developed into a particular postcolonial blues.

In the pages of its *Boletim*, SBAT members cast themselves as flag bearers of the nation and defenders against foreign interlopers. In the mid-1920s, the society sponsored a project to construct a mausoleum for Francisco Manuel da Silva, the author of Brazil's *Hino Nacional*. At a weekly meeting, one member voiced opposition to recognizing the death of a Portuguese actress, arguing, "In Brazil, there should not be [such] acts for foreigners, who never remember us on identical occasions."[23] The SBAT observed important national holidays, a practice that its members saw as part of its larger educative and civilizing mission. One society president implored, "It is necessary that Brazilians do not think only about Carnival and *foot-ball*, but that they also care about the *patria*'s important holidays."[24] Patriotism was tempered by the belief that Brazil had fallen behind "civilized" Europe, which the SBAT saw as not just an exploiter, but also as a model and important ally. With much fanfare, the society welcomed "illustrious visitors" from abroad, including writers, musicians, diplomats, and representatives of counterpart associations. Members gave lectures about famous European playwrights, and most issues of the *Boletim* dedicated at least one full page to the latest goings-on in international theater. In 1932, the society acquired a "luxury edition" copy of Dante's *Inferno*.[25]

The SBAT paid close attention to developments in European and North American intellectual property law. After Hungary centralized and bolstered its system, an SBAT writer asked, "Will we have one day in Brazil the guarantees announced [there]?"[26] Another member openly wished for nationwide enforcement of all "legal dispositions guaranteeing the Author's Right," which he called "one of the most legitimate property rights, and as such recognized and respected in all civilized nations."[27] While pining after European-style regulations, the SBAT actively pursued relationships with foreign societies, which could secure payments for Brazilian music played abroad in return for the same treatment of foreign pieces played in Brazil. By 1933, the SBAT had pacts with associations in nineteen countries throughout Europe and the Americas.

Relationships with foreign societies functioned as a double-edged sword, bolstering the society's revenue, strength, and prestige while also highlighting its low global station. In 1925, lack of money prevented SBAT representatives from attending an international intellectual property conference. In 1927, the American Society of Composers, Authors, and Publishers sent a letter to the SBAT, inquiring about possibilities for protecting works by North American artists in Brazil. In exchange, the American organization offered to advertise but not necessarily protect Brazilian songs, which the association claimed were unknown in the United States. In 1928, an invitation to attend a conference in Paris arrived two days before the event began, making attendance all but impossible.[28] By the early 1930s, associations in France, Italy, England, Germany, and Austria had formed a kind of European author's rights G-5. The SBAT referred to the group as a "cartel" and monitored its deliberations.[29]

The SBAT also drew on European models to advocate for better protection at home. Referring to ineffective enforcement of intellectual property law, the *Boletim* lamented, "In Brazil, in contrast to what goes on in other countries, there is no respect for the right of the author."[30] After Pope Pius XI ordered the Catholic Church to remunerate composers for songs played at Mass and religious celebrations, Rosa wrote in a *Diário de Notícias* column, "In Brazil, everybody thinks that the simple fact of printing or recording a composition on disc makes it available for any sort of use. Just yesterday, the director of one of our radio societies told me quite calmly that the record he just bought would be played however and whenever he wished." Author's rights were respected all over the world, the article concluded, "now even in Vatican City. Only in Brazil is that not the case."[31]

Member of the SBAT saw enemies not only in foreign "cartels" but also much closer to home. In letters to the prefect and the municipal council, the society protested taxes paid by theater companies, highlighting the economic and moral benefits provided by those companies, which gave sustenance to "hundreds of artists." By contrast, movies and radio kept money in the hands of a few.[32] Even worse, the society claimed, cinema's "dark theaters" bred vice.[33] In his treatise "Cinema: Theater's Greatest Enemy," Alvarenga Fonseca, the SBAT president in the mid-1920s, referred to "all kinds of licentiousness" that took place in darkened movie houses and accused the industry of favoring foreign interests at the expense of local artists and entrepreneurs.[34] An article from a São Paulo newspaper, reproduced in the *Boletim*, protested the increasingly frequent transformation of theaters into movie venues. A recent law in Portugal, which prohibited that kind of renovation, prompted the article's author to ask, "When will we have in our land a government which takes the same interest in theater?"[35]

Complaints about theater's decline were connected to sobering realities. In 1934, the Instituto Brasileiro de Geografia e Estatística (Brazilian Institute of Geography and Statistics, IBGE) counted almost 13 million paid spectators at theaters and *casas de espetáculos* (show houses) in Rio. Nearly 11 million of those spectators saw movies; the rest attended operas, plays, and the teatro de revista. The ratio of movie to theater audiences was even higher in the state of São Paulo, where more than 20.7 million of 21.5 million customers saw movies.[36] Similar developments caused parallel concerns among musicians, who saw obstacles not only in the rise of movies but also in the unregulated use of music on the radio, in bars, and in live shows. In their 1930 letter to Vargas, the musicians from Juiz de Fora named talking movies as among the worst enemies of national music. The Pixinguinha- and Donga-led march in Rio asked Vargas for stricter enforcement of author's rights law, regulation of the film industry, and an act to protect "national musicians" by requiring that at least two-thirds of all public repertoires consist of Brazilian music.[37] Though underrepresented within the SBAT, musicians could agree with playwrights that Brazilian artists of all kinds needed greater protection of their author's rights.

Rights Large and Small

On the surface, the individuals at the marche aux flambeaux appeared to be part of a unified collective. The press referred to the participants as representatives of the "musical class," and one article suggested that the march brought together "all of the elements of [that] class." Another suggested that the demonstration was "composed of a near totality of Brazilian musical artists."[38] On the way to Catete, the procession stopped at the Palace Hotel, where the opera singer Bidú Sayão handed over a letter addressed to "the illustrious promoters of the 'marche-aux-flambeaux'":

> Anything representing the artistic and economic aspirations of musicians from my country will always find my most decided solidarity, convinced as I am that only through mutual and agreed support from the various categories of our profession will the musical triumph of Brazil one day surge.[39]

The support of Sayão, a highly decorated artist who performed in Italy and at the Paris Opera, Carnegie Hall, and the Met, carried great symbolic value, as did the presence of Donga, Pixinguinha, and Abadie Farias Rosa.[40] All parties appeared united in the desire to protect Brazilian music.

In the absence of a union or society dedicated exclusively to the protection of musicians' rights, the SBAT would seem to have been a natural ally for musicians. Regular exchange and overlap between theater and music made the fit logical. But while the SBAT ostensibly defended all theater and musical artists — and intellectual property more generally — it also embraced a clear hierarchy. In a letter to the prefect, Fonseca described how theater provided work for "hundreds of artists — musicians, carpenters, electricians, choir members, doormen, dressmakers, tailors, etc."[41] By lumping musicians together with blue-collar workers, Fonseca revealed an assumption about artistic value. While the masses of workers and artists (artistas) were to be valued, they were also held in relief against the society's "cultured" core. In 1926, the *Boletim* boasted, "It is known

TABLE 8. SBAT Author's Rights Payments (1917–32)

Year	Total Payments Made (mil-réis)	Miscellaneous (mil-réis)	Grandes Direitos (mil-réis)	Pequenos Direitos (mil-réis)	Pequenos as % of Total
1917–24*	76:368$400	—	—	—	—
1925	274:410$130	—	—	—	—
1926	289:288$300	—	—	—	—
1927	247:256$450	—	—	—	—
1928	186:035$100	—	—	—	—
1929	277:052$370	3:245$000	243:023$090	30:784$280	11
1930	612:318$000	10:478$120	422:217$690	179:622$190	29
1931	464:841$220	23:808$860	257:523$510	183:508$850	40
1932	419:003$200	5:474$100	192:267$500	221:261$600	53

*Annual average.
Source: *Boletim da SBAT*. Various.

that today the SBAT counts among it a great number of associates, not a small percentage of whom are men of letters" (*homens de letras*).[42]

The disparity between theater and music manifested itself in the way that the SBAT classified the money it collected and distributed. Proceeds from musical performances were called *pequenos direitos* (small rights), and those from theater *grandes direitos* (big or great rights). As those categories suggest, the SBAT was primarily concerned with the latter. In its annual report for 1926, the SBAT acknowledged its inability to enforce payment for musical rights. Collecting pequenos direitos, Fonseca said, "depends exclusively on the functioning of a large oversight apparatus, which we still do not possess."[43] Five years later, the *Boletim* called pequenos direitos "a new thing among us" and "a product of the 'grande direito.'"[44]

The SBAT's 1929 financial report was the first to separate payments of pequenos and grandes direitos. That year, the society's distribution of grandes direitos exceeded that of pequenos by a ratio of approximately 8 to 1. But in 1930, pequenos grew to almost one-third of the total amount distributed by the SBAT. By 1932, they accounted for more than half (see table 8). Casa Edison data provide further evidence that the late 1920s were a turning point in terms of the volume and regularity in which popular composers were paid. The entire available Casa Edison collection contains 1,054 contracts, 465 of which were signed between 1910 and 1928 and 575 between 1929 and 1932.[45] The convergence of Estácio Samba, Carnival, electromagnetic recording, and the Lei Getúlio Vargas made the late 1920s and early 1930s a time of great promise for musicians. With the market rapidly expanding, the SBAT (theoretically) standing behind them, and Vargas in the presidential palace, popular musicians seemed poised to unite and collect. But even as the collection and distribution of peque- nos direitos improved, only some individuals prospered, and the SBAT continued to favor theater artists over popular musicians. Despite the in- creased revenue and the opportunity to become *sócios filiados* (affiliated members), popular musicians rarely found full protection and support in the SBAT.

The perception that musical rights were an offshoot of grandes direitos was reflected in the society's membership, which was dominated by "men of letters." Through the early 1930s, Ary Barroso was the only popular musician to appear with any frequency in meeting minutes or the *Boletim*. Sinhô was a member but had a fractious relationship with the society's leaders. Aside from Barroso and Sinhô, Pixinguinha, Donga, Francisco Alves, Benedito Lacerda, Noel Rosa, João da Baiana, and Ismael Silva all became associated with the SBAT. But with the exception of Pixinguinha and perhaps Alves, most of those musicians appear to have joined the society after 1928, and only as sócios filiados, a category created in early 1929. The new category allowed individuals to seek the SBAT's assistance in collecting payments while exempting them from membership dues and withholding the right to vote. In 1929 and into the early 1930s, just as samba entered its golden age, the SBAT saw a spike in membership ap- plications, most of which appear to have been for filiado status. Like "ar- tista," the sócio filiado category comprised a hodgepodge of "composers, musicistas, authors of popular song, sambistas," record label owners, and representatives of foreign societies—"all," as the *Boletim* put it, "who have a stake in defending Author's Rights."[46] Despite the expansive language, sócios filiados remained marginalized within the organization.

Two 1928 laws—the Lei Getúlio Vargas and Decree 18.527, which called for close relationships between the SBAT and police censors—helped crystallize divisions in the entertainment world. The Getúlio Vargas Law (Decree 5.492) bolstered author's rights protections and regulated rela- tionships between artistas and theater managers and owners.[47] In com- mon and legal parlance, "artista" was a flexible term that referred to any one of a number of occupations, including musicians, painters, and composers. An initial draft of Decree 5.492, written by SBAT members, defined artistas as "the artistic cast of [theater] companies and assistants [*auxiliares*] of the same companies: set designers, secretaries, administrators, propagandists, ticket takers, choir members, dancers, cast members, prompters, musicians, stage managers, ward robe managers, archivists, electricians, carpenters, fashion designers, doormen, and tailors." The final version classified them with similarly broad terms, and Decree 18.527 lumped musicians together with actors, magicians, comedians, dancers, and singers.[48] Both laws separated authors from instrumentalists, artists, and assistants. While Decrees 5.492 and 18.527 restated and expanded existing author's rights provisions, neither law enumerated obligations for composers or playwrights. In contrast, both laws listed responsibilities that artistas, auxiliares, and theater owners had to fulfill to enjoy their rights. While an author's intellectual property would be honored without question, the rights of musicians who played music but did not necessarily write it were guaranteed only through the fulfillment of specific obligations.

In theory, a 1931 law that regulated unions chipped away at the wall between authors and artistas and between intellectual and manual labor. "There is no distinction," the law held, between, "manual laborers and intellectual laborers."[49] In reality, de facto assumptions about the relative value of different kinds of work were entrenched and widespread. In the mid-1920s, the National Labor Council suggested that "intellectual workers" should receive holidays to provide respite from their "intense mental effort." Manual laborers, by contrast, were prone to "latent vices" and could not be trusted with free time. It would be unnecessary, the council reasoned, to provide rest for "a manual worker, whose brain does not expend energy."[50] Even Rio's Metropolitan Football League separated clubs into tiers based on type of employment. The first level included teams whose players earned more than 300 mil-réis per month and "drew no means" from manual labor, which the league contrasted with work that demanded "intelligence." Teams whose players worked as day laborers, errand boys, and in other menial jobs constituted a second level.[51]

Musicians hoped that Vargas might help shatter this kind of hierarchy. During the marche aux flambeaux and through much of his reign, the law named for him was hailed as a foundational text for musicians' rights. But while extending protections for composers, it also limited musicians' ability to perform where and for whom they liked and tempered important rights with obligations and punishments. The law combined and altered several earlier drafts, one of which was conceived in 1925 by SBAT leaders working under the guidance of an honorary member, Armando Vidal (Leite Ribeiro); Vidal was a powerful lawyer and an auxiliary district chief of police who, during the 1910s and '20s, zealously championed police anti-vice campaigns.[52] The drafts eventually found their way to the desk of Vargas, at the time a representative from Rio Grande do Sul. In 1928, after nearly three years of stunted debate and bureaucratic delay, the law was signed into effect.

The final version of the law demanded greater transparency from the owners of theaters and show houses, who had frustrated composers, playwrights, and authorities with lax and uneven payment of royalties and salaries. The law made all theater companies subject to Brazil's Commercial Code, provided for greater oversight of all public performances with "lucrative ends," held *empresários* (club managers/owners) responsible for author's rights payments and salaries, and provided artistas and auxiliares with access to theater financial records.

In exchange for these things, artistas and auxiliares would adhere to a strict code of conduct. An initial draft of the Lei Getúlio Vargas held that any employee who missed a show for an avoidable cause or who did not give forty-eight hours' notice would not only forfeit a full 20 percent of his or her monthly salary but also be forced to spend eight days in jail! At Vidal's urging, the jail stay was removed, but the fine was increased to 30 percent. Performers were forbidden from diverging from original scripts, a rule that the law's architects suggested would protect the sanctity of an author's creation. In his own first draft of the law, Vargas acknowledged abuses not only on the part of empresários, but also artistas, who, he wrote, "with the offer of better earnings, or for inferior motives, break agreements, abandoning one company and going to work for another." The law's final version required theaters and show houses to provide employees with a signed statement acknowledging that all obligations had been fulfilled. Without such proof, individuals would be barred from future employment elsewhere.

Author and State

In bringing musicians, authors, and the state closer together, the Lei Getúlio Vargas represents something of a culmination of processes two decades in the making. In 1912 and 1915, the protections outlined in Law 496, Brazil's original author's rights law, were extended to foreign authors, an important step in formalizing Brazil's international and commercial music relations.[53] In 1916, after nearly a century of debate, a civil code was passed. The code extended the period for which an author (or author's heirs) maintained ownership over a piece to sixty years from the former fifty. One section delineated general rules regarding authorship and, for the most part, either reproduced or bolstered Law 496. A second section regulated relations between authors and the companies that published their work—and frequently owned rights to it. Once sold, a song could be marketed per the desires of the record label, which set the price and the number of copies issued. The label could not, however, make changes to the piece without the author's approval. A third section in the civil code provided guidelines for the theater, where authors were forbidden from making changes to their work without the theater owner's approval.[54]

While the civil code provided more details than previous legislation, it did not settle all debates. Law 496 required authors to register their pieces at the National Library. In addition to creating problems for individuals who did not live in Rio or otherwise lacked the means to register their compositions, the law made no provisions for pieces written before 1898. As they drafted the civil code, some jurists and legislators sought to do away with the registration requirement, which, they felt, unfairly made registration "the origin of the right." The final version of the civil code included only an ambiguous reference to registration, prompting varying interpretations and further confusion.[55] The case of "Pelo telefone" highlights the problems that plagued the system. Donga's author's right petition left doubt about who he thought the song belonged to, but the registration process itself rewarded Donga at the expense of those who claimed to have created the song but were not involved in writing the petition. The larger question of registration was not definitively answered until 1932 in a case concerning "Teu cabelo não nega" (Your hair doesn't lie), an immensely popular Carnival song that helped extend long-standing racist and misogynist depictions of *mulata* figures.[56] The case ended with the judge concluding that authorship could exist without registration.[57] In theory, the ruling would help artists without the means to register a song, but in reality the literate, well-connected, wealthy residents of Rio continued to enjoy distinct advantages over others.

In 1920, the federal government made the SBAT an utilidade pública, and in 1925 Rio's local government did the same. As a public entity, the SBAT maintained a unique relationship with the government, not quite a union and tied only informally to the state. A federal decree conferred upon the association three important functions: to represent its members in legal matters, to request payment on their behalf from theater companies, and to sign accords with foreign associations.[58] The society became a public entity thanks largely to the efforts of Armando Vidal. In his police post, Vidal was responsible for monitoring show houses, a task through which he "came to appreciate the necessity of defending literary property in theater." In 1919, he drafted a bill to make the SBAT a public entity and then passed it to a politician friend who presented it to the Senate. When a letter informing the SBAT of Vidal's actions was read, assembled members broke into applause. The society hung his portrait at their headquarters. To Vidal, the SBAT represented an ideal ally in the uphill battle of enforcing intellectual property law. In an article in *Revista Policial*, he wrote, "It is impossible for the author to be omnipresent in defending his rights. Only societies of authors, with branches throughout the Nation, will be able to effectively achieve this end. Among us, this noble duty falls to the SBAT. . . . The Society can lend great services to the police."[59]

Two years after the SBAT became a public entity, Brazil ratified the 1908 Bern Convention, an international accord that regulated the protection of literary and artistic work.[60] Doing so bolstered the SBAT's relations with foreign societies and paved the way for more comprehensive domestic laws.[61] The adoption of Bern and the utilidade pública designation preceded legislation that would shape intellectual property defense for years to come. In 1924, Decree 4.790 gave authors the right to review the records of any establishment playing their music. The decree also stated that no composition or theatrical piece could be executed in an establishment charging entrance fees without the composer's prior authorization. Authors could also request the closure of unauthorized shows, but to do so they were required to present an advertisement for the show, evidence that was not always easy for them to obtain because bar and club owners did not advertise every performance.[62] In theory, as representatives of composers and playwrights, the SBAT was responsible for calling upon theater owners to open their books, but it does not seem that the society possessed much leverage to do so. That would have to come from the police, and, Vidal's support aside, SBAT leaders frequently complained about both the impunity of theater owners and police inaction. But while the society lacked muscle, it was still able to secure payments through other means. Political connections helped, as did close relationships with prominent entertainment moguls.

Decree 4.790 solidified the SBAT's policing role and made censorship and author's rights two parts of the same machine. All theater pieces were made to undergo a censor's scrutiny. Theater owners presented the censor with set, unalterable scripts and programs and with proof that the work's author had approved the performance in question.[63] In 1928, Decree 18.527 brought censorship and intellectual property defense even closer by calling for cooperation between police censors and author's rights societies like the SBAT and by extending the principal of prior censorship. Under the 1928 law, theaters and clubs were required to furnish the police with programs for all shows as well as contracts signed by the authors. As a result, performances came to be screened for inappropriate content through the same process used to secure payments and verify composers and playwrights' authorization.[64]

While the SBAT called on police to enforce payments from club and theater owners, the society also embraced its own mediating role and openly encouraged censorship as a means for maintaining decency and protecting property rights. Throughout the 1920s, the society communicated with authorities through letters and face-to-face meetings, often several times a week. In 1928, the prefect met with several SBAT representatives and asked the society to monitor plays at the Teatro Casino and to limit casino performances to theater companies "comprised of good elements."[65] A year earlier, authorities requested that the SBAT serve as "intermediary" in the enforcement of a recently devised payment procedure for cinemas.[66] In 1930, the association received an invitation to attend a penal and penitentiary conference.[67]

The SBAT had various motivations for enthusiastically encouraging censorship. To begin, the association used its relationship with the police as leverage for gaining state patronage. At an SBAT-sponsored conference in 1924, participants advocated a tax on foreign theater companies to fund national ones. In return, authorities would receive "reasonable favors," including "instructive" and "patriotic" shows for children and a 6PM end time for all performances. In addition, the SBAT would "edit morally offensive pieces" and support censorship "in liberal molds and in accordance with our social and political culture."[68] The society also embraced censorship because its members saw themselves as defenders of national interests and cultural values. To SBAT leaders, censorship was vital to both. Further, without knowing who was performing what, enforcing author's rights payments would be impossible. As a result, the censor's office became a barometer for the health of local theater. In 1925, the SBAT cited the number of plays censored during the year as a sign of "encouraging" growth of national theater.[69]

In 1933, the society protested what it saw to be the impunity of radio stations, which were not subject to the same oversight as theater and often avoided making author's rights payments.[70] When the SBAT became increasingly vocal in its demands, Rio's radio stations went silent for several days in protest. Though securing payments from radio stations was a continuous challenge, the SBAT came out on top in this standoff thanks to the police, who successfully pressured stations to make payments.[71] Radio's ability to withhold payments not only threatened the SBAT's economic health but also offended some members' notions of decency. In 1932, the *Boletim* reprinted an article from the *Correio da Manhã*, which pointed out how easy it was to tell that radio shows were not subjected to the censor. "Singers of sambas and modinhas have a great time and outdo themselves with their improvisations . . . their licentiousness [is] poorly hidden by the rapidity of their beat." With radios accessible to "maybe half of Rio de Janeiro," the author continued, this was no small concern. The medium, he concluded, should be subjected to the same regulations as theater and cinema.[72] The SBAT saw in most forms of entertainment lucrative, educational, and moralizing potential, but theater was unique. The society held playwriting competitions to honor "theater's good name," and leadership took every opportunity to publicly celebrate their craft's contribution to national progress. In this context, censorship was not just an economic tool that aided tracking and collecting payments, but also a cultural one that guaranteed decency and helped separate "licentious" sambistas from theater's "good elements."

The Limits of Synthesis and Progress

As a kind of proto–police force bent on establishing and maintaining theater's good name and protecting national artistic production, the SBAT both fostered and hindered the projects of Rio's Afro-Brazilian musicians. While the society counted among its members several influential black artists, including Donga, Pixinguinha, and Benjamin de Oliveira, the distinction that the *Correio da Manhã* article drew between samba and theater is indicative of larger divisions within the entertainment class, which marginalized or pigeon-holed popular musicians, black male artists of all genres, and most women, black or white.

In 1925, on its eighth anniversary, the society honored Chiquinha Gonzaga by unveiling her portrait during a festival at society headquarters. Various members of the leadership spoke, pointing out Gonzaga's many accomplishments and emphasizing the role that women should play in developing Brazilian theater. The ceremony included a number of symbolic gestures, such as the portrait's presentation by female members and the reading of a poem written for Gonzaga. In the keynote address, the society treasurer Avelino de Andrade enthusiastically described the "heat" of Gonzaga's notes, which "rise to the clouds, illuminating nighttime serenades, snatching away souls, igniting hearts." "Gonzaga," he declared, "is a musical volcano!" Her oeuvre was "hot" and otherworldly, full of "enchanted" chords and "mysterious music that could make even the trees dance, if the author wished, one day transforming the forest into a dance hall!" One of her compositions, Andrade said, was "magnetized by a strange spiritual force, receiving from the heavens the revelation of a beautiful polka, sung by angels during an Edenic dream."[73]

Gonzaga was said to represent not only a magical musical force, but also a particular brand of feminism linked to national progress. A vocal abolitionist and proponent of women's rights, Gonzaga often stepped outside the bounds of expected female behavior. After she separated from her husband, her parents disowned her and forbade her to see her children. The SBAT leadership presented her in less threatening terms. Especially during the 1880s, supporters of abolition often heralded the end of slavery as a sign of national advancement and of Brazil's burgeoning, racially mixed republic. It was in a similar unifying spirit that the society celebrated Gonzaga's past militancy and her role as an "educator" of women. Andrade noted how Gonzaga's career could serve to inspire "superior women" and compared her to the "mystical maiden" Joan of Arc, who proved that women were not "simply defenseless, human dolls." Gonzaga "honored the feminist cause," Andrade said,

> not with that feminism that exposes the nude flesh of virgins to
> dust on the street—that obscures the conscience, that attacks modesty, that provokes ridicule, that blows wide open the abyss, that, in
> the end, renders useless man's companheira, stripping her, slowly,
> of even her physical enchantments—but instead the feminism that
> demands posts of responsibility in the government, in the selection
> of leaders, in the elaboration of laws, in the guarantee of order, in
> the spiritual fight for the progress and honor of povos![74]

Andrade also lauded Gonzaga as a staunch defender of author's rights. "No one [could] imitate" her "mysterious" music, and she would never stoop to plagiarism. "In her artistic conscience, the appropriation of someone else's thoughts is a capital crime." As a symbol of acceptable feminism and a defender of author's rights, Andrade saw in Gonzaga a true patriot.[75] In recounting the story about her music being played surreptitiously in Europe, he borrowed from Eduardo das Neves's famous song about Alberto Santos Dumont and commented, "Once again, Europe bowed before Brazil." In closing, Andrade appealed to all Brazilian women, asking them to carry Gonzaga's banner and "prove to the world, the value of the Brazilian woman." Doing so, he said, would require a "nationalization" of music halls and careful cultivation of Brazilian music.

The roles that the SBAT ascribed to Gonzaga and other women diverged sharply from those it reserved for men. While addressing the General Assembly in 1925, Alvarenga Fonseca called himself a "disciplined soldier."[76] Women, by contrast, were spiritual, childlike beings, prone to stray from their assigned task of preserving and transmitting Brazilian culture. Officer Iveta Ribeiro wrote, "It is necessary to teach the Brazilian woman that a career in theater is not made glorious through the triumphs of physical beauty, nor should it lead to a path that deviates from the one traced by God for all women."[77] Though Gonzaga and several other women held important positions within the SBAT, the membership was largely male. In 1935, nearly two-thirds of registered theater workers were men, though that gap soon closed considerably. Similar disparities pervaded other fields of intellectual production. Between 1935 and 1939, nine out of every ten individuals who registered and claimed authorship of original works of music, art, or literature in Rio were male (see table 9).

One SBAT member asserted that the association defended "the things and people of our land." Theater, he continued, is "*synthesis* . . . the union of thought of hundreds and thousands of people animated by the most varied and contradictory feelings and viewpoints."[78] In 1925, a delegation from São Paulo visited SBAT's Rio headquarters, where Fonseca noted that Europe was watching Brazil for innovation not only in theater but all "artistic manifestations." "We are," he said, "messengers of a new idea, representatives of a new race, caretakers of a young land which blossoms and flowers magnificently towards the future." Fonseca's comments were largely unexceptional, just one more example of the growing belief that Brazil was home to a special new race. His speech became more note-

TABLE 9. Works Registered (Organized by Author's Gender) (1935, 1937–39)

	1935		1937		1938	
	Male	Female	Male	Female	Male	Female
BN	92	12	97	9	124	19
ENBA	11	0	28	1	12	0
INM	25	1	20	5	21	5
Annual Total/(%)	128/(91)	13/(9)	145/(91)	15/(9)	157/(87)	24/(13)

BN: Biblioteca Nacional; ENBA: Escola Nacional de Belas Artes; INM: Instituto Nacional de Música.
Source: ESXX. Cultura, Various.

worthy when it turned to São Paulo. "Who better to lead this movement of spiritual emancipation than this brilliant Pleiad of men of letters and artists from São Paulo . . . ?" São Paulo, he continued, "is distinguished in the history of civilizers of our country with the mark of great precursor. The epic of territorial *bandeirismo* corresponds today with the shining epic of mental bandeirismo."[79] Bandeirismo refers to the *bandeirantes*, São Paulo–based bands of men, who as early as the seventeenth century explored the hinterlands in search of precious metals and Indians to enslave, staking territorial claims along the way. The fact that some bandeirantes were themselves of Portuguese and indigenous descent did not prevent São Paulo intellectuals from later constructing a regional history that treated people of color as anomalies in a march to progress. This construction, Barbara Weinstein shows, "created a highly successful 'fictive ethnicity.'"[80] Considering Brazil's regional rivalries, it is significant and perhaps surprising that the Rio-based SBAT would publicly and enthusiastically celebrate the São Paulo faction. The bandeirantes were part of São Paulo "exceptionalism," which depicted the homonymous city and state as a white, civilized island in multiracial Brazil.

While Rio continued to be the center of Brazil's entertainment world, São Paulo was also a crucial, populous center for theater, radio, and recording. As the SBAT grew, it struggled to assert itself throughout the vast national territory as regional factionalism, poor transportation and communication, and independent and corrupt regional agents hampered the enforcement of rules and the collection of payments. Of all the locales outside Rio, the SBAT focused its greatest energy on São Paulo, where it established a permanent headquarters. If partially meant to curry favor with individuals there, Fonseca's speech also indicates that São Paulo ex-

1939		Total Works Registered		
Male	Female	Male/(%)	Female/(%)	Total/(%)
117	11	430/(89)	51/(11)	481/(100)
7	0	58/(98)	1/(2)	59/(100)
16	3	82/(85)	14/(15)	96/(100)
140/(91)	14/(9)	570/(90)	66/(10)	636/(100)

ceptionalism, paradoxically, had adherents elsewhere in Brazil. Fonseca expressed confidence that Brazil's "new race" could incorporate and even be led by "white" São Paulo. That imagined identity and the age of "mental bandeirismo" linked up nicely with the images cultivated by the SBAT's homens de letras, who held their cerebral and intellectual work in contrast with what was repeatedly portrayed as the more spiritual production of Afro-Brazilians and women.

Members of the SBAT frequently marked the difference between high and low art in racial terms. Vagalume, who listed the SBAT presidents Abadie Farias Rosa and Alvarenga Fonseca among his *grandes amigos* in *Na roda do samba*, noted a "certain prejudice" among theater artists, whom, he recalled, tended to look down upon those who worked in the circus.[81] A 1928 *Boletim* article discussed *mambembes*, a word of Kimbundu origin that, in Brazil, refers to traveling theater troupes, generally understood to be black and of modest or mediocre quality.[82] A dictionary of popular slang defined mambembes as "insignificant," "vulgar," and constituted by *atores ambulantes*.[83] The SBAT writer used the word to refer to theater groups that surreptitiously avoided paying the society for plays and compositions by its members. The equation of Afro-Brazilian theater with amateurism and the evasion of author's rights payments resonated with deep-rooted and long-lasting assumptions about blackness and authorship. The article ran at a particularly auspicious time, just after the brief heyday of the Companhia Negra de Revistas, the black theater troupe launched in the mid-1920s by De Chocolat. The Companhia enjoyed a short period of success in 1926 and 1927. In 1927, during a meeting of the SBAT's Conselho Deliberativo, the society president Manuel Bastos Tigre urged the organization to do all that it could to prevent the Companhia from touring in

TABLE 10. Registered Artistas and Auxiliares (Organized by Color and Gender) (1935–37)

	Color				Gender	
Year	% Branca (White)	% Mestiça (Mixed)	% Amarela (Yellow)	% Preta (Black)	% Male	% Female
1935 (n = 1,924)	< 89	< 9	< 1	< 3	65	35
1936 (n = 519)	< 96	< 4	0	< 2	54	46
1937* (n = 352/356)	< 97	< 3	0	< 1	50.3	49.7
Total (n = 2,795/2,799)	< 91	< 7	< 1	< 3	61	39

*Racial data are not provided for auxiliares. 352 artistas + 4 auxiliares listed.
Source: ESXX. Cultura, Various.

Argentina and Uruguay, which, Bastos Tigre remarked, would represent an "attack on the pillars of our civilization." A series of letters and articles printed in the press, combined with behind-the-scenes pressure, nixed the trip.[84]

On the Outside Looking In

Between 1935 and 1937, the IBGE counted 2,710 registered artistas and aux-iliares in Rio, less than 3 percent of whom were black. The vast majority of those counted by the IBGE were semiliterate white men, and nearly all were said to support themselves on artistic work alone (see tables 10 and 11).[85] In theory, registered workers were easier to keep track of and therefore less likely to disregard contracts and bounce from establishment to establishment. Registration also provided artistas and auxiliares with proof of employment, no small thing in a city where vagrancy codes were still enforced and where personal identification, property titles, and other written forms of documentation helped solidify a hierarchy that dramati-cally favored legal over extralegal resources and spheres.[86]

Whatever form of identification the Afro-carioca actor João Felippe carried with him in 1931, it was not enough to prevent a neighbor from reporting him to the police as a feiticeiro. According to the *Diário Ca-rioca*, the neighbor called authorities as Felippe prepared himself for a

TABLE 11. Registered Artistas and Auxiliares by Source of Income and
Literacy/Education (1935–37)

Year (artistas/auxiliaries)	Source of Income*		Literacy/Education			
	% A	% B	% X	% Y	% Z	% R
1935 (n = 1,835/1,924)	89.5	10.5	< 1	< 58	< 40	< 3
1936 (n = 515/519)	93.8	6.2	0	< 46	< 52	< 3
1937* (n = 352)	< 100	< 1	< 3	< 61	< 37	0
Total (n = 2,702/2,795)	< 92	< 9	< 1	< 56	< 42	< 3

*Artistas only; A = None besides theater (*Vivendo só da profissão*); B = Outside resources (*Vivendo com outros recursos*); X = Illiterate (*Analfabeto*); Y = Limited literacy (*Sabendo mal ler e escrever*); Z = Literate (*Sabendo ler e escrever bem*); R = Higher education (*Com instrução superior*). *Source*: ESXX. Cultura, Various.

show with the theater troupe Companhia Mulata Brasileira. Upon seeing a "black rooster" inside Felippe's rented room, the neighbor feared that he had stumbled upon a witch's den, but the police soon found that the rooster was made of paper, and they released Felippe. Throughout the false alarm, the paper reported, the actor remained in good spirits, "laughing a lot" as he recounted the incident. A photo above the article displayed the dark-skinned actor, described as *de cor preta*, dressed in a dark suit, bowtie, and crisp white shirt. "In the end," Felippe told the paper, "I'm happy because this just gives more publicity to our show, and all I suffered was a little fright."[87]

Noel Campos, a white actor from São Paulo, did not fare so well in his own brush with the carioca police. On 13 March 1934 at 3:30 in the afternoon, Campos was arrested for what an officer and witness both described as "wandering in [a state of] laziness."[88] The police and witnesses also asserted that Campos was homeless and that he lacked gainful employment, but their real complaint was that he was a "passive pederast."[89] In a written statement, an advocate protested the "humiliation" that Campos had experienced while "at the mercy" of the police's "perverse instincts." Campos was known, the statement read, "in theater circles as a prestigious actor," having performed for years at various theaters, recently as a dancer at Rio's Teatro Municipal. A playbill and the actor's identification card were attached to the statement. A police investigator also testified that he had visited Rio's Teatro Municipal and verified that Campos once worked there. All of this was enough to convince the judge to dismiss the case and release Campos.

On the surface, it would seem that the fact that Campos was white, employed as an actor, and in possession of legal, written proof of employment helped him avoid the kind of punishment reserved for less fortunate individuals. However, here again, the judge's decisions proved to be a poor indicator of individual experience. Like countless others who were acquitted of vagrancy charges, Campos spent weeks in jail. In Rio, where the process, more than the sentence, was the punishment, even a solid career and a state-issued identification card could help only so much.[90] Being a registered actor might provide cachet and income, but dark skin or sexual orientation could trump all and leave individuals like Felippe and Campos at the whim of the police.

THE RISE OF THE SBAT had several important implications for Rio's Afro-Brazilian musicians. Perhaps most significant is that the organization facilitated the approximation between censorship and author's rights protection. In Rio, where the censor's office had the support of a number of influential artists, censorship was not simply a tool imposed by an authoritarian government. It was also embraced and implemented through SBAT artists, who functioned as both a proto-police force and a proto-corporatist association, responsible for creating a buffer between citizen and state. The society's cozy relationship with the police also further dismantled received wisdoms reproduced again and again through the punishment paradigm. As the history of the SBAT makes clear, a surprising degree of cooperation and alliance linked police and entertainers and inspired artists to seek assistance from even the notorious anti-vice officer Vidal.

The formation of the SBAT also suggests how professionalization was marked by competing and often divisive projects. When Pixinguinha and Donga took their places at the front of the marche aux flambeaux and presented their demands to Vargas, they held themselves as representatives of all Brazilian artists. But despite the appearance of a unified entertainment class, most popular musicians and Afro-Brazilian entertainers were sidelined, if not excluded altogether. Ascendant black artists like Donga and Pixinguinha had options and opportunities largely unavailable to Afro-Brazilian women like Tia Ciata or Deo Costa, but few official structures through which to promote or protect their interests. The SBAT was, at its core, an institution of and for playwrights and homens de letras, categories widely equated with whiteness.

The SBAT's role in institutionalizing and exacerbating divisions within the entertainment industry is particularly significant when considered in the context of the rich web that linked popular theater, circus, and music in early twentieth-century Rio. The examples of Benjamin de Oliveira and Eduardo das Neves, who owned and ran circus troupes and fostered vibrant exchanges among circus, theater, and music, suggest that there existed at one time the potential, however tenuous, for the emergence of a larger, more democratic entertainment class. That potential was severely blunted by the SBAT and the distinctions made between artistas and authors. Our knowledge of João Felippe's brush with the law is limited. But even if he took the incident in stride, as the *Diário Carioca* reported, the fact that a neighbor called the police to report him for "witchcraft" suggests that nineteenth- and early twentieth-century fears continued to follow black entertainers—even those who were well dressed and employed—deep into samba's golden age. The divisions and distinctions that the SBAT helped institutionalize continued to shape the entertainment world even during the late 1930s and early 1940s, when, as I will show in the next chapter, musicians broke away from the SBAT and formed their own associations.

8

EVERYWHERE AND NOWHERE

The UBC and the Consolidation of Racial and Gendered Difference

Between 1934 and 1937, Vargas effectively subordinated regional and state interests beneath a centralized federal government and elaborated a corporatist structure around which to organize society. A slew of laws and decrees, and separate constitutions signed in 1934 and 1937, shaped the relationship between capital and labor and between employers and employees.[1] Musicians occupied an awkward, ill-defined place within the Vargas labor structure. Some worked in radio, or at clubs, casinos, and bars. Composers' work continued to be catch-as-catch-can. One moment they were riding high with a successful hit, the next moment out of work or struggling to assert ownership of a disputed work. The categories around which the labor codes were organized rarely matched the experience of most artists. The SBAT was an unreliable institution for anyone outside theater, and there existed few regulations regarding payments to composers. Most singers and dancers bounced from venue to venue on short contracts. While record executives were in some sense bosses, their relationship with composers and entertainers hardly resembled the employer-employee bonds that governed factory work, for example.

With the help of journalists and record executives, during the 1930s and 1940s musicians created their own author's rights organizations. One of their intentions was to clearly define musicians as mental laborers and to gain distance from blue-collar workers. But most legislation either lumped artists together with other workers or ignored them entirely. As noted in the previous chapter, a landmark 1931 unionization law declared there to be no distinction between "manual" and "intellectual" laborers (*operários manuais* and *operários intelectuais*). And while the SBAT clearly distinguished theater artists from musicians, the Consolidation of the Brazil Labor Laws blithely referred to all entertainers as "theater artists and similar persons" (*artistas de teatros e congêneres*).[2] The 1934 constitution prescribed that the Câmara dos Deputados be composed of 350 elected members and 50 others chosen by professional, employer, and labor associations. Of those final 50 spots, only 3 were reserved for all "liberal professions."[3] Vargas's stated desires to "homogenize" national culture, to structure society around large, symbiotic classes, and to elevate communal, collective interests over those of the individual provided few obvious clues about how composers would delineate or protect their artistic creations.[4]

While musicians did not have a clear place in Vargas's labor schema, in other respects they were front and center, the stars of a lucrative samba wave that definitively linked the music to national identity. In the first three years that the SBAT distinguished between the pequenos and grandes direitos in its records, music property rights rose dramatically, from 11 percent of the money distributed to members and affiliates in 1929 to more than half in 1932 (see table 8 in chapter 7). That increase coincided with the rise of the Estácio Sound, the beginning of samba's golden age, the birth of commercial radio, and the "officialization" of Carnival, a process described below. The sum of all of this was not an integrated, more equitable system of distribution, but rather a collection of new and expanding arenas of opportunity for composers and performers, some of whom were well positioned to capitalize and others who were not.

The "Officialization" of Carnival

Rio's fist samba schools came into existence during the late 1920s, just before Vargas ascended to power. During the 1930s, as formal political avenues closed, the schools became crucial, if ultimately limited, vehicles for organization and expression. The escolas built on foundations laid in place by earlier Carnival groups: the ranchos, cordões, and clubs that had animated the city's festivals for years. In the early 1930s, federal and local government agencies in Rio made available to samba schools funding previously provided only to the city's grandes sociedades. The money, part of a larger push to attract tourists to Carnival and Rio, accompanied rules about the content of each school's parade entry. Wind instruments were prohibited, and each school had to base its performances on a "national theme."[5] The schools also had to include an *ala das baianas*, a group of women dressed in clothing associated with Afro-Brazilian women from Bahia. The "officialization" of Carnival began in earnest in 1932, during soccer's off-season, when the sports publication *Mundo Sportivo* sponsored the first formal Carnival parade competition among schools. In 1934, the Rio City Council did the same, awarding cash prizes for the top three finishers.

While these events signaled an important shift, they were not altogether new. Like their predecessors, the samba schools developed brand appeal, fostering loyalty akin to that seen in sports. Some schools produced and sold musical instruments in order to raise funds and provide greater visibility and name recognition.[6] Even *Mundo Sportivo*'s landmark 1932 competition was not without precedent. Similar events were staged among ranchos and cordões as early as 1906. Escola composers competed against one another in 1929, but without a parade.[7] Formal and informal contests among composers and Carnival groups had existed for years, and the press had long taken interest in delineating Carnival successes and failures, often through competitions with monetary prizes attached.[8]

In 1933, a group of samba school directors and members met to brainstorm ways to protect and advance their interests. The initial meeting led to the creation, more than a year later, of the União das Escolas de Sambas (Union of Samba Schools, UES), an organization that comprised some thirty schools and perhaps twelve thousand members.[9] The group's statutes include the regulations about wind instruments, baianas, and "national themes," but it is difficult to know how or where the regulations first originated.[10] It is possible that the União merely vetted guidelines proposed by the administration of Getúlio Vargas. But UES actions suggest that the organization did not simply embrace or accept rules imposed from above.[11] In a 1935 letter, Flávio Costa, a UES co-founder and an Afro-Brazilian escola pioneer, described to the prefect Pedro Ernesto the UES's dedication to "cultivate real national music" and requested assistance in protecting the city's "true authors."[12] The works of those authors, Costa wrote, was being exploited and stolen by "third parties." In Ernesto, Costa had a friendly and powerful ally. Ernesto gained popularity for his work in Rio's favelas and enjoyed several escolas' support and Vagalume's admiration.[13] Ernesto responded quickly to Costa, three days later issuing a decree that made the union responsible for distributing municipal funds to each school. In its statutes, the UES defined itself as "an organ to defend and fight for the interests and aspirations of samba and its schools."

The group's stated purposes included control of the Carnival festivities and of all "propaganda" related to samba. Article 1b stated the organization's intention "to communicate directly with the Federal and Municipal authorities in order to obtain favors and other acts which will benefit our members."[14] Though hardly intent on confronting or subverting state authority, the UES was adept at molding itself in a way that allowed it to survive where other organizations could not. In November 1937, Vargas established his dictatorial Estado Novo and several weeks later abolished all political parties. Frederico Trota, a vocal supporter of government funding for the schools, was among the political figures whose careers were cut short by the Estado Novo. The UES named the trophy for its parade after him. In a public statement, the union declared that with the trophy "the people of the escolas de samba show that we can still elect someone as our representative."[15]

Symbolic acts like the "election" of Trota, important as they were, did little to chip away at the Vargas administration's remarkable ability to deflect and redirect potential critiques and challenges. In April 1937, eight samba schools filed a civil complaint against the directorate of the UES. The schools accused the UES directors of malfeasance and asked a judge to intervene on their behalf. The trouble began at Carnival when Dulcídio Gonçalves, the supervising police official, abruptly halted the parade, sending his officers home and cutting off the nearby electricity supply. Per government-UES stipulations, a panel judged the procession and issued cash prizes to the top three schools. But because the parade ended early, only half of the escolas were able to perform. The reasons behind Gonçalves's actions are unclear, but he was already persona non grata in some samba circles, believed to have forced Paulo da Portela to change his escola's name from Vai Como Pode (Come as You Can) to the more formal sounding Grêmio Recreativo Escola de Samba Portela (Portela Recreational Union and Samba School). Whatever Gonçalves's intentions in 1937, the results of his actions were clear to the schools not allowed to march: no prize money and a bitter, unsatisfying conclusion to months of work and preparation.[16]

While the escolas criticized Gonçalves of acting "tempestuously," it was the UES that they formally accused of violating their right to compete for the prize money. That right, the aggrieved schools pointed out in a court petition, was guaranteed by the union. "The gesture of the [UES]," the complaint read, "represents an attack on the rights of the claimants, who wish to make those rights stand up through the appropriate channels."[17] Available documents do not indicate how or whether the case was resolved, but the claim itself is instructive. Rather than directing their complaint against Gonçalves and the police, the schools targeted the UES, which was founded and maintained by escola directors and members. At least in the minds of the complainants, the union had departed from its mission "to defend and fight for the interests and aspirations of samba and its schools." As a result, some schools missed out on the prestige and publicity that the parade could provide, as well as the lucrative winner's earnings. The schools also felt deprived of a larger investment. To join the union, schools had to pay a 100$000 fee (US $8.67 in 1937), plus 15$000 (US $1.30) per month. In 1937, Rio's tourist board provided 40:000$000 (US $3,457) for the parade, to be divided among the union's thirty-two schools and to cover UES "administrative expenses." That sum was scant compared to the 150:000$000 (US $12,966) provided to the city's storied grandes sociedades, but significantly larger than the 2:500$000 (US $207) that the union received in 1935.[18] The first-place prize for the parade was almost enough to cover a year of dues to the union. Though conceptualized and created independently of Vargas's corporatist machinery, in 1937 the organization served a valuable function for the state. Despite the fact that the police shut down the parade and prevented half of the schools from participating, it was the UES that faced the brunt of the ensuing complaints and legal action.

"Dissidents"

Like the UES, the SBAT had an awkward relationship with the state that ultimately made it a shield against critiques that might otherwise have been directed at the government. As the party responsible for collecting and distributing royalties, it received the brunt of complaints from artists who felt they were not receiving their fair share. Vagalume urged the organization to do more to protect "unknown sambistas," a plea that largely fell on deaf ears.[19] In 1938, a group of musicians and journalists, frustrated with their marginal position within the SBAT, parted ways with the organization and founded the Associação Brasileira de Compositores e Autores (Brazilian Association of Composers and Authors, ABCA). Three years later, a separate group established a Composers' Department within the SBAT (Departamento dos Compositores, SBAT-DC). In 1942, under the guidance of ABCA leaders, members from the two splinter groups remade the ABCA into the União Brasileira de Compositores (Union of Brazilian Composers, UBC). During the 1940s, the UBC became the most significant and influential musician organization in Brazil. It collected and distributed vast amounts of cash, advocated for its members, developed ties with foreign associations, shaped legislation, and established outposts throughout the country.[20]

Many of the ABCA's founding members developed strategies and goals while at the SBAT, and they carried these with them after they left the organization. Nonetheless, the ABCA defined itself in opposition to the SBAT and frequently accused it of wrongdoing. Like the SBAT, the ABCA was overwhelmingly white and male. Of the 411 individuals whose names appeared on its member list in 1941, less than twenty were women and even fewer were mixed-race or black. Buci Moreira and Príncipe Pretinho (Little Black Prince, José Luiz da Costa) were the two most well-known members of color. The society's directorate was dominated by a small cast of white musicians and journalists, including Alberto Ribeiro, Lamartine Babo, Carlos Braga, and Oswaldo Santiago.

A photo in the tenth-anniversary issue of the UBC's *Boletim Social* depicts two white members dressed in suits, poised with serious expressions etched on their faces. One stares down at a checkerboard, while the other, pen in hand, appears to work on either a musical score or association business. The caption below the image describes the two men "disputando damas, isto é:—uma partida de damas." The caption plays on the double meaning of the word *damas*, which can mean either "ladies" or "checkers." The background is dominated by a large painting of black men, dressed in rustic clothes, joyously singing and playing a pandeiro, a scraper, and an afoxê. The men could be longshoremen or slaves.[21] The painting, the suited men, and the damas reflect long-standing racialized and gendered hierarchies—white male leaders and authors, female objects, and black raw material—that were reproduced within the UBC and other author's rights associations.

Members of the ABCA and then the UBC declared themselves to be nothing less than architects of a revolution, one that would lift composers to new heights. A pamphlet printed to commemorate the ABCA's third anniversary accused the SBAT of handing out "crumbs" and likened the society's attempt to "destroy" its musicians to Saturn devouring his children.[22] The ABCA members called themselves "dissidents" but only within the music world. In a clear act of deference to the Estado Novo and the ban on political parties, the ABCA declared that it would "not involve itself in politics, religion, or any other subject unrelated to its mission."[23] The first page of the anniversary publication displayed a regal photo of Vargas, dressed in tuxedo and white tie. The caption below called him "the greatest American statesmen . . . patron of Brazilian laws which protect the right of the author, and the [ABCA's] only honorary member." Like the SBAT, the ABCA was granted status as an utilidade pública, a clear sign of government approval but also an indication of its ill-defined space within the corporatist system.

Founding members relied on publicity and money to lift the ABCA off the ground. For the first, they turned to local journalists who either played or wrote music themselves, or were simply fans, friends, or aficionados. Oswaldo Santiago, who would soon take control of the UBC, was a journalist who dabbled in poetry and music. As a writer for O Malho, he helped launch a public campaign against the SBAT that laid the groundwork for the creation of the ABCA. The search for seed money took the ABCA's founders in a somewhat more surprising direction. Record executives from Rio, São Paulo, and even the United States provided money to the association in return for membership, voting rights, and influence. Among the most important were the Mangione and Vitale families, each of whom built musical empires in Rio and São Paulo. Wallace Downey, a powerful North American movie producer and Columbia Records executive, also belonged to the ABCA.

The marriage of musicians, journalists, and record executives gave the ABCA capital and power but also tied composers to parties that were not always on their side. In some cases, the interests of label owners and musicians dovetailed. Wringing author's rights payments from clubs and bars was an ongoing challenge for musicians and record labels alike. In scores of cases litigated during the 1940s and 1950s, artists and executives sought more effective enforcement of intellectual property law. In other situations—when negotiating contracts or the terms of sale for a given song—composers and executives had decidedly opposite interests. Nonetheless, the resources and influence offered by the likes of the Mangiones, the Vitales, and Downey proved indispensable for musicians seeking to strike out on their own and escape the SBAT's shadow. The alliances produced immediate results for the ABCA and its members. After distributing 133:184$150 (US $7,995) in author's rights payments in 1939, the association distributed more than 200 contos de reis (about US $12,112) to its members in 1940 and nearly the same amount during the first half of 1941.[24]

Though they traded barbs in the press, the ABCA and the SBAT shared common needs and interests and sometimes collaborated to collect and distribute musical property rights. As the creation of the SBAT's Departamento dos Compositores suggests, some musicians preferred to stay with a known entity rather than venture outside. Ironically, though housed within the overwhelmingly white SBAT, the SBAT-DC was more racially diverse than the ABCA. Pixinguinha, Ataulfo Alves, Bide, Wilson Batista, Armando Marçal, and Heitor dos Prazeres all became members of the Departamento.

The contrast between the commission that Vargas received during the marche aux flambeaux—a group fronted by Pixinguinha and Donga—and the overwhelmingly white leadership of the ABCA reflects a larger dynamic affecting Rio's Afro-Brazilian musicians and societal definitions of authorship. As we have seen, the heady rhetoric about entertainment class unity on display in 1930 contrasted with internal tensions and divisions. Donga, Pixinguinha, and other Afro-Brazilian artists surely saw themselves as equals to the most accomplished white artists. But hierarchies within the new author's rights associations reproduced the narrow, racialized definitions of authorship, ownership, and creative genius that marked larger discussions and debates.

The UBC promised to provide an independent institutional home for musicians, while protecting and representing Brazil and its national culture. On both counts, the organization was at least partially successful. Author's rights revenues shot up, and the society provided a welcome alternative to the SBAT. But full institutional autonomy of any kind was elusive in Vargas's Brazil, and while musicians gained power and independence unknown under the SBAT, their livelihood was tied to the state and record executives. The UBC's first president was Ary Barroso, the iconic composer of "Aquarela do Brasil" (Brazilian watercolor) who later became a city councilman. After a falling-out with other leaders, he left the União and in 1946 helped found the UBC's first rival, the Sociedade Brasileira de Autores, Compositores e Editores de Música (Brazilian Society of Musical Authors, Composers, and Label Owners, SBACEM).[25]

Following in the footsteps of the SBAT and the ABCA, the UBC publicly honored men of influence. In June 1943, the society named Israel Souto, Rui Almeida, Abadie Farias Rosa, and the prominent lawyer Miguel Timponi honorary members. As director of the DIP's Cinema and Theater Division, Souto helped regulate the fees paid for musical property rights. Almeida proposed a law to the Rio City Council calling for at least half of the songs played at any performance to be composed by Brazilian musicians. The UBC noted in its *Boletim* that as president of the SBAT, Rosa laid the groundwork for "the establishment of respect for composers' rights."[26] In 1949, the UBC became an utilidade pública.[27]

Throughout the 1940s and 1950s, the UBC, the SBAT, and the SBACEM publicly traded accusations of corruption and wrongdoing. But while the organizations competed for control of what seemed to be an ever-expanding music market—fueled especially by the continued rise of Carnival and radio—they shared a need for protection against foreign interests and for the enforcement of domestic intellectual property law. In the first issue of its *Boletim*, the UBC lauded a recent agreement with the SBAT that reflected the societies' "economic understanding."[28] Souto orchestrated the pact, which prevented the SBAT or the UBC from plundering one another's foreign repertoires. In addition to SBAT and UBC officials, Souto, Vicente Mangione, and Wallace Downey (acting as a representative for the American Society of Composers, Authors and Publishers) were on hand for the signing of the SBAT-UBC agreement.

The inclusion of record executives hardly created a level playing field with them. As an article in the UBC's *Boletim* put it, "The author, almost always, ceded all of his rights [to record companies] in exchange for singular and immediate remuneration." In 1943, a commission formed by the SBAT and the UBC put together a six-point plan to strengthen artists' hands. The proposal suggested that contracts between musicians and editores no longer guarantee the "cession of [all] rights" and instead simply guarantee the label the right to publish a given work. The commission also sought stable price controls, an end to the practice of labels purchasing the rights to songs and never producing them, and more power for musicians and author's rights societies to control relationships with one another and to take action against parties who illegally reproduced protected works.[29] Their proposals went unheeded. Extant laws provided few regulations for the relationship between record companies and authors, and the language in most contracts ceded all rights to the companies. It was not until 1955 that legislation would explicitly state that control of any public presentation of artistic work belonged exclusively to the composer or the author's rights society to which he or she belonged.[30] The UBC hoped that the 1955 law would have "momentous" effect, but the legislation's vague language prompted legal decisions that alternately favored authors and labels and ultimately provided little resolution. Publicly, the

Domestic growth coincided with international expansion. As the SBAT had done for theater, the UBC became Brazil's principal negotiator with foreign music societies. During the 1940s and '50s, the União cultivated relationships with author's rights societies throughout the world. International entertainment magnates such as Downey and Ralph Todd made frequent trips to Rio and often visited the UBC when they did. Leaders of the UBC traveled to Europe, the United States, and throughout Latin America to attend meetings and international intellectual property conferences. In theory, the political and economic pacts signed by the UBC would aid Brazilian composers. With new venues in which their music could be heard and with a formal system for collecting payments in those venues, the future looked bright. Reacting to the creation of Downey's Todámerica Música label, the UBC looked forward hopefully to "an exchange between samba and fox-trot, especially the spread of the first among Uncle Sam's nephews."[42]

On a certain level, such a back-and-forth did take place. Foreign stars came to Brazil, and the UBC's rise coincided with Carmen Miranda's famous trips to the United States and a general increase in the visibility of Brazilian music abroad.[43] In 1957, the União proudly displayed photos from a visit by a distinguished North American who lunched at the presidential palace with Brazilian composers and left behind an autograph that read, "To the UBC. The Best Compliments, Louis Armstrong."[44] Some artists and members of the UBC leadership profited handsomely from international exchanges. Waldir Azevedo's "Delicado" earned more than 1 million cruzeiros from foreign payments alone.[45] The Ministry of Education and Culture gave the UBC 2 million cruzeiros in 1957 (US $26,329) and 3 million in 1958 (US $23,267) to spread Brazilian music abroad.[46]

Though money poured in, distribution and foreign relationships remained uneven. Between 1946 and 1953, thirty-three of every thirty-four cruzeiros that the UBC collected came from songs played in Brazil. While details for distribution are less complete, it is clear that a disproportionately large percentage of the money was sent abroad. In many years, payments to foreign associations and musicians equaled between about one-half and three-quarters of the amount paid to national artists. Overall, the UBC collected many more author rights payments for their international associates than those associates collected for the UBC (see tables 13 and 14). Administrative costs, not all of which were clearly enumerated in the União's records, sucked money from the collection pot before it could be distributed. Thirty-five percent of domestic receipts and 30 percent

TABLE 13. UBC Author's Rights Receipts, Domestic vs. Foreign (1946–53)*

	1946	1947	1948	1949	1950
Domestic (collected in Brazil)	8,011	8,049.9	8,674.7	10,725	12,197.5
Foreign (collected abroad by associate societies)	197	324.6	669.8	210.3	229.3
Misc.	—	—	—	197.6	192.3
Total Receipts	8,208	8,374.5	9,344.5	11,132.9	12,619.1
Domestic: Foreign	41:1	25:1	13:1	51:1	53:1

*Amounts in contos.
Source: AUBC, various.

TABLE 14. Author's Rights Payments (ARPS) vs. Other UBC Payments (1943–53)*

	7/'43–6/'44	7/'44–6/'45	7/'45–12/'45	'46	'47
ARPS	1,648	2,415	1,061	5,566	3,828
To Domestic Authors/ Editores	—	—	—	3,361	2,204
To Foreign Authors/ Editores	—	—	—	2,098	1,137
To Misc. Recipients	—	—	—	107	487
Other Payments	1,682	1,903	1,407	3,341	6,752
To "Social"	—	—	—	2,996	2,915
To the SBAT	—	—	—	345	425
To Misc., incl. payments made to the society's endowment fund	—	—	—	—	3,412
Total Payments	3,330	4,318	2,468	8,907	10,580

*Amounts in contos.
Source: AUBC, various.

of foreign receipts went toward what UBC bookkeepers called "social" funds, ostensibly a collection of administrative salaries, start-up costs for building an endowment, and miscellaneous expenses required to keep the society functioning. An additional 3 percent to 5 percent of proceeds were paid annually to the SBAT. Beginning in 1949, about the same portion went into a Community Chest (Caixa Beneficente), meant to defray

1951	1952	1953	Total
15,865.1	21,111.7	23,542.8	108,178
479.7	452	718	3,281
106.2	143.2	1,966.2	2,606
16,451	21,706.9	26,227	114,065
33:1	47:1	33:1	33:1

'48	'49	'50	'51	'52	'53	Total
5,115	5,963	4,944	7,368	12,401	16,376	66,685
—	—	—	—	7,052	8,329	—
—	—	—	—	5,349	6,307	—
—	—	—	—	—	1,740	—
7,641	9,228	13,135	16,607	8,442	9,853	79,991
3,237	3,818	4,338	5,704	7,175	8,456	—
349	497	809	492	603	706	—
4,055	4,913	7,988	10,411	664	691	—
12,756	15,191	18,079	23,975	20,843	26,229	146,676

the costs of funerals, judicial proceedings, and hospital stays for members and their families. Some years, total payments exceeded receipts, but the UBC leadership kept the society afloat through investments, savings accounts, and an endowment. In a typical year, after all accounts had been settled, Brazilian composers received about one-third of the payments collected by the UBC (see table 15).

TABLE 15. UBC Author's Rights Receipts vs. Payments (1941–53)*

	1–6/1941	7/1942–6/1943	7/1943–6/1944	7/1944–6/1945	7/1945–12/1945
Total Receipts : Total Payments	2.7:1	—	1.9:1	1.6:1	1.8:1
Total Receipts : Payments to National Artists	—	—	—	—	—
National Receipts : Payments to National Artists	—	—	—	—	—

*Amounts in contos.

Source: AUBC, various.

   Two of the organization's greatest challenges were the enforcement of author's rights laws and the collection of payments from tight-fisted club owners. Both proved to be especially difficult in distant states and regions. In 1948, the organization sent Alexandrino Rosas to Rio Grande do Sul to put the UBC office of Brazil's southernmost state in order. Upon arriving in Porto Alegre, Rosas found "many irregularities" and promptly fired the local representative. The trip apparently had good effect: the state's receipts soon skyrocketed (see table 16).[47] Traveling agents like Rosas and more permanent local representatives forged relationships with state DIP officials, who proved to be capricious allies. In 1946, a representative in Minas Gerais complained that the state DIP impeded his work by failing to enforce the law.[48] Such were the difficulties that came with the UBC's expanding web. Nonetheless, receipts continued to rise, and the UBC grew. Looking at the big picture, it seemed that business was good.

Old Allies, New Enemies

The UBC performed a policing role similar to the SBAT's. Like the SBAT, the UBC and the SBAT-DC used their bulletins to announce and remind readers about author's rights legislation and to honor politicians and police officials. In a 1941 article, "What Composers Owe to the DIP," the SBAT-DC praised the censorship department as a "sentinel" for author's rights.[49] State DIP officials and UBC co-founder and president Oswaldo Santiago were on hand for the 1944 opening of the União's Minas Gerais

1946	1947	1948	1949	1950	1951	1952	1953
1.5:1	2.2:1	1.8:1	1.9:1	2.6:1	2.2:1	1.8:1	1.6:1
2.4:1	3.8:1	—	—	—	—	3.1:1	3.1:1
2.4:1	3.7:1	—	—	—	—	3.0:1	2.8:1

office, held on 19 April to coincide with Vargas's birthday. Santiago said that every UBC office and affiliate should display Vargas's portrait. "More than any other entities or unions," he said, "societies of Brazilian authors have the obligation" to honor Vargas, an honorary member and "patron of the intellectual worker."[50] Several months earlier, the UBC honored Souto in similar fashion, prominently displaying his photo in the society's Rio headquarters.[51]

In 1945, when Vargas resigned, the UBC was careful not to take sides. The ascension of José Linhares as president in 1945, and then of Eurico Gaspar Dutra in 1946, did little to change the UBC's relationship with the police.[52] The União welcomed José Pereira Lira, Dutra's appointee as Rio's police chief, with a *Boletim* article titled "Composers Find a Friend." The piece recounted encouraging remarks that Lira made during a recent meeting with UBC leadership:

> He said, among other things, that the days of police only working to catch robbers and murderers is a thing of the past. . . . The police . . . have much more advanced social ends, conducive to an era of economic readjustment and the valorization of human work. He also said that he considers works of art, theater, and music to be objects that deserve the same protection as a necklace or a piece of Madame Lupescu's or Lana Turner's jewelry.[53]

Leaders of the UBC frequently communicated with DIP and police offices and visited the presidential palace. The organization so valued its rela-

TABLE 16. Author's Rights Receipts by State/Region (1939–51)*

	1939	1940	1–6/1941	7/'42–6/'43	7/'43–6/'44	7/'44–6/'45
Alagoas	—	—	—	—	7	12
Amazonas	—	—	—	7	14	9
Bahia	—	3	1	—	17	114
Ceará	—	—	—	—	2	11
Dist. Federal	145	178	140	551	983	1,047
Esp. Santo	—	—	—	—	4	5
Goáis	—	—	—	—	—	—
Maranhão	—	—	—	—	—	—
M. Gerais	—	3	—	71	184	278
Pará	—	—	—	—	28	28
Paraíba	—	—	—	—	8	5
Paraná	—	—	6	18	73	87
Pernambuco	—	—	—	4	97	128
Piauí	—	—	—	—	—	—
R. de Janeiro	8	—	—	19	185	273
RG do Norte	—	—	—	—	13	5
RG do Sul	—	—	20	71	278	376
Sta Catarina	—	—	—	—	2	8
São Paulo	123	202	172	713	1,187	1,377
Sergipe	—	—	—	—	2	3
Total	276	386	339	1,454	3,084	3,766

*Amounts in contos.
Source: AUBC, various.

tionship with the police that in the late 1950s it took the extraordinary measure of momentarily joining forces with the SBACEM to oppose the transfer of censorship responsibilities from the police to the Ministry of Education. Though the Ministry of Education provided the UBC with a large annual stipend to promote Brazilian music abroad, musicians and composers felt that the police could best handle the twin tasks of censorship and author's rights protection. The proposed transfer, the UBC insisted, would be "contrary to the interests of the Nation and prejudicial to the large class of authors and composers."[54] While politicians and the police were seen as allies, they often stood in the UBC's way. In 1951, the union sent a letter to Vargas, who had recently regained the presidency through popular election, asking "His Excellency" for assistance with a litany of problems including ineffective and corrupt censors, police

7–12/1945	1946	1947	1948	1949	1950	1951	Total
7	22	44	54	58	66	90	360
7	6	—	3	—	42	73	161
57	241	204	136	164	179	274	1,390
3	67	56	55	76	86	89	445
562	2,145	2,159	2,613	3,646	4,161	5,081	23,411
6	26	22	8	56	36	20	183
—	1	1	—	—	—	—	2
—	2	5	9	17	28	32	93
124	520	350	384	489	406	683	3,492
11	35	33	44	52	65	60	356
4	24	17	47	26	37	62	230
43	207	277	222	298	325	422	1,978
64	416	486	445	536	606	826	3,608
—	—	—	2	—	—	4	6
148	496	417	431	605	590	672	3,844
—	38	55	52	69	63	89	384
181	651	514	899	1,189	1,335	1,957	7,471
18	8	23	104	127	131	128	549
670	3,102	3,383	3,161	3,311	4,030	5,284	26,715
2	5	5	6	5	10	19	57
1,907	8,012	8,051	8,675	10,724	12,196	15,865	74,735

complacency, and the failure of state-run radio stations to make author's rights payments.[55] Similar complaints appeared regularly in the *Boletim*.

To UBC leaders, author's rights laws were nothing less than the ultimate sign of a civilized country. Failure to enforce the law was therefore detrimental not only to musicians, but also the larger nation. In *Aquarela do direito autoral* (Author's rights watercolor, 1946), Santiago described author's rights as a quintessential "modern right." "With the advance of time and the progress of humanity," he envisioned that someday it would be respected in "every corner of the globe, regardless of race, religion, custom, and ideology."[56] Criminals were no longer the street hustlers or the músicos ambulantes whom João do Rio criticized at the turn of the century; they were scoundrels who misused an author's or composer's property. In 1941, the journalist and composer David Nasser described this view in an article about Donga, who told Nasser about an incident that had taken place years before:

> I was tired of composing so that others could sing, listen, enjoy, and not pay. So, I decide to start demanding compensation for my work. . . . In Niterói, they were putting on a show, during which my music was sung a dozen times and with a dozen parodies. The empresário bought a Ford and his wife got a fur. . . . Everything with my money, with my music, with my inspiration!

When Donga complained, the manager gruffly refused to reimburse him. "Pay for that silly little music called samba, the music of criminals and vagabonds? . . . No way." According to Donga, someone called the police, who took *him* to jail, but not before the officer called Donga an "extortionist" and a "thief" who "tried to exchange musical notes for bank notes." Fortunately, Nasser suggested, times were changing, and composers would no longer be depicted as criminals. "The next time around," he was sure, the empresário would be the one sent to jail.[57] A separate *Boletim* article concluded that plagiarism was a euphemism for something more serious: "theft" and "crime forbidden in the Penal Code."[58]

To secure payments, the UBC often relied on its legal team, directing lawsuits and criminal complaints against offending parties. More often than not, those cases appeared in the *Boletim* with dramatic headlines: "Crimes Against the Author," or "To the Judge Goes the Criminal." "Criminals" were not just murderers, gamblers, or malandros, but anyone who flouted author's rights law: plagiarists, exploitative empresários, or even fellow musicians. Reporting on criminal charges it had brought against Nasser, who left the UBC for the SBACEM in 1946, the union gleefully declared in its *Boletim*, "David Nasser Stands Accused."[59] In the years ahead, the UBC and the SBACEM seemed to spend as much time and energy fighting each other as they did struggling against club owners or plagiarists.

Musicians' "Real Professions"

In contrast to enemies like Nasser, the UBC depicted its own members as wholesome, upstanding working men. The first installment of a five-part *Boletim* series titled "Composers and Their Real Professions" suggests how the organization sought to pull off the tricky balancing act of emphasizing their members' professionalism while also drawing attention to their financial hardships.[60] "Rare is the Brazilian composer," the series began, "who lives exclusively from music because in Brazil Author's Rights are still in a state of development." Another article held, "In any other civilized country, [our successful composers] . . . would be rich." Each of the men featured in the series worked a regular job to supplement a small income from music. Alberto Ribeiro was a homeopathic doctor. Antonio Nâssara was a journalist and cartoonist, and Alcyr Pires Vermelho a banker. The *Boletim* described all as Renaissance men: gifted artists with multiple talents and interests. Despite Vermelho's numerous successes in music, the UBC lamented, he had to put creativity aside and plunge into mindless "daily work" to "sustain his family."

The men portrayed in the "Real Professions" series were not born into poverty. Instead, they suffered a bourgeois malaise, forced upon them by a cruel market and a lack of necessary protections. Geraldo Costa could write music only during his limited "free time." Others faced similar plights. Their problems, the *Boletim* made clear, were the product of global hierarchies and a nation that still did not fully appreciate artistic creation. "As it only happens for the popular composer in Brazil," the money that Nâssara earned through music did not allow him "to dedicate himself professionally to composition." For Vermelho, the only way to "live decently" was to work in banking, "where he is loved and well respected, but where he also becomes so fatigued and stressed that he does not have time to produce . . . [musical] jewels." The *Boletim* went on to praise Vermelho who, as UBC secretary, shunned rest and dedicated what little spare time he had to working for fellow musicians and serving "the collective interest." The composer José Maria de Abreu, who was also a dedicated chef, was more fortunate. "In his leisure time, [he] is one of the happiest fellows in the world. A respectable *Gourmant*, he satisfies himself with a Filet Mignon or Lobster Remoulade."

The "Real Professions" profiles departed from common associations between music and free time. Instead of being lazy or prone to vice, musicians were respectable, severely underappreciated geniuses. Had the series profiled a more representative cross-section of Rio's large and diverse entertainment class, this might have been an innovative, even revolutionary suggestion. Instead, the featured composers were all white middle-class men. As the UBC grew, its membership became more diverse, but photos in the *Boletim* continued to feature white musicians and officials. The most notable exception was Ataulfo Alves, who rose through the UBC leadership while cultivating a decidedly button-down image that contrasted the malandro vogue. His song "É negocio casar!" (Marriage is a great deal!) implored listeners to work hard and marry.[61]

The occupations in the "Real Professions" series contrast with the hodgepodge of low-paying occupations that many UBC members held to keep themselves and their families afloat. As noted in chapter 2, when the Afro-Brazilian musician Geraldo Pereira was arrested in 1948, he described himself to police as a professional motorist. Pereira, a UBC member at the time of his arrest, was charged with possession of an illegal firearm and threatening a café owner at gunpoint. The judge was unconvinced by Pereira's argument that he did not threaten the proprietor and that the firearm belonged to a friend whose name he could not recall. But Pereira posted bail (Cr$ 400, US $21) and, in lieu of prison time, was required to pay court costs and a small fine, which together totaled nearly Cr$ 600 (US $32).

As they did for other suspects, the police recorded details about Pereira's life, appearance, and general behavior:

> Black in color (de cor preta) . . . married, Catholic, childless . . . and a professional driver. . . . Being a samba composer, he is fairly well-known on the airwaves. He does not smoke, but likes to drink and does not gamble. He has a robust complexion and enjoys perfect health. . . . He earns, on average, Cr$ 1,500 [US $79]. In custody he was calm and well mannered.[62]

This is the only mention of Pereira's musical career. On all other occasions, including his own testimony, he is described as a motorista, a significant point considering that by 1948 he was a well-established musician, having composed and released popular hits such as "Falsa baiana" (False baiana) and "Bolinha de papel" (Little ball of paper).[63]

Pereira's experience and his work as a driver placed him somewhere between the men featured in "Real Professions" sketches and the unemployed. Though he did not hire a lawyer to challenge the charges brought against him, Pereira clearly had access to cash, given that he posted bail and paid his fine. Though the UBC does not appear in the case notes, the organization very well may have provided assistance. In 1945, the organization furnished Cr$ 600 to Pereira for "contusions suffered during an accident," and its Caixa Beneficente regularly helped defray legal fees for members.[64] Whatever temporary assistance his affiliation with the UBC provided, his income as a composer did not allow him to avoid blue-collar work. Chauffeuring others through the streets of Rio, he could only dream of the white-collar malaise described in the *Boletim*.[65]

Hierarchy and Difference

The contrast between Pereira and the white musicians profiled by the UBC (and between Pereira and wealthier Afro-Brazilian artists such as Ataulfo Alves) emphasizes the fact that disparities among musicians did not disappear with the rise of the UBC. Alves owned a small record label and was frequently pictured in the pages of the *Boletim*, on one occasion sharing a light moment with Vargas and the future president João Goulart. He went on to hold numerous leadership positions within the UBC. In 1955, Rio's journalists voted him "Best Composer," an award that the UBC proudly acknowledged in the *Boletim*.[66] Months earlier, Pereira had died, and his passing hardly received mention in the press. While the UBC cast itself as representative of a larger artistic class, a large portion of the "unknown sambistas" whom Vagalume urged the SBAT to better represent remained marginalized in the new organization.

Pereira's trajectory also diverged from that of Jamelão (José Bispo Clementino dos Santos), another accomplished Afro-Brazilian musician, who was apprehended by police in 1949.[67] Jamelão's arrest stemmed from an altercation in Praça Tiradentes, a downtown hub of entertainment and nightlife. According to all parties, the fight began as a joke among friends. Out carousing, Jamelão and Romulo Lemos dos Santos, who performed together regularly on the radio, traded playful insults. At around 2:30 in the morning, the exchange became heated. Romulo, a white artist, called Jamelão a "piece of shit singer," told him that he was not "good enough" to play in his band, and insulted his mother. Jamelão responded in kind, and Romulo then called him a "son of a whore" and "a faggot." According to the police report, it was at that moment that Jamelão "lost his cool" and punched Romulo.

As they did with Pereira, the police made detailed observations about Jamelão's appearance, character, and habits:

> He is black in color, [with] black eyes, and black kinky hair . . . strong constitution, [and a] genteel disposition. He . . . works as a professional musician (singer), performing on the carioca stations Tupi and Rádio Clube do Brasil, where he has worked for almost six years. . . . He earns around Cr$ 2,000.00 [US $105] per month.

He is single, but supports his mother and a sister. The father is separated from the mother and does not contribute anything for the maintenance of the home. . . . [His] economic/financial system appears precarious. He smokes, drinks in moderation, [and] does not gamble. [He has] a regular social circle because he has recruited his friends among radio personnel.

Witnesses and the police noted that Romulo had been drunk, and that Jamelão conducted himself in a calm, respectful manner before and after the altercation. In a final note, an officer observed that Jamelão's bosses at both radio stations confirmed his high character and described him as a "kid with upright manners." Though the judge found him guilty, Jamelão's punishment was limited to a fine of 220 cruzeiros (US $11.60). Neither Jamelão and Romulo's friendship nor their altercation was treated as an assault against a color line. Instead, the relationship indicated that Jamelão ran in the right circles. He did not "recruit" his friends from groups of street musicians or malandros, but instead in the safe confines of radio. That an attack against his manhood was what brought Jamelão to violence surely did not hurt his cause.

Jamelão's monthly salary of Cr$ 2,000 (US $105) was far above the typical earnings of a single carioca male at the time. Even spread thin by family obligations, he probably enjoyed a more comfortable life than most of the city's inhabitants.[68] But his salary did not compare to the income of Rio's most prolific entertainers. Francisco Alves's earnings around the same time ranged between thirteen thousand and twenty-five thousand cruzeiros per month (US $685 and $1,316). Herivelto Martins, the UBC's top earner in 1944, received nearly Cr$ 40,000 (US $2,040) in royalty payments, almost twice the amount that Jamelão earned as a radio singer five years later. In 1944, Ataulfo Alves ranked sixth in total earnings and collected Cr$ 25,161.10 (US $1,283). He earned additional money as a successful performer. Pereira's 1944 earnings, Cr$ 11,256 (US $574) were the twenty-first highest in the UBC, but he did not enjoy the lucrative performing career that Ataulfo Alves did.[69]

Almost all of the UBC's top thirty earners in 1944 were white. Racial divisions were strengthened by a conscious desire to distinguish upstanding composers from malandros. In December 1948, the UBC reprinted an article in the *Boletim* that appeared days earlier in a popular city newspaper.[70] The article "What Is a Composer?" was written by the journalist, composer, and radio personality Fernando Lobo. Lobo maintained that "all classes" of musicians should be recognized for their service to the nation. "Brazil," he wrote, "is a country of inspired men, of poets from every class. . . . To be a poet, one only needs to look at nature, make a rhyme, and repeat it." "In other times," he continued, "the malandro's shirt, his knife, and his clogs gave color to samba." More recently, Brazil and its musicians had evolved. "Today, these kids live in a more organized manner, each one making music and not for two or three free drinks, but as a source of income, as honest as any other." Those "composers," he concluded, "may not [know how to] write, but they say it better than anyone else."

While Lobo could find room even for poor, illiterate "kids" in his expansive definition of what it meant to be a productive Brazilian artist, he was hardly above reproducing stereotypes or offensive racial markers. In 1950, he released "Nega maluca" (Crazy black girl), which he cowrote with Evaldo Rui. The song became a Carnival hit and won a contest sponsored by the mayor's office. The *Dicionário Cravo Albin* calls it "one of the classics of the Carnival repertoire." The song describes a barroom confrontation between a male pool player and a "crazy black girl":

'Tava jogando sinuca
Uma nega maluca me apareceu
Vinha com um filho no colo,
E dizia pro povo, que o filho era meu.
—"Não senhor."
—"Tome, que o filho é seu."
—"Não senhor."
—"Guarde que Deus lhe deu."
—Há tanta gente no mundo,
Mas meu azar é profundo,
Veja você meu irmão,
A bomba, estourou na minha mão,
Tudo acontece comigo,
Eu que nem sou do amor
Até parece castigo,
Ou então influência da cor!

I was playing pool
A crazy black girl came up to me
A child in her arms,
She said to the crowd, this one belongs to him.

—"No, siree."

—"Take him, he's yours."

—"No, siree."

—"Take care of what God gave you."

—Out of all the people in the world

I've got the worst luck

As you can see, man,

the bomb blew up in my hand.

Everything happens to me,

and I'm not after love, as you can see.

It must be punishment, brother,

or else the influence of color!

The lyrics leave the pool player and the baby's skin color in doubt. The man's apparent admission to fathering the child—"the bomb blew up in my hand"—seems to suggest that both he and the baby are white. Thanks to this stroke of "bad luck," the baby looks like him. But according to Jairo Severiano and Zuza Homem de Mello, the song was inspired by a different, "curious scene" that Rui witnessed one night in a bar: "Enter a pool player and a crioula, cradling a child. The woman desperately insisted on handing the baby to the man . . . [but] he said that she was crazy and that the child could not be his."[71] The black woman is "crazy" to single out the white pool player, who obviously could not (but in all reality probably did) father a dark-skinned baby. While the recorded version of "Nega maluca" leaves some details to the imagination, Carnival renderings of the song made others brutally clear. A local store sold "Nega maluca" costumes, which Lobo helped design. He earned a share of the profit from sales and based the costume on clothes worn by Topsy, the young female slave character in Harriet Beecher Stowe's *Uncle Tom's Cabin*.[72] Severiano and Mello note that the costume's bright red-and-white suit could be complemented with "a wig of kinky hair and, if necessary, the user's face could be painted black." Linda Batista (Florinda Grandino de Oliveira), a popular white singer who recorded the song, did just that, posing and smiling widely behind thick dark black face paint in a photograph that appeared in the SBACEM's *Boletim*. A caption below the image credited Batista for her "special pose" and called her the "creator" of "Nega maluca." A cartoon two pages later depicts the pool-hall scene. A woman with jet-black skin and five sprouts of curly hair on her head presents a baby with the same skin color to a stunned and hapless white pool player.[73]

"Nega maluca" and Lobo's appreciation for uneducated, naturally talented musicians are good examples of a kind of informal compromise that was broached during and after samba's golden age. Instead of recognizing malandro-musicians as serious intellectual forces, Lobo and the UBC embraced them as "natural talents" and insisted that their lack of education was something good, something that helped them "say it better than anyone else." By treating malandragem as a thing of the past and observing the subsequent shift toward professionalization and "organization," Lobo's ideas linked up with others. In a preface to Lobo's article, the UBC explained why it appreciated his expansive definition of "composer":

> As composers, we are used to seeing ourselves . . . through a
> legendary prism. Every time [the press] talks about composers,
> they also mention the "malandro de morro," the "box of matches"
> (*caixa de fósforos*), "plagiarism," and "bought music." For this rea-
> son, when a cronista like Fernando Lobo takes it upon himself to
> describe the more serious side of the composer, from a human view
> and without forgetting the artistic side . . . we feel vindicated.[74]

The caixa de fósforos, an enduring symbol of "authentic" samba, represented the kind of music that the UBC sought to both access and keep in its proper place. Sitting in a café or on the street with nothing more than a box of matches, even the poorest musician can strike a beat by shaking the box in time.[75] Nestor de Holanda recalled how a pimp with no musical training would kill time by "beating samba" (*batendo samba*) with a box of matches.[76]

Authorship and sophisticated, creative genius were also constructed through gendered language and imagery. While promoting its own, male-centered definition of authorship, the UBC oversaw a stratified gender hierarchy within its ranks that furthered the ongoing erasure of female musical contributions. In 1952, UBC officials traveled with their wives to Amsterdam for a conference. Two photographs in the *Boletim* pictured the men gathered around two tables and the women in a tour boat. The caption read, "The men work. . . . The women sight-see."[77] Hierarchies within the UBC matched the discursive erasure of female authorship writ large. In his memoirs, Holanda recalls amorous encounters with a "morena singer," who despite her lack of talent "recorded a relatively successful Carnival marcha." Two male composers chose her instead of an accomplished artist to perform their song. As Holanda retold it, one of the composers exchanged the favor for a late-night rendezvous. In one of the book's semipornographic scenes, Holanda described how the second musician, upon learning of the arrangement, insisted that he join in on the fun.[78] In this and other less salacious examples, male property and power were constructed through reaffirmations that women, especially those with dark skin, were objects, not authors or composers.

Responses

The UBC's economic might and its rigid definitions of authorship presented a dilemma for musicians who incorporated malandragem into their repertoires and identities. On the one hand, malandragem could bolster popularity and increase earnings. On the other hand, it deviated from the image of upstanding composers profiled in the *Boletim*. The predicament was particularly acute for Afro-Brazilians. The remarkable career of Wilson Batista (Wilson Batista de Oliveira) provides a good example of the creative strategies employed by some black artists in response to double standards and contradictions. To most scholars, Batista was the consummate malandro. Muniz Júnior calls him "one of the most perfect examples of the carioca malandro. . . . He was not a friend of work, sleeping during the day and making his rounds in the bohemian circuit at night." McCann writes, "He survived on any number of odd jobs, including lamplighter and messenger, while training for the only two occupations for which he showed any true inclination, malandro and sambista."[79]

As was the case with Eduardo das Neves, whose dynamic career contrasts with the often one-dimensional treatment he has been afforded in the literature, a close examination of Batista's life reveals a depth not captured with the labels often applied to him. Like Neves, Batista was an enterprising artist who also reveled in and profited from his malandro persona. He was an active UBC member, though his participation at meetings was somewhat erratic.[80] For a time, he left the UBC for the SBACEM but soon returned. In 1960 he was elected as one of four alternates to the UBC's directorate.[81] With both the SBACEM and the UBC, he enjoyed periods of solid income. According to an article printed in a local paper and reproduced in the UBC's *Boletim*, he received a yearly stipend equivalent to US $1,000 from the SBACEM for author's rights payments collected abroad.[82] This substantial sum was less than a quarter of what Ary Barroso and Vicente Mangione each received through similar arrangements, but significantly more than most others made in 1948. His song "Mundo de zinco" (World of zinc) won second place in the mayor's 1952 Carnival competition and a Cr$ 3,000 (US $158) prize.[83]

To keep a leg up on the competition, author's rights societies and record companies usually required a musician to sign an exclusive contract, which prohibited him or her from working for their rivals. If Batista wanted the UBC to collect payments for him, he could not ask the SBACEM to do the same. Because each society had allegiances with individual labels and power brokers, exclusivity limited artists' recording options. To get around this, musicians often created pseudonyms or registered their work under the name of a friend or relative. Over time, this could create problems, especially when an artist switched societies, as Batista did, or fell out of favor with the person who legally owned his or her work. When one such case arose in 1950, the UBC's Conselho Deliberativo granted a member's request to transfer rights to a song back to him. In considering the petition, the council cited a similar case initiated by Batista as justification for granting the request.

Several months later, Batista wrote a letter to the council to complain about a recent decrease in earnings. In a closed session, the council reviewed the society's recent payments to Batista: Cr$ 4,064 (US $214) in June 1950, Cr$ 5,154 (US $271) in August, Cr$ 5,432 (US $286) in October, Cr$ 6,603 (US $348) in December, Cr$ 6,760 (US $356) in February 1951, and Cr$ 6,408 (US $337) in April. The council agreed that his earnings had indeed dipped slightly from February to April. The decrease, a member explained, reflected the high cost of tracking and distribution during Carnival. Besides, the official continued, Batista still ended up with one of the UBC's largest Carnival payouts. The complaint was tabled.[84] Batista and most other artists had little way of knowing how many times their songs were played or even how much money the UBC collected on their behalf. But Batista clearly kept close tabs on his earnings, and even the 5 percent difference between February and April was enough to ignite feelings of injustice. Carnival was a lucrative time, and musicians who received little pay, or less than they thought they deserved, felt exploited as they saw money flowing around them. Despite the murky nature of the way pay was calculated, Batista had a keen sense of how much money he *should* make and was willing to go through formal avenues to express his grievance. In 1955, he and a colleague purchased a small record label, gaining the company's repertoire and all the property rights associated with it. In 1960, he was elected vice president of the Clube do Compositor Brasileiro (CCB), one of a handful of new organizations formed during the 1950s and

1960s. Before dying in 1968, Batista left behind an unpublished, hand-written memoir.[85]

The CCB and its peer organizations blended aspects of author's rights societies and Carnival clubs. Income came from parties, performances, and membership fees. Some of the new associations were conceived to be extensions or allies of the UBC. Others sought to challenge the union. Most of the new societies had limited success and lasted only a few years. Pixinguinha was the CCB's honorary president, and its founder was an Afro-Brazilian musician named Geraldo Queiróz.[86] In 1958, Ataulfo Alves helped found the Associação Defensora de Direitos Artísticos e Fonome-cânicos (Association to Defend Artistic and Phono-Mechanical Rights). In a letter published in the UBC *Boletim*, he explained that the new organization, for which he served as president, would "fill a lacuna" related to the collection and distribution of payments from record labels. Rather than "indiscriminately" attack the record companies, he explained, the new society sought to "discipline" and calm the "chaotic state" of relations between artists and labels. In closing, he expressed his respect for the "glorious" UBC, a source of "national pride."[87]

Alves and his organization focused specifically on one aspect of author's rights payments—records—and in doing so were able to establish a niche that kept the association relevant. The predominance of Afro-Brazilian musicians in the association and the CCB suggests that many were unhappy with the general state of things under the UBC and the SBACEM. But neither the CCB nor Alves's association was conceived or projected as a vehicle of racial uplift, at least not explicitly. The CCB counted among its leaders a diverse cast that included the Afro-Brazilian artists Queiróz, Alves, Batista, and Pixinguinha and the white musicians Ary Barroso, Joracy Camargo, and Lamartine Babo. As it had been years earlier for the UBC, the inspiration for these groups was to forge a more equitable system of author's rights defense. While the UBC and the other organizations created during and after samba's golden age took important steps toward that goal, significant inequalities persisted. Despite the fact that the fight to defend intellectual property in Brazil originally galvanized around Chiquinha Gonzaga, the idea that women could own or create musical property gained little public support. The same was true for dynamic Afro-Brazilian artists who sought to control and access samba's "authentic" side without being turned into caricatures. Doing so was exceedingly difficult in an environment that clearly distinguished racially coded malandros and matchbox players from cultured and sophisticated white authors and composers.

THE UBC BECAME PART of a corporatist structure, and party to discourses, that helped make both the state and Rio's Afro-Brazilian musicians appear to be everywhere and nowhere at once. By establishing outposts throughout Brazil, cooperating with the DIP and the police, and attempting to regulate live performances down to the minute, the union helped promote the kind of constant state presence that Luiz Simões Lopes saw in Germany in 1934 and that some in the Vargas regime sought to reproduce in Brazil. Ultimately, though, state omnipresence failed to materialize in Brazil. Perpetual underfunding made the DIP ineffectual, and, as McCann has shown, pronouncements about totalitarian state censorship under Vargas are exaggerated.[88] But the UBC still delivered an invaluable service to Vargas. It faithfully made him, along with Souto and other government officials, the public "patrons" of author's rights in Brazil, even while taking on the grunt work required to make those rights a reality. Though the organization could sometimes count on legislators to pass laws, judges to rule in their favor, and local officials to enforce the rules, the messy process of tracking and distributing payments fell largely onto its shoulders.[89] When a musician such as Wilson Batista felt that the system was not serving him as it should, he directed his anger and his complaints not toward the state but toward the organization to which he belonged. While the UBC used its *Boletim* to encourage the government to afford better protections to Brazilian artists, real anger was channeled inward. Rather than hold Vargas accountable to the promises he made in 1930, musicians lionized him as their friend while hurling venom at one another, exemplified in the acrimonious exchanges between the UBC and the SBACEM. Much like the UES member schools did in 1937 when the police cut short their parade, in times of trouble the author's rights associations and their members confronted each other, not the state.

In quite a different way, the UBC also helped make Rio's Afro-Brazilian musicians everywhere and nowhere. As the union grew, black performers, singers, and dancers remained prominent staples of Carnival celebrations and the larger music world. As the "Nega maluca" costumes suggest, that presence often took the form of racial stereotype. But even while baianas, dark-skinned malandros, and other stock figures were becoming further engrained in the popular psyche, Afro-Brazilian entrepreneurs and composers were all but absent from high-level discussions of author's rights and from societal definitions of authorship and creative genius. The net effect was division, fragmentation, internal rivalries, and the absorption of Afro-Brazilian musicians into a larger class of composers and entertainers. This was not an orchestrated process or one directed solely from outside or above. Indeed, it was Donga and Pixinguinha who had taken the lead at the marche aux flambeaux, a manifestation meant to demonstrate the force and unity of all Brazilian musicians. In the next chapter, this story closes with a discussion of how the divisions and distinctions that were consolidated through organizations like the UBC and the SBAT were also fortified, challenged, and shaped through less formal projects and discourses as Donga, Pixinguinha, and other members of the Pelo Telefone Generation engineered a series of dramatic self-reinventions.

9

AFTER THE GOLDEN AGE

Reinvention and Political Change

The UBC's foundational years occurred during an era of great political change in Brazil. Within the União's first twenty years of existence, Vargas fell from power, reclaimed it, and then took his own life in 1954. The same years saw the crystallization of de facto urban segregation in Rio and of a conservative "social peace," sealed in 1964 with a military coup.[1] The most brutal phase of military rule commenced in late 1968 with the enactment of Institutional Act No. 5 and Supplementary Act No. 38, which resulted in the dissolution of Congress, harsh censorship, and the purging and suspension of local legislatures and the judiciary. In 1969, the Brazilian National Security Council identified academic studies that documented racial discrimination as examples of "leftist subversion," and the military forcibly retired seventy professors, most of whom taught at the University of São Paulo.[2] In the face of criticism, the regime remained tenaciously optimistic. Its *ufanismo*, or hyperpatriotic love for Brazil, was bolstered by the nation's 1970 World Cup victory and summarized by the government slogan "Brazil: Love It or Leave It."

During the 1950s, 1960s, and 1970s, samba ceded space to newer rhythms, among them bossa nova, *música cafona*, rock 'n' roll, soul, and *tropicália*.[3] Debates about those forms frequently overlapped with larger political and economic discussions. Especially during the late 1960s and early 1970s, censors combated offenses that included explicit critiques of the military, protests wrapped in code, and the flouting of religious, sexual, and social mores. Under the administration of Ernesto Geisel (1974–79), the military altered its approach to music and focused less on censorship. Among other initiatives, it created a National Arts Foundation (Fundação Nacional de Artes) and administered the Pixinguinha Project, a program designed to provide low-cost musical entertainment to working-class audiences and also bolster the international visibility of Brazilian artists.[4] Meanwhile, now-elderly Afro-Brazilian musicians reinvented themselves, often in collaboration with journalists. In some cases, reinvention returned the musicians to familiar places. At other times, members of the Pelo Telefone Generation adopted identities and postures that might well have made their younger selves cringe.

Music at a Crossroads

In 1960, President Juscelino Kubitschek, well known for his passion for music, signed Law 3.857, which created the Ordem dos Músicos do Brasil (Order of Brazilian Musicians), a body meant to resolve long-standing issues regarding professionalization and music. For all the responsibilities that the UBC held—collecting and distributing author's rights payments, collaborating with police and censors, courting politicians on behalf of composers, leading public campaigns and legal battles to ensure the enforcement of intellectual property law—its relationship with the state remained unstable and poorly defined. Law 3.857 used the Order of Brazilian Musicians to bring musicians more formally into the state's fold. The law granted it jurisdiction throughout the country and made it officially responsible for "the selection, discipline, and defense of the [musician] class," tasks that the UBC and other author's rights societies had performed for years.[5]

While Law 3.857 extended to professional musicians the protections afforded to other workers, the legislation, like many earlier laws, provided more details about musicians' responsibilities to the state than about the state's obligations to musicians. The majority of the agency's funding would come from its members, who could only "exercise the profession" after registering with two separate government offices. The musician's workday was limited to five hours, except in the cases of "popular celebrations" or "national interest." At least eleven hours of break had to separate one performance from the next. The law recognized four categories of employers and nine categories of professional musicians, including composers, instructors, instrumentalists, singers, conductors, and arrangers. Law 3.857 also prescribed a list of activities and responsibilities that musicians were expected to pursue on their own in the interest of the common good. Singers and instrumentalists, for example, should hold private recitals, participate in various bands and groups, and provide musical instruction. It is significant that Law 3.857 did not address author's rights, a topic that the government would not revisit fully until thirteen years later. Meanwhile, the music market was experiencing yet another period of phenomenal growth. Between 1970 and 1976, the record industry grew by a whopping 1,375 percent, and annual record sales rose from 25 million to 66 million. Between 1967 and 1980, record player sales skyrocketed 813 percent. The staggering growth helped make Brazil one of the largest record markets in the world.[6]

The music behind that growth sounded quite different from the rhythms and styles of the first half of the century. Bossa nova, which enjoyed an intense period of wild popularity from 1958 to 1964, transformed both the content and image of Brazilian music. So did tropicália, soul, and música cafona, each of which garnered large followings during the 1960s and 1970s. Around 1965, *Música Popular Brasileira* (Brazilian popular music) came into use as an umbrella term for numerous musical genres. Initially, Brazilian popular music excluded genres with overt foreign influences and served, in the words of Paulo Cesar de Araújo, as "a kind of flag for the nationalist fight against music that was effectively popular and produced in [Brazil], but considered 'alien,' 'un-Brazilian.'"[7]

In 1966, the music critic José Ramos Tinhorão published a polemical collection of essays that criticized bossa nova, linked it to jazz, denounced foreign music in general, valorized "traditional" cultural values, and highlighted the difference between "cerebral" white music and "authentic" black and mixed-race forms.[8] Tinhorão was not the only one to target bossa nova. Many of the genre's first and most prominent artists were white, educated, and affluent, and some critics called the music's dreamy, romantic lyrics "escapist." The magazine *Revista Civilização Brasileira* published a debate among musicians, writers, and entertainers titled "What Road to Follow in Brazilian Popular Music?"[9] The magazine described the forum as a response to the "current crisis." Brazilian music was at a crossroads, and there was no shortage of opinions about which way to go.

One musician responded to Tinhorão by shredding copies of his text onstage and depositing the tattered remains in a trash can.[10] The poet and music critic Augusto de Campos derisively called Tinhorão and his supporters the "traditional music family" and argued for an embrace of "modern" music. He insisted that if Tinhorão had his way, Brazil "would continue to export 'macumba for tourists.' . . . It's necessary to put an end to this defeatist mentality which holds that an underdeveloped country can only produce underdeveloped art."[11] Campos's comments echoed those made by Tom Jobim, the famous bossa nova musician, who said:

> We're not going to "sell" the aspect of the exotic, of coffee, of Carnival anymore. We're not going to keep going back to the same old themes of underdevelopment. We're going to move from "agriculture" to "industry." We're going to present our popular music with conviction not only of its unique characteristics, but also its technical brilliance.[12]

Similar ideas marked debates surrounding música cafona, a genre of ballads and love songs popular from the late 1960s through the 1980s. Christopher Dunn translates cafona as a term used "to describe any cultural manifestation that is banal, cheap, overly sentimental, or otherwise 'lower class.'"[13] The genre is often associated with ufanismo, but Araújo shows that that association can be misleading. While cafona musicians composed mainly romantic and often patriotic songs, some also depicted harsher realities, flouted morals embraced by the military and the Catholic Church, and were harassed, arrested, and ostracized for doing so.[14] Cafona artists, especially Afro-Brazilian ones, were largely excluded from the Brazilian music canon. Between 1965 and 2002, the Museum of Image and Sound (MIS) interviewed 839 musicians, none of whom were cafona artists.[15] When pointedly asked why she sang love ballads instead of samba, Carmen Silva, a cafona musician whose grandparents and father were slaves, said, "Just because I'm black, I have to sing sambas? We have to sing what's in our heart, and I liked romantic music."[16]

The widespread idea that música cafona was apolitical distanced it from more explicitly edgy forms, especially tropicália and soul music. Soul assumed special significance in black communities, where albums by James Brown circulated alongside such books as Stokely Carmichael's *Black Power*. Brown's "Say It Loud (I'm Black and I'm Proud)" carried particular cachet. Artists who challenged the notion that racism did not exist in Brazil were accused of embracing divisive and foreign political agendas. Like the discourses surrounding música cafona, those surrounding soul produced what Paulina Alberto calls "narrow and rigid spaces of 'national authenticity' to which Brazilians of African descent and their cultural manifestations were confined during the dictatorship."[17] Soul music's link to black militancy, the valence of U.S. icons, and exaggerated claims about the influence of money, crime, drugs, and foreign infiltration placed soul opposite the values embraced by the military. By contrast, black sambistas were portrayed as apolitical, authentic, and unconcerned with money: perfect symbols of a racially harmonious nation. To Gilberto Freyre, soul threatened to replace "happy and fraternal" samba with songs of "'melancholy' and revolt."[18]

Revivals

In the decades preceding these changes, Donga and Pixinguinha's careers went through highs and lows. The rise of the Estácio Sound and samba's heyday nudged both men somewhat out of the spotlight. Pixinguinha, who preferred choro to samba, was less of a public star during the 1930s through mid-1940s than he had been during the 1920s. But his presence at the 1930 marche aux flambeaux and the letter he wrote on Ismael Silva's behalf in 1939 reflect his enduring, influential presence. As members of the Pelo Telefone Generation approached and then entered old age, they reinvented themselves in creative and sometimes surprising ways. Pixinguinha remade himself twice: as part of a choro revival movement in the 1950s, and then again in the late 1960s and early 1970s, the final years of his life. For Donga, revival and reinvention were more constant processes, that took on multiple forms over many years.

For much of his adult life, Pixinguinha drew steady if modest income working as an inspector for the city's department of sanitation. Both careers—as a musician and as a municipal employee—received a positive jolt during the late 1940s and 1950s, when Almirante led a movement to revive choro. His radio show *O Pessoal da Velha Guarda* (The Personnel, or Gang, of the Old Guard) helped restore the star power of Pixinguinha, Donga, and João da Baiana by recasting them as defenders of authentic music from a bygone era.[19] Almirante invited his listeners to accompany him to a distant place. "One more time," he would say, "the melodies of the past return . . . join us on a voyage to the land of nostalgia."[20] It is noteworthy that Almirante chose choro rather than samba as the focus of his program. When the show began in the late 1940s, the market and the airwaves were saturated with sambas. With choro, Almirante not only sought to evoke an earlier era but also to elevate what he considered to be a truly Brazilian music unpolluted by commercialism or foreign interlopers. In Almirante's hands, choro took on a racial character quite different from that of samba. McCann writes, "Samba made its Afro-Brazilian roots explicit, and these were crucial to its appeal. Choro did not exactly obscure its Afro-Brazilian characteristics; it simply made no issue of them." To Almirante and others, choro was "racially blank."[21] The elevation of choro, a musical form described as racially indeterminate, resonated with growing confidence that undesirable racial elements could be smoothly incorporated into and eventually erased within a larger, uniquely Brazilian amalgamation.[22]

Almirante's show brought mixed results for Pixinguinha. In 1949, thanks in part to his once-again rising musical star, he was promoted from his sanitation job to an administrative post in the city's Department of Education, a position that carried an impressive title and a sizable salary. A few years later, the prefect awarded him an even more prestigious position teaching and conducting in the city's musical education program.[23] His time on Almirante's show also led to a series of recordings with Benedito Lacerda and RCA Victor. While the recordings were in some sense a boon, they came at a price. In exchange for a cash advance, Pixinguinha granted Lacerda joint legal ownership on all of the songs they produced, including compositions that Pixinguinha crafted years earlier. He also had to take a musical back seat to Lacerda, who for years carried the title of Brazil's second best flautist. In the new recordings, Lacerda played flute and Pixinguinha backed him up on tenor saxophone.[24]

Across his long career, Pixinguinha sought to balance his desire to be received as a serious, intellectual composer with the public's taste for emotive, authentic, raw black music. A 1939 *O Cruzeiro* article describes how Pixinguinha's masterpiece "Carinhoso" came into being: "Bar table. Two men. Two pieces of paper. A bottle, almost empty. João de Barros [*sic*], Alfredo Vianna (Pixinguinha). . . . The music of the povo is born like that. Spontaneously. Without subterfuge. Free of prejudice." By depicting Pixinguinha together with João de Barro, a white musician, *O Cruzeiro* portrayed the song as a product of interracial collaboration and solidarity, which, the magazine noted, extended throughout Brazil. But the article also used *pinga* (strong alcohol) and vaguely African references to describe what it considered to be Pixinguinha's unique upbringing. "He was born . . . in the '*zona do Xuxú*.' A place of noise. Of huge, raucous parties. Where pinga fertilizes guitar. Where pinga produces melody." The "most beautiful instrumentations," the article concludes, "come from his brain. From a brain that never stops to think."[25]

If the choro revival returned Pixinguinha to the spotlight, it was his second rebirth during the 1960s and 1970s that sealed his legacy together with Donga's and João da Baiana's. In 1962, with musical, social, and political landscapes rapidly changing around them, a group of "composers, intérpretes, sambistas, scholars, friends of samba, and other interested parties" convened in Rio at the First National Samba Conference (I Congresso Nacional do Samba). Edison Carneiro, an Afro-Brazilian scholar long dedicated to the study of national history and culture, presided over the event and summarized its proceedings in a manifesto titled "Carta do samba" (Samba charter).[26] The congress was held at the Palácio Pedro Ernesto, a downtown landmark named for the prefect who helped secure government funding to samba schools in the 1930s. Donga and Pixinguinha were among ten individuals selected to chair committees. Organizers and participants included Ary Barroso, Sérgio Cabral, Tinhorão, Almirante, several samba school leaders, and representatives from the Ordem dos Músicos.

One committee, charged with discussing "the positive and negative aspects of commercialization," found that the benefits of market growth and new technologies were "annulled" by "an unjust, unequal competition of economic power." To balance the playing field, the committee suggested that composers and singers record with labels that were "actually national, or those foreign ones which sincerely favor the development of our music." Like many musicians and critics before them, those who attended the conference sought to adapt samba to a "modern" market and allow its "natural evolution" while honoring what was described as a deep, unified history. Though they acknowledged the existence of many forms of samba, participants felt that the music was at its best when it highlighted what they considered to be its most basic elements: drums and syncopated rhythm. "To preserve samba's traditional elements," Carneiro wrote, "means to valorize syncopation." The Choreography Committee recommended that samba schools continue to place baianas and percussion instruments front and center. The Committee to Preserve Samba's Traditional Elements emphasized the importance of rhythm. Composers and performers were urged to mix samba with other styles to create new genres—samba-bolero, for example—but in such combinations, samba should always be the dominant influence. "Otherwise," the committee concluded, "we could have a denationalization and decharacterization of samba . . . [that would] turn Brazil's own music into a generic form, indistinguishable from any other."[27]

Though participants acknowledged and valorized samba's diversity, they traced the music's origins back to a single root. Samba, Carneiro declared, was "bequeathed by the black in Angola and brought to Brazil through slavery." The *Carta* recommended that the escolas' Carnival performances remain "simple, direct, easy, and intelligible, without grandiloquent or bombastic phrases." One committee focused on the protection of author's rights, and another, headed by Pixinguinha, proposed strategies for marketing samba abroad. Pixinguinha's committee expressed its desire that samba not be treated as a "rudimentary exoticism."[28]

Three years later, in 1965, the MIS began interviewing musicians who had helped pioneer popular music decades earlier. In 1970, the project yielded a collection of interviews with Pixinguinha, Donga, and João da Baiana titled *As vozes desassombradas do museu* (roughly, Voices taken from the shadows).[29] Within four years of the volume's publication, all three artists had passed away. Recorded while the military strengthened its grip on power, the MIS interviews both served as a means to indirectly oppose authoritarianism and as a vehicle to reinforce regime ideologies, especially the notion that racism did not exist in Brazil. The book's title underscores the MIS's desire to shine light upon and rescue from history's dark recesses the stories of elderly black musicians. Some perceived that act to be a radical form of opposition. The journalist, music critic, and underground communist Sérgio Cabral famously said, "I don't know of anything more revolutionary than researching Brazilian popular music."[30] This notion gained momentum when many of the musicians interviewed by the MIS recounted incidents of police repression decades earlier. Their stories provided means for critiquing authoritarianism without mentioning the current regime. Others saw elderly samba musicians as symbols of authentic Brazil, but in a way that placed sambistas in line with, rather than in opposition to, the values espoused by the military. From this viewpoint, samba's success was proof of Brazil's "racial democracy." Elderly musicians also served as foils to a newer generation of artists, who were said to be mutilating traditional Brazilian musical and social values. Gilberto Gil, at the time a young, pioneering musician and counterculture icon, rejected an award given to him by the MIS. In a scathing critique of the museum and Brazil, he insisted that he had not become the "good Negro samba player" that the museum wanted.[31] If Gil criticized the museum's paternalism and rejected the small boxes in which others tried to confine him, he also imposed similarly reductive ideas on the Pelo Telefone Generation. For Pixinguinha and others, collaborating with the MIS did not simply mean assuming the role of the "good Negro." Rather, they saw the institution as an opportunity to seal their legacies and secure long-overdue recognition and respect.

The MIS memory project and the First National Samba Conference helped consolidate long-standing tropes about race and music. In a 1974 article, Jota Efegê described João da Baiana's music as "primitive, perhaps ingenious."[32] In a separate piece, he preferred not to call the musician a "virtuoso" because "that word does not work well with samba." Instead, João da Baiana was "an able hand at the réco-réco, the agôgô, and even a simple kitchen plate, which he scratches with any sort of utensil." He also noted that João da Baiana's special talents were reinforced through the power of Afro-Brazilian deities and explained that João da Baiana's work was fueled by "inspiration without . . . intellectuality."[33] That characterization echoed the suggestion that Pixinguinha's brain "never stops to think" and also linked up with larger discussions. Bossa nova musicians, Tinhorão suggested, employed "cerebral rhythmic patterns," and could not "feel, in their own skin, the asymmetry characteristic of black rhythms."[34]

Others made similar distinctions. In 1971, Cabral and several other reporters from the leftist publication *Pasquim* interviewed Madame Satã (Madam Satan, João Francisco dos Santos). Though not a musician, Santos was an integral figure in the lore surrounding samba and malandragem. He and Geraldo Pereira had a physical confrontation just before Pereira died, though the legend that Santos killed Pereira is an exaggeration.[35] Madame Satã became an icon in part because of his exposure in *Pasquim*.[36] Born into poverty in the Brazilian Northeast, Santos was sold as a servant by his mother at a young age. He later escaped and made his way to Rio de Janeiro, where he lived first as a cook and cleaner at brothels, and then as a prostitute. He served several prison sentences. He was proudly homosexual, a fierce street fighter, and a widely renowned malandro. This combination made him a unique threat to authority. *Pasquim* declared Satã to be representative of "the true Brazilian counterculture." The magazine also described him as an irrepressible force oozing up from the asphalt of Rio de Janeiro. To *Pasquim*, Madame Satã was an "authentic" Brazilian, but this did not prevent the magazine from critically examining his intellect and knowledge of current affairs. "Are you always up to speed with national politics?" the writers asked him. "Do you know, for example, who the President of the Republic is? Who is Aristotle Onassis . . . Charles de Gaulle, do you know who he is? . . . Do you know what a supersonic plane is?" Addressing Santos after the rapid-fire questions, one journalist said, "Maybe you won't know who this person is, but this is meant as a compliment. You are much more authentic and sophisticated than Jean Genet."[37] To *Pasquim*, the difference between Madame Satã and Genet, the French criminal and male prostitute-turned-poet and playwright, represented all that was wrong with Brazil. Santos's authenticity derived from his lack of education, his dark skin, and his criminal exploits. One of the interviewers told him, "Your conscience comes from the same cloth that they cut great men and leaders from. You became marginalized. If you had been literate, you could have been a leader."[38] The *Pasquim* writers treated Santos's failed potential as a means for critiquing greater inequalities in Brazil and also as an opportunity to position themselves as arbiters between Brazil's "wild" and "civilized" sides.

Pasquim's treatment of Satã, like Jota Efegê's depiction of João da Baiana, was highly patronizing and illustrates how authenticity could be constructed in more than one way. While João da Baiana was depicted playing rudimentary instruments that linked him to an idyllic past, Madame Satã symbolized a hardscrabble life of crime and prostitution. Cabral and the other journalists who spoke with Santos understood themselves to be rescuing part of the nation from obscurity. In doing so, and by hurling questions at Santos, they not only linked themselves to him but also drew a clear line of distinction between themselves and uneducated, "authentic" Brazilians. Valorizations of authentic blackness came from across the political spectrum. Like the writers of *Pasquim*, some of whom still thought in Marxist terms, Freyre and other conservative commentators saw organic, noncommercial black music as a counter to cultural imperialism and other external threats.

The perceived distance between samba and other musical genres was often measured in gendered terms. Compared to Madame Satã or young, virile soul musicians, the elderly João da Baiana was weak and unthreatening. Suffering from rheumatism and living in poverty, his age was marked by his lost sexual potency. Asked by a reporter if he planned to find a female companion, João da Baiana replied, "I'm 84 years old and can't manage a woman anymore" (see figure 8).[39] By contrast, soul musicians were often defined in terms of testosterone. Militants often pro-

FIGURE 8. An elderly João da Baiana. Courtesy Museu da Imagem e do Som.

nounced the "power" in "Black Power" as "pau," slang for penis, thus infusing the movement with additional masculine potency.⁴⁰ The elderly João da Baiana cut a decidedly unthreatening appearance when held up against black pau.

Bossa nova presented a different kind of contrast to samba. While critics accused soul of being too black, opponents of bossa nova complained about just the opposite, suggesting that the white composers had isolated themselves from what Tinhorão called the "social promiscuity" of the lower classes. Samba, he said, was born from that promiscuity and had been forsaken by white bossa nova. The new music had thus distanced itself from samba and, by extension, mixed-race, authentic Brazil. While the elderly João da Baiana stood opposite younger black figures, it was a João da Baiana from another era, João da Baiana the malandro, who provided a counterpoint to the "soft" white bossa nova musicians whom Tinhorão and others charged with emasculating traditional samba and denigrating Brazil's virile racial democracy.⁴¹

Bossa nova artists represented a stark contrast to the young, virile malandro João da Baiana, whose image ran alongside photos of the now emaciated artist. Dressed in a crisp suit and hat, and often with his trademark red tie matching the handkerchief tucked into his breast pocket, the snappily dressed João da Baiana cut an attractive and powerful figure (see figure 2). The contrast between the virile João da Baiana of the past and the impotent contemporary version not only illustrated how far he had fallen but also graphically depicted the damage wrought by bossa nova and other new musical forms. Whether masculine or feeble, and whether held up against black revolutionaries or affluent white sell-outs, João da Baiana symbolized the heart of racially mixed Brazil. Glaringly absent from these depictions was any mention of his political beliefs.

The perceived distance between samba and politics resonated with what was at the time a burgeoning body of scholarly research pioneered by Florestan Fernandes and his students at the University of São Paulo. Fernandes, who was among those sent into exile by the military in 1969, identified political isolation and economic and cultural "anomie" among black Brazilians as legacies of slavery and indicators of systemic inequalities.⁴² In his classic text *The Negro in Brazilian Society*, Fernandes described anomie in four ways. First, from an economic perspective, the transition from slavery to capitalism — or, as Fernandes put it, from a caste to a class system — was disastrous for blacks. After centuries of servitude, he argued, blacks were unequipped for capitalism.⁴³ Second, Fernandes noted an integrationist rather than a revolutionary political philosophy among post-emancipation blacks. Instead of attempting to overthrow the new system, they tried to fit in.[44] Third, after slavery, blacks lacked access to, and a full appreciation of, formal education.[45] Fourth, sexual behavior and the lack of stable families made all of this worse. To Fernandes, black "social disorganization" was the result of what he called the "erotic explosion" or "sexual obsession" that had developed in crowded, filthy, and subhuman conditions during slavery and its aftermath.[46] In journalists' hands, those same traits were interpreted not as a sign that something was wrong, but as just the opposite. João da Baiana's supposed lack of political conviction was not a product of racism or slavery, but an intrinsic part of his being. Tinhorão underlined the political significance inherent in the boundary drawn between samba on the one hand and bossa nova and soul on the other during an interview in 2004. "Politics," he told me plainly, "did not exist in Brazilian music before Chico Buarque."[47]

Critiques of politically conscious musicians were also often coded in economic terms. The soul band Black Rio was derided not only for embracing divisive perspectives on race, but also for pursuing economic interests. Rio de Janeiro's municipal secretary of tourism called the group "a commercial movement with a racist philosophy" and lamented its lack of authenticity.[48] Others accused bossa nova musicians of courting foreign capital. By contrast, João da Baiana was a true musician. The fact that he found himself in poverty at the end of his life was proof that he had not sold out and a signifier of his authentic Brazilianness. This idea reverberated with Fernandes's influential work. After slavery, Fernandes argued, "the Negro" was not

> oriented toward the future and thus did not fit in. . . . He was not sufficiently industrious to develop the habit of thrift based on countless unseemly deprivations and to make it a springboard to wealth and success. . . . And above all, he did not crave wealth or power. Whenever he held positions that conferred status . . . whenever he secured promising employment he clung to standards which were either precapitalist or anticapitalist.[49]

Reporters insisted that João da Baiana was not a "professional" musician and that he instead had come to music naturally, thanks to his African and Bahian lineage. One article held, "He was born a composer because he is the son of Bahian parents and was always disposed to samba."[50] In a separate article, a reporter assumed the voice of all Brazilians and called samba and malandragem "our natural tendencies."[51] A few years later, Chico Buarque highlighted how the difference between the authentic past and the professional present could be understood in gendered and economic terms. In his musical *Ópera do malandro*, set in Vargas's Brazil, Buarque declared that authentic malandros had been replaced by false ones, identifiable by their neckties, steady contracts, access to capital, and wife and children.[52]

In 1973, João da Baiana commented to a *Jornal do Brasil* reporter, "Our time passed. Now things are modern."[53] Mired in debt and ill in a run-down apartment, he had good reason to feel that he had been left behind. In 1970, a number of musicians and journalists, including Cabral and Donga's daughter Lygia dos Santos, organized a concert to raise money on his behalf.[54] His poverty made it easy for journalists and peers to define him in opposition to what they saw to be the ills of contemporary music. Donga told a reporter, "Music is full of nothing but the rich. . . . Samba's been taken over." João da Baiana, the journalist wrote, "sadly agreed."[55] Commenting on the artist's resilience to the commercialization of popular music, a reporter for the *Jornal do Brasil* proclaimed, "For him [João da Baiana], everything is okay, even samba. He spoke to us about the transformation of Carnival, the professionalization of samba schools, and the tourist industry and he did not complain. He has the old samba in his memory."[56]

The irony of separating "old samba" from money and politics is fully appreciated only when considered as part of the long arc described in the preceding chapters. The '60s and '70s did, in fact, witness significant changes. After the first Brazilian broadcast in 1950, television sped images from Carnival to audiences far and wide.[57] In 1962, the Department of Tourism began to charge admission to the Carnival parade, and television and radio stations competed to secure rights to the ever-lucrative collection of Carnival songs.[58] And yet, years earlier, Donga had been pilloried for being a self-interested entrepreneur. As we have seen, the "professionalization of samba schools, and the [rise of the] tourist industry" were, in fact, processes long in the making. Nonetheless, by collaborating in their own reinvention and linking themselves to a bygone era during which money and music did not mix, members of the Pelo Telefone Generation deftly secured for themselves valuable cultural capital, if not much in the way of hard currency. In 1971, *O Globo* wrote that João da Baiana possessed "little more than memories of the struggles and sacrifices he made . . . to give Brazil the samba, one of the universe's greatest rhythms." Those efforts, the paper concluded, "continue to be ignored by young people, by the State, and above all . . . by the UBC."[59] Similar sentiments marked coverage of the benefit concert:

> Donga and Pixinguinha both receive pensions from the SBACEM in honor of their years in samba. They left the UBC, but João da Baiana preferred to stay with them and now regrets it: "The UBC doesn't want to help me retire. If I had known, I would have gone with [Donga and Pixinguinha], but I'm not a prophet."[60]

Sometimes the SBACEM was on the receiving end of analogous critiques, an indication of the widely held notion that all author's rights associations were corrupt and that the system itself was broken. While the benefit concert provided short-term relief, João da Baiana died four years later with little money to his name.

Donga and the Tricks of Time

Like João da Baiana and Pixinguinha, Donga reinvented himself to mixed effect. Though the initial furor over "Pelo telefone" was intense, and though Vagalume brought the controversy back into view in *Na roda do samba*, for the most part, the 1920s and '30s were good to Donga, whose ownership of the song came to be generally accepted, even if widely resented. A 1920 article referred to "Donga's 'Pelo telephone,'" and another called him the "author of 'Pelo telefone.'" Even as early as October 1917, the *Jornal das Moças* published a picture of him with a caption that referred to him as the song's author.[61] That kind of tacit acknowledgment did not last forever. "Pelo telefone," Almirante wrote in the early 1960s, was created not just by Donga, but others who frequented Tia Ciata's house. "Who composed the melody?" Almirante asked, "João da Mata, maestro Germano, Tia Ciata, Hilário Jovino, Sinhô, and Donga. . . . All of them."[62]

While Almirante was probably correct to recognize multiple composers, his conclusions were influenced by his own feelings toward Donga. Newspaper clippings in Almirante's personal archive (now housed at the MIS) are pocked with handwritten notes saying "Donga's lies" and "more of Donga's errors." Meanwhile, despite Mauro de Almeida's original admission that he plucked the song's lyrics from popular ballads, Almirante concluded that Almeida was the song's "indisputable" lyricist. Almirante also lamented that Almeida "never received any royalties," ignoring a 1956 interview in which Almeida bragged that he and Donga each received "a ton of money" (*um dinheirão*) for their work.[63] In that same interview, Almeida doubled back on his earlier insistence that the lyrics were not his, claiming decades after the initial controversy that he in fact had written the words himself. Almeida's role in the song has received little scrutiny, and his authorship has aroused few challenges, a stark contrast to the doubts and vitriol directed at Donga.

Accounts of Donga and "Pelo telefone" evolved over the better part of the twentieth century and eventually formed into three main narratives: accidental success, Donga as a savior, and Donga as a malandro. The narrative of accidental success was iterated clearly and forcefully during an interview I conducted with Donga's daughter, Lygia dos Santos. For decades, Santos has defended her father against what have often been scathing critiques. When we spoke at her home in Rio in 2004, she emphasized how those critiques have often been tainted by racism. "Prejudice is everywhere in Brazil," she said. Then she explained that the song's success was completely "unexpected."[64] Her father often adopted a similar tone. As noted earlier, in 1966 he explained how he tried to keep "Pelo telefone" close to maxixe to make the song as familiar and enjoyable to as many people as possible. This intention, he insisted, represented nothing more than a "suggestion," weighed and considered by his friends and colleagues who helped create the song. In the same interview, recorded eight years before his death, he dismissed the notion that the song belonged solely to him. He was simply a facilitator who provided input and helped put all the musicians in sync with Almeida, the lyricist. "I gathered a melodic theme that didn't belong to anyone and developed it." The success and controversy that followed, he insisted, were unforeseeable.[65]

The narrative of accidental success is related to a second line of explanation, which portrays Donga as a savior. According to this line of thinking, Donga registered and marketed "Pelo telefone" to gain respect for Afro-Brazilians and their music. While he might not have been able to foresee the song's immense success, he consciously sought to reach elite cariocas and alter their perception of black Brazil. In 1966 and then again three years later during his MIS interview, he emphasized that this action should be understood in part as a response to police persecution. He also downplayed his own financial interests and wherewithal. "I wasn't thinking about money because I didn't have the slightest notion about what making a record would mean. I did the deal by instinct and for the group. . . . We had to show those people that samba was not what they thought it was. We used to play samba and then were immediately summoned to the police station."[66] Here the punishment paradigm functions as an explanatory tool for actions otherwise cast in an unfavorable light. By registering and recording the song, Donga was not asserting his individuality or advancing his own economic interests. Instead, he was simply trying to protect and gain respect for his community.

Despite his pointed attempts to downplay it, Donga's entrepreneurialism continues to attract attention. Flávio Silva and Carlos Sandroni have helped move discussions about "Pelo telefone" beyond the bitter back-and-forth that often surrounds the song by embracing Donga's role as the song's "creator"—a pointedly vague term—while still questioning his role as the sole composer. But even Silva could not resist calling him *muito experto*, a phrase that can carry positive implications but that is also often applied to hustlers, tricksters, and other sly "experts" who do well for themselves through theft or subterfuge.[67] In this narrative, Donga the malandro is cast in the same light that Vagalume saw him in and that inspired the journalist to chastise him.

Decades after the initial success and controversy of "Pelo telefone" and years after he helped organize and manage the Oito Batutas, Donga explained to MIS interviewers his motivation for forming and marketing the group. The band began to assert itself commercially, he said, when "I got tired of playing everywhere for free."[68] Asked during the same interview whether, when registering "Pelo telefone" as a samba, he knew that it would be the first disc recorded with that word,[69] he lapsed momentarily from his narrative of accidental success and struck a different chord. Taking a step back from his urgent insistence that the song's success had taken him completely by surprise, and leaving behind the idea that he never really knew much about records, he paused and then told his interviewers, "Everything I did was conscious."[70]

CONCLUSION

When Donga died in 1974, Brazilian musicians were in the process of adapting themselves to life under the Escritório Central de Arrecadação e Distribuição (Central Office of Collection and Distribution, ECAD), a central clearinghouse established by the military government in 1973 to regulate the collection and dispersal of author's rights payments and the center of vigorous debates today. The agency was set in place with Law 5.988, a large piece of legislation meant to provide the final word on all questions related to intellectual property.[1] Today, the ECAD serves as an umbrella organization that coordinates, regulates, and oversees the collection and distribution of music royalties, tasks still executed on the ground mainly by the UBC, the SBACEM, and newer organizations.

Law 5.988 seemed to draw to a close a process of professionalization many decades in the making. But today, enforcement of author's rights law remains still a Sisyphean task, and the ECAD has done little to clarify the murky calculus that governs artists' payments. Collecting and distributing author's rights remains an extrastate obligation, revised by Law 5.988 to match what was, in 1973, an emerging neoliberal order. The first entry in an ECAD pamphlet entitled "Important Points about Author's Rights" explains that the organization is a "private entity—it is not a public organization."[2] Nor has the ECAD significantly altered long-standing assumptions about music. In 2006, a law student wrote, "Unfortunately, for a large swath of society, musicians are always seen as bohemians, malandros, and even vagabundos. In other words, musicians are stereotyped as people who work with no legal responsibilities."[3]

Though much has changed in the last one hundred years, in some ways the challenges facing musicians of the twenty-first century look a lot like those of the twentieth. We can understand today's déjà-vu-all-over-again feeling more clearly by briefly returning to the comments that the UBC president Fernando Brant made about Gilberto Gil in 2007. By equating the UBC's approach to intellectual property rights with modernity and civilization, Brant recycled the same rhetoric that the organization's leadership has used since its inception. More troublesome is his reference to Gil as "the barbarian minister" and his incendiary (if confusing) comments about slavery and Afro-Brazilian culture. Separated by nearly a century, and triggered for different reasons, Donga's "Pelo telefone" controversy and Gil's embrace of Creative Commons suggest how history indeed often moves in a circular fashion. With this circularity in mind, I conclude with several final points.

Race, Gender, and Brazil's Everywhere-Nowhere State

Between the final days of slavery and the rise of the military dictatorship, subtle tensions between musician control and agency were institutionalized via the music market and through the defense of artists' financial interests and intellectual property rights. Songs were tracked and turned into money. Instruments were claimed, and ownership was disputed. Bodies were marked and probed, and blackness was squeezed, stretched, and skewed. The actors in all of this were rarely on level playing fields. But for the most part they were after the same thing: a stake in Brazil and the right to map their own definitions of samba, race, and nation.

As Afro-Brazilian musicians collectively transformed themselves from human property into professionals, they rarely faced the kind of straightforward repression depicted in the punishment paradigm. More often they struggled against less obvious though hardly less onerous projects, some of which they helped construct and preserve. Through collaboration and confrontation with others, they produced conceptual maps of race, gender, and Brazil. Though the exact coordinates often varied, certain lines remained firm. Despite repeated attempts to define themselves as intellectuals and professionals, Rio's black musicians found a surer path to inclusion and acceptance, however limited, through the embrace of long-standing stereotypes that emphasized the emotive, spiritual, apolitical, and anticommercial. That embrace did not necessarily mean full capitulation, but it did effectively marginalize the bolder and more radical personas and projects advanced by the likes of Eduardo das Neves, Pixinguinha, and Wilson Batista, each of whom challenged (in very different ways) popular definitions of blackness, masculinity, and malandragem.

Standard depictions of Rio's black musicians paper over internal differences—especially in terms of class and social background—and present an overwhelmingly male picture. If Neves and Batista's entrepreneurialism and Pixinguinha's relative affluence and rejection of samba have been obscured, the lives and ideas of Brazil's black female musicians are all but erased. In snapshots of Tia Ciata, in Deo Costa's audacious letter to the editor, and even in Donga's insistence that it was his mother, not his father, who shaped his interest in music, we find fragmentary evidence of a much larger world of female creation, which, like the scars on Arlinda Maria da Conceição's face and arm, have been effectively hidden from view. The silencing of female musical contributions operates in concert with the marginalization of certain masculine expressions in favor of others. In the press treatment of Moreno and Dora, in the enthusiastic celebration of Donga's "rosary of crioulas," and in the UBC's depiction of male workers and female sightseers, definitions of normative male and female sexualities fed off of each other.

If race and sexuality were disciplined through a combination of informal projects and discourses, more institutionalized forms of surveillance and control were set in place through the anti-vagrancy campaign and, ironically, through the formal laws and mechanisms used to track and distribute musical property rights. Musicians had clear motivation for ensuring that responsible parties monitored the number of times and the venues in which their songs were played. But protecting intellectual property rights did not just mean tacitly accepting the principle of prior censorship. It also required a delineation between "real" authors and composers—for the most part, white men—and Afro-Brazilian "quasi-authors" such as Donga and Neves, who had limited success in asserting and claiming author's rights and who had to survive bitter public challenges to do so. Both forms of control—the construction and strengthening of normative categories of race and gender, and the discursive and legal construction of music authorship—were quintessential tools of nation building, and the story of Rio's Afro-Brazilian musicians is, at bottom, about the formation of postabolition, twentieth-century Brazil.

As they propelled samba's rise, Rio's black musicians found the state to be everywhere and nowhere. The Vargas era began with hope, promises, and state funding, all of which helped launch samba to national and international renown. Meanwhile, some artists stumbled into isolation and hard times. The letter that Pixinguinha wrote on behalf of Ismael Silva in 1939 says less about the state than it does about Silva's particular challenges and the hierarchical spheres that divided and organized the city's musicians. But the UBC, the marche aux flambeaux, Tio Faustino's 1933 interview, and the 1937 Carnival lawsuit brought against the Union of Samba Schools all tell a different story, one in which politicians and the police repeatedly opened doors only to then slam them shut. Tio Faustino diligently registered "his" instruments through the appropriate channels but then had to rely on the informal support network provided by sympathetic writers at the *Diário Carioca*. While the police made their presence felt at Carnival, they were nowhere to be found when the schools that were denied the right to participate in the 1937 parade sought indemnification. And while the UBC hung Vargas's portrait in its offices and frequently quoted the Lei Getúlio Vargas in its *Boletim*, the society was generally left on its own to track, collect, and distribute author's rights payments. In some ways, things got worse for black stars during samba's golden age. Whereas entertainers like Eduardo das Neves and Benjamin de Oliveira starred in the circus during the first two decades of the twentieth century, the rise of radio and cinema favored white headliners and, sometimes, black supporting casts. For Ismael Silva and Brancura, jailed repeatedly during the late 1920s and '30s, samba's halcyon days were times of great anguish and pain.

In the UBC, Afro-Brazilian musicians found an imperfect and limited ally. Like the SBAT before it, the UBC promoted narrow definitions of authorship, professionalism, race, and nation. The organization's mechanisms for collection and distribution provided Wilson Batista with significant earnings, but he remained skeptical about whether those earnings represented his fair share. Geraldo Pereira benefited from the Community Chest but could not make a living entirely from music. Ultimately, Brazil's Everywhere-Nowhere state shifted concerns about fair distribution away from official government organs and onto the shoulders of utilidades públicas like the SBAT and the UBC. While *O Globo* lamented that "the State" did not take more interest in protecting João da Baiana and other sambistas, in the end it was the UBC that was held responsible for the musicians' dire condition.

The Missing Middle, Culturalism, and the Ambivalent Slide

Years after being shunned or criticized for what was deemed to be an inappropriate interest in money, some of the savviest and most accomplished artists embraced the role of purveyors of authenticity and purity, untainted by politics or money. That was hardly a perfect fit for an artist like Pixinguinha, who dismissed and distanced himself from samba years earlier, or Donga, a gifted, persistent entrepreneur. And yet the match was not entirely misconceived or completely new. It was Pixinguinha, after all, who insisted that he and the Oito Batutas played nothing more than simple, sincere melodies.

The actions and words of Pixinguinha and other black musicians help begin to fill spaces in Brazilian historiography's "missing middle." The lines surrounding Rio's Afro-Brazilian musicians were remarkably fluid. Privileged and powerful mediators like Donga and Pixinguinha, who came from wealthier families than some of their counterparts in Estácio, retained strong (though sometimes strained) ties with larger black communities, while also maintaining and cultivating close (if uneven) relationships with white journalists, intellectuals, and politicians. On some occasions—the marche aux flambeaux, for example—Rio's black mediators publicly courted and cultivated cross-racial alliances. On other occasions they rallied themselves in less integrationist fashion. In 1917, Vagalume did not direct his charge against whites and instead toward Donga, whose position and influence gave him access to white power brokers and institutions. While that kind of access could bolster one's social standing, black men who traversed worlds also attracted criticism from multiple directions. Vagalume accused Donga of "selling out." Whites and self-styled light-skinned *mulatos* saw in Donga and other upwardly mobile, entrepreneurial-minded black artists a challenge to familiar orders and reassuring stereotypes.

The fact that Donga and other entrepreneurs were open to attacks from multiple directions may be explained, at least in part, by the contradictory values often assigned to the production of culture and cultural commodities. As I wrote in the introduction, "culturalism" is often held up as opposite to, and even in conflict with, political activism. But when Eduardo das Neves, Tio Faustino, Donga, and others sought to turn culture into money—undeniably political acts in a postabolition milieu where the ways that black men accumulated wealth constantly came under the microscope—they met the seemingly inevitable response of being told that they were straying too far away from their appropriate place.

If the successes and challenges of Rio's Afro-Brazilian musicians suggest the need to embrace a more expansive and flexible understanding of the relationship between culture and politics, the lives of such multitalented individuals as Neves, Oliveira, Vagalume, Pixinguinha, and Tio Faustino also inform and expand our understanding of the familiar phenomenon—what Homi Bhabha calls the "ambivalent slide"—of elites alternately embracing and rejecting marginalized groups and cultural forms. Bhabha's framework is useful for understanding how Neves and Moreno and others were tugged and pulled by a public that both adored and scorned them. But if it is clear that discourses slide between "enunciatory positions," what triggers them to do so? The obvious response is that Moreno's and Neves's brazen masculine displays, for example, presented a clear threat to the established order and discouraged an already tentative white elite from embracing racial mixture. Both Moreno and Neves violated cherished norms and were attacked for doing so. Beyond this simple answer is a more profound statement about the significance of both men's actions and those of the larger cohorts of black musicians who shaped postabolition Brazil. Bhabha and others have argued that national projects and discourses are conceived at the margins of society, amid its "fragments"—in "the space of liminality, in the 'unbearable ordeal of the collapse of certainty.'"[4] Rio's Afro-Brazilian musicians came from and occupied such liminal spaces. They neither wholly belonged to the city's elite sectors nor entirely to the impoverished masses they are almost invariably associated with. As middlemen, they neither simply reproduced nor entirely rejected discourses handed down from above or pressed upon them from below. Rather, they engaged those discourses in such a way that allowed them to tweak them and incorporate them into their own identities and ideas. In their performances, their lives, and their interpretations of what it meant to be male, black, and Brazilian, Moreno and Neves embodied an "unbearable ordeal of the collapse of certainty." But others lined themselves up with much less threatening images. From Pixinguinha defining himself and the Batutas as simple and sincere to João da Baiana and Donga lamenting the passing of the halcyon days when money and music did not mix, the most successful members of the Pelo Telefone Generation were adept at providing a counterbalance to more dramatic, boundary-pushing actions and pulling back just before reaching the abyss.

Final Remarks: Of Paradigm and Power

The newspaper article that featured the dramatic photograph of João da Baiana standing behind bars, pandeiro in hand, provides an appropriate conclusion to this book. The article also featured a second image, iconic in its own right (figure 9). Here, João da Baiana is seated next to the reporter Lourival Coutinho, the article's author. Both men hold a pandeiro said to be the one that Pinheiro Machado gave the musician after he was

FIGURE 9. João da Baiana (right) and Lourival Coutinho.
Courtesy Museu da Imagem e do Som.

apprehended on the way to the senator's house. This second image is just as staged as the jail photograph: two men—one black, one white—in an apparent display of interracial fraternity.

Both men have their hands on the pandeiro, and though they are not quite tugging on the instrument, it is clear that each man has his own story to tell. Coutinho noted that João da Baiana "witnessed the birth of samba" and described how the musician recounted "in the colorful language of samba initiates" the history of "our characteristic music." During the interview, Coutinho alternated between encouraging that "colorful language" and pushing João da Baiana toward points and ideas that he wanted to hear. Sometimes João da Baiana pushed back. To Coutinho's declaration, "people are saying that samba was born in the favelas," the musician responded, "Listen, samba was born in Bahia." At another point João da Baiana said that samba "was inspired by African motifs. Is that what you wanted to know?" "No, João," Coutinho replied, "we want you to tell us the history of samba." The musician took a sip of coffee, lit his cigarette, and then continued. "'Look, my man, I'm from the Old Guard. I come from the era of *capadócios*, precursors to the malandros." Capadócios, João da Baiana explained, were groups of men who socialized, organized, and worked together. They were identifiable by their white shirts, silk scarves, baggie pants, and colorful hats. Popular memory defines them as capoeiras, fighters, and criminals, associations that João da Baiana refuted. "History," he said, "has erred once again. . . . We passed into posterity along with the rest of society's bad elements. But what was our crime? We worked." To this, Coutinho responded, "Capadócios were quarrelsome." "That's not true," João da Baiana replied. "We only fought when we were provoked."[5]

If João da Baiana's narrative did not line up with the more familiar story that Coutinho wanted to hear, the two men found common ground when the conversation turned to police abuse. "It was not only Strauss's waltzes that were repudiated when they entered noble and aristocratic salons during the last century," Coutinho told readers. "No, sir. The pioneers of our samba suffered much more than that genius Viennese composer. And what suffering! . . . The least that happened to a sambista when he was arrested was getting thrown in jail!"[6] When João da Baiana referred to the police's intolerance for samba, the journalist urged him to continue. "To what do you attribute society's aversion for samba during that era?" João da Baiana fell silent. "Across his face," Coutinho wrote, "paraded the bitter memories of sufferings that samba brought him." The journalist then urged him to continue. "Go on, João."

He recalled a particularly twisted police officer who would dress up as a thug and play music in poor areas of town. Doing so would attract neighborhood musicians, whom the officer would lure into joining him before springing other police on them and carting the men to jail. "And then?" Coutinho asked. In jail, the officer would order his assistant, whom João da Baiana described as "a gigantic crioulo," to slash the prisoners' pants and paint them with bright stripes of paint. Looking "like clowns," they were then released onto the streets, where well-dressed "dandies" ridiculed them. This humiliated João da Baiana, who earlier in the interview proudly described the way he and others dressed: "Naturally, we couldn't dress like the 'dandies' of the era because our low paying jobs didn't allow us to. . . . Only the '*gran-finos*' could pay for clothes made abroad. So, we created our own 'models,' purely national, which really, at the time, guided our spirit: a certain nationalist tendency."[7] Both Coutinho and João da Baiana spoke of samba's early days as a bygone era, and both emphasized the music's eventual acceptance and success. "Police persecution," João da Baiana insisted, "could not prevent samba from reaching its destiny." As long as repression and violence were things of the past, they could be incorporated into a story of national progress. It was in this spirit that João da Baiana concluded, "Values change. What society once rejected later gains acceptance, even among blue bloods."

The interview and article were as much about Coutinho casting himself as a friend and protector of samba as it was a forum for João da Baiana to have his own story heard. While João da Baiana probably posed for the jail photo, he was not the only one who performed for the camera. Coutinho mugged for the second photograph and portrayed himself in the article as a guide who could render João da Baiana's exotic story legible to readers. Coutinho's dismissal of João da Baiana's point that capadócios worked hard is not surprising. While work was a crucial part of João da Baiana's identity, to Coutinho it was a distraction from the story that he wanted to tell. And yet the two men eventually found common language in the punishment paradigm. While recounting stories of police abuse was surely a more intimate and painful experience for João da Baiana than it was for Coutinho, each agreed that punishment was a thing of the past. Within their exchange we find a clear indication of how and why racial democracy and the punishment paradigm—two narratives often put to very different uses—continue to wield power and sway. Neither myth could retain strength or validity if large sectors of the population, even those whose lives and stories have been distorted or marginalized by those myths, did not believe in them. More to the point, neither myth could last as long as they have without competition between parties fighting tooth and nail to shape them and, above all, to make them their own.

NOTES

A Note about Terminology

1 When unitalicized, the Portuguese word *mulato* may appear to be a typo of the English word "mulatto." For this reason, and because *mulato* is still in common use in Brazil, whereas in the United States "mulatto" sounds more antiquated, I have left *mulato* in italics throughout.

2 For three useful approaches to the perennial dilemma of racial language and categories in Brazilian historical documents, see Alberto, *Terms of Inclusion*, 22; T. Gomes, *Um espelho no palco*, 40–44; and Seigel, *Uneven Encounters*, xvii–xviii.

3 K. Miller, "Segregating Sound," 13.

4 See, Agawu, "The Invention of 'African Rhythm'"; Davis, *White Face, Black Mask*, 197; Radano, *Lying up a Nation*. For an important alternative view, see Floyd, *The Power of Black Music*.

5 For convenience, I have chosen to use commas and periods for currency notations in such a way that will be familiar to U.S. readers: 1.00 instead of 1,00, as is more common in Brazil.

6 Conversions to dollars were made by using the exchange rates listed in Duncan, "Public and Private Operation of Railways in Brazil," 183, and Levine, *The Vargas Regime*, 193, and by using the conversion tools at http://measuringworth.com. I am grateful to Steve Topik for his help on this.

Introduction

1 During an interview near the end of his life, Donga provided two given names, Ernesto Joaquim Maria and Ernesto dos Santos. Museu da Imagem e do Som (MIS), *As vozes desassombradas do museu*, 73. Brazilians frequently refer to public figures (including musicians, models, athletes, and presidents) by their first name or nickname.

2 See http://creativecommons.org/about.

3 Eliane Costa, "'Com quantos *gigabytes*,'" 46, 155, 163.

4 Fernando Brant, "No baile do ministro banda larga, autor não entra," *O Globo*, 7 September 2007. On the history of capoeira, see Holloway, "A

'Healthy Terror'"; C. Soares, *A capoeira escrava e outras tradições rebeldes no Rio de Janeiro, 1808–1850*; C. Soares, "Festa e violência"; C. Soares, *A negregada instituição*; and Talmon-Chvaicer, *Hidden History of Capoeira*. Unless otherwise noted, all translations are my own.

5 Eliane Costa, "'Com quantos *gigabytes*,'" 24–43; C. Lopes, "A re-caricatura de Gilberto Gil"; Risério, "Zelberto Zel."

6 For an introduction to contemporary debates surrounding intellectual property and digital culture in Brazil, see Branco, *O domínio público no direito autoral brasileiro*; G. Castro, "Consumindo música, consumindo tecnologia"; Eliane Costa, "'Com quantos *gigabytes*'"; Dibbell, "We Pledge Allegiance to the Penguin"; Herschmann, "A indústria da música como 'laboratório'"; Lemos, https://freedom-to-tinker.com/blog/rlemos/legacy -risk-how-new-ministry-culture-brazil-reversed-its-digital-agenda; Lemos et al, *Tecnobrega*; Savazoni and Cohn, *Cultura digital.br*; and Shaver, *Access to Knowledge in Brazil*.

7 Per convention, "Rio" is used here to refer to the city (but not the state) of Rio de Janeiro.

8 A small sampling of representative works on authorship and intellectual property includes Barthes, "Death of an Author"; Coombe, *Cultural Life of Intellectual Properties*; Foucault, "What Is an Author?"; Lemos et al, *Tecnobrega*; Manuel, "Saga of a Song"; McLeod, *Owning Culture*; Sherman and Benty, *Making of Modern Intellectual Property Law*; Toynbee, "Music, Culture, and Creativity"; Woodmansee and Jaszi, *Construction of Authorship*.

9 Florentino, "Alforrias e etnicidade no Rio de Janeiro oitocentista," 10–11; Klein and Luna, *Slavery in Brazil*, 296; Slenes, "Demography and Economics of Brazilian Slavery," 2:688, 697. It is notoriously difficult to gauge the precise accuracy of Brazil's nineteenth-century censuses, particularly regarding race. The numbers presented here, though approximate, represent scholarly consensus.

10 Karasch, *Slave Life in Rio de Janeiro, 1808–1850*, 60–66, 336, 337, 368.

11 Conrad, *Destruction of Brazilian Slavery, 1850–1888*, 231; Klein and Luna, *Slavery*, 183, 296; Slenes, "Demography," 688, 697.

12 Karasch, *Slave Life*, 362; Klein and Luna, *Slavery*, 285.

13 In his dissertation and forthcoming book, Bruno Carvalho shows that while "Little Africa" was a meaningful label indicative of a large black presence, Cidade Nova was also home to, and popularly associated with, a number of other groups, including gypsies and a large Jewish community. Roberto Moura helped coin the phrase "Little Africa," though only decades after the musician and artist Heitor dos Prazeres likened the area to an *"África em miniatura."* B. Carvalho, "New City in the New World"; B. Carvalho, "Porous City"; Lirio and Prazeres Filho, *Heitor dos Prazeres*, 47; R. Moura, *Tia Ciata*.

14 White employers outnumbered black employers 12:1, with 19,091 whites to 848 blacks. See L. Pinto, *O negro no Rio de Janeiro*, 100–114, 121.

15 Arantes, "Negros do porto"; Arantes, "O porto negro"; Cruz, "Da tutela"; Cruz, "Puzzling Out"; Cruz, "Tradições negras na formação de um sindicato"; Cruz, "Virando o jogo"; McPhee, "'Immigrants with Money Are No Use to Us'"; McPhee, "'New 13th of May'"; McPhee, "'Standing at the Altar of the Nation.'"

16 For example, Alberto, *Terms of Inclusion*; Alberto, "When Rio Was *Black*"; Hanchard, *Orpheus and Power*.

17 Two important recent exceptions are Alberto, *Terms of Inclusion*, 69–109, and Seigel, *Uneven Encounters*, 95–135.

18 For Salvador, see Alberto, *"Para africano ver"*; Alberto, *Terms of Inclusion*; Albuquerque, *O jogo da dissimulação*; Bacelar, *A hierarquia da raças*; Butler, *Freedoms Given, Freedoms Won*; Cooper, "Freedoms Betwixt and Between"; Ickes, "Salvador's Transformist Hegemony"; Kraay, *Afro-Brazilian Culture and Politics*; Matory, *Black Atlantic Religion*; Parés, *A formação do candomblé*; and Pinho, *Mama Africa*. On São Paulo, see Alberto, *Terms of Inclusion*; Andrews, *Blacks and Whites*; Bastide, "A Imprensa negra no Estado de São Paulo"; M. Cardoso, "Representações sociais e práticas políticas do movimento negro paulistano"; Domingues, "Uma história não-contada"; Hanchard, *Orpheus and Power*; Leite, . . . *E disse militante Jose Correia Leite*; M. Lopes, "Beleza e ascensão social na imprensa negra paulistana"; C. Moura, *Organizações negras/São Paulo*; R. Pinto, "O movimento negro em São Paulo"; and Seigel, *Uneven Encounters*.

19 Portuguese-language literature on Rio's black communities far exceeds what exists in English, though work in both languages still tends to focus on either the nineteenth century or the second half of the twentieth. In addition to the works cited above, see Chalhoub, "Solidariedade e liberdade"; Chalhoub, *Visões da liberdade*; Farias, "Entre identidades e diásporas"; T. Gomes, "Para além da casa da Tia Ciata"; R. Moura, *Tia Ciata*; L. Pinto, *O negro*; and Velloso, "As tias baianas tomam conta do pedaço." Of special note here is the work of Maria Clementina Pereira Cunha, whose work on musicians has greatly informed my own. See M. Cunha's "De sambas e passarinhos," "Não me ponha no xadrez com esse malandrão," and "'Acontece que eu sou baiano.'"

20 Nonetheless, to avoid clunky alternatives (e.g., "individual who played music"), I employ the term throughout.

21 The artists discussed in this book represent an important part, but just a part, of a larger set of individuals and communities. For reasons related to space, documentation, or both, a number of important figures and institutions (the magnificent flautist Patápio Silva, the Orquestra Afro-Brasileira,

for example) are not discussed here. It is also worth mentioning that the
famous writer Paulo Lins published a new novel about samba (*Desde que o
samba é samba*) just as this book was going to press. I was unable to incorporate it into my analysis.

22 T. Azevedo, *As elites de côr*; Frank, *Dutra's World*; Matory, *Black Atlantic
Religion*; Owensby, *Intimate Ironies*.

23 The Federação dos Homens de Cor (Federation of Men of Color), a group
about which little has been written, published its own paper for a time, but
otherwise Rio lacked the kind of vibrant black press that flourished in São
Paulo. See Alberto, *Terms of Inclusion*, 83–84, 87.

24 See Farias et al., *No labirinto da nações*.

25 Alberto, *Terms of Inclusion*.

26 M. Cunha, "'Acontece'"; Farias et al., *No labirinto*, 108–9.

27 Alberto shows in *Terms of Inclusion* how the category of "intellectual" was
constructed with exceptionally limiting terms and largely to the exclusion of
nonwhite groups.

28 Hanchard, *Orpheus and Power*, 21. Paul Gilroy embraces a similarly cynical
view of commodification, and Kim Butler sets up a culture-versus-politics
binary that closely resembles Hanchard's. See Butler, *Freedoms Given, Freedoms Won*, esp. 166–67, and Gilroy, *Darker Than Blue*, 120–77.

29 McCann, *Hello, Hello Brazil*, 15–16; Hobsbawm, *Jazz Scene*. João Baptista Borges Pereira's pioneering work *Cor, profissão e mobilidade* provides
a useful template for studying the social meanings of professionalization
within the music world.

30 Van Young, "New Cultural History Comes to Old Mexico," 204.

31 Abercrombie, "To Be Indian, to Be Bolivian"; Bhabha, *Location of Culture*;
Foucault, *Discipline and Punish*; Foucault, "Governmentality"; Foucault,
History of Sexuality; Foucault, "Nietzsche, Genealogy, History"; Foucault,
"What Is an Author?"; Wade, *Music, Race, and Nation*. Ann Stoler's well-
known work *Race and the Education of Desire* deserves mention too. For a
useful discussion of the profitable tensions that arise when considering Fou-
cault (among others) in Latin American and other postcolonial settings, see
Mallon, "Promise and Dilemma of Subaltern Studies."

32 Abercrombie, "To Be Indian," 105, 111.

33 See note 21 above.

34 F. Silva, "Origines de la Samba Urbain à Rio de Janeiro," 235; F. Silva, "Pelo
telefone e a história do samba," 71, 72.

35 Sandroni, *Feitiço decente*.

36 Gilberto Freyre's 1933 *Casa grande e senzala* is the text most often associated
with the idea, though the phrase itself came into popular use years later. For
an excellent overview of racial democracy as both a popular concept and

an object of scholarly inquiry, see Alberto, *Terms of Inclusion*, 5–17. Also see Guimarães, *Classes, raças e democracia*, 137–68.

37 The association has dropped the theater designation, though it still goes by the acronym SBAT.

One. Between Fascination and Fear

1 Kidder, *Sketches of Residence*, 69.

2 Ewbank, *Life in Brazil*, 92, 185–86.

3 See Karasch, *Slave Life*, 204, 233–35, 238, 241.

4 Ibid., 242. One placed the attendance at closer to ten thousand or even fifteen thousand. See Robertson and Robertson, *Letters on Paraguay*, 164–65.

5 Karasch, *Slave Life*, 232–33, 243n85. For examples of slave-era prohibitions outside Rio, see F. Cardoso and Ianni, *Côr e mobilidade social em Florianópolis*, 126–27; Fryer, *Rhythms of Resistance*; and Reis, "Batuque."

6 Reis, *Slave Rebellion in Brazil*; Reis and Gomes, "Repercussions of the Haitian Revolution."

7 Borges, "Healing and Mischief," 183; Conrad, *Children of God's Fire*, 254–67.

8 Borges, "Healing and Mischief"; Harding, *Refuge in Thunder*; Lühning, "'Acabe com este santo,'"; Maggie, *Medo do feitiço*.

9 Ewbank, *Life in Brazil*, 92.

10 Debret, *Viagem pitoresca e histórica ao Brasil*, tomo 2: vol. 3, prancha 12, p. 165.

11 Robertson and Robertson, *Letters on Paraguay*, 164, 165, 168–69.

12 Agawu, "Invention of 'African Rhythm'"; Radano, *Lying Up a Nation*, 49–105.

13 For example, Brazilian *tango* and *modinha*. See M. Andrade, *Dicionário musical brasileiro*, 291–94; M. Andrade, *Modinhas imperiais*; M. Araújo, *A modinha e o lundu no século XVIII*; Cascudo, *Dicionário do folclore brasileiro*, 446–47; Chasteen, "Prehistory of Samba," 35–36; Frange, "A modinha e o lundu no período colonial"; Fryer, *Rhythms of Resistance*, esp. 116–26, 142–47; Kiefer, *A modinha e o lundu*; R. Miller, "African Rhythms in Brazilian Popular Music"; Sandroni, *Feitiço decente*, 39–61; Sweet, "Evolution of Ritual in the African Diaspora"; Tinhorão, *História social da música popular brasileira*, 99–114; and Tinhorão, *Pequena história da música popular*, 47–57.

14 For years, scholars doubted the etymological relationship between calundu and lundu, but James Sweet, in *Recreating Africa*, uncovered clear indications that Portuguese-speaking Luso-Brazilians used lundu as an abbreviation for calundu as early as the late seventeenth century (146, 219).

15 Bastide, *African Religions of Brazil*; Capone, *Searching for Africa in Brazil*; Carneiro, *Candomblés da Bahia*; Harding, *Refuge in Thunder*; Matory, *Black Atlantic Religion*; Parés, *A formação do candomblé*.

16 The ceremonial umbigadas were used to initiate and conclude dances and have often been misinterpreted as purely sexual displays.

17 Tinhorão, *Fado*, 29–30. In *Rhythms of Resistance* (117, 118, 121), Peter Fryer suggests that the widely cited 1780 text refers to lundu in Portugal, not Brazil. But he and others produce additional references that provide overwhelming evidence that lundu was a widely popular dance with blacks and whites in Brazil. The German artist Johann Moritz Rugendas, who traveled through Brazil during the early nineteenth century, produced drawings of blacks and whites dancing "landu." See Rugendas, *Viagem pitoresca através do Brasil*, 171 (prancha 68), 239 (prancha 97).

18 Morais, "Domingos Caldas Barbosa (Fl. 1775–1800)"; Sandroni, *Feitiço decente*, 41–47.

19 Cited in Sandroni, *Feitiço decente*, 53.

20 Livingston-Isenhour and Garcia, *Choro*, 27.

21 M. Abreu, "*Mulatas, Crioulos* and *Morenas.*" Oneyda Alvarenga writes in *Música popular*, "Lundu was the first form of black music that Brazilian society accepted" (172). Two other works emphasize lundu's "black-African" roots: Cascudo, *Dicionário*, 446, and Marcondes, *Enciclopédia da música brasileira*, 1:430. Though not specifically concerned with lundu, a somewhat more nuanced theoretical approach—one that allows for variety and change in Brazil and Africa—is offered by Gerhard Kubik in *Angolan Traits in Black Music, Games and Dances of Brazil*.

22 New Grove II provides a useful definition that indicates why the firm equation of Africa and syncopation is misleading: "The regular shifting of each beat in a measured pattern by the same amount ahead of or behind its normal position in that pattern. . . . A texture in which every part conflicts with the sense of the prevailing metre, or even overcomes it, is also called syncopated (an example occurs in the first movement of Beethoven's Third Symphony at bars 248–80)" ("Syncopation," in Macy, *Grove Music Online*).

23 Sandroni, *Feitiço decente*, 19–28.

24 Ibid., 56.

25 There has been little written about this phenomenon in Brazil, and it was probably less common there than in the United States. See M. Andrade, *Música, doce música*, 74–80, and Davis, *White Face, Black Mask*, 79–80.

26 Schwarcz, *Emperor's Beard*, 103, 122; Williams, *Culture Wars in Brazil*, 27.

27 Mariz, *História da música no Brasil*, 52, 65.

28 Lino de Almeida Cardoso suggests in "O som e o soberano" that musical patronage under Pedro I was, in fact, more vigorous than previously believed.

29 Marcondes, *Enciclopédia*, 1:352–63; Sandroni, *Feitiço decente*, 51.

30 Schwarcz, *Emperor's Beard*, esp. 91–92, 109; Williams, *Culture Wars*, 29–30.

31 Needell, "Domestic Civilizing Mission"; Schwarcz, *Emperor's Beard*.

32 Williams, *Culture Wars*, 30.

33 Needell, "Domestic Civilizing Mission."

34 Mariz, *História da música*, 70; Schwarcz, *Emperor's Beard*, 115.

35 Schwarcz, *Emperor's Beard*, 103.

36 Needell, "Domestic Civilizing Mission"; Schwarcz, *Emperor's Beard*, 93–94, 110–11; Sommer, *Foundational Fictions*, 138–71.

37 Magaldi, "Music for the Elite," 8; Mariz, *História da música*, 65.

38 Mariz, *História da música*, 53. Details of José Maurício's life are found in Hazan, "Raça, nação e Jose Maurício Nunes Garcia"; Mariz, *História da música*; C. Mattos, *José Maurício Nunes Garcia*; Muricy et al., *Estudos mauricianos*; Porto Alegre, "Iconographia brazileira."

39 Porto Alegre, "Iconographia brazileira," 359.

40 Ibid., 360.

41 Ibid., 368–69.

42 Peard, *Race, Place, and Medicine*; Schwarcz, *Spectacle of the Races*; Skidmore, *Black into White*; Stepan, "Hour of Eugenics."

43 Schwartz, "Formation of a Colonial Identity in Brazil."

44 Karasch, *Slave Life*, 202, 204.

45 The vast majority of references to barber-musicians came from urban centers. Marieta Alves ("Música de barbeiros," 8) argues that barber-musicians did not exist outside Bahia and Rio de Janeiro, but Mário de Andrade (*Dicionário*, 356) cites an example from Pernambuco. José Ramos Tinhorão (*História social*) contrasts urban barber bands to rural musical groups, which, because of the desires of large landholders, often mimicked European orchestras. By contrast, he argues, urban barbers normally played "under the direction of a maestro of the same condition, necessarily producing a musical style more spontaneous and popular" (161).

46 While it is well established that most barber-musicians were black or mixed-race, it is more difficult to know how many were slaves and how many free. See M. Abreu, *O império do divino*, 54; Alves, "Música de barbeiros," 11; Moraes Filho, *Festas e tradições populares do Brasil*, 117; and Tinhorão, *História social*, 164–65, 169–70.

47 Debret, *Viagem pitoresca*, tomo 1: vol. 2, prancha 12, p. 151.

48 See Tinhorão, *História social*, 166–67, and Tinhorão, *Música popular*, 106.

49 M. Abreu, *O império*, 54; Alves, "Música de barbeiros," 10, 12; Fryer, *Rhythms of Resistance*, 136; Tinhorão, *História social*, 155, 157, 160, 170–71.

50 M. Abreu, *O império*, 54.

51 Debret, *Viagem pitoresca*, tomo 1: vol. 2, prancha 12, p. 151.

52 M. Abreu, *O império*, 56; M. Andrade, *Dicionário*, 355; Frank, *Dutra's World*, 112, 135–36; Fryer, *Rhythms of Resistance*, 140.

53 Alves, "Música de barbeiros," 10; Tinhorão, *História social*, 161–62.

54 Moraes Filho, *Festas e tradições*, 151.

55 Wetherell, *Brasil*, 30, cited in M. Andrade, *Dicionário*, 356.

56 Avé-Lallemant, *Viagem*, 1:59.

57 Macedo, *As mulheres*, 2:161, quoted in Tinhorão, *História social*, 162–63.

58 Moraes Filho, *Festas e tradições*, 151.

59 M. Andrade, *Dicionário*, 356; F. Costa, "Folklore Pernambucano," 441n1.

60 Tinhorão, *História social*, 160.

61 Frank (*Dutra's World*) prefers "middle groups" and "middling wealth-holders" to "middle class" because the latter term "connotes a form of class-consciousness for which evidence is scarce in [nineteenth-century] Rio de Janeiro." This middle sector—which Frank defines as the "middle 60 percent of the distribution of wealthholders"—includes "urban professionals" ranging from barbershop owners to public servants (8–9).

62 Frank, *Dutra's World*, 111. For more on the economic significance of slave musicians, see M. Abreu, *O império*, 54, and A. Santos, *Os músicos negros*, esp. 99–122.

63 Alves, "Música de barbeiros," 11; Fryer, *Rhythms of Resistance*, 136; Koster, *Travels in Brazil*, 1:232–33, 269; Tannenbaum, *Slave and Citizen*, 91–92.

64 Frank, *Dutra's World*, 135–36; Mattoso, *To Be a Slave in Brazil, 1550–1888*, appendix A, esp. 216, 219.

65 Karasch, *Slave Life*, 204–6.

66 M. Andrade, *Dicionário*, 355.

67 J. Silva, *Crônica dos tempos coloniais*, 184, cited in Tinhorão, *História social*, 164.

68 Querino, *A Bahia de outrora*, cited in Alves, "Música de barbeiros," 10.

Two. Beyond the Punishment Paradigm

1 Rio Novo is now called Avaré.

2 On fandango in Brazil, see M. Andrade, *Dicionário*, 215–19, and Moraes Filho, *Festas e tradições*, 117n54.

3 "A novidade do samba em Avaré," *O Estado de São Paulo*, 12 December 1937, 9; M. Andrade, *Dicionário*, 454.

4 Lourival Coutinho, "O samba nasceu na Baía?" *Carioca* (n.d.). I read most of the newspaper articles about João da Baiana mentioned in this chapter at the Museu da Imagem e do Som-Praça XV, Pastas "João da Baiana (1–2)."

5 On the museum's creation, see Mesquita, *Um museu para a Guanabara*.

6 "João da Baiana vem do tempo em que o samba era proibido," *O Globo*, 23 March 1970.

7 Malandro is often awkwardly translated as "rogue" or "scoundrel," neither of which captures the full meaning of the word. "Hustler" is perhaps the best English approximation, but I believe that the word is best left untranslated. For extensive citations, see Hertzman, "Making Music and Masculinity in Vagrancy's Shadow," 593n7.

8 Bollig, "White Rapper/Black Beats," 164.

9 Frota, *Auxílio luxuoso*, 44.

10 Tramonte, *O samba conquista passagem*, 21.

11 Shaw, *Social History of Brazilian* Samba, 10. Punishment paradigm examples abound in scholarly and popular literature. For example, see Adamo, "Race and *Povo*," 202–3; Amaral and Silva, "Foi conta para todo canto," 192–93; Bezerra, "'Sambations,'" 1; Butler, *Freedoms Given*, 40; Davis, *Avoiding the Dark*, 120; Davis, *White Face, Black Mask*, 14, 55; E. Diniz, *Chinquinha Gonzaga*, 77; Dunn, *Brutality Garden*, 25; Fenerick, *Nem do morro, nem da cidade*, 13, 34; Franceschi, *Samba de sambar do Estácio, 1928–1931*, 59–60; Fry, "Feijoada e *Soul Food*," 51; Guillermoprieto, *Samba*, 26; Matos, *Acertei no milhar*, 32; McCann, *Hello, Hello*, 164; R. Moura, *Tia Ciata*, 100; Muniz Jr., *Sambistas imortais*, 28, 120–21, 128, 209; Naves, *O violão azul*, 93; Oliven, "Production and Consumption of Culture in Brazil," 106, 110; Perrone and Dunn, "'Chiclete com Banana,'" 9; Raphael, "*Samba* and Social Control," 16, 52–54, 75, 76–77, 174; Sheriff, "Theft of *Carnaval*," 13, 16; M. Soares, *São Ismael do Estácio*, 97; Valença, *Carnaval*, 56; Vasconcelos, *Panorama da música popular brasileira*, 65; Vasconcelos, *Panorama da música popular brasileira na belle époque*, 16; and Zan, "Popular Music and Policing in Brazil," 206.

12 Butler, *Freedoms Given*, 185; L. Pereira, *Carnaval das letras*, 266n36; Soihet, "Festa da Penha."

13 Bretas, *A guerra da ruas*; Bretas, *Ordem na cidade*; Chalhoub, *Trabalho, lar e botequim*; O. Cunha, *Intenção e gesto*; Holloway, *Policing Rio de Janeiro*; Lauderdale Graham, "Vintem Riot and Political Culture"; Meade, *"Civilizing" Rio*; Needell, "The Revolta Contra Vacina of 1904."

14 In this respect, the punishment paradigm serves a productive purpose similar to that of "sorrow songs" or the "blues continuum" in the United States. See DuBois, *Souls of Black Folk*; Jones, *Blues People*; and Jones, "The Changing Same (R & B and New Black Music)."

15 Berger, *As freguesias do Rio antigo, vistas por Noronha Santos*, 107–18, 123–27; B. Carvalho, "Porous City"; Decreto no. 1030, 11 November 1890. Within Santana and Santo Antônio, cases were chosen randomly. Racial data were available for only 141 of the 424 individuals who were arrested. Most of the time, racial classifications were made in terms of skin color, so that a white suspect would be described as "da cor branca," or "of the color white." Of the 141 suspects for whom skin color was recorded, 60 were identified as white, 39 as brown (*parda* or *morena*), and 33 as black (*preta*). Nine individuals were described with multiple labels. Of the suspects, 77.6 percent were men, and 22.4 percent were women. For a wonderful interactive guide to key locales in Rio's musical and religious landscape, see http://www.unicamp.br/cecult/mapastematicos/.

16 As Keila Grinberg ("Slavery, Liberalism, and Civil Law") and others have shown, it was not until 1916, when Brazil finally adopted a Civil Code (other Latin American countries had done so decades earlier), that the last legal traces of slavery were wiped away.

17 Decreto no. 847, 11 October 1890: Código Penal dos Estados Unidos do Brazil, Article 399. Many laws and decrees are available at www.senado.gov.br. As much as possible, I cite paper copies.

18 One could correctly refer to multiple anti-vagrancy campaigns, with multiple regional and local variants. See C. Azevedo, *Onda negra, medo branco*; Chalhoub, *Trabalho, lar e botequim*; Chalhoub, "Vadios e barões no ocaso do Império"; O. Cunha, *Intenção e gesto*; O. Cunha, "The Stigmas of Dishonor"; Fausto, *Crime e cotidiano*; Flory, "Race and Social Control in Independent Brazil"; Fraga Filho, *Mendigos, moleques e vadios na Bahia do século XIX*; Holloway, *Policing Rio*; Huggins, *From Slavery to Vagrancy in Brazil*; Kowarick, *Trabalho e vadiagem*; Mattos, "Vadios, jogadores, mendigos e bêbados na cidade do Rio de Janeiro do início do século"; and Souza, *Desclassificados do ouro*.

19 For details on police identification and surveillance techniques, see O. Cunha, *Intenção e gesto*, and Hertzman, "Surveillance and Difference," 102–51.

20 Andrews, *Blacks and Whites*, 54–89; C. Azevedo, *Onda negra*; Emilia Viotti da Costa, *Brazilian Empire*, 94–124; Emilia Viotti da Costa, *Da senzala à colônia*, 99–158, 168–71, 212–26; Dean, *Rio Claro*, 88–123; Holloway, *Immigrants on the Land*; Lesser, *Negotiating National Identity*; Skidmore, *Black into White*, 124–44.

21 Andrews, *Blacks and Whites*, 48.

22 Quoted in C. Azevedo, *Onda negra*, 52.

23 Lei no. 2.040, 28 September 1871, in *Collecção das leis do Imperio do Brazil de 1871*, vol. 31, part 1, 147–52 (Rio de Janeiro: Typographia Nacional, 1871); Lei no. 3.270, 28 September 1885, in *Collecção das leis do Imperio do Brazil de 1885*, vol. 32, part 1, 14–20 (Rio de Janeiro: Typographia Nacional, 1886).

24 Decreto no. 847; Piragibe, *Diccionario*, 2:153, 157.

25 Olívia Maria Gomes da Cunha uses the phrase for female suspects, but elsewhere discusses similar stigmas attached to men. See her *Intenção e gesto* and "Stigmas."

26 Green, *Beyond Carnival*.

27 Between 1890 and 1911, Santana and Santo Antônio were separate administrative units. In 1911, they merged into a single police zone, the Terceira Pretoria Criminal. Arquivo Nacional (AN), CODES Instrumentos OI, OT, 7D, 7F, MV, MU, 7J, 7K, 7L, 7M, OR, 7C, T8, 7E, MW, 7G, 6Z, 70, 71, 72, and 73. There are thousands of additional, unindexed records from other districts.

28 AN, CODES Instrumentos OR and 6Z.

29 Chazkel, "Social Life and Civic Education in the Rio de Janeiro City Jail," 697.

30 O. Cunha, *Intenção e gesto*, 111–14. Also see Ribeiro, *Cor e criminalidade*.

31 Beattie, "Measures of Manhood"; Beattie, *Tribute of Blood*; Green, *Beyond Carnival*, 22–23, 252–53; Hertzman, "Making Music and Masculinity."

32 AN, OR.5895; AN, OR.8262; AN, 6Z.1585; AN, 6Z.6392.

33 Foucault, *History of Sexuality*, 44.

34 Lobo, "Capítulo 1." Also see Addor, *A insurreição anarquista no Rio de Janeiro*; B. Costa and Mattos, *Trabalhadores em greve, polícia em guarda*; Góes, *A formação da classe trabalhadora*; McPhee, "'A new 13th of May'"; McPhee, "'Standing at the Altar of the Nation'"; Meade, *"Civilizing" Rio*; and Meade, "'Living Worse and Costing More.'"

35 Quoted and translated in Cruz, "Puzzling Out Slave Origins in Rio de Janeiro Port Unionism," 242, 243.

36 McPhee, "'New 13th of May,'" 151.

37 Quoted and translated in ibid., 158.

38 Ministerio da Agricultura, Industria e Commercio, Directoria Geral de Estatistica, *Recenseamento do Brazil*, cxviii, 514–15.

39 Cited in Damazio, *Retrato social do Rio de Janeiro na virada do século*, 47.

40 Cost-of-living data from nineteenth- and early twentieth-century Rio are sparse. A British man who collected data from local newspapers recorded the 940 percent figure. See Oakenfull, *Brazil (1913)*, 570. Also see Lobo, "Evolução dos preços e do padrão de vida no Rio de Janeiro, 1820–1930"; Lobo, *História da cidade do Rio de Janeiro*, 2:501–9; and Meade, "'Living Worse.'"

41 Popinigis, *Proletários de casaca*.

42 Hahner, *Poverty and Politics*, 242–50 (table 27).

43 Esteves, *Acordes e acordos*.

44 Decreto no. 1.637, 5 January 1907.

45 It is believed that ranchos emerged in Rio during the early 1870s, at least in part as a popular response to the elite and exclusive *grande sociedade* Carnival clubs. Rancho members paraded through the streets wearing colorful costumes, singing, and playing various instruments, including guitar and sometimes flute. Their parades preceded more formal ones organized by samba schools and state officials beginning in the 1930s.

46 Carnival cordões preceded and overlapped with the ranchos. Members paraded wearing masks and were often dressed as devils or clowns. A leader in the front used a whistle to direct their movement. Musical accompaniment featured drums and other percussion instruments.

47 Chalhoub, *Trabalho, lar e botequim*, 62. Between 1890 and 1930, Teresa Meade writes in *"Civilizing" Rio*, "only a fraction of the working class was even employed on a relatively regular basis. . . . A worker in a textile mill might be laid off half of the year, during which time he or she worked as a day laborer, maid, street vendor, numbers runner, or prostitute" (9–10).

48 AN, OR.6474, 3-a.

49 AN, OR.3776; AN, OR.6360; AN, OR.7574; AN, 6Z.1279; AN, 6Z.592; AN, 6Z.1265; AN, OR.3725. Other studies suggest that my sample was not unique. Sueann Caulfield writes, "Prostitutes presented themselves as upstanding citizens with rights to privacy, property, and livelihood, going as far as the Supreme Court to appeal for recognition of the 'inviolability of their homes.'" Cristiana Schettini Pereira found that prostitutes used cases in which they were accused of pandering to advocate for basic rights and privileges such as fair rent. See Caulfield, "Getting into Trouble," 171, and C. Pereira, "Prostitutes and the Law." For more on prostitution in Brazil, see M. Abreu Esteves, *Meninas perdidas*; Caulfield, "The Birth of Mangue"; C. Pereira, *Que tenhas teu corpo*; and Rago, *Os prazeres da noite*. On women accused of vagrancy, see O. Cunha, "Stigmas," and Garzoni, "Raparigas e meganhas em Santana (Rio de Janeiro, 1950)."

50 Nor did suspects use related terms, such as "composer" or "singer."

51 This is not to say that music and work did not often overlap. Coworkers formed bands, and residents across the city founded music and Carnival clubs. It is not unreasonable to imagine an acusado asking a club president to vouch for him or her to the police. Indeed, membership in most clubs was contingent upon proof of moral character and upright behavior. Nonetheless, in my research, I did not come across a single example of a suspect who relied on a club for support against criminal charges.

52 Special thanks to Rachel Soihet for helping me locate this case. AN, "Tereza de Jesus dos Santos e outros, Processo 11133, Caixa 1874, 6a Vara Criminal," 8-a. Cited in Soihet, *Condição feminina e formas de violência*, 214–15.

53 The search encompassed hundreds of individuals, ranging from well-known to obscure artists.

54 The 1890 Penal Code criminalized "deflowering," defined as sexual intercourse with an underage virgin woman. See Caulfield, *In Defense of Honor.*

55 AN, 70.7492, 1927; AN, 70.7685, 1927; AN, 70.7112, 1927; AN, 70.7094, 1927; AN, 70.8665, 1928; AN, 6Z.13226, 1929.

56 AN, Cx. 1096, Proc. 11.901/48, RC 758.789, 20a/18a Vara Criminal, 1948.

57 Baiaco: AN, Processo 69, Caixa 235, Gal. B, 10a Vara Criminal, 1927; AN, Processo 42, Maço 27, Gal. 15, 1928; Brancura: AN, 6a Vara Criminal (CT) (antigo 10a VC), Processo 1551, Caixa 1859, 1926; Lacerda: AN, 6Z.7601, 1923; Jovino: AN, OR.2264, 1902; Jamelão: AN, Proc. no. 600, Caixa 1567, 20a Vara de Execuções Criminais do RJ (D3), 1949; Santiago: AN, M. 265, Proc. 304, Gal BA, 1929; Paulo da Portela: AN, Processo 254, 289, Gal B, 1921; AN, 6a Vara Criminal (CT) (antigo 10a VC), Processo 1551, Caixa 1859; Noel Rosa: AN, no. 742, Caixa 1821, 1934.

58 AN, MW.2044, 13a Pretoria Criminal do Rio de Janeiro. Thanks to Maria Clementina Pereira Cunha for passing this document on to me.

59 AN, OR.2325; AN, 6Z.7310; AN, 6Z.1929; AN, 6Z.18000.

60 B. Gomes, *Wilson Batista e sua época*, 77–78.

61 B. Borges, "The Recognition of Afro-Brazilian Symbols and Ideas, 1890–1940."

62 Quoted in Fausto, *Crime e cotidiano*, 63.

63 Chazkel, "*Crônica*, the City, and the Invention of the Underworld," 90.

64 Quoted and translated in ibid., 94–95.

65 Barbosa, *Bambambã!*; Barbosa, *Na prisão*; Barbosa, *Samba*. For more on Barbosa and his contemporaries, see Bretas, "What the Eyes Can't See"; Chazkel, "*Crônica*"; Coutinho, *Os cronistas de Momo*; and Geraldo, "Histórias e historiadores da música popular no Brasil."

66 Chazkel, "Beyond Law and Order"; Chazkel, *Laws of Chance*.

67 A 1908 decree officially linked jogo and vagrancy, and held that "any individual maintaining himself through jogo will be judged and punished as a vagrant." Decreto no. 6994, article 52, paragraph 7; Piragibe, *Diccionario*, 2:161.

68 Decreto no. 847, articles 401–4.

69 D. Borges, "Healing and Mischief," 203.

70 Ibid., 190–91.

71 Quoted and translated in ibid., 193.

72 Decreto no. 847, articles 156–58.

73 Piragibe, *Diccionario*, 1:314.

74 Ibid., 1:223, 366–67. For an extended discussion about a famous Afro-Brazilian feiticeiro who gained notoriety during the 1870s, see G. Sampaio, "Tenebrosos mistérios."

75 Quoted and translated in D. Borges, "Healing and Mischief," 195.

76 AN, 6Z.3694.

77 Eduardo Silva, *As queixas do povo*, 106, 110.

78 *A Noite*, 10 February 1912.

79 "A questão do dia: o adiamento do carnaval," *A Noite*, 15 February 1912.

80 "O carnaval: o policiamento de hoje," *A Noite*, 17 February 1912; "O carnaval será adiado?" *A Noite*, 14 February 1912.

81 "O carnaval n. 1," *A Noite*, 19 February 1912.

82 "Carnaval: o dia e a tarde," *A Noite*, 19 February 1912.

83 "O carnaval: os preparativos fazem crer que o carnaval será animadíssimo," *A Noite*, 3 April 1912.

84 Detailed income and cost-of-living data are provided in the next chapter.

85 "O carnaval: os preparativos fazem crer que o carnaval será animadíssimo."

86 This does not, of course, discount the many other reasons that revelers enjoyed the event. For extensive citations on Carnival, see Hertzman, "Surveillance and Difference," 76.

87 Instituto de Economia, *Pesquisa sôbre*, 28.

88 AN, Privilégios Industriais (PI).4507; AN, PI.6563; AN, PI.7764.

89 "O carnaval: em plena animação," *A Noite*, 8 April 1912.

90 Concerns about the quality and origins of lança-perfumes persisted all the way up until 1937, when the police banned them. See Coutinho, *Os cronistas*, 155.

91 L. Pereira, *Carnaval das letras*, 67, 81, 85–86.

92 Soihet, "Festa da Penha," 357.

93 AN, 7H.335, 15a Pretoria do Rio de Janeiro.

94 Additional examples of police mediation include AN, MW.0699; AN, OR.8650, 8a Pretoria Criminal do Rio de Janeiro; AN, 6Z.20566, 3a Pretoria Criminal do Rio de Janeiro.

95 L. Pereira, "E o Rio dançou," 419–20, 437.

96 AN, Grupo de Identificação de Fundos Internos (hereafter, GIFI) 6C, Lata 63.

97 AN, GIFI 6C, Lata 170.

98 All from AN, GIFI 6C, Lata 170.

99 MIS, *As vozes*, 57.

100 Fischer, "*Quase pretos de tão pobres*," 59.

101 R. Moura, *Tia Ciata*, 96–97, 100.

102 Ibid., 102–3.

103 MIS, *As vozes*, 20.

104 Oliveira Filho, *Bicho Novo, Carlos Cachaça, Ismael Silva*, 63–100.

105 AN, Acelino dos Santos, Processo 2593, 10a Vara Criminal, 15-a.

106 R. Moura, *Tia Ciata*, 46, 63–67; Eduardo Silva, *Prince of the People*, 60–61.

107 Records reveal that he was arrested many other times, but the specific records for those seem to have disappeared. AN, 6a Vara Criminal (CT) (antigo 10a VC), Processo 1551, Caixa 1859, 1926; AN, Processo 361, No. 28, Maço 143, Gal. BA, 1927; AN, Processo 746, No. 600, Maço 16, Gal. BA, 1929; AN, 6Z.15125, 1930; AN, Processo 128, No. 7, Maço 242, Gal. BA, 1933; AN, Processo 167, No. 26, Maço 242, Gal. BA, 1933; AN, Processo 540, No. 6, Maço 242, Gal. BA, 1933; AN, Processo 133, No. 2, Maço 268, Gal. BA, 1934.

108 Some accounts place his birth around 1908. Court documents hold that he was born several years earlier.

109 http://www.dicionariompb.com.br. Brancura's obscurity is at least partially related to doubts surrounding the authorship of his works. See Rangel, "Um prefácio de 1974," 12.

110 Http://www.dicionariompb.com.br. Also see Máximo and Didier, *Noel Rosa*, 211, 290.

111 AN, 6a Vara Criminal (CT) (antigo 10a VC), Processo 1551, Caixa 1859.

112 Caulfield, *In Defense of Honor*, 174.

113 AN, CT, Processo 742, Caixa 1821, 1934.

114 Pacheco, *Noel Rosa e a sua época*, 104–5.

115 Máximo and Didier, *Noel Rosa*, 283–84.

116 Brooks, *Bodies in Dissent*, 3.

117 *Estado da Bahia*, 15 March 1948; Farias et al., *No labirinto*, 299–301.

1   Meanwhile, Brazilian industry slowly grew. In 1889 there were little more than six hundred factories in the entire country. By the start of World War I, that figure had multiplied more than ten times over, and in 1920 industrial production was five times what it had been in 1907. In 1940, nearly 1.5 million Brazilians worked in some seventy thousand factories. See Burns, *A History of Brazil*, 203, 356, 357. Despite these developments, the agricultural sector dominated the economy well into the twentieth century. As late as 1920, nearly 70 percent of the nation's laborers worked in agriculture. See Leff, *Economic Structure and Change, 1822–1847*, 166.

2   Erminia Silva, *Circo-teatro*.

3   "E o palhaço o que é?" *Revista da Semana*, 7 October 1944.

4   Erminia Silva, *Circo-teatro*; Tinhorão, "Circo brasileiro, local do universo."

5   T. Gomes, *Um espelho no palco*, 71.

6   Erminia Silva, *Circo-teatro*, 264–65.

7   Ibid., 277.

8   "E o palhaço o que é?"

9   Quoted in Erminia Silva, *Circo-teatro*, 231.

10 Ibid., 226–27.

11 Figner's life remains untold in English-language sources. Details and a massive amount of raw material (song tracks, contracts, personal letters, music catalogs, etc.) about Figner and his recording empire have been made available by Humberto Franceschi, a music collector and the current owner of Figner's personal and musical archive, in his *A Casa Edison e seu tempo*. Additional sources include Viriato Corrêa, "Frederico Figner," *A Noite*, 27 January 1947; "Desaparece o pioneiro do disco e do fonógrafo no Brasil," *A Noite*, 20 June 1947; Franceschi, *Registro sonoro por meios mecânicos no Brasil*; and Sá, *A Mansão Figner*.

12 Ord-Hume and Weber, "Recorded Sound."

13 *A Casa Edison e seu tempo* (CEST), Documentos, Catálogos Casa Edison (1902). Digital images of the catalog and a wide array of documents related to Figner and Casa Edison are found on the "Documentos" CD-ROM in Franceschi's *A Casa Edison e seu tempo*. Henceforth, documents included on the "Documentos" CD-ROM will be cited as at the beginning of this note, according to the following format: CEST, Documentos, pasta, image number.

14 Franceschi, *A Casa Edison*, 117.

15 The factory had a short existence, destroyed by a fire soon after its inception. See Franceschi, *A Casa Edison*, 203.

16 Ibid., 90–94.

17 Ibid., 124.

18 Ibid., 75.

19 CEST, Documentos, Cartas Zonophone—F. M. Prescott, images 2, 6.

20 Ibid., image 6.

21 Franceschi, *A Casa Edison*, 96.

22 Ibid., 90–93.

23 Ibid., 21–22.

24 CEST, Documentos, Catálogos Casa Edison (1913), image 2.

25 Quoted in Franceschi, *Registro sonoro*, 75–76.

26 Gitelman, "Reading Music, Reading Records, Reading Race," 283.

27 Sherman and Benty, *Making of Modern*.

28 The foundational, though severely limited, 1898 legislation was modified slightly in 1899, 1900, and 1912. More significant changes were made in 1916, 1928, and beyond. The 1824 constitution and the 1830 Penal Code both included small provisions to protect literary and artistic production. After several failed projects during the 1850s and '70s, the 1890 Penal Code and the 1891 constitution also provided limited protection, but the constitution referred only to literary, and not musical, works. Lei no. 496, 1 August 1898, in *Collecção das leis da Republica dos Estados Unidos do Brazil de 1898*, 4–8 (Rio de Janeiro: Imprensa Nacional, 1900); Lei no. 652, 23 November 1899, in *Collecção das leis da Republica dos Estados Unidos do Brazil de 1899*, 91–127 (Rio de Janeiro: Imprensa Nacional, 1902); Decreto no. 3.836, 24 November 1900, in *Collecção das leis da Republica dos Estados Unidos do Brazil de 1900*, 1104 (Rio de Janeiro: Imprensa Nacional, 1902); Lei no. 2.577, 17 January 1912, in *Collecção das leis da Republica dos Estados Unidos do Brazil de 1912*, 231 (Rio de Janeiro: Imprensa Nacional, 1915); S. Martins, *Direito autoral*, 45–67; and Pimenta, *Princípios de direitos autorais*, 88–97.

29 CEST, Documentos, Direito Autoral, image 58.

30 While the contracts are valuable, they must be used cautiously; it is unclear whether the available documents represent all those that have survived, all that Figner issued in 1911, or simply part of a larger collection. Of the 196 contracts, 192 included the price that Figner paid for the rights to one or a number of songs. The other four ceded privileges, with no mention of the amount that Figner may have surrendered. A fifth contract, discussed later, was signed by two artists and a publishing house for 5:000$000 (5 contos de réis). The remaining 191 pacts were signed by 82 individuals and involved the rights to 367 songs. The contracts are found in CEST, Documentos, Direito Autoral. Franceschi provides no summary or systematic analysis of the contracts; the statistics and information provided here come from my own calculations.

31 The sales helped pay for Figner's mansion, which became a Rio landmark. See Franceschi, *A Casa Edison*, 195, and Sá, *A mansão Figner*, 20.

32 Well-off families spent upward of 300$000 (US $97) each month just on food. See Hahner, *Poverty and Politics*, 205, 209.

33 Franceschi, *A Casa Edison*, 66.

34 Ibid.; Hahner, *Poverty and Politics*, 205, 209.

35 Vasconcelos, *Panorama da música popular brasileira na* belle époque, 20–21.

36 CEST, Documentos, Direito Autoral, image 213.

37 Vasconcelos, *Panorama da música popular brasileira na* belle époque, 113.

38 Details about Cearense are found in Miereles, *Catulo*, and Vasconcelos, *Panorama da música popular brasileira na* belle époque, 115–39.

39 Beattie, "Conscription versus Penal Servitude"; Windler, "City of Children," 143–79.

40 Vasconcelos, *Panorama da música popular brasileira na* belle époque, 106, 337–38.

41 See Hertzman, "Surveillance and Difference," 222, figs. 6–7.

42 Short treatments of his life are found in M. Abreu, "O 'crioulo Dudu'"; M. Abreu, "Eduardo das Neves"; M. Abreu, "Eduardo das Neves (1874–1919)"; Marcondes, *Enciclopédia*, 1:532; Vagalume, *Na roda*, 65–76; and Vasconcelos, *Panorama da música popular brasileira na belle époque*, 282–87.

43 Neves, *Trovador da malandragem*, 64–65.

44 "O malandro," original recording by Neves and Mário Pinheiro, Odeon, ca. 1910; "O sonho dourado do malandro," original recording by Neves, Odeon, ca. 1915.

45 Quaresma was among the most important publishing houses at the turn of the century and published pamphlets and small books, most of which were available at prices as low as the cost of a daily newspaper.

46 Neves, *Trovador da malandragem*, 4.

47 Ibid., 9.

48 Erminia Silva, *Circo-teatro*, 222.

49 W. Martins, "Paschoal Segreto."

50 It is unclear how the 5 contos were distributed. Because of its unique size, I have not included this contract in the quantitative data presented in this chapter.

51 *A caráter* may also mean "dressed to the nines." Special thanks to Bert Barickman and Claudia Tatinge Nascimento for help with this translation.

52 Neves, *Trovador da malandragem*, 3–4.

53 Barreto, *A alma encantadora das ruas*, 178.

54 Emphasis in the original. Vagalume, *Na roda*, 75.

55 Vasconcellos and Suzuki Jr., "A malandragem," 511.

56 M. Abreu, "*Mulatas, Crioulos* and *Morenas*," 279.

57 See B. Carvalho, "Porous City," esp. 95, 102, and Needell, *A Tropical Belle Époque*, 207–9.

58 Green, James N. *Beyond Carnival*, 58.

59 Barreto, *A alma encantadora*, 65–69.

60 Barreto, João Paulo Alberto Coelho (João do Rio), "Negros ricos," *Gazeta de Notícias*, 13 May 1905.

61 João do Rio generally used *alufá* to refer to African-descendant Muslims. The term is also used for spiritual leaders in Candomblé and its offshoots. See Cacciatore, *Dicionário de cultos afro-brasileiros*, 46, and João Rodrigues, *João do Rio*, 51.

62 Alberto, *Terms of Inclusion*, 23–68.

63 A. Lopes, "The Jaguar's Leap," 121.

64 Neves, *Mysterios do violão*.

65 Lacerda, *Diccionario Encyclopedico*, 1:828. Also see Nascentes, *Dicionário etimológico da língua portuguesa*, 223; J. Vasconcellos, *Antroponimia portuguesa*, 364; and Fr. Vieira, *Grande diccionario portugues*, 2:641. During colonial times, the word may have been used infrequently to refer to an individual of European descent born in Brazil, much in the same way that *criollo* was used during the same period to designate Spanish American-born offspring of European parents. Such usage appears to have been rare. Thanks again to Bert Barickman for help here.

66 Barreto, *A alma encantadora*, 178–79.

67 Neves, *Trovador da malandragem*, 123–25.

68 Rebouças's identity underwent a dramatic shift after the fall of the monarchy; see Spitzer, *Lives in Between*. On Machado de Assis, see Emilia Viotti da Costa, *Brazilian Empire*, 241–42.

69 "Othelo caricato: fim de dous canconetistas," *O Malho*, 21 January 1911.

70 "Canconetistas da morte," *O Paiz*, 15 January 1911.

71 Skidmore, *Black into White*.

72 *O Malho* was one of Rio's "most prestigious" daily newspapers, and *O Paiz* was one of its most storied and widely circulating. See N. Sodré, *História da imprensa no Brasil*, 345.

73 Translations by Susan Besse, "Crimes of Passion," 653, 655.

74 Caulfield, *In Defense of Honor*, 88.

75 Besse, "Crimes of Passion," 655.

76 "As tragedias do despeito," *Diário Carioca*, 2 October 1928.

77 Lyrics are found in MIS, *As vozes*, 66.

78 Amado, *O país do carnaval*, 19; Franceschi, CEST, "Documentos," CD-ROM, "Direito Autoral," image 1056.

79 Brancura (Sílvio Fernandes), "Deixa essa mulher chorar," original recording by Francisco Alves and Mário Reis, Odeon, 1930.

80 Martha Abreu suggests in "*Mulatas, Crioulos* and *Morenas*" that caricatured depictions of blacks did not simply reinforce and spread racial prejudice but also contained "a possibility, certainly irreverent and in defiance of

socioracial hierarchies, that not only makes stereotypes and prejudices explicit but also plays with them" (268).

81 By far, the most thorough text on maxixe is Efegê, *Maxixe*. Other useful references include M. Andrade, *Dicionário*, 317–25; Cascudo, *Dicionário*, 486; Chasteen, *National Rhythms*, 17–18, 21–32; Chasteen, "The Prehistory," 38–40; Fryer, *Rhythms of Resistance*, 154–57; Livingston-Isenhour and Garcia, *Choro*, 30–37; Marcondes, *Enciclopédia*, 1:465; McCann, *Hello, Hello*, 44–46; R. Miller, "African Rhythms"; Sandroni, *Feitiço decente*, 62–83; Seigel, *Uneven Encounters*, 67–94; and Tinhorão, *Pequena história*, 58–96.

82 McGowan and Pessanha call it "the first original Brazilian urban dance" (*Brazilian Sound*, 210).

83 Berger, *As freguesias*, 49–50; Caulfield, "Birth of Mangue"; and Gerson, *História das ruas*, 229–39, 246–53.

84 Aoki, in "Authors, Inventors, and Trademark Owners," uses the term to refer to a specific twentieth-century transformation in U.S. trademark law, but I find the term useful for describing the partial, limited nature of authorship rights in turn-of-the-century Rio.

Four. "Our Music"

1 Moraes Filho, *Serenatas e saráus*, 1:vii.

2 The term *tresillo* was coined by Cuban scholars and musicians and adapted by the Brazilian ethnomusicologist Carlos Sandroni. See Sandroni, *Feitiço decente*, 28–32.

3 Cabral, *As escolas*, 242.

4 "Donga recorda o rancho e vê cossacos no frevo," *O Globo*, 5 December 1966.

5 F. Silva, "Pelo telefone e a história do samba," 71.

6 Arlequim, *A Notícia*, 23 January 1917. Reproduced in F. Silva, "Pelo telefone e a história," 70.

7 Beléo, *O Paiz*, 14 February 1917. Reproduced in F. Silva, "Pelo telefone e a história," 70.

8 For a summary of census data on literacy from 1872 to 1890, see Besse, *Restructuring Patriarchy*, 114.

9 Arlequim, "No reinado de Momo . . . uma carta do Mauro," *A Notícia*, 24 January 1917. In F. Silva, "Pelo telefone e a história," 70.

10 "Uma carta do Mauro," *O Paiz*, 15 February 1917. In F. Silva, "Pelo telefone e a história."

11 F. Silva, "Pelo telefone e a história," 66. African-influenced cuisine, like samba, is often held up as a symbol of national identity. See Fry, "Feijoada e soul food," 47–53.

12 In his essay "Pelo telefone e a história" (65), Flávio Silva credits Jota Efegê with uncovering the incident and linking it to the song.

13 Almirante, *No tempo*, 17–20; Sandroni, *Feitiço decente*, 121; F. Silva, "Pelo telefone e a história," 65–66.

14 Sandroni, *Feitiço decente*, 123.

15 M. Andrade, *Dicionário*, 186–90; Cascudo, *Dicionário*, 287–88; N. Lopes, *O negro no Rio de Janeiro*, esp. 95–100; McGowan and Pessanha, *Brazilian Sound*, 144–45; Sandroni, *Feitiço decente*, 123–30.

16 Sandroni, *Feitiço decente*, 130.

17 Ibid., 122; F. Silva, "Pelo telefone e a história," 67; Vasconcelos, *Panorama da música popular brasileira*, 20.

18 Quoted in F. Silva, "Pelo telefone e a história," 69.

19 The lyrics are reproduced in Almirante, *No tempo de Noel Rosa*, 21–22.

20 F. Silva, "Pelo telefone e a história," 73–74n9.

21 Almirante, *No tempo*, 22.

22 Emphasis in the original. Vagalume, *Na roda*, 30–31.

23 Ibid., 75.

24 Cabral, *Pixinguinha*, 17, 22; MIS, *As vozes*, 13, 16; M. Silva and Oliveira Filho, *Filho de Ogum*, 16, 25; Vasconcelos, *Panorama da música popular brasileira*, 85. In the late 1960s, he explained the origins of his nickname (MIS, *As vozes*, 13–14). "It was Pizinguim, not Pixinguinha. Pizinguim was given to me by my African grandmother." After recovering from smallpox (*bexiga*) as a child, others began to call him Bexinguinha, a diminutive of "bexiga," and eventually the two names melded into one. Pixinguinha identified and remembered his grandmother's African-ness through her difficulties speaking Portuguese: "They say that she was African because she spoke halfway mixed-up [*até meio atrapalhado*]." But his sisters recalled things differently. According to Marília T. Barboza da Silva (*Filho de Ogum Bexiguento*, 26), "[They] knew both of their grandmothers well, neither of whom were African, both speaking Portuguese as well as their granddaughters." (According to Silva, a cousin gave Pixinguinha his nickname.)

25 Vasconcelos, *Panorama da música popular brasileira*, 72.

26 MIS, *As vozes*, 89.

27 Cabral, *Pixinguinha*, 35, 40–41.

28 MIS, *As vozes*, 74, 78–79; Vasconcelos, *Panorama da música popular brasileira*, 72.

29 MIS, *As vozes*, 16; Vasconcelos, *Panorama da música popular brasileira*, 85.

30 Nascimento is credited with popularizing the seven-string guitar in Brazil and was a member of Anacleto de Medeiros's Banda do Corpo de Bombeiros.

31 MIS, *As vozes*, 17–18.

32 Cabral, *Pixinguinha*, 44; MIS, *As vozes*, 20–21.

33 Oliveira died soon after the band's formation and was replaced by João Tomás.

34 MIS, *As vozes*, 86. "Spalla" refers to a group's most important musician or instrument.

35 "Donga, general do samba, escreveu: 'o samba é nosso,'" *Diário Carioca*, 26 December 1932.

36 Cabral, *Pixinguinha*, 49.

37 MIS, *As vozes*, 26.

38 The blurry line between jazz and música sertanjea is further evident in the varied use of "jazz" in band names. One group, the Jazz-Band do Cipó, wore sertanejo hats and played large drums and small wooden wind instruments. For differing interpretations of the meanings of "jazz" in 1920s Brazil, see Hertzman, "The Promise," 311–12, and Seigel, *Uneven Encounters*, 95–135.

39 Micol Seigel makes a similar point in *Uneven Encounters*.

40 On their time in Paris, see Bastos, "Brazil in France, 1922"; Cabral, *Pixinguinha*, 71–86; and Seigel, *Uneven Encounters*, 121–35.

41 Quoted in Cabral, *Pixinguinha*, 73.

42 E. Cunha, *Rebellion in the Backlands*; Levine, *Vale of Tears*.

43 Arquivo Sérgio Cabral, "Pasta 'Pixinguinha/Oito Batutas,'" program, 1921; "Theatros," unnamed paper (Recife), 7 July 1921; and "Telos e palcos," *Jornal do Commercio* (Recife), 7 July 1921. Most of the newspaper articles used in the remainder of this chapter were consulted at Arquivo Sérgio Cabral, Pasta Pixinguinha/Oito Batutas.

44 Benjamim Costallat, "Os oito batutas," *Gazeta de Notícias*, 22 January 1922.

45 "O successo de Os Batutas, no Rialto," *Correio da Manhã*, 15 October 1923.

46 Arquivo Sérgio Cabral, "Pasta 'Pixinguinha/Oito Batutas,'" advertisement #1, n.d.

47 "Da platea," *A Noite*, 22 August 1920.

48 "Visões da roça," *Luz e Sombra* (Niterói), 1 November 1920.

49 "A apropriação de músicas brasileira na França," *Vanguarda*, 1 September 1922; Olavo Bilac, *Poesias*, 18th ed. (Rio de Janeiro: Livraria Francisco Alves, 1940), 287. Bilac's poem became a point of reference for writers seeking to define a uniquely Brazilian character at the turn of the century. See Haberly, *Three Sad Races*.

50 McCann, *Hello, Hello*, 22; Moreira, *O rádio no Brasil*, 15.

51 M. Andrade, *Macunaíma*; O. Andrade, "Manifesto antropófago"; Bary, "Oswald de Andrade's Cannibalist Manifesto"; D. Borges, "'Puffy, Ugly, Slothful and Inert,'" 251–54; Dunn, *Brutality Garden*, 12–26; A. Gomes, *Essa gente do Rio . . .* ; McCann, *Hello, Hello*, 7–8, 19; Madureira, "A Cannibal Recipe to Turn a Dessert Country into the Main Course"; Naves, *O violão azul*; Sevcenko, *Orfeu extático*, 269–77; Travassos, *Modernismo e música brasileira*; Velloso, *Modernismo no Rio de Janeiro*. Though beyond my purview here, it is worth calling attention to the parallels between Brazilian attempts

to articulate new relationships between avant-garde and mass culture (and between politics and culture) with similar projects taking place around the same time elsewhere. See Denning, *The Cultural Front*; Garramuño, *Primitive Modernities*; and Huyssen, *After the Great Divide*.

52 Graham, *The Idea*; Stabb, *In Quest of Identity*, 12–33; Stepan, "*The Hour of Eugenics.*"

53 "Música brasileira," unnamed paper (Belo Horizonte), 22 January 1920; "O festival dos 'Oito Batutas', hoje, no Lyrico," *Gazeta de Notícias*, 24 August 1920; "O festival dos 8 Batutas," *A Noite*, 22 August 1920; and "Os '8 Batutas' partirão domingo para a Europa," *Jornal do Brazil*, 26 January 1922.

54 "Notas de Arte: Los ocho batutas," *El Día* (La Plata, Argentina), 22 February 1923.

55 "Os Batutas," unnamed paper (São Paulo), 13 November 1922.

56 Jethro, "Fitas," unnamed paper, 26 February 1920.

57 "Os 'Oito Batutas,'" *Jornal de Minas* (Juiz de Fora), 27 January 1920.

58 *Jornal do Commercio* (São Paulo), undated.

59 "Visões da roça."

60 "O festival dos '8 Batutas,' amanhã," *A Noite*, 10 October 1921.

61 "Visões da roça."

62 Renan, "'A Noite' nos theatros e cinemas," undated.

63 Weinstein, "Racializing Regional Difference."

64 "Varias." *Correio Paulistano* (São Paulo), 28 October 1919.

65 "Chronica social: os Oito Batutas," *Correio Paulistano* (São Paulo), 22 October 1919.

66 Costallat, "Os oito batutas."

67 "A propósito dos 'oito batutas,'" *A Noite*, 25 September 1922.

68 "Vinte minutos de rua do Ouvidor," *A Notícia*, 16 August 1922.

69 A survey of Latin American music treats "music nationalism" and "art music" as distinct from "popular music." The piece mentions Pixinguinha briefly, under the heading "A Note on Popular Music." See Béhague, "Latin American Music."

70 "Écos e novidades," *A Noite*, 16 September 1922.

71 In preparation for the visit, President Epitácio Pessoa and Prefect Carlos Sampaio ordered massive arrests in the hopes of impressing the European royalty. See Caulfield, *In Defense of Honor*, 48–55.

72 Quoted in Cabral, *Pixinguinha*, 61.

73 Emphasis is in the original. Foucault, "What Is an Author?" 101.

74 Also see Amy Chazkel's relevant discussion in *Laws of Chance* regarding the literal and figurative "enclosure" of urban culture and commerce during the early twentieth century.

Five. Mediators and Competitors

1   Seigel, *Uneven Encounters*, 114; Vianna, *Mystery*, 2.
2   *Saludos Amigos*, Disney Gold Classic Collection, Burbank, Calif.: Buena
    Vista Home Entertainment, 1943. Texts that emphasize appropriation and
    exploitation include Candeia and Isnard, *Escolas de samba*; N. Lopes,
    O samba na realidade; Quieróz, *Carnaval brasileiro*; Raphael, "From Popu-
    lar Culture to Microenterprise"; Raphael, "*Samba* and Social Control";
    A. Rodrigues, *Samba negro, espoliação branca*; Shaw, *Social History*; and
    Sheriff, "Theft of *Carnaval*."
3   Vianna, *Mystery*.
4   Ibid., 15. Vianna has been harshly criticized in the United States and Brazil
    for what some consider an overly generous treatment of white intellectuals.
    I consider Vianna's work to be extremely valuable because it questions the
    notion that samba was simply repressed before the birth of samba schools
    in the 1920s and '30s. Even still, he oversimplifies the relationships between
    black musicians and white intellectuals and suggests that white individuals
    mediated on behalf of black musicians.
5   See, for example, Tramonte, *O samba*.
6   Dávila, *Diploma of Whiteness*; MIS, *As vozes*, 15.
7   Along with violins and mandolins, flutes ranked just behind the piano
    as preeminent musical symbols associated with wealth and prestige. See
    Cabral, *Pixinguinha*, 19–20; Freyre, *Order and Progress*, 68–69, 75; and Vas-
    concelos, *Panorama da música popular brasileira*, 85.
8   MIS, *As vozes*, 19, 60.
9   "Ponto de Inhasã" and "Ponto de Ogum," original recordings by Elói Antero
    Dias and Getúlio Marinho, Odeon, 1930.
10 Fischer, *A Poverty of Rights*, 31.
11 MIS, *As vozes*, 62; J. Pereira, *Cor, profissão e mobilidade*, 221.
12 M. Cunha, "'Acontece,'" 327. Also see Rocha, *As nações Kêtu*, 21–28.
13 For example, see T. Pinto and Freitas, *Guia e ritual para organização de te-
    rreiros de Umbanda*; T. Pinto, *O eró (segrêdo) da umbanda*; T. Pinto, *Origens
    da umbanda*; T. Pinto, *Cabala umbandista*; and Souza and Pinto, *Negro e
    branco na cultura religiosa afro-brasileira, os Egbás*.
14 M. Cunha, "'Acontece,'" 327; M. Cunha, "De sambas e passarinhos"; Fa-
    rias et al., *No labirinto*, 265–98; Prandi, "The Expansion of Black Religion in
    White Society"; Vagalume, *Na roda*, 53.
15 Rocha, *As nações Kêtu*, 26.
16 M. Cunha, "'Acontece,'" 329. Also see Fenerick, *Nem do morro*, 203–53;
    T. Gomes, "Para além"; and Velloso, "As tias baianas."
17 Alencar, *Nosso Sinhô*.
18 In addition to "parrot," *louro* can also refer to a person with light colored

skin or hair. Sinhô, "Fala meu louro," original recording by Francisco Alves and Grupo dos Africanos, Popular, ca. 1920.

19 Alencar, *Nosso Sinhô*, 33, 67; M. Cunha, "'Acontece'"; M. Cunha, "De sambas e passarinhos."

20 Sinhô, "Dor de cabeça," original recording by Fernando, Odeon, ca. 1925.

21 Alencar, *Nosso Sinhô*, 69.

22 Sinhô, "Ora vejam só," original recording by Francisco Alves, Odeon, 1927; Sinhô, "Gosto que me enrosco," original recording by Mário Reis, Odeon, 1928.

23 Alencar, *Nosso Sinhô do samba*, 70–71; M. Cunha, "'Acontece,'" 344; M. Cunha, "De sambas e passarinhos."

24 M. Cunha, "De sambas e passarinhos," 571. Sinhô, "O pé de anjo," original recording by Bloco do Fala Meu Louro, Popular, ca. 1919.

25 M. Cunha, "'Acontece,'" 352n42; M. Cunha, "De sambas e passarinhos," 576.

26 Alencar, *Nosso Sinhô*, 68. Sampling in rap and hip-hop raise similar issues. Hebdige, *Cut 'n' Mix*; Lena, "Meaning and Membership"; Marshall, "Giving up Hip-Hop's Firstborn"; Pennycook, "'The Rotation Gets Thick. The Constraints Get Thin'"; Schloss, *Making Beats*.

27 Quoted in M. Cunha, "De sambas e passarinhos," 549.

28 Alencar, *Nosso Sinhô*, 71.

29 ASC, "Os 'oito batutas' estáo sendo prejudicados," *O Globo*, n.d.; ASC, "Uma declaração dos directores da orchestra 'os batutas,'" *O Globo*, n.d.

30 Cabral, *Pixinguinha*, 133.

31 "A acrtiz negra Deo Costa quer 'ver o preto no branco,'" *Folha da Manhã*, 21 November 1926, 8. Cited in Barros, *Corações De Chocolat*, 179–81.

32 The troupe was also directed by Jaime Silva, a white Portuguese. See Barros, *Corações De Chocolat*, and T. Gomes, *Um espelho*, 287–374.

33 "Por que o samba é diferente na voz de cada uma de suas intérpretes," *Carioca*, 12 December 1936. Quoted in G. Lopes, "Samba e mercado de bens culturais," 70.

34 MIS, *As vozes*, 73.

35 M. Cunha, "De sambas e passarinhos," 582n10.

36 M. Cunha, "'Acontece,'" 329.

37 Coutinho, *Os cronistas*; L. Pereira, *Carnaval das letras*.

38 Coutinho, *Os cronistas*; Geraldo, "Histórias e historiadores"; Sandroni, "Adeus à MPB."

39 Coutinho, *Os cronistas*, 90–108; Geraldo, "Histórias e historiadores"; and "Notas biográficas do autor publicadas no jornal 'Ameno Resedá', editado pelo rancho do mesmo nome" in Vagalume, *Na roda*.

40 Coutinho, *Os cronistas*, 101.

41 Coutinho, *Os cronistas*; Efegê, *Figuras e coisas*, 55–57, 223–24.

42 N. Sodré, *História da imprensa*, 424, 453. The paper's history has not been studied in depth, and it is unclear how or why three prominent Afro-Brazilian reporters all ended up working for it. But there is no doubt that their shared desire to write about Carnival and music in the city's poorer regions linked up with the *Diário Carioca*'s self-appointed role as the people's voice.

43 Coutinho, *Os cronistas*, 87–88.

44 Vagalume, *Na roda*, 19.

45 Ibid., 23–26.

46 Ibid., 90.

47 Sandroni, *Feitiço decente*, 148; Cabral, *As escolas*.

48 "A fabulosa herança de Chico Alves," *Boletim Social da* UBC 10, no. 29 (October–December 1952): 15. In 1942, the cruzeiro directly substituted the mil-réis, so that Cr\$ 1.00 equaled 1\$000. For typical salaries and cost of living during the late 1940s, see Instituto de Economia, *Pesquisa sôbre o padrão de vida do comerciário no Distrito Federal*.

49 Vagalume, *Na roda*, 96.

50 Ibid., 120.

51 Ibid., 43, 202.

52 Ibid., 239. Article originally appeared in the *Diário Carioca* on 24 September 1933.

53 Vagalume, *Na roda*, 93–94.

54 See Conniff, *Urban Politics in Brazil*.

55 Emphasis in the original. Vagalume, *Na roda*, 30, 94–95.

56 Ibid., 30, 47, 96 (emphasis in original).

57 Ibid., 88, 92.

58 Ibid., 107–9.

59 Ibid., 150, 204.

60 Ibid., 175, 180, 184, 188, 189.

61 Agache, *Rio de Janeiro*; Fischer, *A Poverty of Rights*, 16, 38–49.

62 Vagalume, *Na roda*, 146.

63 Fischer, *A Poverty of Rights*, 15–17; Sinhô, "A favela vai abaixo," original recording by Francisco Alves, Odeon, 1928.

64 To distinguish himself from another Paulo who lived in nearby Bento Ribeiro, he took the name Paulo da Portela, for Oswaldo Cruz's main thoroughfare, the Estrada da Portela. Paulo's father, Mário Benjamin de Oliveira, was rarely around, and some claim that Paulo was, in fact, the son of the entertainer Benjamin de Oliveira. See M. Silva and Santos, *Paulo da Portela*.

65 Ibid., 40.

66 Ibid., 19, 20, 43–44, 46, 59, 113, 132.

67 Ibid., 86. McCann shows in *Hello, Hello* (52–54) that the distance between morro and cidade was more societal construct than musical reality, a point borne out in *A Nação*'s contest, which billed itself as a competition for musicians who lived in the morros but included individuals who hailed from across the city. Also see Fenerick, *Nem do morro*.

68 M. Silva and Santos, *Paulo da Portela*, 92.

69 Ibid., 72, 78, 87–90, 92.

70 Ibid., 92.

71 Ibid., 132.

72 Holanda, *Memórias do Café Nice*, 52.

73 Daniella Thompson illuminates this story in several detailed entries on her blog, daniellathompson.com/Texts/Stokowski/Stokowski.htm (accessed August 2007).

74 This figure, calculated at http://measuringworth.com, differs dramatically from the one Thompson calculated, which she concedes may not be reliable.

75 It is impossible to quantify the details or significance of informal arrangements brokered between musicians, but interviews recorded by Sérgio Cabral and others strongly suggest that they were as much a part of the music industry as were the written formalized arrangements sealed by Figner and other label owners. See especially Cabral, *As escolas*, and Sandroni, *Feitiço decente*, 143–55.

76 An image of the letter appears in M. Silva and Oliveira Filho, *Filho de Ogum*, 182.

77 Pixinguinha's letter also suggests the enduring importance of individual patronage and the *pistolão* (letter of recommendation). During the late 1930s and '40s, reformers attempted to establish a more equitable and unbiased system of hiring employees by establishing *concursos* (competitive examinations) meant to replace the pistolão. Their efforts had limited success. See Owensby, *Intimate Ironies*, 80–88.

78 A. Garcia, *O circo*, 5; Erminia Silva, *Circo-teatro*, 222.

79 "Ouvindo os 'bachareis' do samba," *Diário Carioca*, 15 January 1933; Vagalume, *Na roda*, 125–26. Tio Faustino and his property claims are discussed further in chapter 6. Also see Hertzman, "A Brazilian Counterweight."

80 Said, *Musical Elaborations*, 7.

81 Ataulfo Alves, and Roberto Martins, "Rei vagabundo," remastered original sound recording performed by Carlos Galhardo, *É quase a felicidade*, Revivendo, 1996.

82 Nelson Cavaquinho, José Ribeiro, and Noel Silva, "Rei vagabundo," remastered original sound recording performed by Nelson Cavaquinho, *Fala Mangueira!* EMI, n.d. (orig. 1968).

83 Wilson Batista, "Lenço no pescoço," original sound recording performed by Silvio Caldas, Victor, 1933.

84 Rerecordings of "Lenço" and the other songs in the Batista-Rosa exchange are available on *Coleção 10 Polegadas: Francisco Egydio, Roberto Paiva, Tom Jobim e Vinícius de Moraes*, CD, EMI, 2003.

85 McCann, "Noel Rosa's Nationalist Logic," 10.

86 Quoted in Olivia Cunha's *Intenção e gesto*, 90.

87 MIS, *As vozes*, 18–19.

88 See McCann, *Hello, Hello*, ninth image between pp. 128 and 129.

89 Joubert de Carvalho, "Seduções de um beijo," original recording by Pedro Celestino, Odeon, 1926.

90 Pixinguinha and João de Barro, "Carinhoso," original recording by Orlando Silva, Victor, 1937.

91 Pixinguinha and Benedito Lacerda, "Vagando," original recording by Pixinguinha and Lacerda, RCA Victor, 1950.

92 A. Pinto, *O choro*.

93 Ibid., 16, 77, 83, 109, 193.

94 Quoted in Barros, *Corações De Chocolat*, 111.

95 Ibid., 113.

96 For example, Bonfíglio de Oliveira, "O malandrinho," original recording by Edgard Freitas and Grupo do Donga, Odeon, ca. 1923; Lamartine Babo and Pixinguinha, "Mulher boêmia," original recording by Benício Barbosa, Parlophon, 1928; Felisberto Martins, "Teus beijos," original recording by Donga and Orquestra Típica Pixinguinha, Parlophon, 1928; De Chocolat and Donga, "Miss Brasil," original recording by Alfredo Albuquerque, Odeon, 1929; Gastão Viana and Pixinguinha, "Mulata baiana," original recording by Patrício Teixeira, Victor, 1938.

97 Assis Pacheco, "Um samba na penha," original recording by Pepa Delgado, Odeon, ca. 1907; "O vendeiro e a mulata," original recording by Mário Pinheiro and Pepa Delgado, Odeon, ca. 1904.

98 That power has much in common with the control and authority wielded by white writers, who incorporated "Africanisms" into their work and assumed the voices of black characters—what Alexandra Isfahani-Hammond, in *White Negritude*, calls "writing black" (45–82).

99 Arlequim, "No reinado de Momo," *A Notícia*, n.d.

100 M. Silva and Santos, *Paulo da Portela*, 59. Many observers associated Carnival and dance halls in fast-growing urban centers like Rio and São Paulo with violence and moral decay. The honor of women who frequented *dancings* (dance halls) or attended Carnival without "appropriate supervision" was often called into question. See Caulfield, "The Changing Politics of Freedom and Virginity in Rio de Janeiro, 1920–1940."

101 M. Silva and Santos, *Paulo da Portela*, 114. It is no coincidence that the centering of the *mulata* coincided with a period during which, to use Susan Besse's apt phrase in *Restructuring Patriarchy*, patriarchy was restructured

but not dismantled. While women entered the workforce and public dia-
logues in increasing numbers between the two world wars, their increased
presence did little to shift long-standing assumptions and hierarchies. For a
related discussion, with particular emphasis on race, see Alberto, *Terms of
Inclusion*, 74–77.

102 M. Silva and Santos, *Paulo da Portela*, 94.

103 Ibid., 19–29.

104 "Os autores dos sambas dos outros . . ." *Diário Carioca*, 22 March 1933.

Six. Bodies and Minds

1 Floriano de Lemos, *Correio da Manha*, 28 November 1943.

2 Béhague, *Heitor Villa-Lobos*; McCann, *Hello, Hello*, 237. For other works on
Villa-Lobos, see Appleby, *Heitor Villa-Lobos*; França, *Villa-Lobos: Sintese
crítica*; Peppercorn, *Villa-Lobos: Collected Studies*; and Wisnik, "Getúlio da
Paixão Cearense."

3 See D. Borges, "Healing and Mischief," 194–96; D. Borges, "'Puffy, Ugly,
Slothful and Inert,'" esp. 240–43; Peard, *Race, Place, and Medicine*, esp. 101–
6; Schwarcz, *Spectacle of the Races*, esp. 234–96; and Skidmore, *Black into
White*, esp. 57–62.

4 R. Rodrigues, *As raças humanas*.

5 Ibid., 8.

6 Ibid., 141–42.

7 Quoted and translated in Grinberg, "Slavery, Liberalism, and Civil Law,"
121.

8 Freyre, *Masters and the Slaves*. The specific reference to "valorization"
comes from an article published by Freyre in 1926.

9 See Stroud, *Defence*, 136–43.

10 The book first appeared in 1929 as the *Compêndio de história da música*.

11 M. Andrade, *Pequena história*, 182, 186.

12 Ibid., 16, 17.

13 Ibid., 182, 187.

14 Ibid., 21.

15 McGowan and Pessanha, *Brazilian Sound*, 210.

16 M. Andrade, *Pequena história*, 186.

17 Ibid., 19, 23, 187–88.

18 Ibid., 193.

19 Ibid., 190.

20 Ibid., 163, 194, 195, 196.

21 For a discussion of similar ideas advanced by Fernando Ortiz and Alejo
Carpentier in Cuba, see Moore, *Nationalizing Blackness*.

22 Haberly, *Three Sad Races*; M. Nunes, "Mário de Andrade in 'Paradise,'"
70–75.

23 Z. Nunes, *Cannibal Democracy*, 59–61. I am grateful to Carlos Sandroni and Barbara Weinstein for helping me track down this example.

24 M. Andrade, *Ensaio sobre a música brasileira*; M. Andrade, *Macunaíma*.

25 Though Tia Ciata's house was in Praça Onze, Andrade sets the ceremony (and her home) a few blocks away in Mangue, the city's red-light district. Bruno Carvalho, in "Porous City," treats this dislocation as an example of how writers like Andrade selectively blurred and blended Cidade Nova's racialized symbols and landmarks (137–38).

26 M. Silva and Oliveira Filho, *Filho de Ogum*, 84–85; Vianna, *Mystery*. Also see Dealtry, *No fio da navalha*, 19–44.

27 J. Pereira, *Cor, profissão e mobilidade*, 206n40.

28 M. Andrade, *Macunaíma*, 54.

29 Ibid., *Macunaíma*, 59.

30 M. Andrade, "Força biológica da música," 47, 50, 56.

31 "Os reis do choro e do samba: Octavio Vianna, 'o China,' violão seguro e voz afinada dos '8 batutas,'" *O Jornal*, 29 January 1925.

32 Quoted and translated in Alberto, *Terms of Inclusion*, 64.

33 Quoted in DuBois, "Brazil," 33. Also see Skidmore, *Black into White*, esp. 65–70.

34 In this sense, he shares much in common with the "ethnicity entrepreneurs" described by Philip Kasinitz (*Caribbean New York*), J. Lorand Matory (*Black Atlantic Religion*), and Stephan Palmié (*Wizards and Scientists*).

35 "Ouvindo os 'bachareis' do samba," *Diário Carioca*, 15 January 1933.

36 Pixinguinha and Donga reportedly chose the name Guarda Velha to indicate their desire to protect "traditional" music. Supporting Pixinguinha on flute and Donga on guitar was a percussion section that included João da Baiana striking a kitchen plate, Tio Faustino and his omelê, and several other men playing agogô, cabaça, pandeiro, and cuíca. See Cabral, *Pixinguinha*, 133–34.

37 Brown, *Umbanda*, 25.

38 Bastide, *African Religions* i Ramos, *O negro brasileiro*.

39 Pierson, *Negroes in Brazil*, 305. Matory, Luis Parés, and Beatriz Dantas have shown how the idea of candomblé purity—and the hierarchical relationship between candomblé and other "dilutions"—have been constructed over time. See Dantas, *Vovó Nagô e Papai Branco*; Matory, *Black Atlantic Religion*; and Parés, *A formação*.

40 Cabral, *Pixinguinha*, 134.

41 Orestes Barbosa, "Na vertigem da cidade: um aspecto da avenida," *A Notícia*, 15 September 1923.

42 "Os reis do choro e do samba: um flautista de valor—Alfredo Vianna, o 'Pixinguinha,'" *O Jornal*, 27 January 1925.

43 Abercrombie's discussion in "To Be Indian" of Aymara constructions of

"savage" and "civilized" spheres within their own history—and the subsequent "cultural pidgin" produced by outsiders—is particularly relevant here.

44 Luciano Gallet, "Reagir!" *O Globo*, 22 March 1930; Gallet, "Reagir!" *Weco: Revista de vida e cultura musical* 2, no. 2 (March 1930): 3–7. The Biblioteca Nacional–Arquivo Sonoro in Rio de Janeiro houses a full run of *Weco*. All other articles and personal communications cited in this section were consulted at the Acervo de Manuscritos, Biblioteca Alberto Nepomuceno da Escola de Música da Universidade Federal do Rio de Janeiro, hereafter AM-BAN.

45 Despite Gallet's achievements, little has been written about him. Biographical details are taken from various documents in AM-BAN.

46 Gallet, "Reagir!"

47 Ibid.

48 Renato Almeida, "Vida musical: a traição da música popular," *Diário de Notícias*, 18 June 1930; AM-BAN, Pasta 29; Luiz Heitor, "Música: reagir!" *A Ordem*, 8 April 1930 and 24 April 1930.

49 Pedro Sinzig, "Música popular," *Jornal do Brasil*, 6 July 1930.

50 Mário de Andrade, "Luciano Gallet e a sua obra," *Diário Nacional* (São Paulo), 8 October 1929. *Música erudita* translates, roughly, as "erudite," "sophisticated," or even "classical" music.

51 Luciano Gallet, "Folclore brasileiro: danças e cantigas," *Weco: Revista de vida e cultura musical* 1, nos. 4–5 (January–March 1929): 13–14.

52 Luciano Gallet, "A missão dos músicos brasileiros de agora," *Weco: Revista de vida e cultura musical* 2, no. 1 (February 1930): 15–17.

53 "Canções populares brasileiras recolhidas e harmonizadas por Luciano Gallet," *Weco: Revista de vida e cultura musical* 1, no. 1 (November 1928): 15.

54 Gallet, *Estudos de folklore*; AM-BAN.

55 For example, Oscar Guanabarino, "Pelo mundo das artes," *Jornal do Commercio*, 16 April 1930.

56 Arnaldo Estella, "O compositor e o interprete brasileiro," *Weco: Revista de vida e cultura musical* 2, nos. 7–8 (August–September 1930): 7–8.

57 Djalma de Vincenzi, "Sinhô: sua vida de artista e seus direitos autoraes," *Weco: Revista de vida e cultura musical* 2, nos. 9–10 (October–November 1930): 8–9.

58 Paavo Nurmi, "O direito autoral em disco," pts. 1 and 2, *Weco: Revista de vida e cultura musical* 1, no. 9 (January 1930): 15–16; 2, no. 1 (February 1930): 20–21.

59 Nurmi, "O direito autoral em disco," pt. 2.

60 "Correio musical," *Correio da Manhã*, 11 February 1931.

61 AM-BAN, Pasta 29, untitled.

62 "Os músicos desempregados," *Democracia*, 23 February 1931; Myriam Dutra, "Em torno de um memorial," *Diário Carioca*, 19 February 1931.

63 "Em prol do nosso carnaval de rua," *Weco: Revista de vida e cultura musical* 1, no. 3 (January 1929): 18; "Uma entrevista com o snr. Walter Mocchi," *Weco: Revista de vida e cultura musical* 2, no. 12 (January 1931): 14–15.

64 AM-BAN, Pasta 29, "Saudação"; Aranha, *A viagem*.

65 "Música & co.," *Weco: Revista de vida e cultura musical* 2, nos. 5–6 (June–July 1930): 3–4.

66 "A nossa capa: Villa Lobos," *Weco: Revista de vida e cultura musical* 1, no. 2 (December 1928): 7.

67 Emphasis in the original. O. Lorenzo Fernandez, "Considerações sobre a música brasileira (excerpto)," *Weco: Revista de vida e cultura musical* 2, no. 4 (May 1930): 11–14.

68 Gallet, *Estudos de folklore*.

69 Barroso was also "virulently anti-Semitic" and a member of the fascist Integralist movement. See Skidmore, *Black into White*, 205.

70 Gallet, *Estudos de folklore*, 50.

71 Ibid., 27.

72 Ibid., 37.

73 Gallet's denial of indigenous influences in favor of African ones was part of a larger shift through which black caricatures replaced Indian ones as national racial mascots, and this is also indicative of a general negation of indigenous musical influences in Brazil. See Bastos, "O índio," and McCann, *Hello, Hello*, 2–4.

74 Gallet, *Estudos de folklore*, 53.

75 Berrien, *Latin American Composers*, 3, 12. In defining blacks as raw material, the author followed in a long line of paternalistic and racist thought embraced by intellectuals across the Americas. In 1918, the prominent Argentine writer Carlos Octavio Bunge wrote, "The Negro has not invented anything, he is not capable of intellectual leadership or of artistic creativity" (quoted and translated in Stabb, *In Quest of Identity*, 16–17). For a trenchant critique of the double standards associated with cultural creation and appropriation, see Clifford, *Routes*, 201–2.

76 Accounts of the event are found at http://www.dicionariompb.com.br and in M. Soares, *São Ismael*.

77 AN, 70.7492, 1927; AN, 70.7685, 1927; AN, 70.7112, 1927; AN, 70.7094, 1927; AN, 70.8665, 1928; AN, 6z.13226, 1929; AN, 70.11771, 1930.

78 AN, 6z.13226; AN, 70.11771.

79 AN, 70.7685.

80 AN, 70.7094.

81 AN, 70.7492; AN, 70.7685; AN, 70.7094; AN, 70.8665.

82 AN, 70.8665.

83 For example, AN, 70.7112; L. Carvalho, *Ismael Silva*, 18.

84 AN, 6z.13226.

85 It is significant that the creation of the first escolas coincided with an in-crease in value attached to education and diplomas, which helped distin-guish white-collar employees from manual laborers. See Owensby, *Intimate Ironies*, 58.

86 AN, Processo 746, no. 600, Maço 16, Gal. BA; AN, Processo 540, no. 6, Maço 242, Gal. BA; AN, Processo 128, no. 7, Maço 242, Gal. BA.

87 AN, Processo 361, no. 28, Maço 143, Gal. BA.

88 AN, Processo 128, no. 7, Maço 242, Gal. BA; AN, Processo 167, no. 26, Maço 242, Gal. BA.

89 The most well-known case of state violence against musicians took place *after* the golden age. In 1960, Carnival festivities were marred when police "settled" a fierce dispute surrounding the parade competition by clubbing and kicking samba school members. See Luis Gardel's *Escolas de samba*, 112–20.

Seven. Alliances and Limits

1 Vagalume, *Na roda*, 126 (emphasis in the original).

2 "Os sem-trabalho," *Diário da Noite*, 1 December 1930.

3 Levine, *Father of the Poor?* Useful guides to literature on the Vargas years include V. Borges, "Anos trinta e política"; Capelato, "Estado Novo"; Hentschke, *Vargas and Brazil*; *Luso-Brazilian Review*, special issue; Pandolfi, *Repensando o Estado Novo*; and Weinstein, "Postcolonial Brazil," 231–42.

4 "A 'marche aux flambeaux' promovida pela classe musical em homenagem ao sr. Getulio Vargas," *O Jornal*, 9 December 1930.

5 "'Marche aux flambeaux,' da classe musical," *Diário da Noite*, 2 December 1930; "A 'marche aux flambeaux' em homenagem ao Sr. Getulio Vargas," *Diário da Noite*, 8 December 1930; "A imponente manifestação da classe musical ao presidente Getulio Vargas," *Diário da Noite*, 9 December 1930; "A imponente manifestação da classe musical ao presidente Getulio Vargas," *Diário da Noite*, 2nd ed., 9 December 1930.

6 CEST, Documentos, Direito Autoral, images 1324–32. As noted earlier, the 1911 data, culled from individual contracts, may be incomplete. By con-trast, the 1930 data are taken from a ledger and appear to be comprehensive. Nonetheless, the vast gap between 1911 and 1930 is indicative of the larger expansion of the music industry that occurred during the 1910s and '20s.

7 Cabral, *Pixinguinha*, 179.

8 McCann, *Hello, Hello*, 23. Also see Cabral, *No tempo*; Casé, *Programa Casé*; Decreto no. 21.111, 1 March 1932, in *Coleção das Leis de 1932*, 1:285–322, Rio de Janeiro: Imprensa Nacional, 1942; Federico, *História da comunicação*;

Ferraretto, *Rádio*; Jambeiro et al., *Tempos de Vargas*; Moreira, *O rádio no Brasil*; Murce, *Bastidores do rádio*; Nascimento, PRA-9 *Rádio Mayrink Veiga*; and J. Vieira, *César de Alencar*.

9 McCann, *Hello, Hello*. On radio as a means for professionalization in music, also see Davis, *White Face, Black Mask*; Fenerick, *Nem do morro*, 166–200; and Pereira, *Cor, profissão*.

10 Franceschi, *A Casa Edison*, 235–41; McCann, *Hello, Hello*, 22–26; Ortiz, *A moderna tradição brasileira*, 39–40; M. Sampaio, *História do rádio e da televisão no Brasil e no Mundo (memórias de um pioneiro)*, 110.

11 Cabral, *Pixinguinha*, 129–30.

12 "A imponente," 2nd ed.

13 "'Marche aux flambeaux,' da classe musical."

14 The exchange rate between Brazil and the United States fluctuated from just less than 4 mil-réis per U.S. dollar in 1917 to a high of 9.7 in 1923 to 9.3 in 1930.

15 João Rodrigues, *João do Rio*, 214.

16 On his way out of power in 1945, he made a "populist gamble," which helped revive some of that earlier hope and ultimately set the stage for his return to power in 1951. See French, "Populist Gamble."

17 Arquivo Gustavo Capanema, Centro de Pesquisa e Documentação da História Contemporânea do Brasil/Fundação Getúlio Vargas, GC/g 1934.09.22.

18 Williams, *Culture Wars*, 82–83.

19 Rosa, Abadie Farias, "Da representação e execução publicas," *Boletim da Sociedade Brasileira de Autores Theatraes*, no. 114 (December 1933): 6–7.

20 "Vida interna da S.B.A.T.," *Boletim da Sociedade Brasileira de Autores Theatraes*, no. 92 (February 1932): 8.

21 "Vida interna da S.B.A.T.," *Boletim da Sociedade Brasileira de Autores Theatraes*, no. 88 (October 1931).

22 E. Diniz, *Chiquinha Gonzaga*, 211–13.

23 "Actas das semanaes realisadas no mez de Março de 1925," *Boletim da Sociedade Brasileira de Autores Theatraes* 2, no. 9 (March 1925).

24 "Datas nacionaes," *Boletim da Sociedade Brasileira de Autores Theatraes* 3, no. 26 (August 1926): 194.

25 "Vida interna da S.B.A.T.," *Boletim da Sociedade Brasileira de Autores Theatraes*, no. 95 (May 1932): 3.

26 "Protecção dos direitos autoraes de musicistas," *Boletim da Sociedade Brasileira de Autores Theatraes* 3, no. 20 (February 1926): 139.

27 "Acção official em defesa do direito do autor," *Boletim da Sociedade Brasileira de Autores Theatraes*, no. 97 (July 1932): 8.

28 "Relatorio referente ao anno de 1925, apresentado aos socios da S.B.A.T. pelo seu presidente, em assembléa geral ordinaria realizada em 13 de abril de 1926," *Boletim da Sociedade Brasileira de Autores Theatraes* 3, no. 22

(April 1926): 153; "Actas das semanaes realizadas no mez de janeiro de 1927," *Boletim da Sociedade Brasileira de Autores Theatraes* 4, no. 31 (January 1927): 250; "Congrès International du Theatre," *Boletim da Sociedade Brasileira de Autores Theatraes* 5, no. 48 (June 1928): 400.

29 "Reunião em Berlim do 'cartel' das grandes sociedades de direitos de execução," *Boletim da Sociedade Brasileira de Autores Theatraes*, no. 79 (January 1931): 10.

30 "O congresso de Roma funda o 'cartel' das sociedades de autores e compositores dramaticos," *Boletim da Sociedade Brasileira de Autores Theatraes*, no. 82 (April 1931): 10.

31 "Notas & informações: o chefe da egreja catholica e seu grande apoio moral ao direito de autor," *Boletim da Sociedade Brasileira de Autores Theatraes*, no. 94 (April 1932): 8–9.

32 The SBAT often clashed publicly with local radio executives over the payment of author's rights. See Fenerick, *Nem do morro*, 184–89.

33 "Os impostos theatraes," *Boletim da Sociedade Brasileira de Autores Theatraes* 3, no. 30 (December 1926): 239–40.

34 Alvarenga Fonseca, "10a these: o cinema, o maior inimigo do theatro," *Boletim da Sociedade Brasileira de Autores Theatraes* 4, no. 35 (May 1927).

35 M.N., "Em defeza do theatro," *Boletim da Sociedade Brasileira de Autores Theatraes* 5, no. 48 (June 1928): 399.

36 ESXX, Cultura, Diversões, Teatros e outras casas de espetáculos, 1934. This and subsequent data labeled "ESXX" are found on the CD-ROM portion of Instituto Brasileiro de Geografia e Estatística, *Estatísticas do século XX*, Rio de Janeiro: IBGE, 2003.

37 "A 'marche aux flambeaux' promovida pela classe musical em homenagem ao sr. Getulio Vargas."

38 "'Marche aux flambeaux,' da classe musical"; "A imponente."

39 "A 'marche aux flambeaux' promovida pela classe musical em homenagem ao sr. Getulio Vargas."

40 On Sayão, see Rasponi, *Last Prima Donnas*, 505–11.

41 "Os impostos theatraes," *Boletim da Sociedade Brasileira de Autores Theatraes* 3, no. 30 (December 1926): 239.

42 "Jornaes dos estados," *Boletim da Sociedade Brasileira de Autores Theatraes* 3, no. 20 (February 1926): 138.

43 "Relatorio da Sociedade Brasileira de Autores Theatraes, lido pelo Sr. Alvarenga Fonseca, na Assembléa Geral Ordinaria realizada a 13 de setembro e referente ao exercicio de 1926, em que foi seu presidente," *Boletim da Sociedade Brasileira de Autores Theatraes* 4, no. 39 (September 1927): 314.

44 "Notas & informações: porque se deve cobrar o 'pequeno direito,'" *Boletim da Sociedade Brasileira de Autores Theatraes*, no. 79 (January 1931): 9. For a

related discussion of hierarchies drawn between "high" and "low" theater, see T. Gomes, *Um espelho*, 121–92.

45 It was impossible to ascertain dates for thirteen of the fourteen remaining contracts; one was signed in 1936.

46 "Actas das reuniões realisadas no mez de Janeiro de 1929," *Boletim da Sociedade Brasileira de Autores Theatraes* 6, no. 55 (January 1929): 462; "Conselho Deliberativo," *Boletim da Sociedade Brasileira de Autores Theatraes* 6, no. 55 (January 1929): 466–67.

47 Decreto no. 5.492.

48 Decreto no. 5.492; Decreto no. 18.527, 10 December 1928, in *Collecção das leis da Republica dos Estados Unidos do Brasil de 1928*, 2:607–20, Rio de Janeiro: Imprensa Nacional, 1929; Vidal, *O teatro e a lei*, 3.

49 Decreto no. 19.770, 19 March 1931, in *Coleção das Leis de 1931*, 1:234–38, Rio de Janeiro: Imprensa Nacional, 1942.

50 Quoted and translated in Owensby, *Intimate Ironies*, 38–39.

51 A final tier included teams of military grunts. See L. Pereira, *Footballmania*, 116, 118.

52 Chazkel, *Laws of Chance*, 211.

53 Lei no. 2.577, 17 January 1912, in *Collecção das leis da Republica dos Estados Unidos do Brazil de 1912*, 1:231, Rio de Janeiro: Imprensa Nacional, 1915; Decreto no. 11.588, 19 May 1915, in *Collecção das leis da Republica dos Estados Unidos do Brazil de 1915*, 3:135–226, Rio de Janeiro: Imprensa Nacional, 1917.

54 *The Civil Code of Brazil*; Pimenta, *Princípios de direitos autorais*, 97–134; Santiago, *Aquarela do direito autoral*, 59–66.

55 Pimenta, *Princípios*, 97, 123–26, 132; Santiago, *Aquarela do direito autoral*, 52.

56 Irmãos Valença and Lamartine Babo, "Teu cabelo não nega!," original sound recording performed by Castro Barbosa, Victor, 1932. See Caldwell, *Negras in Brazil*, 88–90.

57 Pimenta, *Princípios*, 127–28; Santiago, *Aquarela do direito autoral*, 116–17.

58 Decreto no. 4.092, 4 August 1920, in *Collecção das leis da Republica dos Estados Unidos do Brasil de 1920*, 1:235–36, Rio de Janeiro: Imprensa Nacional, 1923; "Prefeitura do districto federal: actos do poder executivo," *Boletim da Sociedade Brasileira de Autores Theatraes* 2, no. 7 (January 1925): 1.

59 Vidal, *O teatro e a lei*, 35–49. On other aspects of Vidal's role in regulating culture and commerce, see Chazkel, *Laws of Chance*, 221.

60 Decreto no. 4.541, 6 February 1922, in *Collecção das leis da Republica dos Estados Unidos do Brasil de 1922*, 1:88–89, Rio de Janeiro: Imprensa Nacional, 1923; Decreto no. 15.530, 21 June 1922, in *Collecção das leis da Republica dos Estados Unidos do Brasil de 1922*, 2:388–400, Rio de Janeiro: Imprensa Nacional, 1923.

61 It also required the society to pay a small annual fee. See "Noticiario: utili-

dade publica municipal," *Boletim da Sociedade Brasileira de Autores Theatraes* 2, no. 11 (May 1925): 44–45.

62 Decreto no. 4.790, 2 January 1924, in *Collecção das leis da Republica dos Estados Unidos do Brasil de 1924*, 1:4–5, Rio de Janeiro: Imprensa Nacional, 1925; Santiago, *Aquarela do direito autoral*, 53, 66–67.

63 "Noticiario," *Boletim da Sociedade Brasileira de Autores Theatraes* 1, no. 4 (October 1924): 31; Decreto no. 16.590, 10 September 1924, in *Collecção das leis da Republica dos Estados Unidos do Brasil de 1924*, 3:161–80, Rio de Janeiro: Imprensa Nacional, 1925; Decreto no. 5.492, 16 July 1928, in *Collecção das leis da Republica dos Estados Unidos do Brasil de 1928*, 1:124–28, Rio de Janeiro: Imprensa Nacional, 1929.

64 Decreto no. 18.527.

65 "Actas das reuniões realisadas no mez de Junho de 1928," *Boletim da Sociedade Brasileira de Autores Theatraes* 5, no. 48 (June 1928): 390.

66 "Noticiario," *Boletim da Sociedade Brasileira de Autores Theatraes* 4, no. 31 (January 1927): 255–56.

67 "Actas das reuniões realisadas no mez de Junho de 1930," *Boletim da Sociedade Brasileira de Autores Theatraes* 7, nos. 70–72 (April–June 1930): 604.

68 "Congresso artistico theatral," *Boletim da Sociedade Brasileira de Autores Theatraes* 2, no. 7 (January 1925): 10–11.

69 "Censura theatral," *Boletim da Sociedade Brasileira de Autores Theatraes* 2, no. 18 (December 1925).

70 "Notas & informações," *Boletim da Sociedade Brasileira de Autores Theatraes*, no. 107 (May 1933): 10–12.

71 G. Lopes, "Samba e mercado de bens culturais," 106–9.

72 "O radio não é censurado?" *Boletim da Sociedade Brasileira de Autores Theatraes*, no. 100 (October 1932): 9.

73 "Noticiario: oitavo anniversario da S.B.A.T. e homenagem á maestrina brasileira D. Francisca Gonzaga," *Boletim da Sociedade Brasileira de Autores Theatraes* 2, no. 16 (October 1925): 90–98.

74 Ibid., 94.

75 The transformation of Gonzaga's more radical actions into palatable and cooperative acts resembles the way that other women in mid- and late nineteenth-century Brazil saw their bold actions reduced and twisted in the public eye. See Ipsen, "Delicate Citizenship."

76 "Nossas Assembléas Geraes," *Boletim da Sociedade Brasileira de Autores Theatraes* 2, no. 17 (November 1925): 105.

77 Iveta Ribeiro, "2a these: da fundação de uma Liga de Protecção á Mulher do Theatro," *Boletim da Sociedade Brasileira de Autores Theatraes* 3, no. 25 (July 1926): iv.

78 "As conferencias na S.B.A.T.," *Boletim da Sociedade Brasileira de Autores Theatraes* 2, no. 18 (December 1925): 113–22.

79 "'O principe dos gatunos': homenagem ao seu autor," *Boletim da Sociedade Brasileira de Autores Theatraes* 2, no. 12 (June 1925): 54–55.

80 Weinstein, "Racializing Regional Difference," 244–45.

81 Vagalume, *Na roda*, 71.

82 "Os mambembes nos Estados," *Boletim da Sociedade Brasileira de Autores Theatraes* 5, no. 44 (June 1928): 360; N. Lopes, *Dicionário*, 157.

83 Pederneiras, *Geringonça carioca*, 42.

84 Barros, *Corações De Chocolat*, 230–32.

85 ESXX, Cultura, Various. The vast majority of those registered were classified as artistas. The overall number of registered individuals declined from 1,924 in 1935 to 519 the next year, and to 356 in 1937. The cause for the decline is unclear.

86 Fischer, *A Poverty of Rights*.

87 "Communicados: A prisão de um actor da Companhia Mulata Brasileira como feiticeiro," *Diário Carioca*, 22 January 1931. The case is mentioned in Raphael, "*Samba* and Social Control." No police report appears to have been filed.

88 AN, 6z.18179.

89 For a discussion of police repression of homosexuals, see Green, *Beyond Carnival*, 17–146.

90 I borrow the phrase "the process is the punishment" from Feeley, *Process Is the Punishment*.

Eight. Everywhere and Nowhere

1 See R. Araújo, *O batismo do trabalho*; Conniff, *Urban Politics in Brazil*; Erickson, *Brazilian Corporative State and Working-Class Politics*; French, *Brazilian Workers' ABC*; French, "The Origin of Corporatist State Intervention in Brazilian Industrial Relations, 1930–1934"; A. Gomes, *Burguesia e trabalho*; Leme, *A ideologia dos industriais brasileiros (1919–1945)*; Levine, *Vargas Regime*; Munakata, *A legislação trabalhista no Brasil*; José Rodrigues, *Sindicato e desenvolvimento no Brasil*; Skidmore, *Politics in Brazil, 1930–1964*; Weinstein, *For Social Peace*; and Wolfe, *Working Women, Working Men*.

2 The original Consolidation of the Brazilian Labor Laws was signed in 1943. The "artistas de teatros e congêneres" phrase comes from that version, which was revised in 1953. See Decreto no. 19.770, 19 March 1931, in *Coleção das leis de 1931*, 1:234–38, Rio de Janeiro: Imprensa Nacional, 1942; *Consolidação das Leis do Trabalho Brasileiras/Consolidation of the Brazilian Labor Laws*, São Paulo: American Chamber of Commerce of São Paulo, 1944; and *Consolidation of the Brazilian Labor Laws/Consolidação das Leis do Trabalho Brasileiras*, 244, Rio de Janeiro: American Chambers of Commerce in Brazil, 1953. Also see French, *Drowning in Laws*.

3 Castro, *A nova constituição brasileira*, 143; Levine, *Vargas Regime*, 9–10.

4 Vargas, *A nova política do Brasil III*, 135–58.

5 The exclusion of wind instruments, it seems, was meant to ensure that the festivities were appropriately "authentic." Coded as African or Afro-Brazilian, percussion—as opposed to wind—instruments would lend Carnival with what organizers felt was the proper feel.

6 Cabral, *As escolas*, 95.

7 Chasteen, "The Prehistory of Samba," 42; Ferreira, *O livro de ouro*, 346.

8 Coutinho, *Os cronistas*, 63, 100.

9 Written documentation about the UES and the early samba schools is sparse. As a result, little is known about relationships among the UES, general escola membership, and the local and federal governments. Sérgio Cabral (*As escolas*) and Nelson da Nobrega Fernandes (*Escolas de samba*) are among the few scholars to seriously treat the UES, and the union remains virtually mentioned in English-language literature.

10 Portions of the statutes are quoted by Cabral and by Fernandes. A pamphlet containing the entire set of statutes is found in documentation of a civil case involving the UES found at the Arquivo Nacional. No author or publisher is given. See *Estatutos da União das Escolas de Sambas*, Rio de Janeiro, 1936; AN, Proc. 2210, Maço 2444–Gal. A, 3a Pretoria Civel do Rio de Janeiro (6L).

11 Most works interpret the Carnival regulations as an example of top-down repression. For an important exception, see Augras, *Brasil do samba-enredo*, 43.

12 The letter is reproduced in Cabral, *As escolas*.

13 The Vargas regime removed him from office in 1936.

14 AN, Proc. 2210, Maço 2444–Gal. A, 3a Pretoria Civel do Rio de Janeiro (6L).

15 Cabral, *As escolas*, 115–16.

16 AN, Processo 2210, Maço 2444–Gal. A, 3a Pretoria Civel do Rio de Janeiro (6L).

17 Ibid.

18 Ibid.; Cabral, *As escolas*, 106, 111.

19 Vagalume, *Na roda*, 129.

20 In 2003 and 2004, the UBC generously granted me access to its archives and thousands of pages of internal meeting minutes and notes, financial data, and the union's *Boletim Social* (the *Boletim* is also available at the National Library), published several times a year beginning in 1943. All non-*Boletim* sources cited below are labeled Arquivo UBC (AUBC). Today, the union retains a prominent place within the Escritório Central de Arrecadação e Distribuição (ECAD, the Central Office for Collection and Distribution), the centralized author's rights system created in 1973. The websites for the ECAD and that of the UBC offer useful information: http://www.ecad.org.br; http://www.ubc.org.br. There is only one substantial work on the history of Bra-

zilian author's rights societies: Morelli's *Arrogantes, anônimos, subversivos*. Also see G. Lopes, "Samba e mercado de bens culturais," 91–128.

21 "Na séde social," *Boletim Social da* UBC 10, no. 27 (April–June 1952): 31.

22 *Associação Brasileira de Compositores e Autores: Edição comemorativa do terceiro aniversario*, n.p., São Paulo: Gráfico Mangione, 1941.

23 Ibid.

24 Ibid.

25 While the SBACEM has maintained the same acronym since its inception, the "E" no longer stands for editores, and instead *escritores* (writers). For more on the SBACEM and the main author's rights associations founded during and after the 1950s, see Morelli, *Arrogantes, anônimos, subversivos*.

26 "Socios honorarios," *Boletim Social da* UBC 1 (October 1943).

27 Decreto no. 26.811, 23 June 1949: Declara de utilidade pública a União Brasileira de Compositores, com sede nesta Capital Federal. Despite a 1935 law meant to circumscribe the powers of public entities, the UBC performed many of the same functions as the SBAT. Lei no. 91, 28 August 1935: Determina regras pelas quaes são as sociedades declaradas de utilidade pública (Determines the laws through which societies are declared to be of public utility).

28 "O acordo com a 'S.B.A.T.,'" *Boletim Social da* UBC 1 (October 1943).

29 "Os contratos de edição," *Boletim Social da* UBC 1 (October 1943).

30 Lei no. 2.415, 9 February 1955: Altera dispositivos dos Decretos nos. 18.527, 10 December 1928, and 20.493, 24 January 1946. Record executives also exercised great power and influence within the SBACEM. See Morelli, *Arrogantes, anônimos, subversivos*, 35–51.

31 "A Lei 2.415," *Boletim Social da* UBC 11, no. 38 (January–March 1955): 1; "A Lei No. 2.415 e seu efeitos," *Boletim Social da* UBC 11, no. 38 (January–March 1955): 2–3; "A Lei 2415 na Justiça," *Boletim Social da* UBC 15, no. 46 (January–March 1957): 9–10; "A Lei 2415 e a Justiça," *Boletim Social da* UBC 15, no. 49 (October–December 1957): 20; AUBC, "Conselho Deliberativo, Livro No. 8, Atas de 24.12.1954 à 27.12.1955," 17–21, 22a, 23a–30, 33–33a, 40–40a, 42–42a, 45a, 49–53, 55–55a, 59a–60; AUBC, "Conselho Deliberativo, Livro No. 9, Atas de 24.01.1956 à 24.04.1957," 61a–2; AUBC, "Diretoria Livro No. 7: Atas de 12-10-1955 a 12-04-1958," 77–78; Gondim Neto, "A Lei 2415 em face dos contratos de edição," *Boletim Social da* UBC 15, no. 47 (April–June 1957): 22–24; Lafayette Stockler, "O serviço de censura e a Lei 2415," *Boletim Social da* UBC 11, no. 41 (October–December 1955): 3–4.

32 UBC and SBAT, *Como e porque se paga direito autoral no Brasil* (Rio de Janeiro: UBC/SBAT, 1943).

33 Decreto no. 847, 11 October 1890: Código Penal dos Estados Unidos do Brazil; Decreto no. 22.120, 22 November 1932: Promulga a Convenção de Berna

para a proteção das obras literarias e artísticas, de 9 de setembro de 1886, revista em Berlim, a 13 de novembro de 1908, e em Roma, a 2 de junho de 1928; Decreto no. 23.270, 24 October 1933: Promulga a Convenção de Berna para a proteção das obras literarias e artísticas, revista em Roma, a 2 de junho de 1928; Decreto no 5.077, 29 December 1939: Aprova o regimento do Departamento de Imprensa e Propaganda (D.I.P.); Juarez de Oliveira and Marcus Cláudio Acquaviva, eds., *Código Penal: Organização dos textos, notas remissivas e índice alfabético-remissivo*, 15th ed., São Paulo: Saraiva, 1978.

34 Maria José (Zezé) Grecco, interview with author, 1 December 2004, Rio de Janeiro.

35 The financial importance and attendant problems of Carnival were not unique to the UBC. In 1952, for example, the SBACEM made nearly 20 percent of its collections for the entire year just during Carnival. See Morelli, *Arrogantes, anônimos, subversivos*, 123.

36 Emphasis in the original. Holanda, *Memórias do Café Nice*, 56, 296.

37 Though receipts continued to climb during the 1950s, their value in relation to the dollar fell dramatically along with that of the cruzeiro.

38 "Representantes nos estados," *Boletim Social da UBC* 1 (October 1943).

39 "A U.B.C., no norte e no nordeste do Brasil," *Boletim Social da UBC* 9, no. 23 (January 1951): 4.

40 "1951 e o direito autoral," *Boletim Social da UBC* 9, no. 25 (December 1951): 1.

41 "Criado o Departamento Interior da U.B.C.," *Boletim Social da UBC* 7, no. 17 (June–September 1948): 9.

42 "Uma nova editora," *Boletim Social da UBC* 6 (June 1945): 2.

43 See G. Castro, *Carmen*; T. Garcia, *O "it verde e amarelo" de Carmen Miranda, 1930–1946*; Gil-Montero, *Brazilian Bombshell*; McCann, *Hello, Hello*, 129–59; Nasser, *A vida trepidante de Carmen Miranda*; Perrone and Dunn, "'Chiclete com Banana'"; and Veloso, "Carmen Mirandada."

44 "Um acontecimento na música popular," *Boletim Social da UBC* 15, no. 49 (December 1957): 10–12.

45 "'Delicado' no estrangeiro," *Boletim Social da UBC* 15, no. 48 (June–September 1957): 2.

46 "O governo brasileiro confiou à UBC a difusão da nossa música no estrangeiro," *Boletim Social da UBC* 15, no. 47 (April–June 1957): 2–4. The cruzeiro-to-dollar exchange rate changed dramatically between 1957 and 1958, from an average of around 76 cruzeiros to 1 dollar in 1957 to nearly 130 cruzeiros the next year. See http://measuringworth.com.

47 "O delegado especial da U.B.C. no Rio Grande do Sul," *Boletim Social da UBC* 7, no. 18 (October–December 1948): 10; "Transformações na nossa representação do Rio Grande do Sul," *Boletim Social da UBC* 7, no. 18 (October–December 1948): 19.

48 "U.B.C. em Minas," *Boletim Social da UBC* 9 (April 1946): 2.

49 "O que devem os compositores ao Departamento de Imprensa e Propaganda," *Boletim do Departamento dos Compositores*, no. 2 (July–September 1941): 12–13.

50 "Direito autoral em Minas Gerais," *Boletim Social da UBC* 2 (June 1944).

51 "Homenagem ao Dr. Israel Souto," *Boletim Social da UBC* 2 (June 1944).

52 Linhares briefly held the presidency after Vargas was ousted. Dutra was elected in December 1945 and took office the following January. Vargas returned to power through democratic elections in 1950 and held the presidency from January 1951 through August 1954, when he committed suicide in the presidential mansion.

53 "Os compositores encontraram um amigo," *Boletim Social da UBC* 9 (April 1946).

54 "Juscelino cumpriu," *Boletim Social da UBC* 16, no. 51 (April–June 1958): 1.

55 "Para que seja cumprida a lei dos direitos autorais," *Boletim Social da UBC* 9, no. 24 (May 1951): 1–2.

56 Santiago, *Aquarela do direito autoral*, 13, 23.

57 "S. Ex. e os compositores," *Boletim do Departamento dos Compositores*, no. 1 (April–June 1941): 3, 31.

58 E. Frazão, "Plagiários," *Boletim Social da UBC* 7, no. 21 (July–September 1949): 1–2.

59 "David Nasser no banco dos réus," *Boletim Social da UBC* 6, no. 15 (February–March 1948): 6.

60 The series appeared in the following issues and pages of the *Boletim*: 8, no. 18: 10; 7, no. 19: 23; 7, no. 20: 16; 7, no. 21: 4; 9; no. 24: 12.

61 Ataulfo Alves and Felisberto Martins, "É negocio casar!," original recording by Ataulfo Alves, Odeon, 1941. At least toward the end of the career, Alves wrote more critical pieces, such as his 1967 "Laranja madura" (Ripe orange), a subtle commentary on Brazilian racism. I am indebted to the insights, time, and material provided by Alves's son, Ataulfo Alves Júnior. For a discussion of "Laranja madura," see Frota, *Auxílio luxuoso*, 187–90.

62 AN, Cx. 1096, Processo 11.901/48, RC 758.789, 20a/18a Vara Criminal, 1948.

63 Geraldo Pereira, "Bolinha de papel," original recording by Anjos do Inferno, RCA Victor, 1945; Geraldo Pereira, "Falsa baiana," original recording by Ciro Monteiro, RCA Victor, 1944.

64 "Compositores da U.B.C. que mais receberam direitos em 1944," *Boletim Social da UBC* 5 (April 1945): 4; "Seguro coletivo de sócio da U.B.C." *Boletim Social da UBC* 7, no. 18 (October–December 1948): 14.

65 For more on Pereira, see Alice Campos et al., *Um certo Geraldo Pereira*; McCann, "Geraldo Pereira"; and L. Vieira and Pimentel, *Um escurinho direitinho*.

66 "O melhor compositor de 1955," *Boletim Social da UBC* 11, no. 41 (October–December 1955): 13.

67 AN, Proc. No. 600, Caixa 1567, 20a Vara de Execuções Criminais do RJ (D3), 1949.

68 Instituto de Economia, *Pesquisa*, 90–991, 108.

69 Earnings figures can be found in "Compositores da U.B.C."

70 "Fernando Lobo e os compositores," *Boletim Social da UBC* 7, no. 18 (October–December 1948): 12.

71 Severiano and Mello, *A canção no tempo*, 278.

72 It is reasonable to think that Lobo would know the icon and base his costume on it. He lived and traveled in the United States, and a silent film version of Stowe's novel was made in Brazil in 1909.

73 "Vitória absoluta da SBACEM no Carnaval dêste ano," *Boletim da SBACEM*, no. 3 (April 1950): 3, 5.

74 "Fernando Lobo e os compositores."

75 The image remains powerful today. In 2004, I attended a conference in Rio called "Lírica e resistência: A voz do samba" (Lyric and resistance: The voice of samba). A poster for the conference depicted a dark set of hands cradling a matchbox.

76 Holanda, *Memórias do Café Nice*, 24.

77 "No congresso de Amsterdam," *Boletim Social da UBC* 10, no. 28 (July–September 1952): 12.

78 Holanda, *Memórias do Café Nice*, 15, 18–19.

79 McCann, *Hello, Hello*, 55; Muniz Jr., *Sambistas imortais*, 187.

80 This is evident not only in the *Boletim* but also in thousands of pages of meeting minutes.

81 "Governo da UBC," *Boletim Social da UBC* 18, no. 61 (October–December 1960): 2.

82 "O dolar vai baixar?" *Boletim Social da UBC* 6, no. 16 (April–May 1948): 7.

83 "A vitoria da 'U.B.C. no carnaval de 1952," *Boletim Social da UBC* 9, no. 26 (January–March 1952): 8–9.

84 AUBC, "Conselho Fiscal, Livro No. 5 (1950–51)," 86.

85 I am indebted to Rodrigo Alzuguir and Luís Fernando Vieira for lending me a copy of the memoir.

86 "Em atividad 'O Clube do Compositor Brasileiro,'" *Boletim Social da UBC* 16, no. 59 (April–June 1960): 14–15. Also see Biblioteca Nacional-Sonoro, Arquivo Paralelo, Pasta "Clube do Compositor Brasileiro, RJ."

87 Ataulfo Alves, "Circular da 'A.D.D.A.F.,'" *Boletim Social da UBC* 16, no. 53 (November–December 1958): 14.

88 McCann, *Hello, Hello*.

89 In this respect, the UBC and the SBACEM had much in common with the National Service for Industrial Training and the Industrial Social Service, national agencies founded in the 1940s that funneled responsibility for

workers' vocational training and social welfare programs into the hands of industrialist associations. See Weinstein, *For Social Peace*.

Nine. After the Golden Age

1 Fischer, *Poverty of Rights*; Weinstein, *For Social Peace*.
2 It was not only arguments about race that made professors at the University of São Paulo dangerous to the military, but also their embrace of Marxism. See Skidmore, *The Politics of Military Rule*, 73–84. Also see Andrews, *Blacks and Whites*, 7; Gaspari, *A ditadura envergonhada*; and Gaspari, *A ditadura escancarada*. For details on the National Security Council, see Andrews, *Blacks and Whites*, 7n11, and T. Azevedo, *Democracia racial*, 53n27.
3 Music from this period has been richly investigated elsewhere. See Alberto, "When Rio Was *Black*"; Araújo, *Eu não sou cachorro, não*; Coelho and Cohn, *Tropicália*; Dunn, *Brutality Garden*; McCann, "Black Pau"; McCann, "Blues and Samba"; McCann, *Hello, Hello*, 160–234; Napolitano, "*Seguindo a canção*"; Perrone, *Masters of Contemporary Brazilian Song*; and Stroud, *Defence*.
4 See Stroud, *Defence*, 111–30.
5 Lei no. 3.857, 22 December 1960: "Cria a Ordem dos Músicos do Brasil e dispõe sobre a regulamentação do exercício da profissão de músico, e dá outras providências."
6 Araújo, *Eu não sou*, 19.
7 Ibid., 32. Also see Sandroni, "Adeus à MPB," and Stroud, *Defence*.
8 Tinhorão, *Música popular: Um tema em debate*.
9 "Que caminho seguir na música popular brasileira?" *Revista Civilização Brasileira* 1, no. 7 (May 1966): 375–85.
10 Araújo, *Eu não sou*, 406n578.
11 Augusto Campos, "A explosão de *Alegria, Alegria*," 144.
12 "Os Americanos verão a 'bossa-nova' Brasileira em suas raízes autênticas," *O Globo*, 12 November 1962. Cited in Schreiner, *Música Brasileira*, 148. My translation differs slightly from Schreiner's.
13 Dunn, "Review," 148.
14 Araújo, *Eu não sou*.
15 Ibid., 23.
16 Ibid., 320.
17 Alberto, "When Rio Was *Black*," 38.
18 Hanchard, *Orpheus and Power*, 115. For more on the contrasts drawn between soul and samba, see Alberto, "When Rio Was *Black*," 18–19, 24, 35–37.
19 McCann, *Hello, Hello*, 160–80.
20 Quoted and translated in ibid., 170.
21 Ibid., 171, 173.

22 That idea was vividly captured in a monument constructed in Rio in 1960 in honor of the nation's World War II veterans. The monument is guarded by three concrete soldiers, each with what Peter Beattie aptly describes in *The Tribute of Blood* as "racially neutral features" (283).

23 Cabral, *Pixinguinha*, 162, 167; McCann, *Hello, Hello*, 176.

24 Cabral, *Pixinguinha*, 160–61; Koidin, "Benedicto Lacerda and the Golden Age of Choro," 40–41; McCann, *Hello, Hello*, 167.

25 Julio Pires, "Como nasce a música do povo: Pixinguinha," *O Cruzeiro*, 21 January 1939, 34–35, 40.

26 Carneiro, *Carta do samba*.

27 Ibid., 3, 8–9.

28 Ibid., 7, 10, 14.

29 MIS, *As vozes*.

30 McCann, "Review: *Auxilio Luxuoso*." Cabral expressed the same sentiment to me during conversations in November and December 2004, and the music scholar Luís Fernando Vieira made a similar point during conversations in 2004.

31 Quoted and translated in Dunn, *Brutality Garden*, 157.

32 Jota Efegê, "João da Baiana nos ranchos Kananga do Japão e Deixa Falar," *O Globo*, 28 January 1974.

33 Jota Efegê, "João da Baiana: um sambista em repouso," *O Globo*, 17 May 1972.

34 Tinhorão, *Música popular*, 37, 64.

35 Pereira's cause of death has never been definitively pronounced, but most accounts agree that he had been struggling with a long-term illness.

36 Francis, "Madame Satã"; Green, *Beyond Carnival*, 85–92; Green, "Madame Satã (Satan)," 267–86; Paezzo, *Memórias de Madame Satã*.

37 Francis, "Madame Satã," 157.

38 Ibid., 156.

39 "João da Baiana, 84 anos de solidão," *O Globo*, 22 July 1971. Images of the emaciated and elderly João da Baiana were ubiquitous in newspaper accounts of the MIS interviews.

40 McCann, "Black Pau."

41 The feminization of male bossa nova musicians may be surprising to readers who associate the music with what Green, in "Madame Satã (Satan)," calls "the hypermasculinized culture of 'beach life, beer, and beautiful women'" (273) that flourished in the chic Zona Sul neighborhoods in which bossa nova was pioneered. Indeed, "Garota de Ipanema" ("The Girl from Ipanema") makes a beautiful woman the object of masculine desire. Tinhorão's association between "white" and jazz is somewhat ironic. In fact, the "cool" jazz style pioneered by African American jazz musicians including Miles Davis had influenced João Gilberto and his cohort more than any other stream from the United States. Tinhorão was, no doubt, aware of this.

42 As Michael Hanchard points out in *Orpheus and Power* (33), Fernandes's treatment of "anomie" resembles arguments made about African American communities in the United States. See F. Fernandes, *Negro*, and Glazer and Moynihan, *Beyond the Melting Pot*.

43 The supposed incongruity—caused, in his estimation, by slavery—between blacks and capitalism is a leitmotif running through *The Negro in Brazilian Society*. See, especially, 55–130 and 239–67.

44 F. Fernandes, *Negro*, esp. 187–233, 380–447.

45 Ibid., 123.

46 Ibid., 84–85. While acknowledging his important contributions, numerous scholars in Brazil and the United States have critiqued Fernandes's bleak depiction of black communities. Most have done so by reinterpreting the post-emancipation period, describing black agency, and providing alternative explanations for black exclusion from politics and the workforce. Little attention has been given to the ways in which Fernandes's ideas linked up with contemporary discourses circulating outside of academia.

47 José Ramos Tinhorão, interview with author, 22 November 2004, São Paulo. As a young star, Buarque became a counterculture icon during the 1960s and '70s. His lyrics were censored by the military.

48 Quoted and translated in Hanchard, *Orpheus and Power*, 114.

49 F. Fernandes, *Negro*, 6.

50 "João da Baiana vem do tempo em que o samba era proibido," *O Globo*, 23 March 1970.

51 "João da Baiana, 84 anos de solidão."

52 Buarque, *Ópera do malandro*.

53 "João da Baiana diz que voltar ao samba é mais difícil sem Pixinguinha," *Jornal do Brasil*, 25 February 1973.

54 "João da Baiana vem do tempo" and "João da Baiana agradece apoio," *O Dia*, 27 March 1970.

55 "João da Baiana fêz 84 anos, e estava triste," *O Globo*, 18 May 1971.

56 "João da Baiana diz que voltar ao samba é mais difícil sem Pixinguinha."

57 For an overview of television's influence on the music industry, see Stroud, *Defence*, 65–88.

58 Cabral, *As escolas*, 185.

59 "João da Baiana, 84 anos de solidão," *O Globo*, 22 July 1971.

60 "João da Baiana fêz 84 anos, e estava triste," *O Globo*, 18 May 1971. Also see "João da Baiana recebe com lágrimas," *Jornal do Brasil*, 1 April 1970.

61 *Jornal das Moças*, 4 October 1917; "O pic-nic de amanhã na Tijuca," *A Noite*, 23 September 1920; *A Noite*, 8 December 1920.

62 Almirante, *No tempo*, 24.

63 That claim contrasts with an assertion made by Donga in 1966 that he "never received a cent" for the song. Almeida's 1956 interview appeared in

the March 22 edition of *A Noite* and was reproduced in the UBC's *Boletim Social*. See Almirante, *No tempo*, 24; "Donga recorda o rancho e vê cossacos no frevo," *O Globo*, 5 December 1966; and "O samba 'Pelo telefone,'" *Boletim Social da* UBC 12, no. 42 (January–March 1956): 18.

64 Lygia dos Santos, interview with author, 28 September 2004, Rio de Janeiro.

65 "Donga recorda o rancho."

66 MIS, *As vozes*, 80.

67 F. Silva, "Pelo telefone e a história do samba," 65.

68 MIS, *As vozes*, 86.

69 As we have seen, "Pelo telefone" was not, in fact, the first recorded song to be called a samba.

70 MIS, *As vozes*, 82.

Conclusion

1 Lei no. 5.988, 14 December 1973: "Regula os direitos autorais e dá outras providências" (Regulates author's rights and provides other [related] measures).

2 The pamphlet was given to me in 2004 when I visited the ECAD's headquarters in Rio.

3 Rhenzo Alexandre Gonçalves de Brito Fernandes de Melo, "O músico brasileiro entre a Lei 3.857/1960 e a Constituição Federal de 1988," *Direito Em Ação* 7, no. 2 (December 2006): 55.

4 Bhabha, *Location of Culture*, 149.

5 In an interview in 1950, he made a similar point, telling the newspaper *A Noite* that police could never arrest him and his friends as vagrants "because we all worked." Quoted in M. Cunha, "'Acontece,'" 335. Also recall his claim that he missed the Batutas' Paris trip to keep his job at the docks.

6 Lourival Coutinho, "O samba nasceu na Baía?" *Carioca* (n.d.).

7 This poignant, painful memory underlines the importance that João da Baiana and other musicians gave to their appearance and also conjures images of the 1943 Zoot Suit Riot in Los Angeles, in which white U.S. servicemen and civilians attacked black and Chicano youth, combining physical violence with a "ritualized stripping" of victims' clothing. See Kelley, "Riddle of the Zoot," 173. Also see Alvarez, *Power of the Zoot*, and Ramírez, *The Woman in the Zoot*.

BIBLIOGRAPHY

Archives

Acervo de Manuscritos, Biblioteca Alberto Nepomuceno da Escola da Música da Universidade Federal do Rio de Janeiro, Rio de Janeiro

Arquivo Edgard Leuenroth, Universidade Estadual de Campinas, São Paulo

Arquivo Geral da Cidade do Rio de Janeiro, Rio de Janeiro

Arquivo Histórico do Ministério das Relações Exteriores, Rio de Janeiro

Arquivo Instituto Moreira Salles, Rio de Janeiro

Arquivo Jairo Severiano, Rio de Janeiro

Arquivo Luís Fernando Vieira, Rio de Janeiro

Arquivo Nacional, Rio de Janeiro

Arquivo Público do Estado do Rio de Janeiro, Rio de Janeiro

Arquivo Sérgio Cabral, Rio de Janeiro

Arquivo Vanissa Santiago, Rio de Janeiro

Biblioteca Nacional, Rio de Janeiro

Biblioteca Nacional Arquivo Sonoro, Rio de Janeiro

Centro de Pesquisa e Documentação, Fundação Getúlio Vargas, Rio de Janeiro

Chefia da Polícia Civil, Setor da Microfilmagem, Rio de Janeiro

Instituto Nacional da Propriedade Industrial, Rio de Janeiro

Museu da Polícia Civil, Rio de Janeiro

Museu de Imagem e da Som-Praça XV, Rio de Janeiro

Museu de Imagem e da Som-Lapa, Rio de Janeiro

Museu de Imagem e da Som-São Paulo, São Paulo

Sociedade Brasileira de Autores Teatrais, Rio de Janeiro

União Brasileira de Compositores, Rio de Janeiro

Wisconsin State Historical Society, Madison

Major Periodicals

Boletim da SBAT (Rio de Janeiro)

Boletim da UBC (Rio de Janeiro)

Boletim do Departamento dos Compositores da SBAT (Rio de Janeiro)

Correio da Manhã (Rio de Janeiro)

Correio Paulistano (São Paulo)

O Dia (Rio de Janeiro)
Diário Carioca (Rio de Janeiro)
Diário da Noite (Rio de Janeiro)
O Estado de São Paulo (São Paulo)
Gazeta de Notícias (Rio de Janeiro)
O Globo (Rio de Janeiro)
O Jornal (Rio de Janeiro)
Jornal do Brasil (Rio de Janeiro)
Jornal do Commercio (São Paulo Ed.)
O Malho (Rio de Janeiro)
A Noite (Rio de Janeiro)
A Notícia (Rio de Janeiro)
A Ordem (Rio de Janeiro)
O Paiz (Rio de Janeiro)
Revista do Instituto Historico e Geographico Brazileiro (Rio de Janeiro)
Weco: Revista de vida e cultura musical (Rio de Janeiro)

Legislation (in Chronological Order)

When no publication information is given, legislation was consulted online at
www.senado.gov.br.

Lei no. 2040, 28 September 1871. In *Collecção das leis do Imperio do Brasil de
1871*. Tomo 31, pt. 1, 147–52. Rio de Janeiro: Typographia Nacional, 1871.

Lei no. 3270, 28 September 1885. In *Collecção das leis do Imperio do Brasil de
1885*. Tomo 32, pt. 1, 14–20. Rio de Janeiro: Typographia Nacional, 1886.

Lei no. 3.353, 13 May 1890.

Decreto no. 847, 11 October 1890: Código Penal dos Estados Unidos do Brazil.

Decreto no. 1.030, 11 November 1890.

Decreto no. 145, 11 July 1893.

Decreto no. 1.794, 11 September 1894.

Lei no. 496, 1 August 1898. In *Collecção das leis da Republica dos Estados Unidos
do Brazil de 1898*, 4–8. Rio de Janeiro: Imprensa Nacional, 1900.

Lei no. 652, 23 November 1899. In *Collecção das leis da Republica dos Estados
Unidos do Brazil de 1899*, 91–127. Rio de Janeiro: Imprensa Nacional, 1902.

Decreto no. 3.836, 24 November 1900. In *Collecção das leis da Republica dos Estados Unidos do Brazil de 1900*, 1104. Rio de Janeiro: Imprensa Nacional, 1902.

Decreto no. 4.753, 18 January 1903.

Decreto no. 4.780, 2 March 1903.

Decreto no. 1.637, 5 January 1907.

Decreto no. 6.994, 19 June 1908.

Decreto no. 8.233, 22 September 1910.

Lei no. 2.577, 17 January 1912. In *Collecção das leis da Republica dos Estados
Unidos do Brazil de 1912*, 1:231. Rio de Janeiro: Imprensa Nacional, 1915.

Decreto no. 11.588, 19 May 1915. In *Collecção das leis da Republica dos Estados Unidos do Brazil de 1915*, 3:135–226. Rio de Janeiro: Imprensa Nacional, 1917.

Decreto no. 4.092, 4 August 1920. In *Collecção das leis da Republica dos Estados Unidos do Brasil de 1920*, 1:235–36. Rio de Janeiro: Imprensa Nacional, 1923.

Decreto no. 4.541, 6 February 1922. In *Collecção das leis da Republica dos Estados Unidos do Brasil de 1922*, 1:88–89. Rio de Janeiro: Imprensa Nacional, 1923.

Decreto no. 15.530, 21 June 1922. In *Collecção das leis da Republica dos Estados Unidos do Brasil de 1922*, 2:388–400. Rio de Janeiro: Imprensa Nacional, 1923.

Decreto no. 4.577, 5 September 1922.

Decreto no. 4.790, 2 January 1924. In *Collecção das leis da Republica dos Estados Unidos do Brasil de 1924*, 1:4–5. Rio de Janeiro: Imprensa Nacional, 1925.

Decreto no. 16.590, 10 September 1924. In *Collecção das leis da Republica dos Estados Unidos do Brasil de 1924*, 3:161–80. Rio de Janeiro: Imprensa Nacional, 1925.

Decreto no. 5.492, 16 July 1928. In *Collecção das leis da Republica dos Estados Unidos do Brasil de 1928*, 1:124–28. Rio de Janeiro: Imprensa Nacional, 1929.

Decreto no. 18.527, 10 December 1928. In *Collecção das leis da Republica dos Estados Unidos do Brasil de 1928*, 2:607–20. Rio de Janeiro: Imprensa Nacional, 1929.

Decreto no. 19.770, 19 March 1931. In *Coleção das leis de 1931*, 1:234–38. Rio de Janeiro: Imprensa Nacional, 1942.

Decreto no. 21.111, 1 March 1932. In *Coleção das leis de 1932*, 1:285–322. Rio de Janeiro: Imprensa Nacional, 1942.

Decreto no. 22.120, 22 November 1932: Promulga a Convenção de Berna para a proteção das obras literarias e artísticas, de 9 de Setembro de 1886, revista em Berlim, a 13 de Novembro de 1908, and em Roma, a 2 de Junho de 1928.

Decreto no. 23.270, 24 October 1933: Promulga a Convenção de Berna para a proteção das obras literarias e artísticas, revista em Roma, a 2 de Junho de 1928.

Lei no. 91, 28 August 1935: Determina regras pelas quaes são as sociedades declaradas de utilidade pública.

Decreto no. 5.077, 29 December 1939: Aprova o regimento do Departamento de Imprensa e Propaganda (DIP).

Decreto no. 26.811, 23 June 1949: Declara de utilidade pública a União Brasileira de Compositores, com sede nesta Capital Federal.

Lei no. 2.415, 9 February 1955: Altera dispositivos dos Decretos nos. 18.527 de 10 Dezembro 1928, e 20.493 de 24 Janeiro 1946.

Lei no. 3.857, 22 December 1960: "Cria a Ordem dos Músicos do Brasil e dispõe sobre a regulamentação do exercício da profissão de músico, e dá outras Providências."

Lei no. 5.988, 14 December 1973: "Regula os direitos autorais e dá outras providências."

Internet Resources

http://daniellathompson.com
http://dictionary.oed.com
http://eh.net
http://www.dicionariocravoalbin.com.br (also dicionariompb.com.br)
http://www.grovemusic.com
http://www.ims.com.br
http://measuringworth.com
www.senado.gov.br.
http://www.unicamp.br/cecult/mapastematicos/
http://www.universoespirita.org.br
http://www.xreferplus.com

Written and Recorded Material

Abercrombie, Thomas A. "To Be Indian, to Be Bolivian: 'Ethnic' and 'National' Discourses of Identity." In *Nation-States and Indians in Latin America*, edited by Greg Urban and Joel Sherzer, 95–130. Austin: University of Texas Press, 1991.

Abreu, Edman Ayres de. *O plágio em música*. São Paulo: Editora Revista dos Tribunais, 1968.

Abreu, Martha. "O 'crioulo Dudu': Participação política e identidade negra nas histórias de um músico cantor (1890–1920)." *Topoi* (Rio de Janeiro) 11, no. 20 (January–June 2010): 92–113.

———. "Eduardo das Neves." In *Encyclopedia of African American Culture and History: The Black Experience in the Americas*, edited by Colin A. Palmer. 2nd ed. Translated by Marc Hertzman, 2:582–83. New York: Macmillan Reference USA, 2006.

———. "Eduardo das Neves (1874–1919): Histórias de um crioulo malandro." In *Resistência e inclusão: História, cultura, educação e cidadania: Afrodescendentes no Brasil e nos Estados Unidos, Vol. 1*, edited by Denise Pini Rosalem da Fonseca, 73–88. Rio de Janeiro: Consulado Geral dos Estados Unidos, 2003.

———. *O império do divino: Festas religiosas e cultura popular no Rio de Janeiro, 1830–1900*. Rio de Janeiro: FAPESP, 1999.

———. "*Mulatas, Crioulos* and *Morenas*: Racial Hierarchy, Gender Relations, and National Identity in Postabolition Popular Song: Southeastern Brazil, 1890–1920." In *Gender and Slave Emancipation in the Atlantic World*, edited by Pamela Scully and Diana Paton, 267–88. Article translated by Amy Chazkel and Junia Claudia Zaidan. Durham: Duke University Press, 2005.

Abreu, Martha, and Carolina Vianna Dantas. "Música popular, folclore e nação no Brasil, 1890–1920." In *Nação e cidadania no Império: Novos horizontes,* edited by José Murilo de Carvalho, 123–51. Rio de Janeiro: Civilização Brasileira, 2007.

Abreu Esteves, Martha de. *Meninas perdidas: Os populares e o cotidiano do amor no Rio de Janeiro da Belle Époque*. Rio de Janeiro: Paz e Terra, 1989.

Acerbi, Patricia. "Slave Legacies, Ambivalent Modernity: Street Commerce and the Transition to Free Labor in Rio de Janeiro, 1850–1925." PhD dissertation. University of Maryland, 2010.

Adamo, Sam. "The Broken Promise: Race, Health, and Justice in Rio de Janeiro, 1890–1940." PhD dissertation. University of New Mexico, 1983.

———. "Race and *Povo*." In *Modern Brazil: Elites and Masses in Historical Perspective*, edited by Michael L. Conniff and Frank D. McCann, 192–208. Lincoln: University of Nebraska Press, 2010.

Addor, Carlos Augusto. *A insurreição anarquista no Rio de Janeiro*. Rio de Janeiro: Dois Pontos Editora, 1986.

Affonseca Jr., Leo de. *O custo da vida na cidade do Rio de Janeiro*. Rio de Janeiro: Imprensa Nacional, 1920.

Agache, Alfred. *Rio de Janeiro: Extensão, remodelação, e embelezamento*. Paris: Foyer Brasilien, 1930.

Agawu, Kofi. "The Invention of 'African Rhythm.'" *Journal of the American Musicological Society* 48, no. 3 (Fall 1995): 380–95.

———. *Representing African Music: Postcolonial Notes, Queries, Positions*. New York: Routledge, 2003.

Alberto, Paulina L. "*Para Africano Ver*: African-Bahian Exchanges in the Reinvention of Brazil's Racial Democracy, 1961–63." *Luso-Brazilian Review* 45 (June 2008): 78–117.

———. "Terms of Inclusion: Black Activism and the Cultural Conditions for Citizenship in a Multi-Racial Brazil, 1920–1982." PhD dissertation. University of Pennsylvania, 2005.

———. *Terms of Inclusion: Black Intellectuals in Twentieth-Century Brazil*. Chapel Hill: University of North Carolina Press, 2011.

———. "When Rio Was *Black*: Soul Music, National Culture, and the Politics of Racial Comparison in 1970s Brazil." *Hispanic American Historical Review* 89, no. 1 (2009): 3–39.

Albuquerque, Wlamyra R. de. *O jogo da dissimulação: Abolição e cidadania negra no Brasil*. São Paulo: Companhia das Letras, 2009.

Alencar, Edigar de. *Nosso Sinhô do samba*. Rio de Janeiro: Civilização Brasileira, 1981. First published 1968.

———. *O carnaval carioca através da música*. 2 vols. Rio de Janeiro: Livraria Freitas Bastos S.A., 1965.

Almirante (Henrique Foréis Domingues). *No tempo de Noel Rosa: A verdade definitiva sôbre Noel e a música popular*. São Paulo: Linográfica Editóra, 1977. First published 1963.

Alvarenga, Oneyda. *Música popular brasileira*. 2nd ed. São Paulo: Duas Cidades, 1982. First published 1950.

Alvarez, Luis. *The Power of the Zoot: Youth Culture and Resistance during World War II*. Berkeley: University of California Press, 2008.

Alves, Marieta. "Música de barbeiros." *Revista Brasileira de Folclore* 7, no. 17 (January–April 1967): 5–14.

Amado, Jorge. *O país do carnaval*. Lisbon: Colecção Livros do Brasil, 1970. First published 1931.

Amaral, Rita, and Vagner Gonçalves da Silva. "Foi conta para todo canto: As religiões afro-brasileiras nas letras do repertório musical popular brasileiro." *Afro-Asia* 34 (2006): 189–235.

Andrade, Mário de. *Compêndio de história da música*. São Paulo: Eugenio Cupolo, 1929.

———. *Dicionário musical brasileiro*. Compiled and edited by Oneyda Alvarenga and Flávia Camargo Toni. Belo Horizonte: Editora Itatiaia, 1999.

———. *Ensaio sobre a música brasileira*. 3rd ed. São Paulo: Livraria Martins, 1972. First published 1928.

———. "Força biológica da música." *Publicações Médicas* 8, nos. 3–4 (October–November 1936): 47–56.

———. "Lundu do escravo." In *Música, doce música*, 74–80. São Paulo: Livraria Martins, 1963. First published 1928.

———. *Macunaíma*. Translated by E. A. Goodland. London: Quartet Books, 1984.

———. *Modinhas imperiais*. São Paulo: Livraria Martins, 1964.

———. *Música de feitiçaria no Brasil*. 2nd ed. Belo Horizonte: Editora Itatiaia, 1983.

———. *Música, doce música*. São Paulo: Livraria Martins, 1963.

———. *Pequena história da música*. 10th ed. Belo Horizonte: Editora Itatiaia, 2003. First published 1944.

Andrade, Oswald de. "Manifesto antropófago." In *Vanguarda européia e modernismo brasileira*, edited by Gilberto Mendonça Teles, 226–32. Petrópolis: Editora Vozes, 1972.

Andrews, George Reid. *The Afro-Argentines of Buenos Aires, 1800–1900*. Madison: University of Wisconsin Press, 1980.

———. *Blacks and Whites in São Paulo, Brazil 1888–1988*. Madison: University of Wisconsin Press, 1991.

Aoki, Keith. "Authors, Inventors, and Trademark Owners: Private Intellectual Property and the Public Domain. Part II." *Columbia–VLA Journal of Law and the Arts* 18 (1994): 191–267.

Appadurai, Arjun, ed. *The Social Life of Things: Commodities in Cultural Perspective*. Cambridge: Cambridge University Press, 1986.

Appleby, David P. *Heitor Villa-Lobos: A Life (1887–1959)*. London: Scarecrow Press, 2002.

Aranha, José Pereira da Graça. *A viagem maravilhosa*. 3rd ed. Rio de Janeiro: F. Briguiet, 1944.

Arantes, Erika Bastos. "Negros do porto: Trabalho, cultura e repressão policial no Rio de Janeiro, 1900–190." In *Trabalhadores na cidade: Cotidiano e cultura no Rio de Janeiro e em São Paulo, séculos XIX e XX*, edited by Elciene Azevedo et al., 107–56. Campinas, Brazil: Editora da Universidade Estadual de Campinas, 2009.

———. "O porto negro: Cultura e trabalho no Rio de Janeiro dos primeiros anos do século XX." M.A. thesis. Universidade Estadual de Campinas, 2005.

Araújo, Mozart de. *A modinha e o lundu no século XVIII (Uma pesquisa histórica e bibliográfica)*. São Paulo: Ricordi Brasileira, 1963.

Araújo, Paulo Cesar de. *Eu não sou cachorro, não: Música popular cafona e ditadura militar*. 2nd ed. Rio de Janeiro: Editora Record, 2002.

Araújo, Rosa Maria Barboza de. *O batismo do trabalho: A experiência de Lindolfo Collor*. 2nd ed. Rio de Janeiro: Civilização Brasileira, 1990. First published 1981.

Araújo Júnior, Samuel Mello. "Acoustic Labor in the Timing of Everyday Life: A Critical Contribution to the History of Samba in Rio de Janeiro." PhD dissertation. University of Illinois at Urbana-Champaign, 1992.

Augras, Monique. *O Brasil do samba-enredo*. Rio de Janeiro: Editora Fundação Getúlio Vargas, 1998.

Avé-Lallemant, Robert. *Viagem pelo norte do Brasil no ano de 1859*. 2 vols. Translated into Portuguese by Eduardo de Lima Castro. Rio de Janeiro: Ministério da Educação e Cultura, Instituto Nacional do Livro, 1961. First published 1860.

Azevedo, Célia Maria Marinho de. *Onda negra, medo branco: O negro no imaginário das elites, século XIX*. Rio de Janeiro: Paz e Terra, 1987.

Azevedo, Thales de. *As elites de côr: Um estudo de acensão social*. São Paulo: Companhia Editora Nacional, 1955.

———. *Democracia racial: Ideologia e realidade*. Petrópolis: Editora Vozes, 1975.

Bacelar, Jefferson. *A hierarquia das raças: Negros e brancos em Salvador*. Rio de Janeiro: Pallas, 2001.

Barbosa, Orestes. *Bambambã!* Rio de Janeiro: Coleção Biblioteca Carioca, 1993.

———. *Na prisão: Chronicas*. 2d ed. Rio de Janeiro: Jacintho Ribeiro dos Santos, 1922.

———. *Samba: Sua história, eus poetas, seus músicos e seus cantores*. 2nd ed. Rio de Janeiro: Fundação Nacional de Artes, 1978. First published 1933.

Barreto, João Paulo Alberto Coelho (João do Rio). *A alma encantadora das ruas*. Rio de Janeiro: Biblioteca Carioca, 1987. First published 1908.

———. *As religiões no Rio*. Rio de Janeiro: Organização Simões, 1951.

Barros, Orlando de. *Corações De Chocolat: A História da Companhia Negra de Revista*. Rio de Janeiro: Livre Expressão, 2005.

Barthes, Roland. "The Death of an Author." In *Image-Music-Text*, 142–48. Edited and translated by Stephen Heath. New York: Hill and Wang, 1977.

Bary, Leslie. "Oswald de Andrade's Cannibalist Manifesto." *Latin American Literary Review* 19, no. 38 (1991): 35–47.

Bastide, Roger. *The African Religions of Brazil: Toward a Sociology of the Interpenetration of Civilizations*. Translated by Helen Sebba. Baltimore, Md.: Johns Hopkins University Press, 2007. First published 1960.

———. "A imprensa negra no Estado de São Paulo." In *O negro na imprensa e na literatura*, edited by José Marques de Melo, 50–78. São Paulo: Escola de Comunicações e Artes, 1972.

Bastos, Rafael José de Menezes. "Brazil in France, 1922: An Anthropological Study of the Congenital International Nexus of Popular Music." *Latin American Music Review* 29, no. 1 (2008): 1–28.

———. "O índio na música brasileira: Recordando quinhentos anos de esquecimento." In *Músicas africanas e indígenas no Brasil*, edited by Rosângela Pereira de Tugny and Ruben Caixeta de Queiroz, 115–30. Belo Horizonte: Editora da Universidade Federal de Minas Gerais, 2006.

Beattie, Peter M. "Conscription versus Penal Servitude: Army Reform's Influence on the Brazilian State's Management of Social Control, 1870–1930." *Journal of Social History* 32, no. 4 (Summer 1999): 847–78.

———. "Measures of Manhood: Honor, Enlisted Army Service, and Slavery's Decline in Brazil, 1850–1890." In *Changing Men and Masculinities in Latin America*, edited by Matthew C. Gutmann, 233–55. Durham: Duke University Press, 2003.

———. *The Tribute of Blood: Army, Honor, Race, and Nation in Brazil, 1864–1945*. Durham: Duke University Press, 2001.

Béhague, Gerard. "Bossa and Bossas: Recent Changes in Brazilian Urban Popular Music." *Ethnomusicology* 17, no. 2 (May 1973): 209–33.

———. *Heitor Villa-Lobos: The Search for Brazil's Musical Soul*. Austin: Institute of Latin American Studies, 1994.

———. "Latin American Music, c. 1920–c.1980." In *Latin America Since 1930: Ideas, Culture and Society*, edited by Leslie Bethell, 307–64. Vol. 10 of *The Cambridge History of Latin America*. Cambridge: Cambridge University Press, 1995.

Benjamin, Walter. "The Work of Art in the Age of Mechanical Reproduction." In *Illuminations*, edited and with an introduction by Hannah Arendt, 217–52. New York: Schocken Books, 1968.

Berger, Paulo. *As freguesias do Rio antigo, vistas por Noronha Santos*. Rio de Janeiro: Edições o Cruzeiro, 1965.

Berrien, William. *Latin American Composers and Their Problems*. Pamphlet. Fine Arts Series, no. 10. Washington, D.C.: Pan American Union, 1938.

Besse, Susan K. "Crimes of Passion: The Campaign against Wife Killing in Brazil, 1910–1940." *Journal of Social History* 22, no. 4 (Summer 1989): 653–66.

———. *Restructuring Patriarchy: The Modernization of Gender Inequality in Brazil, 1914–1940*. Chapel Hill: University of North Carolina Press, 1996.

Bezerra, Riselia Duarte. "'Sambations': Samba and the Politics of Syncopation." PhD dissertation. University of California–Riverside, 2000.

Bhabha, Homi K. *The Location of Culture*. London: Routledge, 1994.

Bittar, Carlos Alberto. *A lei de direitos autorais na jurisprudência*. São Paulo: Editora Revista dos Tribunais, 1988.

Bobbio, Pedro Vicente. *O direito de autor na creação musical: Ensaio teórico e pratico*. São Paulo: Editora Lex, 1951.

Bollig, Ben. "White Rapper/Black Beats: Discovering a Race Problem in the Music of Gabriel o Pensador." *Latin American Music Review* 23, no. 2 (Fall/Winter 2002): 159–78.

Borges, Dain. "Healing and Mischief: Witchcraft in Brazilian Law and Literature, 1890–1922." In *Crime and Punishment in Latin America: Law and Society since Late Colonial Times*, edited by Carlos Aguirre, Ricardo D. Salvatore, and Gilbert Joseph, 181–210. Durham: Duke University Press, 2001.

———. "'Puffy, Ugly, Slothful and Inert': Degeneration in Brazilian Social Thought, 1880–1940." *Journal of Latin American Studies* 25, no. 2 (May 1993): 235–56.

———. "The Recognition of Afro-Brazilian Symbols and Ideas, 1890–1940." *Luso-Brazilian Review* 32, no. 2 (Winter 1995): 59–78.

Borges, Vavy Pacheco. "Anos trinta e política: História e historiografia." In *Historiografia brasileira em perspectiva*, edited by Marcos Cezar de Freitas, 159–82. São Paulo: Editora Contexto, 1998.

Bourdieu, Pierre. "The Forms of Capital." In *Handbook of Theory and Research for the Sociology of Education*, edited by John G. Richardson, 241–58. Article translated by Richard Nice. New York: Greenwood Press, 1986.

Branco, Sérgio. *O domínio público no direito autoral brasileiro: Uma obra em domínio público*. Rio de Janeiro: Editora Lumen Juris, 2011.

Bretas, Marcos Luiz. *A guerra das ruas: Povo e polícia na cidade do Rio de Janeiro*. Rio de Janeiro: Arquivo Nacional, 1997.

———. *Ordem na cidade: O exercício da autoridade policial no Rio de Janeiro: 1907–1930*. Rio de Janeiro: Rocco, 1997.

———. "A Polícia das Culturas." In *Entre Europa e África: A invenção do carioca*, edited by Antônio Herculano Lopes, 245–60. Rio de Janeiro: TopBooks, 2000.

———. "What the Eyes Can't See: Stories from Rio de Janeiro's Prisons." In *The Birth of the Penitentiary in Latin America: Essays on Criminology, Prison Reform, and Social Control, 1830–1940*, edited by Ricardo D. Salvatore and Carlos Aguirre, 101–22. Austin: University of Texas Press, 1996.

Brooks, Daphne A. *Bodies in Dissent: Spectacular Performances of Race and Freedom, 1850–1910*. Durham: Duke University Press, 2006.

Brown, Diana Degroat. *Umbanda: Religion and Politics in Urban Brazil*. New York: Columbia University Press, 1994.

Buarque, Chico. *Ópera do malandro*. São Paulo: Livraria Cultura Editora, 1978.

Burns, E. Bradford. *A History of Brazil*. 2nd ed. New York: Columbia University Press, 1980.

Butler, Kim D. *Freedoms Given, Freedoms Won: Afro-Brazilians in Post-Abolition São Paulo and Salvador*. London: Rutgers University Press, 1998.

Cabral, Sérgio. *Ataulfo Alves: Vida e obra*. São Paulo: Lazuli Editora, 2009.

———. *As escolas de samba do Rio de Janeiro*. 2nd ed. Rio de Janeiro: Lumiar, 1996. First published 1974.

———. *No tempo de Almirante: Uma história do rádio e da MPB*. Rio de Janeiro: Francisco Alves, 1990.

———. *Pixinguinha: Vida e obra*. Rio de Janeiro: Lumiar Editora, 1997.

Cacciatore, Olga Gudolle. *Dicionário de cultos afro-brasileiros*. Rio de Janeiro: Forense Universitária, 1977.

Caldwell, Kia Lilly. *Negras in Brazil: Re-Envisioning Black Women, Citizenship, and the Politics of Identity*. New Brunswick, N.J.: Rutgers University Press, 2007.

Campos, Alice Duarte Silva de, et al. *Um certo Geraldo Pereira*. Rio de Janeiro: Fundação Nacional de Artes, 1983.

Campos, Augusto de, ed. *Balanço da bossa: Antologia crítica da moderna música popular brasileira*. São Paulo: Editora Perspectiva, 1968.

———. "A explosão de *Alegria, Alegria*." In *Balanço da Bossa: Antologia crítica da moderna música popular brasileira*, edited by Augusto de Campos, 139–45. São Paulo: Editora Perspectiva, 1968.

Candeia (Antônio Candeia Filho) and Isnard. *Escolas de samba: A árvore que esqueceu a raiz*. Rio de Janeiro: Editora Lidador, 1978.

Capelato, Maria Helena. "Estado Novo: Novas histórias." In *Historiografia brasileira em perspectiva*, edited by Marcos Cezar de Freitas, 183–213. São Paulo: Editora Contexto, 1998.

Capone, Stefania. *Searching for Africa in Brazil: Power and Tradition in Candomblé*. Durham: Duke University Press, 2010.

Cardoso, Fernando Henrique, and Octávio Ianni. *Côr e mobilidade social em Florianópolis: Aspectos das relações entre negros e brancos numa comunidade do Brasil meridional*. São Paulo: Companhia Editora Nacional, 1960.

Cardoso, Lino de Almedia. "O som e o soberano: Uma história da depressão musical carioca pós-abdicação (1831–1843) e de seus antecedentes." PhD dissertation. Universidade de São Paulo, 2006.

Cardoso, Maria Claudia Ferreira. "Representações sociais e práticas políticas do movimento negro paulistano: As trajetórias de Correia Leite e Veiga dos Santos (1928–1937)." M.A. thesis. Universidade Estadual do Rio de Janeiro, 2005.

Carneiro, Edison. *Candomblés da Bahia*. Salvador: Secretaria de Educação e Saúde, 1948.

———. *Carta do samba*. Campanha de Defesa do Folclore Brasileiro, 1962.

———. *Religiões negras: Notas de etnografia religiosa*. Rio de Janeiro: Civilização Brasileira, 1936.

Carvalho, Bruno. "New City in the New World: Literary Spaces of an Afro-Jewish Brazilian Neighborhood." PhD dissertation. Harvard University, 2009.

———. "Porous City: Rio de Janeiro's 'Little Africa,' 'Jewish Neighborhood,' and the Formation of Brazilian Culture (1808–1945)." Unpublished book manuscript.

Carvalho, Luiz Fernando Medeiros de. *Ismael Silva: Samba e resistência*. Rio de Janeiro: José Olympio, 1980.

Cascudo, Luis da Câmara. *Dicionário do folclore brasileiro*. 5th ed. Belo Horizonte: Editora Itatiaia Limitada, 1984. First published 1956.

Casé, Rafael. *Programa Casé: O rádio começou aqui*. Rio de Janeiro: Mauad, 1995.

Castro, Araujo. *A nova constituição brasileira*. Rio de Janeiro: Livraria Editora Freitas Bastos, 1935.

Castro, Gisela. "Consumindo música, consumindo tecnologia." In *Novos rumos da cultura da mídia: Indústrias, produtos, audiências*, edited by Micael Herschmann and João Freire Filho, 213–26. Rio de Janeiro: Mauad X, 2007.

Castro, Ruy. *Bossa Nova: The Story of the Brazilian Music That Seduced the World*. Translated by Lysa Salsbury. Chicago: A Cappella Books, 2000.

———. *Carmen: Uma biografia*. São Paulo: Companhia das Letras, 2005.

Caulfield, Sueann. "The Birth of Mangue: Race, Nation, and the Politics of Prostitution in Rio de Janeiro, 1850–1942." In *Sex and Sexuality in Latin America*, edited by Daniel Balderston and Donna Guy, 86–100. New York: New York University Press, 1997.

———. "The Changing Politics of Freedom and Virginity in Rio de Janeiro, 1920–1940." In *Honor, Status, and Law in Modern Latin America*, edited by Sueann Caulfield, Sarah C. Chambers, and Lara Putnam, 223–45. Durham: Duke University Press, 2005.

———. "Getting Into Trouble: Dishonest Women, Modern Girls, and Women-Men in the Conceptual Language of *Vida Policial*, 1925–1927." *Signs: Journal of Women in Culture and Society* 19, no. 1 (Autumn 1993): 146–76.

———. *In Defense of Honor: Sexual Morality, Modernity, and Nation in Early-Twentieth-Century Brazil*. Durham: Duke University Press, 2000.

Cavalcanti, Maria Laura Viveiros de Castro. *Carnaval carioca: Dos bastidores ao desfile*. Rio de Janeior: Editora da Universidade Federal do Rio de Janeiro, 1995.

Chalhoub, Sidney. *Cidade febril: Cortiços e epidemias na corte imperial*. São Paulo: Companhia das Letras, 1996.

————. "Medo branco de almas negras: Escravos, libertos e republicanos na cidade do Rio." *Revista Brasileira de História* 8, no. 16 (1988): 83–103.

————. "Solidariedade e liberdade: Sociedades beneficentes de negros e negras no Rio de Janeiro na segunda metade do século XIX." In *Quase-cidadão: Histórias e antropologias da pós-emancipação no Brasil*, edited by Olívia Maria Gomes da Cunha and Flávio dos Santos Gomes, 219–40. Rio de Janeiro: Editora Fundação Getúlio Vargas, 2007.

————. *Trabalho, lar e botequim: O cotidiano dos trabalhadores no Rio de Janeiro da belle époque*. São Paulo: Brasiliense, 1986.

————. "Vadios e barões no ocaso do Império: O debate sobre a repressão da ociosidade na Câmara dos Deputados em 1888." *Estudos Ibero-Americanos* 9, nos. 1–2 (1983): 53–67.

————. *Visões da liberdade: Uma história das últimas décadas da escravidão na corte*. São Paulo: Companhia das Letras, 1990.

Chasteen, John Charles. *National Rhythms, African Roots: The Deep History of Latin American Popular Dance*. Albuquerque: University of New Mexico Press, 2004.

————. "The Prehistory of Samba: Carnival Dancing in Rio de Janeiro, 1840–1917." *Journal of Latin American Studies* 28, no. 1 (February 1996): 19–47.

Chazkel, Amy. "Beyond Law and Order: The Origins of the Jogo do Bicho in Republican Rio de Janeiro." *Journal of Latin American Studies* 39, no. 3 (August 2007): 535–65.

————. "The *Crônica*, the City, and the Invention of the Underworld: Rio de Janeiro, 1889–1922." *Estudios Interdisciplinarios de América Latina y el Caribe* 12, no. 1 (January–June 2001): 79–106.

————. *Laws of Chance: Brazil's Clandestine Lottery and the Making of Urban Public Life*. Durham: Duke University Press, 2011.

————. "Social Life and Civic Education in the Rio de Janeiro City Jail." *Journal of Social History* 42, no. 3 (Spring 2009): 697–731.

The Civil Code of Brazil. Translated by Joseph Wheless. St. Louis: Thomas Law Book Co., 1920.

Clifford, James. *Routes: Travel and Translation in the Late Twentieth Century*. Cambridge, Mass.: Harvard University Press, 1997.

Coelho, Frederico Oliveira, and Sergio Cohn. *Tropicália*. Rio de Janeiro: Beco do Azougue Editorial, 2008.

Collier, Simon, et al. *Tango! The Dance, the Song, the Story*. London: Thames and Hudson, 1995.

Conniff, Michael L. "The Populists of Brazil, 1945–1966." *Review of Latin American Studies* 4, no. 1 (1991).

————. *Urban Politics in Brazil: The Rise of Populism, 1925–1945*. Pittsburgh: University of Pittsburgh, 1981.

Conrad, Robert Edgar. *Children of God's Fire: A Documentary History of Black Slavery in Brazil*. Princeton, N.J.: Princeton University Press, 1984.

――――. *The Destruction of Brazilian Slavery, 1850–1888*. Berkeley: University of California Press, 1972.

Coombe, Rosemary. *The Cultural Life of Intellectual Properties: Authorship, Appropriation, and the Law*. Durham: Duke University Press, 1998.

Cooper, Elizabeth. "Freedoms Betwixt and Between: Work, Revelry and Race in the Urban Post-Emancipation Atlantic World: Salvador da Bahia and Havana, 1880–1930." PhD dissertation. University of Chicago, 2007.

Costa, Branna Hocherman, and Marcelo Badaró Mattos, eds. *Trabalhadores em greve, polícia em guarda: Greves e repressão policial na formação da classe trabalhadora carioca*. Rio de Janeiro: FAPERJ, 2004.

Costa, Eliane Sarmento. "'Com quantos *gigabytes* se faz uma jangada, um barco que veleje': O Ministério da Cultura, na gestão Gilberto Gil, diante do cenário das redes e tecnologias digitais." M.A. thesis. Fundação Getúlio Vargas. 2011.

Costa, Emilia Viotti da. *The Brazilian Empire: Myths and Histories*. 2nd ed. Chapel Hill: University of North Carolina, 2000.

――――. *Da senzala à colônia*. 3rd ed. São Paulo: Editora Brasiliense, 1989.

Costa, Francisco Augusto Pereira da. "Folklore Pernambucano: Cancioneiro." *Revista do Instituto Historico e Geographico Brazileiro* 116, no. 70 (part 2, 1908): 429–74.

Coutinho, Eduardo Granja. *Os cronistas de Momo: Imprensa e carnaval na Primeira República*. Rio de Janeiro: Editora Universidade Federal do Rio de Janeiro, 2006.

Cruz, Maria Cecília Velasco e. "Da tutela ao contrato: 'Homens de cor' brasileiros e o movimento operário carioca no pós-abolição." *Topoi* (Rio de Janeiro) 11, no. 20 (January–June 2010): 114–35.

――――. "Puzzling Out Slave Origins in Rio de Janeiro Port Unionism: The 1906 Strike and the Sociedade de Resistência dos Trabalhadores em Trapiche e Café." Translated by Sabrina Gledhill. *Hispanic American Historical Review* 86, no. 2 (May 2006): 205–45.

――――. "Tradições negras na formação de um sindicato: Sociedade de Resistência dos Trabalhadores em Trapiche e Café, Rio de Janeiro, 1905–1930." *Afro-Ásia* (Salvador) 24 (2000): 243–90.

――――. "Virando o jogo: Estivadores e carregadores no Rio de Janeiro da Primeira República." PhD dissertation. Universidade de São Paulo, 1998.

Cunha, Euclides da. *Rebellion in the Backlands*. Translated by Samuel Putnam. Chicago: University of Chicago Press, 1944.

Cunha, Maria Clementina Pereira. "'Acontece que eu sou baiano': Identidades em Santana—Rio de Janeiro, no início do século XX." In *Trabalhadores na cidade: Cotidiano e cultura no Rio de Janeiro e em São Paulo, séculos xix e xx,* edited by Elciene Azevedo et al., 313–56. Campinas, Brazil: Editora da Universidade Estadual de Campinas, 2009.

———, ed. *Carnavais e outras f(r)Estas: Ensaios de história social da cultura.* Campinas, Brazil: CECULT, 2002.

———. "De sambas e passarinhos: As claves do tempo nas canções de Sinhô." In *História em cousas miúdas: Capítulos de história social da crônica no Brasil,* edited by Margarida de Souza Neves et al., 547–88. Campinas, Brazil: Editora da Universidade Estadual de Campinas, 2005.

———. *Ecos da folia: Uma história social do carnaval carioca entre 1880 e 1920.* São Paulo: Companhia das Letras, 2001.

———. "Não me ponha no xadrez com esse malandrão." Paper presented at the 9th meeting of the Brazilian Studies Association. New Orleans, La., 2008.

Cunha, Olívia Maria Gomes da. *Intenção e gesto: Pessoa, cor e a produção da (in) diferença no Rio de Janeiro, 1927–1942.* Rio de Janeiro: Arquivo Nacional, 2002.

———. "The Stigmas of Dishonor: Criminal Records, Civil Rights, and Forensic Identification in Rio de Janeiro, 1903–1940." In *Honor, Status, and Law in Modern Latin America,* edited by Sueann Caulfield, Sarah C. Chambers, and Lara Putnam, 295–315. Durham: Duke University Press, 2005.

Cunha, Olívia Maria Gomes da, and Flávio dos Santos Gomes, eds. *Quase-cidadão: Histórias e antropologias da pós-emancipação no Brasil.* Rio de Janeiro: Fundação Getúlio Vargas, 2007.

Damazio, Sylvia F. *Retrato social do Rio de Janeiro na virada do século.* Rio de Janeiro: Editora da Universidade Estadual do Rio de Janeiro, 1996.

Dantas, Beatriz Góis. *Vovó Nagô e Papai Branco: Usos e abusos da África no Brasil.* Rio de Janeiro: Graal, 1988.

Dávila, Jerry. *Diploma of Whiteness: Race and Social Policy in Brazil, 1917–1945.* Durham: Duke University Press, 2003.

Davis, Darién J. *Avoiding the Dark: Race and the Forging of National Culture in Modern Brazil.* Aldershot, England: Ashgate, 1999.

———. *White Face, Black Mask: Africaneity and the Early Social History of Popular Music Performance in Brazil.* East Lansing: Michigan State University Press, 2009.

Dealtry, Giovanna. *No fio da navalha: Malandragem na literature e no samba.* Rio de Janeiro: Casa da Palavra, 2009.

Dean, Warren. *Rio Claro: A Brazilian Plantation System, 1820–1920.* Stanford, Calif.: Stanford University Press, 1976.

Debret, Jean-Baptiste. *Viagem pitoresca e histórica ao Brasil.* 3 vols. Translated and edited by Sérgio Millet. São Paulo: Livraria Martins Editora S.A., 1972. First published 1839.

Deloria, Phillip. *Playing Indian.* New Haven, Conn.: Yale University Press, 1998.

Denning, Michael. *The Cultural Front: The Laboring of American Culture in the Twentieth Century.* London: Verso, 1998.

Dibbell, Julian. "We Pledge Allegiance to the Penguin." *Wired* 12, no. 11 (2004). Accessed 18 December 2011, at http://www.wired.com/wired/archive/12.11/linux.html.

Diniz, André. *O Rio musical de Anacleto de Medeiros: A vida, a obra e o tempo de um mestre do choro.* Rio de Janeiro: Jorge Zahar Editor, 2007.

Diniz, Edinha. *Chiquinha Gonzaga: Uma história de vida.* 6th ed. Rio de Janeiro: Editora Rosa dos Tempos, 1999.

Domingues, Petrônio. "Uma história não-contada: Negro, racismo e trabalho no pós-abolição em São Paulo (1889–1930)." M.A. thesis. Universidade de São Paulo, 2000.

DuBois, W. E. B. "Brazil." In *African-American Reflections on Brazil's Racial Paradise*, edited by David J. Hellwig, 31–34. Philadelphia: Temple University Press, 1992.

———. *The Souls of Black Folk.* Edited with an introduction by David W. Blight and Robert Gooding-Williams. Boston: Bedford Books, 1997. First published 1903.

Duncan, Julian Smith. "Public and Private Operation of Railways in Brazil." PhD dissertation. Columbia University, 1932.

Dunn, Christopher. *Brutality Garden: Tropicália and the Emergence of a Brazilian Counterculture.* Chapel Hill: University of North Carolina Press, 2001.

———. "Review: *Eu não sou cachorro, não: Música popular cafona e ditadura.*" *Luso-Brazilian Review* 40, no. 2 (Winter 2003): 148–50.

Efegê, Jota. *Figuras e coisas do carnaval carioca.* Rio de Janeiro: Fundação Nacional de Artes, 1982.

———. *Maxixe: A dança excomungada.* Rio de Janeiro: Conquista, 1974.

Erickson, Kenneth Paul. *The Brazilian Corporative State and Working-Class Politics.* Berkeley: University of California Press, 1977.

Esteves, Eulícia. *Acordes e acordos: A história do sindicato dos músicos profissionais do Estado Rio de Janeiro, 1907–1941.* Rio de Janeiro: Multiletra, 1996.

Ewbank, Thomas. *Life in Brazil; or, a Journal of a Visit to the Land of the Cocoa and the Palm.* New York: Harper and Brothers Publishers, 1856.

Farias, Juliana Barreto. "Assumano Mina do Brasil: Personagens e Áfricas ocultas, 1892–1927." In *No labirinto das nações: Africanos e identidades no Rio de Janeiro, século XIX.* Edited by Juliana Barreto Farias, Carlos Eugênio Soares, and Flávio Gomes, 265–97. Rio de Janeiro: Arquivo Nacional, 2005.

———. "Entre identidades e diásporas: Negros minas no Rio de Janeiro (1870–1930)." M.A. thesis. Universidade Federal do Rio de Janeiro, 2004.

Farias, Juliana Barreto, Carlos Eugênio Soares, and Flávio Gomes, eds. *No labirinto das nações: Africanos e identidades no Rio de Janeiro, século XIX.* Rio de Janeiro: Arquivo Nacional, 2005.

Fausto, Boris. *Crime e cotidiano: A criminalidade em São Paulo (1880–1924).* 2nd ed. São Paulo: Editora da Universidade de São Paulo, 2000. First published 1984.

Federico, Maria Elvira Bonavita. *História da comunicação: Rádio e TV no Brasil.* Petrópolis: Vozes, 1982.

Feeley, Malcolm. *The Process Is the Punishment: Handling Cases in a Lower Criminal Court.* New York: Russell Sage Foundation, 1979.

Fenerick, José Adriano. *Nem do morro, nem da cidade: As transformações do samba e a indústria cultural (1920–1945).* São Paulo: Annablume, 2005.

Ferlim, Uliana Dias Campos. "A polifonia das modinhas: Diversidade e tensões musicais no Rio de Janeiro na passagem do século XIX ao XX." M.A. thesis. Universidade Estadual de Campinas, 2006.

Fernandes, Florestan. *The Negro in Brazilian Society.* Translated by A. Brunel Jacqueline D. Skiles and Arthur Rothwell. New York: Columbia University Press, 1969.

Fernandes, Nelson da Nobrega. *Escolas de samba: Sujeitos celebrantes e objetos celebrados, Rio de Janeiro, 1928–1949.* Rio de Janeiro: Prefeitura da Cidade do Rio de Janeiro, 2001.

Ferrareto, Luiz Artur. *Rádio: O veículo, a história e a técnica.* Porto Alegre: Sagra Luzzatto, 2001.

Ferreira, Felipe. *O livro de ouro do carnaval brasileiro.* Rio de Janeiro: Ediouro, 2004.

Fischer, Brodwyn M. *A Poverty of Rights: Citizenship and Inequality in Twentieth-Century Rio de Janeiro.* Stanford: Stanford University Press, 2008.

———. "*Quase pretos de tão pobres*? Race and Social Discrimination in Rio de Janeiro's Twentieth-Century Criminal Courts." *Latin American Research Review* 39, no. 1 (February 2004): 31–59.

Florentino, Manolo. "Alforrias e etnicidade no Rio de Janeiro oitocentista: Notas de pesquisa." *Topoi* (Rio de Janeiro) (September 2002): 9–40.

———. *Em costas negras: Uma história do tráfico Atlântico de escravos entre a África e o Rio de Janeiro (séculos XVIII e XIX).* Rio de Janeiro: Arquivo Nacional, 1995.

Flory, Thomas. "Race and Social Control in Independent Brazil." *Journal of Latin American Studies* 9, no. 2 (1977): 199–224.

Floyd, Samuel A., Jr. *The Power of Black Music: Interpreting Its History from Africa to the United States.* New York: Oxford University Press, 1995.

Foucault, Michel. *Discipline and Punish: The Birth of the Prison.* Translated by Alan Sheridan. New York: Vintage, 1995.

———. "Governmentality." In *The Foucault Effect: Studies in Governmentality with Two Lectures by and an Interview with Michel Foucault,* edited by Colin Gordon, Graham Burchell, and Peter Miller, 87–104. Chicago: University of Chicago Press, 1991.

————. *The History of Sexuality. Vol. 1: An Introduction*. Translated by Robert Hurley. New York: Vintage Books, 1990. First published in English in 1978; first published in French in 1976.

————. "Nietzsche, Genealogy, History." In *Language, Counter-Memory, Practice: Selected Essays and Interviews*, edited by D. F. Bouchard, 139–64. Ithaca, N.Y.: Cornell University Press, 1977.

————. "What Is an Author?" In *The Foucault Reader*, edited by Paul Rabinow, 101–20. New York: Pantheon Books, 1984.

Fraga Filho, Walter. *Mendigos, moleques e vadios na Bahia do século XIX*. São Paulo: Hucitec, 1996.

França, Eurico Nogueira. *Villa-Lobos: Síntese crítica e biográfica*. Rio de Janeiro: Museu Villa-Lobos, 1970.

Franceschi, Humberto Moraes. *A Casa Edison e seu tempo*. Rio de Janeiro: Sarapuí, 2002.

————. *Registro sonoro por meios mecânicos no Brasil*. Rio de Janeiro: Studio HMF, 1984.

————. *Samba de sambar do Estácio, 1928–1931*. São Paulo: Instituto Moreira Salles, 2010.

Francis, Paulo. "Madame Satã." In *As grandes entrevistas do Pasquim*, edited by Jaguar (Sérgio de Magalhães Gomes Jaguaribe), 149–60. Rio de Janeiro: Editora Codecri, 1975.

Frange, Olga. "A modinha e o lundu no período colonial: Uma pesquisa bibliográfica." In *A música no Brasil colonial*, edited by Rui Vieira Nery, 330–62. Lisbon: Serviço de Música, 2000.

Frank, Zephyr L. *Dutra's World: Wealth and Family in Nineteenth-Century Rio de Janeiro*. Albuquerque: University of New Mexico Press, 2004.

French, John D. *The Brazilian Workers' ABC: Class Conflict and Alliances in Modern São Paulo*. Chapel Hill: University of North Carolina Press, 1992.

————. *Drowning in Laws: Labor Law and Brazilian Political Culture*. Chapel Hill: University of North Carolina Press, 2004.

————. "The Origin of Corporatist State Intervention in Brazilian Industrial Relations, 1930–1934: A Critique of the Literature." *Luso-Brazilian Review* 28, no. 2 (Winter 1991): 13–26.

————. "The Populist Gamble of Getúlio Vargas in 1945: Political and Ideological Transitions in Brazil." In *Latin America in the 1940s: War and Postwar Transitions*, edited by David Rock, 141–65. Berkeley: University of California Press, 1994.

Freyre, Gilberto. *Casa grande e senzala: Formação da família brasileira sob o regimen de economia patriarchal*. Rio de Janeiro: Maia and Schmidt, 1933.

————. *The Masters and the Slaves: A Study in the Development of Brazilian Civilization*. 2nd English-language ed. Translated by Samuel Putnam. Berkeley: University of California Press, 1986.

————. *Order and Progress: Brazil from Monarchy to Republic*. Translated by Rod W. Horton. New York: Knopf, 1970.

Frota, Wander Nunes. *Auxílio luxuoso: Samba símbolo nacional, geração Noel Rosa e indústria cultural*. São Paulo: Annablume, 2003.

Fry, Peter. "Feijoada e *soul food*: Notas sobre a manipulação de símbolos étnicos e nacionais." In *Para inglês ver: Identidade e política na cultura brasileira*, 47–53. Rio de Janeiro: Zahar Editores, 1982.

Fryer, Peter. *Rhythms of Resistance: African Musical Heritage in Brazil*. Hanover, Conn.: Wesleyan University Press, 2000.

Gallet, Luciano. *Estudos de folclore*. Rio de Janeiro: Carlos Wehrs, 1934.

Garcia, Antolim. *O circo: A pitoresca turnê do Circo Garcia, através à África e países asiáticos*. São Paulo: Edições DAG, 1976.

Garcia, Tânia da Costa. *O "it verde e amarelo" de Carmen Miranda, 1930–1946*. São Paulo: Annablume, 2004.

Gardel, André. *O encontro entre Bandeira e Sinhô*. Rio de Janeiro: Biblioteca Carioca, 1996.

Gardel, Luis D. *Escolas de Samba: An Affectionate Descriptive Account of the Carnival Guilds of Rio de Janeiro*. Rio de Janeiro: Kosmos Editôra, 1967.

Garramuño, Florencia. *Primitive Modernities: Tango, Samba, and Nation*. Translated by Anna Kazumi Stahl. Stanford, Calif.: Stanford University Press, 2011.

Garzoni, Lerice de Castro. "Raparigas e meganhas em Santana (Rio de Janeiro, 1950)." In *Trabalhadores na cidade: Cotidiano e cultura no Rio de Janeiro e em São Paulo, séculos xix e xx*, edited by Elciene Azevedo et al., 157–88. Campinas, Brazil: Editora da Universidade Estadual de Campinas, 2009.

Gaspari, Elio. *A ditadura envergonhada*. São Paulo: Companhia das Letras, 2002.

————. *A ditadura escancarada*. São Paulo: Companhia das Letras, 2002.

Geraldo, José. "Histórias e historiadores da música popular no Brasil." *Latin American Music Review* 28, no. 2 (Fall/Winter 2007): 271–99.

Gerson, Brasil. *História das ruas do Rio*. 4th ed. Rio de Janeiro: Livraria Brasiliana, 1965.

"Getúlio Vargus and His Legacy." Special issue of *Luso-Brazilian Review* 31, no. 2 (Winter 1994).

Gil-Montero, Martha. *Brazilian Bombshell: The Biography of Carmen Miranda*. New York: D. I. Fine, 1989.

Gilroy, Paul. *The Black Atlantic: Modernity and Double-Consciousness*. Cambridge, Mass.: Harvard University Press, 1993.

————. *Darker Than Blue: On the Moral Economies of Black Atlantic Culture*. Cambridge, Mass.: Harvard University Press, 2010.

Gitelman, Lisa. "Reading Music, Reading Records, Reading Race: Musical Copyright and the U.S. Copyright Act of 1909." *Musical Quarterly* 81, no. 2 (Summer 1997): 265–90.

Glazer, Nathan, and Daniel Patrick Moynihan. *Beyond the Melting Pot: The*

Negroes, Puerto Ricans, Jews, Italians, and Irish of New York City. Cambridge, Mass.: MIT Press, 1963.

Góes, Maria Conceição Pinto de. *A formação da classe trabalhadora: Movimento anarquista no Rio de Janeiro, 1888–1911*. Rio de Janeiro: Jorge Zahar Editor, 1988.

Gomes, Angela Maria de Castro. *Burguesia e trabalho: Política e legislação social no Brasil, 1917–1937*. Rio de Janeiro: Editora Campus, 1979.

———. *Essa gente do Rio . . . : Modernismo e nacionalismo*. Rio de Janeiro: Fundação Getúlio Vargas, 1999.

Gomes, Bruno Ferreira. *Wilson Batista e sua época*. Rio de Janeiro: Fundação Nacional de Artes, 1985.

Gomes, Tiago de Melo. *Um espelho no palco: Identidades sociais e massificação da cultura no teatro de revista dos anos 1920*. Campinas, Brazil: Editora da Universidade Estadual de Campinas, 2004.

———. "Lenço no pescoço: O malandro no teatro de revista e na música popular—'Nacional,' 'popular' e cultura de massas nos anos 1920." M.A. thesis. Universidade Estadual de Campinas, 1998.

———. "Negros contando (e fazendo) sua história: Alguns significados da trajetória da Companhia Negra de Revistas (1926)." *Estudos Afro-Asiáticos* 23, No. 1 (January–June 2001): 53–83.

———. "Para além da casa da Tia Ciata: Outras experiências no universo cultural carioca, 1830s–1930s." *Afro-Ásia* 29/30 (2003): 175–98.

Graden, Dale Torston. *From Slavery to Freedom in Brazil: Bahia, 1835–1900*. Albuquerque: University of New Mexico Press, 2006.

Graham, Richard, ed. *The Idea of Race in Latin America, 1870–1940*. Austin: University of Texas Press, 1990.

Green, James N. *Beyond Carnival: Male Homosexuality in Twentieth-Century Brazil*. Chicago: University of Chicago Press, 1999.

———. "Madame Satã (Satan): The Black 'Queen' of Rio's Bohemia." In *The Human Tradition in Modern Brazil*, edited by Peter M. Beattie, 267–86. Wilmington, Del.: Scholarly Resources Books, 2004.

Grinberg, Keila. "Slavery, Liberalism, and Civil Law: Definitions of Status and Citizenship in the Elaboration of the Brazilian Civil Code (1855–1916)." In *Honor, Status, and Law in Modern Latin America*, edited by Sueann Caulfield, Sarah C. Chambers, and Lara Putnam, 109–27. Durham: Duke University Press, 2005.

Gronow, Pekka, and Ilpo Saunio. *An International History of the Recording Industry*. Translated by Christopher Moseley. London: Cassell, 1998.

Guillermoprieto, Alma. *Samba*. New York: Vintage, 1991.

Guimarães, Antonio Sérgio Alfredo. *Classes, raças e democracia*. São Paulo: Editora 34, 2002.

Guy, Donna J. *Sex and Danger in Buenos Aires: Prostitution, Family, and Nation in Argentina*. Lincoln: University of Nebraska Press, 1991.

Haberly, David T. *Three Sad Races: Racial Identity and National Consciousness in Brazilian Literature.* Cambridge, Mass.: Cambridge University Press, 1983.

Hahner, June E. *Poverty and Politics: The Urban Poor in Brazil, 1870–1920.* Albuquerque: University of New Mexico Press, 1986.

Hanchard, Michael. *Orpheus and Power: The* Movimento Negro *of Rio de Janeiro and São Paulo, Brazil, 1945–1988.* Princeton, N.J.: Princeton University Press, 1994.

Harding, Rachel E. *A Refuge in Thunder: Candomblé and Alternative Spaces of Blackness.* Bloomington: Indiana University Press, 2000.

Hazan, Marcelo Campos. "Raça, nação e Jose Maurício Nunes Garcia." *Estudios—Resonancias,* no. 24 (May 2009): 23–40.

Hebdige, Dick. *Cut 'n' Mix: Culture, Identity and Caribbean Music.* London: Methuen, 1987.

Hentschke, Jens R., ed. *Vargas and Brazil: New Perspectives.* New York: Palgrave Macmillan, 2006.

Herschmann, Micael. "A indústria da música como 'laboratório.'" *Observatório Itaú Cultural* (São Paulo), no. 9 (January–April 2010): 21–30.

Hertzman, Marc A. "A Brazilian Counterweight: Music, Intellectual Property, and the African Diaspora in Rio de Janeiro (1910s–1930s)." *Journal of Latin American Studies* 41, no. 4 (November 2009): 695–722.

———. "Making Music and Masculinity in Vagrancy's Shadow: Race, Wealth, and *Malandragem* in Post-Abolition Rio de Janeiro." *Hispanic American Historical Review* 90, no. 4 (November 2010).

———. "The Promise and Challenge of Transnational History." *A Contracorriente* 7, no. 1 (Fall 2009): 305–15.

———. "Surveillance and Difference: The Making of *Samba,* Race, and Nation in Brazil (1880s–1970s)." PhD dissertation. University of Wisconsin–Madison, 2008.

Hobsbawm, Eric. *The Jazz Scene.* 3rd ed. New York: Pantheon, 1993.

Holanda, Nestor de. *Memórias do Café Nice: Subterrâneos da música popular e da vida boêmia do Rio de Janeiro.* Rio de Janeiro: Conquista, 1970.

Holloway, Thomas H. "A 'Healthy Terror': Police Repression of 'Capoeiras' in Nineteenth-Century Brazil." *Hispanic American Historical Review* 69, no. 4 (1989): 637–76.

———. *Immigrants on the Land: Coffee and Society in São Paulo, 1886–1934.* Chapel Hill: University of North Carolina Press, 1980.

———. *Policing Rio de Janeiro: Repression and Resistance in a 19th-Century City.* Stanford, Calif.: Stanford University Press, 1993.

Huggins, Martha Knisely. *From Slavery to Vagrancy in Brazil: Crime and Social Control in the Third World.* New Brunswick, N.J.: Rutgers University Press, 1985.

Huyssen, Andreas. *After the Great Divide: Modernism, Mass Culture, Postmodernism*. Bloomington: Indiana University Press, 1987.

Ickes, Scott Alan. "Salvador's Transformist Hegemony: Popular Festivals, Cultural Politics and Afro-Bahian Culture in Salvador, Bahia, Brazil, 1930–1952." PhD dissertation. University of Maryland, 2003.

Instituto Brasileiro de Geografia e Estatística. *Estatísticas do século xx*. Rio de Janeiro: IBGE, 2003.

Instituto de Economia. *Pesquisa sôbre o padrão de vida do comerciário no Distrito Federal*. Rio de Janeiro, 1949.

Ipsen, Wiebke. "Delicate Citizenship: Gender and Nationbuilding in Brazil, 1865–1891." PhD dissertation. University of California–Irvine, 2005.

Isfahani-Hammond, Alexandra. *White Negritude: Race, Writing, and Brazilian Cultural Identity*. New York: Palgrave Macmillan, 2008.

Jambeiro, Othon, et al. *Tempos de Vargas: O rádio e o controle da informação*. Salvador: Editora da Universidade Federal da Bahia, 2003.

Jones, LeRoi (Amiri Baraka). *Blues People: Negro Music in White America*. New York: W. Morrow, 1963.

———. "The Changing Same (R & B and New Black Music)." In *The Black Aesthetic*, edited by Addison Gayle, 112–25. Garden City, N.Y.: Anchor Books, 1971.

Karasch, Mary C. *Slave Life in Rio de Janeiro, 1808–1850*. Princeton, N.J.: Princeton University Press, 1987.

Kasinitz, Philip. *Caribbean New York: Black Immigrants and the Politics of Race*. Ithaca, N.Y.: Cornell University Press, 1992.

Kelley, Robin D. G. "The Riddle of the Zoot: Malcolm Little and Black Cultural Politics during World War II." In *Race Rebels: Culture, Politics, and the Black Working Class*. New York: Free Press, 161–81.

Kidder, Daniel P. *Sketches of Residence and Travels in Brazil, Embracing Historical and Geographical Notices of the Empire and Its Several Provinces*. London: Wiley and Putnam, 1845.

Kiefer, Bruno. *A modinha e o lundu: Duas raízes da música popular brasileira*. Porto Alegre: Movimento, 1977.

Klein, Herbert S., and Francisco Vidal Luna. *Slavery in Brazil*. New York: Cambridge University Press, 2010.

Koidin, Julie. "Benedicto Lacerda and the Golden Age of Choro." *Luso-Brazilian Review* 48, no. 1 (June 2011): 36–60.

Koster, Henry. *Travels in Brazil: In the Years from 1809 to 1815*. 2 vols. Philadelphia: M. Carey and Son, 1817.

Kowarick, Lúcio. *Trabalho e vadiagem: A origem do trabalho livre no Brasil*. São Paulo: Editora Brasiliense, 1987.

Kraay, Hendrik, ed. *Afro-Brazilian Culture and Politics: Bahia, 1790s to 1990s*. Armonk, N.Y.: M. E. Sharpe, 1998.

Kubik, Gerhard. *Angolan Traits in Black Music, Games and Dances of Brazil: A Study of African Cultural Extensions Overseas.* Estudos de Antopologia Cultural. Lisbon: Junta de Investigações Científicas do Ultramar, Centro de Estudos de Antopologia Cultural, 1979.

Lacerda, José Maria de Almeida e Araujo Corrêa de. *Diccionario encyclopedico, ou novo diccionario da lingua portugueza para uso dos portuguezes e brazileiros.* 5th ed. Lisbon: Francisco Arthur da Silva, 1878.

Lauderdale Graham, Sandra. *House and Street: The Domestic World of Servants and Masters in Nineteenth-Century Rio de Janeiro.* Cambridge: Cambridge University Press, 1988.

———. "The Vintem Riot and Political Culture: Rio de Janeiro, 1880." *Hispanic American Historical Review* 60, no. 3 (1980): 431–49.

Lazzari, Alexandre. *Coisas para o povo não fazer: Carnaval em Porto Alegre (1870–1915).* Campinas, Brazil: Editora da Universidade Estadual de Campinas, 2001.

Leff, Nathaniel H. *Economic Structure and Change, 1822–1947.* Vol. I of *Underdevelopment and Development in Brazil.* London: George Allen and Unwin, 1982.

Leite, Jose Correia. *. . . E disse o velho militante Jose Correia Leite.* São Paulo: Secretaria Municipal de Cultura, 1992.

Leme, Marisa Saenz. *A ideologia dos industriais brasileiros (1919–1945).* Petrópolis: Vozes, 1978.

Lemos, Ronaldo, et al. *Tecnobrega: O Pará reinventando o negócio da música.* Rio de Janeiro: Aeroplano, 2008.

Lena, Jennifer C. "Meaning and Membership: Samples in Rap Music, 1979–1995." *Poetics* 32 (2004): 297–310.

Lesser, Jeffrey. *Negotiating National Identity: Immigrants, Minorities, and the Struggle for Ethnicity in Brazil.* Durham: Duke University Press, 1999.

Levine, Robert M. *Father of the Poor? Vargas and His Era.* New York: Cambridge University Press, 1998.

———. *Vale of Tears: Revisiting the Canudos Massacre in Northeastern Brazil, 1893–1897.* Berkeley: University of California Press, 1992.

———. *The Vargas Regime: The Critical Years, 1934–1938.* New York: Columbia University Press, 1970.

Linhares, Maria Yedda, and Maria Bárbara Lévy. "Aspectos da história demográfica e social do Rio de Janeiro (1808–1889)." In *L'Histoire Quantitative du Brésil de 1800 a 1930,* 123–42. Paris: Éditions du Centre National de La Recherche Scientifique, 1973.

Lins, Paulo. *Desde que o samba é o samba.* São Paulo: Planeta, 2012.

Lipsitz, George. *Time Passages: Collective Memory and American Popular Culture.* Minneapolis: University of Minnesota Press, 1990.

Lirio, Alba e Heitor dos Prazeres Filho. *Heitor dos Prazeres: Sua arte e seu tempo.* Rio de Janeiro: SESC, 2003.

Livingston-Isenhour, Tamara Elena, and Thomas George Caracas Garcia. *Choro: A Social History of a Brazilian Popular Music.* Bloomington: Indiana University Press, 2005.

Lobo, Eulalia Maria Lahmeyer. "Capítulo 1: A situação do operariado no Rio de Janeiro em 1930." In *Rio de Janeiro operário: Natureza do estado e conjuntura econômica, condições de vida e consciência de classe (1930–1970)*, 20–46. Rio de Janeiro: Access Editora, 1992.

———. "Evolução dos preços e do padráo de vida no Rio de Janeiro, 1820–1930: Resultados preliminares." *Revista Brasileira de Economia* 25, no. 4 (October–December 1971): 235–65.

———. *História da cidade do Rio de Janeiro: Do capital industrial ao capital industrial e financeiro.* 2 vols. Rio de Janeiro: IBMEC, 1978.

———, ed. *Rio de Janeiro operário: Natureza do estado e conjuntura econômica, condições de vida e consciência de classe (1930–1970).* Rio de Janeiro: Access Editora, 1992.

Lopes, Antonio Herculano. "The Jaguar's Leap: Musical Theater in Rio de Janeiro, 1900–1922." PhD dissertation. New York University, 2000.

Lopes, Cássia. "A re-caricatura de Gilberto Gil: Zelberto Zel." Paper presented at IV Encontro de Estudos Multidisciplianres em Cultura, 28–30 May 2008, Salvador, Bahia.

Lopes, Gustavo Gomes. "Samba e mercado de bens culturais (Rio de Janeiro, 1910–1940)." M.A. thesis. Universidade Federal Fluminense, 2001.

Lopes, Maria Aparecida Oliveira. "Beleza e ascensão social na imprensa negra paulistana: 1920–1940." M.A. thesis. Pontifícia Universidade Católica de São Paulo, 2002.

Lopes, Nei. *Dicionário banto do Brasil.* Rio de Janeiro: Prefeitura da Cidade do Rio de Janeiro, 1995.

———. *O negro no Rio de Janeiro e sua tradição musical: Partido-Alto, calango, chula e outras cantorias.* Rio de Janeiro: Pallas, 1992.

———. *O samba na realidade: A utopia da ascensão social do sambista.* Rio de Janeiro: Editora Codecri, 1981.

Loveman, Mara. "Nation-State Building, 'Race,' and the Production of Official Statistics: Brazil in Comparative Perspective." PhD dissertation. University of California–Los Angeles, 2001.

Lühning, Angela. "'Acabe com este santo, Pedrito vem aí . . .': Mito e realidade da perseguição policial ao candomblé baiano entre 1920 e 1942." *Revista USP* 28 (December–February 1995–96): 194–220.

Macedo, Joaquim Manuel de. *As mulheres de mantilha: Romance histórico.* Rio de Janeiro: Oficinas Gráficas do Jornal do Brasil, 1931. First published 1870.

Madureira, Luís. "A Cannibal Recipe to Turn a Dessert Country into the Main Course: Brazilian 'Antropofagia' and the Dilemma of Development." *Luso-Brazilian Review* 41, no. 2 (2005): 96–125.

Magaldi, Cristina. "Music for the Elite: Musical Societies in Imperial Rio de Janeiro." *Latin American Music Review* 16, no. 1 (1995): 1–41.

Maggie, Yvonne. *Medo do feitiço: Relações entre magia e poder no Brasil*. Rio de Janeiro: Arquivo Nacional, 1992.

Mallon, Florencia E. "The Promise and Dilemma of Subaltern Studies: Perspectives from Latin American History." *American Historical Review* 99, no. 5 (1994): 1491–1515.

Manuel, Peter. "The Saga of a Song: Authorship and Ownership in the Case of 'Guantanamera.'" *Latin American Music Review* 27, no. 2 (Fall/Winter 2006): 121–47.

Marcondes, Marcos Antônio, ed. *Enciclopédia da música brasileira: Erudita, folclórica e popular*. 2 vols. São Paulo: Art Editora, 1977.

Mariz, Vasco. *História da música no Brasil*. 5th ed. Rio de Janeiro: Editora Nova Fronteira, 2000.

Marshall, Wayne. "Giving up Hip-Hop's Firstborn: A Quest for the Real after the Death of Sampling." *Callaloo* 29, no. 3 (Summer 2006): 868–92.

Martins, Samuel. *Direito autoral: Seu conceito, sua historia e sua legislação entre nós*. Recife: Officinas da Livraria Franceza, 1906.

Martins, William de Souza Nunes. "Paschoal Segreto: 'Ministro das Diversões' do Rio de Janeiro (1883–1920)." M.A. thesis. Universidade Federal do Rio de Janeiro, 2004.

Matory, J. Lorand. *Black Atlantic Religion: Tradition, Transnationalism, and Matriarchy in the Afro-Brazilian Candomblé*. Princeton, N.J.: Princeton University Press, 2005.

Matos, Cláudia. *Acertei no milhar: Malandragem e samba no tempo de Getúlio*. Rio de Janeiro: Paz e Terra, 1982.

Mattos, Cleofe Person de. *José Maurício Nunes Garcia: Biografia*. Rio de Janeiro: Ministério da Cultura, 1997.

Mattos, Marcelo Badaró. "Vadios, jogadores, mendigos e bêbados na cidade do Rio de Janeiro do início do século." M.A. thesis. Universidade Federal Fluminense, 1991.

Mattoso, Katia M. Querós. *To Be a Slave in Brazil, 1550–1888*. Translated by Arthur Goldhammer. New Brunswick, N.J.: Rutgers University Press, 1986.

Máximo, João, and Carlos Didier. *Noel Rosa: Uma biografia*. Brasilia: Linha Gráfica, 1990.

McCann, Bryan. "Black Pau: Uncovering the History of Brazilian Soul." In *Rockin' Las Américas: The Global Politics of Rock in Latin/o America*, edited by Héctor Fernández L'Hoeste, Deborah Pacini Hernandez, and Eric Zolov, 68–90. Pittsburgh: University of Pittsburgh Press, 2004.

———. "Blues and Samba: Another Side of Bossa Nova History." *Luso-Brazilian Review* 44, no. 2 (2007): 21–49.

———. "Geraldo Pereira: Samba Composer and Grifter." In *The Human Tradition in Modern Brazil*, edited by Peter M. Beattie, 127–46. Wilmington, Del.: Rowman and Littlefield, 2004.

———. *Hello, Hello Brazil: Popular Music in the Making of Modern Brazil*. Durham: Duke University Press, 2004.

———. "Noel Rosa's Nationalist Logic." *Luso-Brazilian Review* 38, no. 1 (2001): 1–16.

———. "Review: *Auxílio Luxuoso*." *Luso-Brazilian Review* 40, no. 2 (Winter 2003): 146–47.

———. "Thin Air and the Solid State: Radio, Culture, and Politics in Brazil's Vargas Era." PhD dissertation. Yale University, 1999.

McGowan, Chris, and Ricardo Pessanha. *The Brazilian Sound*: Samba, Bossa Nova, *and the Popular Music of Brazil*. 2nd ed. Philadelphia: Temple University Press, 1998.

McLeod, Kembrew. *Freedom of Expression: Overzealous Copyright Bozos and Other Enemies of Creativity*. New York: Doubleday, 2005.

———. *Owning Culture: Authorship, Ownership, and Intellectual Property Law*. New York: P. Lang, 2001.

McLeod, Kembrew, and Peter DiCola, eds. *Creative License: The Law and Culture of Digital Sampling*. Durham: Duke University Press, 2011.

McPhee, Kit. "'Immigrants with Money Are No Use to Us': Race and Ethnicity in the *Zona Portuária* of Rio de Janeiro, 1903–1912." *Americas* 62, no. 4 (April 2006): 623–50.

———. "'A New 13th of May': Afro-Brazilian Port Workers in Rio de Janeiro, Brazil, 1905–18." *Journal of Latin American Studies* 38, no. 1 (2006): 149–77.

———. "'Standing at the Altar of the Nation': Afro-Brazilians, Immigrants and Racial Democracy in a Brazilian Port City, 1888–1937." PhD dissertation. University of Melbourne, 2004.

Meade, Teresa A. *"Civilizing" Rio: Reform and Resistance in a Brazilian City, 1889–1930*. University Park: Pennsylvania State University Press, 1997.

———. "'Living Worse and Costing More': Resistance and Riot in Rio de Janeiro, 1890–1917." *Journal of Latin American Studies* 21, no. 2 (May 1989): 241–66.

Mencarelli, Fernando Antonio. *Cena aberta: A absolvição de um bilontra e o teatro de revista de Arthur Azevedo*. Campinas, Brazil: Editora da Universidade Estadual de Campinas, 1999.

Mendoza, Zoila S. *Creating Our Own: Folklore, Performance, and Identity in Cuzco, Peru*. Durham: Duke University Press, 2008.

Mesquita, Cláudia. *Um museu para a Guanabara: Carlos Lacerda e a criação do Museu da Imagem e do Som (1960–1965)*. Rio de Janeiro: FAPERJ, 2010.

Miereles, Mario M. *Catulo: Seresteiro e poeta*. São Luis, Maranhão: Tipografia São José, 1963.

Miller, Karl Hagstrom. "Segregating Sound: Folklore, Phonographs, and the Transformation of Southern Music, 1888–1935." PhD dissertation. New York University, 2002.

———. *Segregating Sound: Inventing Folk and Pop Music in the Age of Jim Crow*. Durham: Duke University Press, 2010.

Miller, Richard. "African Rhythms in Brazilian Popular Music: *Tango Brasileiro, Maxixe* and *Choro*." *Luso-Brazilian Review* 48, no. 1 (June 2011): 6–35.

Ministerio da Agricultura, Industria e Commercio, Directoria Geral de Estatistica. *Recenseamento do Brazil: Realizado em 1 de setembro de 1920, Volume II (1a Parte), população do Rio de Janeiro (Districto Federal)*. Rio de Janeiro: Typografia da Estatistica, 1923.

Moore, Robin. *Nationalizing Blackness*: Afrocubanismo *and Artistic Revolution in Havana, 1920–1940*. Pittsburgh, Pa.: University of Pittsburgh Press, 1997.

Moraes, Eneida de. *História do carnaval carioca: Nova edição, revista e ampliada*. Edited by Haroldo Costa. Rio de Janeiro: Editora Record, 1987. First published 1957.

Moraes Filho, Mello. *Festas e tradições populares do Brasil*. Edited by Câmara Cascudo. São Paulo: Livraria Itatiaia, 1979. First published 1895.

———. *Serenatas e saráus: Collecção de autos populares, lundús, recitativos, modinhas, duetos, serenatas barcarolas e outras producções brasileiras antigas e modernas*. 3 vols. Rio de Janeiro: H. Garnier, 1901–2.

Morais, Manuel. "Domingos Caldas Barbosa (Fl. 1775–1800): Compositor e tangedor de viola?" In *A música no Brasil colonial*, edited by Rui Vieira Nery, 305–29. Lisbon: Serviço de Música, 2000.

Moreira, Sonia Virgínia. *O rádio no Brasil*. Rio de Janeiro: Rio Fundo Editora, 1991.

Morelli, Rita de Cássia Lahoz. *Arrogantes, anônimos, subversivos: Interpretando o acordo e a discórdia na tradição autoral brasileira*. São Paulo: Mercado de Letras, 2000.

Moura, Clovis. *Organizações negras/São Paulo: O povo em movimento*. Petrópolis: Vozes, 1980.

Moura, Roberto. *Tia Ciata e a Pequena África no Rio de Janeiro*. Rio de Janeiro: Secretaria da Cultura, 1995. First published 1983.

Moura, Roberto M. *No princípio era a roda: Um estudo sobre samba, partido-alto e outros pagodes*. Rio de Janeiro: Rocco, 2004.

Munakata, Kazumi. *A legislação trabalhista no Brasil*. São Paulo: Brasiliense, 1981.

Muniz Jr., J. *Sambistas imortais: Dados biográficos de 50 figuras do mundo do samba*. Vol. 1: *1850–1914*. São Paulo: Cia. Brasileira de Impressão e Propaganda and Cia. Lithographica Ypiranga, 1976.

Murce, Renato. *Bastidores do rádio: Fragmentos do rádio de ontem e de hoje*. Rio de Janeiro: Imago, 1976.

Muricy, José Cândido de Andrade, et al. *Estudos mauricianos*. Rio de Janeiro: Fundação Nacional de Artes, 1983.

Museu da Imagem e do Som. *As vozes desassombradas do museu*. Rio de Janeiro: MIS, 1970.

Napolitano, Marcos. *"Seguindo a canção": Engajamento político e indústria cultural na MPB, 1959–1969*. São Paulo: Annablume, 2001.

Napolitano, Maros, and Maria Clara Wasserman. "Desde que o samba é o samba: A questão das origens no debate historiográfico sobre a música popular brasileira." *Revista Brasileira de História* (São Paulo) 20, no. 39 (2000): 167–89.

Nascentes, Antenor. *Dicionário etimológico da língua portuguesa*. Rio de Janeiro: Livraria Francisco Alves, 1932.

Nascimento, Marcio. *PRA-9 Rádio Mayrink Veiga: Um lapso de memória na história do rádio brasileiro*. Rio de Janeiro: Litteris Editora, 2002.

Nasser, David. *A vida trepidante de Carmen Miranda*. Rio de Janeiro: O Cruzeiro, 1966.

Naves, Santuza Cambraia. *O violão azul: Modernismo e música popular*. Rio de Janeiro: Editora Fundação Getúlio Vargas, 1998.

Needell, Jeffrey D. "The Domestic Civilizing Mission: The Cultural Role of the State in Brazil, 1808–1930." *Luso-Brazilian Review* 36, no. 1 (Summer 1999): 1–18.

———. "The Revolta Contra Vacina of 1904: The Revolt against 'Modernization' in Belle-Epoque Rio de Janeiro." *Hispanic American Historical Review* 67, no. 2 (May 1987): 233–69.

———. *A Tropical* Belle Époque: *Elite Culture and Society in Turn-of-the-Century Rio de Janeiro*. Cambridge: Cambridge University Press, 1987.

Neves, Eduardo das. *Mysterios do violão*. Rio de Janeiro: Livraria do Povo and Editora Quaresma, 1905.

———. *Trovador da malandragem*. 2nd ed. Rio de Janeiro: Editora Quaresma, 1926.

Nunes, Maria Luisa. "Mário de Andrade in 'Paradise.'" *Modern Language Studies* 22, no. 3 (Summer 1992): 70–75.

Nunes, Zita. *Cannibal Democracy: Race and Representation in the Literature of the Americas*. Minneapolis: University of Minnesota Press, 2008.

Oakenfull, J. C. *Brazil in 1910*. Devonport, England: R. T. White Stevens, 1910.

———. *Brazil in 1911*. London: Butler and Tanner, 1912.

———. *Brazil in 1912*. London: Robert Atkinson, 1913.

———. *Brazil (1913)*. Frome, England: Butler and Tanner, n.d.

Oliveira Filho, Arthur Loureiro de. *Bicho Novo, Carlos Cachaça, Ismael Silva: Pioneiros do samba*. Rio de Janeiro: MIS Editorial, 2002.

Oliven, Ruben George. "The Production and Consumption of Culture in Brazil." Special issue, *Latin American Perspectives* 11, no. 1 (Winter 1984): 103–15.

Ord-Hume, Arthur W. J. G., and Jerome F. Weber. "Recorded Sound." In *Grove Music Online*, edited by L. Macy. Accessed July 6, 2006, at http://www .grovemusic.com.

Ortiz, Renato. *A moderna tradição brasileira: Cultura brasileira e indústria cultural*. São Paulo: Editora Brasiliense, 1988.

Owensby, Brian P. *Intimate Ironies: Modernity and the Making of Middle-Class Lives in Brazil*. Stanford, Calif.: Stanford University Press, 1999.

Pacheco, Jacy. *Noel Rosa e a sua época*. Rio de Janeiro: G. A. Penna, 1955.

Paezzo, Sylvan. *Memórias de Madame Satã*. Rio de Janeiro: Lidador, 1972.

Palmié, Stephan. *Wizards and Scientists: Explorations in Afro-Cuban Modernity and Tradition*. Durham: Duke University Press, 2002.

Pandolfi, Dulce Chaves, ed. *Repensando o Estado Novo*. Rio de Janeiro: Editora Fundação Getúlio Vargas, 1999.

Parés, Luis Nicolau. *A formação do candomblé: História e ritual da Nação Jeje na Bahia*. Campinas, Brazil: Editora da Universidade Estadual de Campinas, 2006.

Peard, Julyan G. *Race, Place, and Medicine: The Idea of the Tropics in Nineteenth Century Brazilian Medicine*. Durham: Duke University Press, 1999.

Pederneiras, Raul. *Geringonça carioca: Verbêtes para um dicionário da gíria*. 2nd ed. Rio de Janeiro: F. Briguet and Cia, 1946.

Pennycook, Alastair. "'The Rotation Gets Thick. The Constraints Get Thin': Creativity, Recontextualization and Difference." *Applied Linguistics* 28, no. 4 (2007): 579–96.

Peppercorn, Lisa M. *Villa-Lobos: Collected Studies*. Aldershot, England: Scolar Press, 1992.

Pereira, Cristiana Schettini. "Prostitutes and the Law: The Uses of Court Cases over Pandering in Rio de Janeiro at the Beginning of the Twentieth Century." In *Honor, Status, and Law in Modern Latin America*, edited by Sueann Caulfield, Sarah C. Chambers, and Lara Putnam, 273–94. Durham: Duke University Press, 2005.

———. *Que tenhas teu corpo: Uma história social da prostituição no Rio de Janeiro das primeiras décadas republicanas*. Rio de Janeiro: Arquivo Nacional, 2006.

Pereira, João Baptista Borges. *Cor, profissão e mobilidade: O negro e o rádio de São Paulo*. 2nd ed. São Paulo: Editora da Universidade de São Paulo, 2001. First published 1967.

———. "O negro e a comercialização da música popular brasileira." *Revista do Instituto de Estudos Brasileiros* (São Paulo) no. 8 (1970): 7–15.

Pereira, Leonardo Affonso de Miranda. *Carnaval das letras: Literatura e folia no*

Rio de Janeiro do século XIX. Campinas, Brazil: Editora da Universidade Estadual de Campinas, 2004.

———. *Footballmania: Uma história social do futebol no Rio de Janeiro, 1902–1938.* Rio de Janeiro: Editora Nova Fronteira, 2000.

———. "E o Rio dançou: Identidades e tensões nos clubes recreativos." In *Carnavais e outras f(r)Estas: Ensaios de história social da cultura*, edited by Maria Clementina Pereira Cunha, 419–44. Campinas, Brazil: CECULT, 2002.

Perrone, Charles A. *Masters of Contemporary Brazilian Song: MPB, 1965–1985.* Austin: University of Texas Press, 1989.

Perrone, Charles A., and Christopher Dunn. "'Chiclete com Banana': Internationalization in Brazilian Popular Music." In *Brazilian Popular Music and Globalization*, edited by Charles Perrone and Christopher Dunn, 1–38. New York: Routledge, 2002.

Pierson, Donald. *Negroes in Brazil: A Study of Race and Contact in Bahia.* Carbondale: Southern Illinois University Press, 1967. First published 1942.

Pimenta, Eduardo. *Princípios de direitos autorais: Um século de proteção autoral no Brasil, 1898–1998, Livro I.* Rio de Janeiro: Editora Lumen Juris, 2004.

Pimentel, Luís, and Luís Fernando Vieira. *Wilson Batista: Na corda bamba do Samba.* Rio de Janeiro: Relume Dumará, 1996.

Pinho, Patricia de Santana. *Mama Africa: Reinventing Blackness in Bahia.* Durham: Duke University Press, 2010.

Pinto, Alexandre Gonçalves. *O choro: Reminiscências dos chorões antigos.* Rio de Janeiro: Fundação Nacional de Artes, 1978. First published 1936.

Pinto, Luiz de Aguiar Costa. *O negro no Rio de Janeiro: Relações de raça numa sociedade em mudança.* 2nd ed. Rio de Janeiro: Editora Universidade Federal do Rio de Janeiro, 1998.

Pinto, Regina Pahim. "O movimento negro em São Paulo: Luta e identidade." PhD dissertation. Universidade de São Paulo, 1993.

Pinto, Tancredo da Silva. *Cabala umbandista.* Rio de Janeiro: Editora Espiritualista, 1971.

———. *O eró (segrêdo) da umbanda.* Rio de Janeiro: Editora Eco, 1968.

———. *Origens da umbanda.* Rio de Janeiro: Editora Espiritualista, 1970.

Pinto, Tancredo da Silva, and Byron Tôrres de Freitas. *Guia e ritual para organização de terreiros de umbanda.* Rio de Janeiro: Editora Eco, 1968.

Piragibe, Vicente. *Diccionario de jurisprudencia penal do Brasil.* São Paulo: Saraiva and Cia, 1931.

Popinigis, Fabiane. *Proletários de casaca: Trabalhadores do comércio carioca (1850–1911).* Campinas, Brazil: Editora da Universidade Estadual de Campinas, 2007.

Porto Alegre, Manuel de Araújo. "Iconographia brazileira." *Revista do Instituto Historico e Geographico do Brasil* 19, no. 34 (Third Trimester 1856): 349–78.

Prandi, Reginaldo. "The Expansion of Black Religion in White Society: Brazilian Popular Music and Legitimacy of Candomblé." Paper delivered at the 20th International Congress of the Latin American Studies Association, Guadalajara, Mexico, 1997.

Querino, Manuel. *A Bahia de outrora*. Salvador: Livraria Progresso Editora, 1955.

Quieróz, Maria Isaura Pereira de. *Carnaval brasileiro: O vívido e o mito*. São Paulo: Editora Brasiliense, 1992.

———. "Escolas de samba do Rio de Janeiro, ou a domesticação da massa urbana." *Ciência e Cultura* 6, no. 36 (1984).

Radano, Ronald. *Lying up a Nation: Race and Black Music*. Chicago: University of Chicago Press, 2003.

Rago, Margareth. *Os prazeres da noite: Prostituição e codigos da sexualidade feminina em São Paulo, 1890–1930*. Rio de Janeiro: Paz e Terra, 1991.

Ramírez, Catherine S. *The Woman in the Zoot Suit: Gender, Nationalism, and the Cultural Politics of Memory*. Durham: Duke University Press, 2009.

Ramos, Arthur. *O negro brasileiro*. 3rd ed. São Paulo: Companhia Editora Nacional, 1951. First published 1934.

Rangel, Lúcio. "Um prefácio de 1974." In Sérgio Cabral, *As escolas de samba do Rio de Janeiro*, 11–13. 2nd ed. Rio de Janeiro: Lumiar, 1996. First published 1974.

Raphael, Allison. "From Popular Culture to Microenterprise: The History of the Brazilian *Samba* Schools." *Latin American Music Review* 11, no. 1 (June 1990): 73–83.

———. "*Samba* and Social Control: Popular Culture and Racial Democracy in Rio de Janeiro." PhD dissertation. Columbia University, 1981.

Rasponi, Lanfranco. *The Last Prima Donnas*. New York: Knopf, 1982.

Reis, João José. "Batuque: African Drumming and Dance between Repression and Concession, Bahia, 1808–1855." *Bulletin of Latin American Research* 24, no. 2 (2005): 201–14.

———. *Slave Rebellion in Brazil: The Muslim Uprising of 1835 in Bahia*. Baltimore, Md.: Johns Hopkins University Press, 1993.

Reis, João José, and Flávio dos Santos Gomes. "Repercussions of the Haitian Revolution in Brazil, 1791–1850." In *The World of the Haitian Revolution*, edited by David Patrick Geggus and Norman Fiering, 284–314. Bloomington: Indiana University Press, 2009.

Ribeiro, Carlos Antonio Costa. *Cor e criminalidade: Estudo e análise da justiça no Rio de Janeiro (1900–1930)*. Rio de Janeiro: Editora da Universidade Federal do Rio de Janeiro, 1995.

Risério, Antonio. "Zelberto Zel: Uma caricatura racista." In *O poético e o político, e outros escritos*, edited by Antonio Risério and Gilberto Gil, 191–93. Rio de Janeiro: Paz e Terra, 1988.

Robertson, J. P., and W. P. Robertson. *Letters on Paraguay: Comprising an Ac-*

count of a Four Years' Residence in That Republic, Under the Government of the *Dictator Francia*. New York: AMS Press, 1970. First published 1839.

Rocha, Agenor Miranda. *As nações Kêtu: Origens, ritos e crenças: Os candomblés antigos do Rio de Janeiro*. 2nd ed. Rio de Janeiro: Mauad, 2000.

Rodrigues, Ana Maria. *Samba negro, espoliação branca*. São Paulo: Editora Hucitec, 1984.

Rodrigues, João Carlos. *João do Rio: Uma biografia*. Rio de Janeiro: Topbooks, 1996.

Rodrigues, José Albertino. *Sindicato e desenvolvimento no Brasil*. 2nd ed. São Paulo: Edições Símbolo, 1979. First published 1968.

Rodrigues, Raimundo Nina. *As raças humanas e a responabilidade penal no Brazil*. Rio de Janeiro: Editora Guanabara, n.d. First published 1894.

———. *O animismo fetichista dos negros bahianos*. Rio de Janeiro: Civilização Brasileira, 1935.

Rugendas, João Maurício. *Viagem pitoresca através do Brasil*. 8th ed. Translated by Sérgio Millet. São Paulo: Editora Itatiaia Limitada, 1979. First published 1835.

Sá, Marcos Moraes de. *A Mansão Figner: O ecletismo e a casa burguesa no início do século XX*. Rio de Janeiro: SENAC, 2002.

Said, Edward W. *Musical Elaborations*. New York: Columbia University Press, 1991.

Sampaio, Gabriela dos Reis. "Tenebrosos mistérios: Juca Rosa e as relações entre crença e cura no Rio de Janeiro imperial." In *Artes e ofícios de curar no Brasil: Capítulos de história social*, edited by Sidney Chalhoub et al., 387–426. Campinas, Brazil: Editora da Universidade Estadual de Campinas, 2003.

Sampaio, Mario Ferraz. *História do rádio e da televisão no Brasil e no Mundo (memórias de um pioneiro)*. Rio de Janeiro: Achiamé, 1984.

Sandroni, Carlos. "Adeus à MPB." In *Decantando a república: Inventário histórico e político da canção popular moderna brasileira*, edited by Berenice Cavalcante and José Eisenberg Heloisa Starling, 1:23–36. São Paulo: Nova Fronteira, 2004.

———. "Dois sambas de 1930 e a constituição do gênero: *Na Pavuna* e *Vou te abandonar*." *Cadernos do Colóquio* 4 (2001): 8–21.

———. *Feitiço decente: Transformações do samba no Rio de Janeiro, 1917–1933*. Rio de Janeiro: Jorge Zahar Editor, 2001.

Santiago, Oswaldo. *Aquarela do direito autoral: História, legislação, comentários*. 3rd ed. Rio de Janeiro: UBC, 1985. First published 1946.

Santos, Antônio Carlos dos. *Os músicos negros: Escravos da Real Fazenda de Santa Cruz no Rio de Janeiro (1808–1832)*. São Paulo: Annablume, 2009.

Santos, Myrian Sepúlveda dos. "A prisão dos ébrios, capoeiras e vagabundos no início da era republicana." *Topoi* 5, no. 8 (June 2004): 138–69.

———. "Samba Schools: The Logic of Orgy and Blackness in Rio de Janeiro."

In *Representations of Blackness and the Performance of Identities*, edited by
Jean Muteba Rahier, 69–90. London: Bergin and Garvey, 1999.

Savazoni, Rodrigo, and Sergio Cohn. *Cultura digital.br*. Rio de Janeiro: Beco do
Azougue, 2009.

Schloss, Joseph Glenn. *Making Beats: The Art of Sample-Based Hip-Hop*. Middle-
town, Conn.: Wesleyan University Press, 2004.

Schreiner, Claus. *Música Brasileira: A History of Popular Music and the People
of Brazil*. Translated from German by Mark Weinstein. New York: Marion
Boyars, 2002.

Schwarcz, Lilia Moritz. *The Emperor's Beard: Dom Pedro II and the Tropical Monarchy of Brazil*. Translated by John Gledson. New York: Hill and Wang, 2004.

———. *The Spectacle of the Races: Scientists, Institutions, and the Race Question
in Brazil, 1870–1930*. Translated by Leland Guyer. New York: Hill and Wang,
1993.

Schwartz, Stuart B. "The Formation of a Colonial Identity in Brazil." In *Colonial Identity in the Atlantic World, 1500–1800*, edited by Nichals Canny and
Anthony Pagden, 15–50. Princeton, N.J.: Princeton University Press, 1989.

Seigel, Micol. *Uneven Encounters: Making Race and Nation in Brazil and the
United States*. Durham: Duke University Press, 2009.

Seigel, Micol, and Tiago de Melo Gomes. "Sabina's Oranges: The Colors of Cultural Politics in Rio de Janeiro, 1889–1930." *Journal of Latin American Cultural
Studies* 11, no. 1 (March 2002): 5–28.

Sevcenko, Nicolau. *Orfeu extático na metrópole: São Paulo, sociedade e cultura
nos frementes anos 20*. São Paulo: Companhia das Letras, 1992.

Severiano, Jairo. *Getúlio Vargas e a música popular*. Rio de Janeiro: Fundação
Getúlio Vargas, 1983.

———. *Uma história da música popular brasileira: Das origens à modernidade*.
São Paulo: Editora 34, 2008.

Severiano, Jairo, and Zuza Homem de Mello. *A canção no tempo: 85 anos de
músicas brasileiras*. Vol. 1: *1901–1957*. 5th ed. São Paulo: Editora 34, 1997.

Shaver, Lea, ed. *Access to Knowledge in Brazil: New Research in Intellectual Property, Innovation and Development*. London: Bloomsbury Academic, 2010.

Shaw, Lisa. *The Social History of Brazilian Samba*. Aldershot, England: Ashgate,
1999.

Sheriff, Robin E. "The Theft of *Carnaval*: National Spectacle and Racial Politics
in Rio de Janeiro." *Cultural Anthropology* 14, no. 1 (1999): 3–28.

Sherman, Brad, and Lionel Benty. *The Making of Modern Intellectual Property
Law: The British Experience, 1760–1911*. Cambridge: Cambridge University
Press, 1999.

Silva, Eduardo. *As queixas do povo*. Rio de Janeiro: Paz e Terra, 1988.

———. *Prince of the People: The Life and Times of a Brazilian Free Man of
Colour*. Translated by Moyra Ashford. London: Verso, 1993.

Silva, Erminia. *Circo-teatro: Benjamin de Oliveira e a teatralidade circense no Brasil.* São Paulo: Editora Altana, 2007.

Silva, Flávio. "Origines de la Samba Urbain à Rio de Janeiro." PhD dissertation. Paris, École Pratique des Hautes Études, 1975.

———. "Pelo telefone e a história do samba." *Cultura* 8, no. 28 (January–June 1978).

———. "Pelo telefone." Segundo Encontro de Pesquisadores de Música Popular Brasileira. Rio de Janeiro, 1976.

Silva, Ildefonso Mascarenhas da. *Direito do autor.* Rio de Janeiro: Editora Aurora, 1947.

Silva, J. M. Velho da. *Crônica dos tempos coloniais—Gabriela, romance brasileiro.* Rio de Janeiro: Imprensa Nacional, 1875.

Silva, Marília T. Barboza da, and Arthur L. de Oliveira Filho. *Filho de Ogum Bexiguento.* Rio de Janeiro: Fundação Nacional de Artes, 1979.

Silva, Marília T. Barboza da, and Lygia Santos. *Paulo da Portela: Traço de união entre duas culturas.* Rio de Janeiro: Fundação Nacional de Artes, 1980.

Siqueira, Baptista. *Origem do termo samba.* São Paulo: IBRASA, 1978.

Skidmore, Thomas E. *Black into White: Race and Nationality in Brazilian Thought.* 2nd ed. Durham: Duke University Press, 1993. First published 1974.

———. *Politics in Brazil, 1930–1964: An Experiment in Democracy.* New York: Oxford University Press, 1967.

———. *The Politics of Military Rule in Brazil, 1964–1985.* New York: Oxford University Press, 1988.

Slenes, Robert W. "The Demography and Economics of Brazilian Slavery: 1850–1888." PhD dissertation. Stanford University, 1976.

Soares, Carlos Eugênio Líbano. *A capoeira escrava e outras tradições rebeldes no Rio de Janeiro, 1808–1850.* Campinas, Brazil: Editora da Universidade Estadual de Campinas, 2001.

———. "Festa e violência: Os capoeiras e as festas populares na corte do Rio de Janeiro (1809–1890)." In *Carnavais e outras f(r)Estas: Ensaios de história social da cultura,* Maria Clementina Pereira Cunha, 281–310. Campinas, Brazil: CECULT, 2002.

———. *A negregada instituição: Os capoeiras na Corte Imperial, 1850–1890.* Rio de Janeiro: Access Editora, 1999.

Soares, Maria Thereza Mello. *São Ismael do Estácio: O sambista que foi rei.* Rio de Janeiro: Fundação Nacional de Artes, 1985.

Sodré, Muniz. *Samba: O dono do corpo (ensaios).* Rio de Janeiro: Editora Codecri, 1979.

Sodré, Nelson Werneck. *História da imprensa no Brasil.* Rio de Janeiro: Civilização Brasileira, 1966.

Soihet, Rachel. *Condição feminina e formas de violência: Mulheres pobres e ordem urbana, 1890–1920.* Rio de Janeiro: Forense Universitária, 1989.

————. "Festa da Penha: Resistência e interprenetração cultural (1890–1920)." In *Carnavais e outras f(r)Estas: Ensaios de história social da cultura*, Maria Clementina Pereira Cunha, 341–70. Campinas, Brazil: CECULT, 2002.

————. *A subversão pelo riso: Estudos sobre o carnaval carioca da* Belle Époque *ao tempo de Vargas*. Rio de Janeiro: Fundação Getúlio Vargas, 1998.

Sommer, Doris. *Foundational Fictions: The National Romances of Latin America*. Berkeley: University of California Press, 1993.

Souza, Gérson Ignez de, and Tancredo da Silva Pinto. *Negro e branco na cultura religiosa afro-brasileira, os Egbás: Umbanda, cabala e magia*. Rio de Janeiro: Gráfica Editora Aurora, 1976.

Souza, Laura de Mello e. *Desclassificados do ouro: A pobreza mineira no século XVIII*. Rio de Janeiro: Graal, 1982.

Spitzer, Leo. *Lives in Between: Assimilation and Marginality in Austria, Brazil, West Africa, 1780–1945*. Cambridge: Cambridge University Press, 1989.

Stabb, Martin S. *In Quest of Identity: Patterns in the Spanish American Essay of Ideas*. Chapel Hill: University of North Carolina Press, 1967.

Stepan, Nancy Leys. *"The Hour of Eugenics": Race, Gender, and Nation in Latin America*. Ithaca, N.Y.: Cornell University Press, 1991.

Stephens, Thomas M. *Dictionary of Latin American Racial and Ethnic Terminology*. 2nd ed. Gainesville: University of Florida Press, 1999.

Stoler, Ann Laura. *Race and the Education of Desire: Foucault's* History of Sexuality *and the Colonial Order of Things*. Durham: Duke University Press, 1995.

Stroud, Sean. *The Defence of Tradition in Brazilian Popular Music: Politics, Culture, and the Creation of* Música Popular Brasileira. Aldershot, England: Ashgate, 2008.

Sweet, James H. "The Evolution of Ritual in the African Diaspora: Central African *Kilundu* in Brazil, St. Domingue, and the United States, Seventeenth-Nineteenth Centuries." In *Diasporic Africa: A Reader*, edited by Michael A. Gomez, 64–80. New York: New York University Press, 2006.

————. *Recreating Africa: Culture, Kinship, and Religion in the African-Portuguese World, 1441–1770*. Chapel Hill: University of North Carolina Press, 2003.

Talmon-Chvaicer, Maya. *The Hidden History of Capoeira: A Collision of Cultures in the Brazilian Battle Dance*. Austin: University of Texas Press, 2007.

Tannenbaum, Frank. *Slave and Citizen*. Boston: Beacon Press, 1992. First published 1946.

Tinhorão, José Ramos. "Circo brasileiro, local do universo." In *Cultural popular: Temas e questões*, 55–84. São Paulo: Editora 34, 2001.

————. *Fado: Dança do Brasil, cantar de Lisboa: O fim de um mito*. Lisbon: Caminho da Música, 1994.

————. *História social da música popular brasileira*. São Paulo: Editora 34, 1998.

————. *Música popular de índios, negros e mestiços*. Petrópolis: Editora Vozes, 1972.

————. *Música popular: Os sons que vêm da rua*. Rio de Janeiro: Edições Tinhorão, 1976.

————. *Música popular: Um tema em debate*. 3rd ed. São Paulo: Editora 34, 1997.

————. *Os negros em Portugal: Uma presença silenciosa*. Lisbon: Caminho da Música, 1988.

————. *Pequena história da música popular: Da modinha ao tropicalismo*. 5th ed. São Paulo: Art Editora, 1986.

Toynbee, Jason. "Music, Culture, and Creativity." In *The Cultural Study of Music: A Critical Introduction*, edited by Trevor Herbert Martin Clayton and Richard Middleton, 102–12. New York: Routledge, 2003.

Tramonte, Cristiana. *O samba conquista passagem: As estratégias e a ação educativa das escolas de samba*. Petrópolis: Editora Vozes, 2001.

Travassos, Elizabeth. *Modernismo e música brasileira*. Rio de Janeiro: Jorge Zahar, 2000.

Vagalume (Francisco Guimarães). *Na roda do samba*. Rio de Janeiro: Fundação Nacional de Artes, 1978. First published 1933.

Valença, Rachel T. *Carnaval: Para tudo se acabar na quarta-feira*. Rio de Janeiro: Relume Dumará, 1996.

Van Young, Eric. "The New Cultural History Comes to Old Mexico." *Hispanic American Historical Review* 79, no. 2 (May 1999): 211–47.

Vargas, Getúlio. *A nova política do Brasil III: A realidade nacional em 1933 retrospecto das realizações do govêrno, em 1934*. Rio de Janeiro: Livraria José Olympio, 1938.

Vasconcellos, Gilberto, and Matinas Suzuki Jr. "A malandragem e a formação da música popular brasileira." In *História geral da civilização brasileira (Tomo III: O Brasil republicano: Ecônomia e cultura, 1930–1964, Vol. IV)*, edited by Sérgio Buarque de Holanda, 501–23. São Paulo: Difel, 1984.

Vasconcellos, J. Leite de. *Antroponimia portuguesa: Tratado comparativo da origem, significação, classificação, e vida do conjunto dos nomes proprios, sobrenomes, e apelidos, usados por nós desde a Idade-Média até hoje*. Lisbon: Imprensa Nacional, 1928.

Vasconcelos, Ary. *Panorama da música popular brasileira*. São Paulo: Martins, 1964.

————. *Panorama da música popular brasileira na belle époque*. Rio de Janeiro: Livraria Sant-Anna, 1977.

Velloso, Mônica Pimenta. *A cultura das ruas no Rio de Janeiro (1900–1930): Mediações, linguagens e espaço*. Rio de Janeiro: Casa Rui Barbosa, 2004.

————."As tias baianas tomam conta do pedaço: Espaço e identidade cultural no Rio de Janeiro." *Estudos Históricos* 6 (1990).

————. *Mário Lago: Boemia e política*. Rio de Janeiro: Fundação Getúlio Vargas, 1998.

————. *Modernismo no Rio de Janeiro: Turunas e quixotes*. Rio de Janeiro: Fundação Getúlio Vargas, 1996.

Veloso, Caetano. "Carmen Mirandadada." In *Brazilian Popular Music and Globalization*, edited by Charles A. Perrone and Christopher Dunn, 39–45. New York: Routledge, 2002.

Vianna, Hermano. *The Mystery of Samba: Popular Music and National Identity in Brazil*. Edited and translated by John Charles Chasteen. Chapel Hill: University of North Carolina Press, 1999.

————. *O mistério do samba*. Rio de Janeiro: Jorge Zahar, 1995.

Vidal, Armando. *O teatro e a lei: Estudos*. Rio de Janeiro: Sociedade Brasileira de Autores Teatrais, 1932.

Vieira, Fr. Domingos. *Grande diccionario portugues, ou thesouro da lingua portugueza*. 5 vols. Porto, Portugal: Imprensa Litterario-Commercial, 1873.

Vieira, Jonas. *César de Alencar: A voz que abalou o rádio*. Rio de Janeiro: Valda, 1993.

Vieira, Luís Fernando, and Luís Pimentel. *Um escurinho direitinho: A vida e obra de Geraldo Pereira*. Rio de Janeiro: Relume Dumará, 1995.

Wade, Peter. *Music, Race, and Nation: Música Tropical in Colombia*. Chicago: University of Chicago Press, 2000.

Weinstein, Barbara. *For Social Peace in Brazil: Industrialists and the Remaking of the Working Class in São Paulo, 1920–1964*. Chapel Hill: University of North Carolina Press, 1996.

————. "Not the Republic of Their Dreams: Historical Obstacles to Political and Social Democracy in Brazil." *Latin American Research Review* 29, no. 2 (1994): 262–73.

————. "Postcolonial Brazil." In *The Oxford Handbook of Latin American History*, edited by José C. Moya, 212–56. Oxford: Oxford University Press, 2011.

————. "Racializing Regional Difference: São Paulo Versus Brazil." In *Race and Nation in Modern Latin America*, edited by Anne S. Macpherson Nancy Appelbaum, and Karin Alejandra Rosemblatt, 237–62. Chapel Hill: University of North Carolina Press, 2003.

Wetherell, James. *Brasil: Stray Notes from Bahia; Being Extracts from Letters, &c., During a Residence of Fifteen Years*. Liverpool: Webb and Hunt, 1860.

Williams, Daryle. *Culture Wars in Brazil: The First Vargas Regime, 1930–1945*. Durham: Duke University Press, 2001.

Windler, Erica M. "City of Children: Boys, Girls, Family and State in Imperial Rio de Janeiro, Brazil." PhD dissertation. University of Miami, 2003.

Wisnik, José Miguel. "Getúlio da Paixão Cearense: Villa-Lobos e o Estado Novo." In *Música: O nacional e o popular na cultura brasileira*, edited by Enio Squeff and José Wisnik, 129–91. São Paulo: Brasiliense, 2004.

Wolfe, Joel. *Working Women, Working Men: São Paulo and the Rise of Brazil's Industrial Working Class, 1900–1955*. Durham: Duke University Press, 1993.

Woodmansee, Martha. *The Author, Art, and the Market: Rereading the History of Aesthetics*. New York: Columbia University Press, 1994.

Woodmansee, Martha, and Peter Jaszi, eds. *The Construction of Authorship: Textual Appropriation in Law and Literature*. Durham: Duke University Press, 1994.

Zan, José Roberto. "Popular Music and Policing in Brazil." In *Policing Pop*, edited by Martin Cloonan and Reebee Garofalo, 205–20. Philadelphia: Temple University Press, 2003.

INDEX

Note: *Page numbers in italics indicate figures, tables, and a map.*

Alfredo (Alfredo José de Alcântara), 138

Almeida, Aracy Teles de, 118, 139

Almeida, Hilária Batista de (Tia Ciata): constraints on, 62; death of, 120; musical gatherings and influence of, 59–61, 125, 246; "Pelo telefone" lyrics and, 102

Almeida, Irineu de, 103, 117

Almeida, João Mauro de (Mauro): authorship renounced by, 97–98, 101, 102; Donga's connection to, 118; earnings of, 242; lyrics credited to, 3, 96–97, 100, 241–42; as SBAT member, 173

Almeida, Renato, 159

Almeida, Rui, 201–2

Almirante (Henrique Foréis Domingues): choro revival of, 231–32; excluded from Vagalume's roda, 130; on "Pelo telefone," 241–42; samba conference role of, 233; on song appropriations, 122–23

alufá, use of term, 83, 270n61

Alvaiade (Oswaldo dos Santos), 119

Alves, Ataulfo: background of, 119; as CCB member, 224; connections and success of, 217, 218; later writing of, 293n61; music composed by, 139; as SBAT-DC member, 201; style of, 215–16

Alves, Francisco (Chico Alves, Chico Viola, the Rei da Voz [the King of Voice]): circle of, 165; Donga and, 132; earnings of, 129, 171, 218; favela song performed by, 133, 139; Ismael Silva and, 129; as SBAT member, 179; tactics of, 128, 137

Alves, Marieta, 259n45

Alves, Nelson, 104

Amaral, Norberto, Jr. (Morcego), 97, 100

"ambivalent slide" concept, 10, 249

Ameno Resedá (rancho), 126–27

American Society of Composers, Authors, and Publishers, 175

Amor (Getúlio Marinho da Silva), 118

Andrade, Avelino de, 186–87

Andrade, Basilio de Assis, 77

Andrade, Mário de: background and position of, 152–153153; on barber-musicians, 28, 259n45; on lundu, 22; on musical

colonialism and classification, 160; on national and music history, 149–53; on place of nonwhites, 164; symbols and locations blurred by, 281n25

Andrews, George Reid, 38

anti-vagrancy measures: approach to studying, 13; bicheiros arrested under, 51; call for harsher, 148–49; cases studied, 36–37, 39, 261n15, 264n49; defenses against, 40, 43–45, 46, 47, 165–66; fortuneteller arrested under, 52–53; goals of, 37–38; implications of, 246; incidents of musicians arrested under, 38–40, 43, 44–48, 62; judicial treatment of, 40–41, 44–45, 165, 191–92; literacy at issue in, 166–67; public image strategies in context of, 91–92; Reagir! campaign and, 165; regional and local varieties of, 262n18; registration of artistas and auxiliares as proof against, 190. See also policing and social control; stereotypes and caricatures; vagrants

Aoki, Keith, 92–93, 271n84

"Aquarela do Brasil" (Brazilian watercolor), 201, 204

Aquarela do direito autoral (Author's rights watercolor, Santiago), 213

Aranha, José Pereira da Graça, 163

Araújo, Mozart de, 137

Araújo, Paulo Cesar de, 229, 230

Areda, Luis, 171

Argentina: Batutas' tours in, 105, 107, 109; Black Brazilian Pandeirista in, 138; radio in, 171

Arlequim (Paulo Cabrita): on Almeida, 96, 97; Donga's connection to, 118; on Donga's manhood, 143–44; on "Pelo telefone," 100, 101

Armstrong, Louis, 207

Arquivo Nacional (National Archive): Bicho Novo case files in, 61–62; defloramento case files in, 62–64; physical reports on prisoners, 165, 167; vagrancy case files in, 37–41, 165, 262n15, 262n27

arreglador (music arranger), 97–98

Brasil Operário (periodical), 42

Braz, Wenceslau, 60

Brazil: amalgamation of race in, 232,
296n22; coup in (1930), 169–70; economic inflation in (1900–1920s), 5;
greatest love song of, 141; *Hino Nacional*
(national anthem) of, 169, 174; independence anniversary in, 108; industrialization in, 267n1; political changes summarized (1888–1960s), 12; Portuguese
royal court's exile in, 23–24; as racial
democracy (*see* racial democracy); regional differences of, 20, 188; separated
from other Latin American countries,
147, 148; "social peace" and military
coup in (1964), 227; struggles over right
to define, 114–15; terminology explained,
ix–x. *See also* definitional projects; national identity; sertão; *and specific cities
and regions*

Brazilian Association of Composers and
Authors. *See* Associação Brasileira de
Compositores e Autores

Brazilian Institute of Geography and
Statistics (Instituto Brasileiro de Geografia e Estatística, IBGE), 176, 190, *190*,
191

Brazilian Ministry of Education, 212

Brazilian National Security Council, 227,
295n2

Brazilianness (*brasilidade*), 11, 114–15. *See
also* Afro-Brazilianness

Brazilian Press Association, 105

Brazilian Society of Musical Authors,
Composers, and Label Owners/Writers.
See Sociedade Brasileira de Autores,
Compositores e Editores/Escritores de
Música

Brazilian Spiritist Federation, 51

Brazilian Symphonic Orchestra, 137

Brooks, Daphne, 64

Brown, James, 230

"Brown" (*Marrom*; Luís Correia de Barros), 126, 127

Buarque, Chico, 240, 297n47

Bunge, Carlos Octavio, 283n75

Butler, Kim, 256n28

caboclos, Batutas as, 110

Cabral, Sérgio: on arrangements between
musicians, 278n75; benefit concert for
João da Baiana, 240; Donga's album
held by, 105; Madame Satã interviewed
by, 235–36; on popular music's history,
234; samba conference role of, 233; on
UES, 290nn9–10

Cabrita, Paulo. *See* Arlequim

Cadete (Manoel Evêncio da Costa
Moreira), 77–79

Caetano, Antônio da Silva, 134, 135

Café Nice (Rio), 136, 205

caipira (hick), 109–11, 160

caititu, use of term, 205

caixa de fósforos (box of matches) symbol,
221, 294n75

calundu, use of term, 20–21, 22, 257n14.
See also *lundu*

Camargo, Joracy, 224

Campo de Santana, 18, 19–20

Campos, Augusto, 229–30

Campos, Noel, 191–92

"Canção de Dixie" (Dixieland song), 152

cançonetas, 78

Candeia Filho, Antônio, 138

candomblé practices, 51–52, 156, 158,
270n61, 281n39. *See also* macumba

Caninha (José Luiz de Morais), 138

cantoras (female singers), 125

Capela Real (Royal Chapel), 23, 25–26, 29

capoeira (combination of dance and martial arts), 2, 51, 78, 251

Cardoso, Lino de Almeida, 258n28

"Carinhoso," 141, 232

Carioca (periodical), 125

Carlos, Décio Antônio (Mano Décio da
Viola), 118, 119, 120, 122, 128

Carlos Cachaça (Carlos Moreira de
Castro), 119

Carmichael, Stokely, 230

Carneiro, Edison, 233, 234

Carnival: admissions and rights to televise, 240; "authentic" instruments for, 195–96, 290n5; Cidadão Samba of (1936), 47; classic song of, 219–21; Disney film about, 116; dual celebrations of (1912), 53–55; funds for, 131, 198; journalists' role in promoting songs and musicians of, 125–27; King of (Cidadão Momo), 135; marketing frenzy and earnings in, 205, 223, 292n35; masks for, 55; objects for, 53, 54–56, 266n90; "officialization" of, 195–98; "Pelo telefone" as success during, 96, 101; police involvement in, 13, 53–59, 197–98; reputation of, 279n100; samba as music of, 12; song competition of, 223. *See also* clothing

Carnival clubs, working-class, 56–59

Carnival *cordões*, 43, 196, 263n46

Carnival *grandes sociedades* (elite clubs): competition and money-raising by, 56; costumes of, 54–55; promotional role of, 125, 126; ranchos vs., 263n45; requested to postpone activities, 43

Carnival *ranchos* (dancing and social clubs): of Carlos's family, 120; emergence of, 263n45; members of, 43, 103, 104; newsletter of, 126–27; parade competition of, 196

"Carta do samba" (Samba charter), 233–34

Cartola (Angenor, or Agenor de Oliveira), 119, 139

cartomante (fortuneteller), 52–53

Carvalho, Bruno, 254n13, 281n25

Casa de Detenção (Rio), 45, 50, 167. *See also* anti-vagrancy measures

Casa Edison: award for misogynist song, 90; composers' contracts and earnings of, 73, *74*, *75*, 76–77, 81, 268n28; decline of, 172; early samba recordings of, 96; favela song recorded by, 139; Francisco Alves associated with, 130; Neves associated with, 80–85; patent rights to two-sided records, 70–72; payments to musicians and composers, 171, 178–79;

"Pelo telefone" recorded by, 98–100, *99*; products of, 69; sources on, 267n13; top drawing artists and genres of, 77–79, *78*. *See also* Figner, Fred

Casa Editora Carlos Wehrs, 103–4

Casa grande e senzala (Freyre), 149

casas de espetáculos (show houses), 183–85. *See also* movie houses; theater

Castro, Carlos Moreira de (Carlos Cachaça), 119

Catholic Church, composers remunerated by, 175–76

Caulfield, Sueann, 63, 264n49

CCB (Clube do Compositor Brasileiro), 223–24

Cearense, Catulo da Paixão, 78, 81, 113–14, 151

censorship: author's rights linked to, 183–85, 192–93; under military rule, 227–28; principle of prior, 184, 203, 246; SBAT and, 179–81; SBAT's role in, 179–81; UBC-SBAT pamphlet and, 203–5; UBC's role in, 210–14. *See also* Departamento de Imprensa e Propaganda

Central Office for Collection and Distribution (Escritório Central de Arrecadação e Distribuição, ECAD), 244, 290–91n20

Centro Musical do Rio de Janeiro, 42

Chalhoub, Sidney, 44

Chávez, Carlos, 112

Chazkel, Amy, 39–40, 50

Chico Viola. *See* Alves, Francisco

China (Otávio Littleton da Rocha Viana): in Batutas, 104; as mediator, 137, 158; on samba, Africa, and Brazil, 153–55; Sinhô's attack on, 122

choro: in hierarchy of genres, 60–61; Pixinguinha's use of, 117, 141–42, 231; revival of, 231–33

O Choro (Pinto), 142

Cidade Nova (New City, neighborhood), 4, 119, 254n13. *See also* Santana and Santo Antônio

Cinema Palais, 104, 105

circuses: costumes in, 68, 81, 251, 263n46; Oliveira's role in, 67–69; white stars discovered in, 137–38

Civil Code (1916), 182, 262n16

"civilizing missions": definition of author and ownership in, 151–52; mixed-race composer in context of, 24–26; SBAT's role in, 174–75

class: complexities of, 6; defloramento cases and, 62–64; of Figner's composers, 76–77; hierarchy and display of, 17–18. *See also* intellectuals and elites; poor people; working class

Clementina de Jesus, 125

clothing: a caráter, 81, 269n51; of clowns and circus performers, 68, 81, 251, 263n46; informal trademarks of, 138; mediation function of, 138, 139–40; murderer disguised by finery, 86, 87, *87*; parade requirements of, 196; professionalism in, 140–41, *142*; of slaves at Campo de Santana gathering, 19–20; of theater performer, 190–91; of Zoot Suiters (U.S.), 298n7. See also *malandragem*

Club Carnavalesco Caprichosos de Jacarepaguá, 57

Clube Carnavalesco dos Vagalumes, 126

Clube do Compositor Brasileiro (CCB), 223–24

code of conduct, 181

Colombia, *costeño* music of, 10

Columbia Records (label): as ABCA member, 200; Figner's dealings and, 71, 72; *Native Brazilian Music* album of, 136–37; recording patents of, 69

Commercial Code, 181

commercialization and commodification: authenticity juxtaposed to, 239, 240, 247–48; of Carnival objects, 53, 54–56; contradictory values of, 248; cynical approach to, 256n28; meaning of process of, 8–9; mixed and overlapping relationships in, 4–8; samba conference discussion of, 233–34; whitening projects

in, 116–17. *See also* advertisements and marketing; music market; professionalization

communities, black and mixed-race: development of, 4–5; Frank's "middling groups" in, 260n61; "missing middle" of, 5–8, 248; property claims controversy in, 3

Companhia de Menores do Arsenal de Guerra, 78–79

Companhia Mulata Brasileira, 191

Companhia Negra de Revistas (Black Theater Company), 124–25, 142–43, 189–90

Composers' Department (Departamento dos Compositores, SBAT-DC), 198. *See also* União Brasileira de Compositores

compositores (composers): accused of criminality, 214; contracts and earnings from Casa Edison recordings, 73, *74*, *75*, 76–77, 268n28; copyright protection of, 72–73; difficulties of, 194; earnings of recording artists vs., 129; hierarchy and differences among, 217–22; jobs of, to supplement music income, 46, 214–17; music purchased from, 136–37; newspaper contests for, 134–35, 278n67; pamphlet on problems of, 164–65; patronage for (mid-nineteenth century), 24–25; as productive artists, 218–19, 221; "real" vs. "quasi," 246; SBAT department for, 198; visibility of vocalists vs., 79. *See also* Associação Brasileira de Compositores e Autores; authorship; author's rights receipts; Direitos Autorais; União Brasileira de Compositores

comprositores, use of term, 136

Conceição, Arlinda Maria da, 61–62, 64, 246

Conceição, Faustino Pedro da (Tio Faustino): as ethnicity entrepreneur, 281n34; in Guarda Velha, 281n36; instrument designs claimed by, 138, 155–57, 247; racial and cultural challenges for, 165; religious and musical activities of, 120

Conservatório de Música (later Instituto Nacional de Música; then Escola Nacional de Música): establishment of, 23; Gallet's position at, 158–59; Medeiros as student at, 79; Oliveira as student at, 118; Pixinguinha as student at, 117

Conservatório Dramático e Musical (São Paulo), 149

Consolidation of the Brazil Labor Laws (1943, revised 1953), 195

Constança, Perciliana Maria (Tia Perciliana), 59, 62

corporatist state structure: anger deflected by, 225; authors and, 181–85; centralized interests in, 194; entertainment class oversight by, 181; Estado Novo (New State) and, 173–74, 197, 199–200; as everywhere and nowhere, 246–47; performance regulations of, 203–5; samba school funding under, 195–96; slogan under military rule, 227; UBC as part of, 225–26; UBC connections in, 205–6, 207; vocational training and, 294–95n89. *See also* censorship; Departamento de Imprensa e Propaganda; police; *utilidades públicas*; Vargas, Getúlio

Correio da Manhã (newspaper), 146, 185

Costa, Deo, 124, 125, 246

Costa, Flávio, 196

Costa, Geraldo, 215

Costa, José Luiz da (Príncipe Pretinho; Little Black Prince), 199

Costallat, Benjamin, 107, 111–12

Coutinho, Lourival, *250*, 250–52

Creative Commons controversy, 1–2, 244–45

"creator," use of term, 243

criminal cases: gambling and, 50–51, 53, 265n67; men exonerated of violence against women, 90; murder-suicide (*see* Moreno); musicians identified in, 43, 45–48; studies of social problems and, 148–49; underworld and, 49–50. *See also* anti-vagrancy measures; police

criollo, use of term, 270n65

crioulo, use of term, 84–85, 86

cronistas (writers and journalists who chronicled daily life): ABCA promoted by, 200; on Batutas as national, authentic symbol, 107–12; definitional projects of, 148–49; misreadings of musicians by, 116–17; musicians promoted by, 67, 125–27, 136; music promoted by, 96–97; Paulo da Portela's relationship with, 134–36; underworld invented by, 50. *See also* newspapers and media

O Cruzeiro (periodical), 232

cuíca (instrument), 156, 169

culturalism concept, 8, 248

culture: avant-garde linked to mass culture, 273–74n51; good vs. bad, defined, 159–61; hierarchy and difference mapped in, 163–64; high vs. low, marked by race, 189–90; homogenization of, 195; policing and censorship of, 183–85; samba as metonym for, 1; Tio Faustino as arbiter of, 156–57; valorization of Afro-Brazilian, 49–50, 149; warnings about impact of talkies and gramophones on, 102, 128, 172; white mediators in, 116–17. *See also* commercialization and commodification; definitional projects

Cunha, Euclides da, 107

Cunha, Maria Clementina Pereira, 7, 121, 255n19

Cunha, Olívia Maria Gomes da, 40, 262n25

curandeirismo (folk healing), 52

currency: changes in (1942), 277n48; exchange rate between Brazil and U.S., 285n14, 292n37, 292n46; explained, x, 253nn5–6

dancers and dance: capoeira, 2, 51, 78, 251; at Carnival working-class clubs, 58–59; maxixe style music, 91, 95, 96, 271nn81–82; reputation of dance halls, 279n100; shift to instrumentalists separated from, 66; of slaves at Campo de Santana gathering, 20

Donga (*continued*)

name and logo, 123–24; on author's rights, 214; background and privilege of, 5, 103, 116, 117, 118; clothing and style of, 141, 143; entrepreneurialism of, 242–43, 248; given names of, 253n1; in Guarda Velha, 281n36; marginalization of, 246; as mediator, 136, 137, 248; on parents and music, 125, 246; pension of, 241; on popular music, 240; racial and cultural challenges for, 165; reinventions of, 231, 233, 234, 241–43; on rhythmic forms, 96; as SBAT member, 179, 185; Sinhô and, 122–23; status and success of, 103–4, 192–93; on unauthorized incarnation of Batutas, 123; Vagalume on, 3, 128, 131, 132, 243, 248; Vargas welcomed by, 169–70, 171, 176–77. *See also* Oito Batutas; "Pelo telefone"

"Dor de cabeça" (Headache), 121–22

Dornellas, Sophonias, 77

Downey, Wallace, 200, 202, 207

Dragão (Dragon). *See* Donga

drums and drum circles: intelligent vs. natural differences in, 150–51; introduction of African, 138; repression of, 18–19. *See also* lundu; pandeiros

DuBois, W. E. B., 155

Dumont, Alberto Santos, 80–81, 187

Dunn, Christopher, 230

Dutra, Antônio José, 28

Dutra, Eurico Gaspar, 211, 293n52

ECAD (Escritório Central de Arrecadação e Distribuição, Central Office for Collection and Distribution), 244, 290–91n20

Edison, Thomas, 69, 71

Editora Quaresma, 80–81, 269n45

editoras de música, authors' rights acquired from, 72. *See also* traditional music

Efegê, Jota (João Ferreira Gomes), 126, 130, 235, 271n12

elites. *See* Carnival *grandes sociedades*; intellectuals and elites

Elói, Mano (Elói Antero Dias), 47, 118

"É negocio casar!" (Marriage is a great deal!), 216

Enemies of Work (Inimigos do Trabalho, group), 56–58

Ensaio sobre a música brasileira (Essay on Brazilian music, M. Andrade), 152

entertainment class: approach to studying, 14; censorship and policing of, 183–85; divisions in, 177–81; hierarchies and differences of, 173, 217–22; high vs. low, marked by race, 189–90; intellectual rights concerns of, 173–77; of São Paulo vs. Rio, 187–89; SBAT's implications for, 192–93; state organization's definitions of, 228–29

"Entregue o samba aos seus donos" (Give samba back to its owners), 121

Escola Nacional de Música. *See* Conservatório de Música

escolas de samba (samba schools): complaints against UES, 197–98; educational context of early, 284n85; founding and requirements of, 134, 166; funding for, 131, 195–96; members attacked at Carnival by police, 284n89; musician members of, 43; neighborhoods of, 119; newspaper of, 127; president of, imprisoned, 61–62; UES founded to protect, 196–98

Escritório Central de Arrecadação e Distribuição (Central Office for Collection and Distribution, ECAD), 244, 290–91n20

Estácio Sound (or Estácio Samba): connections of, 134; emergence of, 95–96, 165, 231; excluded from Vagalume's roda, 130; musicians from, 138; police abuse of members, 165–68

Estado Novo (New State [Vargas]), 173–74, 197, 199–200

Estudos de folklore (Folklore studies, journal), 163–64

ethnomusicology, emergence of, 149

Europe: Brazilian music's origins linked to, 147, *147*; Brazil watched by, 187–88; continued obsession with culture of, 174–75; intellectual property rights law in, 72; recording stages handled in, 70, 71

Everywhere-Nowhere state, 246–47. *See also* corporatist state structure; policing and social control

Ewbank, Thomas, 18, 19

"Fala meu louro" (Speak, my parrot), 121

"Falsa baiana" (False baiana), 216

fandango, 31–32

Farias, Juliana Barreto, 7

farsa-fantástica, Oliveira's play as, 68–69

favelas and morros (hills): context of, 4; improvements for, 131; recorded songs' origins in, 130; samba composition contests in, 134–35, 278n67; Vagalume's description of, 127, 132–34. *See also* Mangueira; *and specific neighborhoods*

"A favela vai abaixo" (The favela's coming down), 133, 139

Federação dos Homens de Cor (Federation of Men of Color), 256n23

federal government. *See* corporatist state structure

feitiçaria (unorthodox religious or magic practices), 19, 51–52, 153, 190–91

Felippe, João, 190–91, 193

feminism, 186–87. *See also* gender; women

Fernandes, Florestan, 238–39, 297n42, 297n46

Fernandes, Nelson da Nobrega, 290nn9–10

Fernandes, Sílvio (Brancura), 47, 62–63, 167, 247

Fernandez, Oscar Lorenzo, 163

Ferreira, Hilário Jovino: arrested for confrontation, 47; authorship dispute with Sinhô, 121; media connections of, 125; "Pelo telefone" lyrics and, 102; religious role of, 120; Vagalume's book dedicated to, 131

Ferreira, João Cândido. *See* De Chocolat

Festa da Penha, 53, 56, 98, 99, *99*

festivals: Dia de São João (Saint John's Day), 47–48; Festa da Penha, 53, 56, 98, 99, *99*; funds spent for, 55. *See also* Carnival

Figner, Fred (Frederico): background of, 69; business acumen and wealth of, 69–70, 117, 171, 268n31; circle of, 113; composers' contracts and earnings under, 73, *74*, *75*, 76–77, 81, 268n28; intellectual property rights and, 70–73; marketing strategy of, 77–79; Neves's meeting of, 80; as "quasi-author," 92–93, 271n84; sources on, 267n11, 267n13; trademarks held by, 124. *See also* Casa Edison

fire brigade, band connected to, 79

Firefly. *See* Vagalume

First National Samba Conference (I Congresso Nacional do Samba), 233–34, 235

fiscalizadores (auditors), 204

Fischer, Brodwyn, 133

Flor Tapuia (operetta), 108

Fluminense (club), 24

flutes, 117, 118, 157–58, 275n7

folha obscura, police records as, 40, 48

Fonotipia (label of Società Italiana di Fonotipia), 70, 71

Fonseca, Alvarenga, 131, 176–78, 187–89

Fonseca, Hermes de, 54

Fontes, Lourival, 131

Foucault, Michel, 10, 11, 41, 115, 157

Franceschi, Humberto, 267n11, 267n13

Frank, Zephyr, 28, 260n61

"Frankstein" (Frankenstein), 140

free people of color, 4–5, *5*. *See also* Afro-Brazilians

Free Womb Law (1871), 4, 38

Freyre, Gilberto, 149, 231, 236, 256–57n36

Fryer, Peter, 258n17

Fundação Nacional de Artes (National Arts Foundation), 228

Gabriel, Antônio, 31

Galhardo, Carlos (Catello Carlos Guagliardi), 139

Gallet, Luciano: background of, 158–59; Indigenous peoples and blacks dis-

historical context (mid-nineteenth century): barber-musicians in, 26–29;
"civilizing missions" and patronage in,
23–26; diversity of sights and sounds
in, 17–20; lundu roots in, 20–23; summarized, 29–30. *See also* anti-vagrancy
measures; socioeconomic context

Hitler, Adolf, 173–74. *See also* Germany

Hobsbawm, Eric, 8

Holanda, Nestor de (Nestor de Holanda
Cavalcanti Neto), 205, 221–22

*How and Why We Pay Author's Rights in
Brazil* (UBC-SBAT pamphlet), 203–5

Hungary, intellectual property rights in, 175

IBGE (Instituto Brasileiro de Geografia e
Estatística), 176, 190, *190, 191*

I Congresso Nacional do Samba (First National Samba Conference), 233–34, 235

ideologia da vadiagem, 38, 41, 90, 91, 143.
See also anti-vagrancy measures

ideology, "ambivalent slide" of, 10, 249

idleness (*ociosidade*), defined, 37. *See also*
stereotypes and caricatures

Imperial Academy of Music, 24

Indigenous peoples: dismissed as influence, 164, 283n73; essentialized approach to, 152; rhythm of, 150, 151. *See
also* Aymara people

Inferno (Dante), 175

Inimigos do Trabalho (Enemies of Work,
group), 56–58

Instituto Brasileiro de Geografia e Estatística (Brazilian Institute of Geography
and Statistics, IBGE), 176, 190, *190, 191*

Instituto Histórico e Geográfico Brasileiro (Institute of Brazilian History and
Geography), 23–26

Instituto Nacional de Música. *See* Conservatório de Música

instruments: of barber-musicians, 27; resistance to prohibition at Penha, 56;
Tio Faustino's claim to designs of, 138,
155–57, 247; wind, prohibited from
parade, 195–96, 290n5; *specific*: afoxê

(rattle), 138, 155–57; agogô (instrument
with bells), 138, 155–57, 247; cuíca, 156,
169; flutes, 117, 118, 157–58, 275n7; omelê
(friction drum), 138, 155–57, 169; pianos,
159; portable organs, 83; seven-string
guitar, 272n30. *See also* drums and drum
circles; *pandeiros*

intellectual property law: author's rights
defined in, 72–73, 181–82; ECAD established (1973), 244; Getúlio Vargas law on
(1928), 170, 179–81; international cooperation in, 175, 181–82, 183; newslet-
ters on developments in, 210–11; vague
language in (1955), 202–3. *See also* Bern
Convention; Law 496

intellectual property rights: controversies over, 1–3; European models of,
175–76; international context of, 72–73;
international societies for, 175, 181–82,
183, 207–9; as national concern, 3,
174, 175–77; patent rights to two-sided
record, 70–71; struggles over, 14, 114–15;
whites favored in system of, 129. *See also*
authorship; Direitos Autorais; ownership; socioeconomic context

intellectuals and elites: Afro-Brazilian
symbols embraced or criticized by,
49–50; "ambivalent slide" and, 10, 249;
arts patronage of, 24–25; attitudes
toward pan-Africanism, 154–55; category of, 256n27; Gallet's appeal to, 159;
musical gatherings of, 59–61; musicians' engagement with, 7–8; professors
forcibly retired, 227, 295n2

Internet, Creative Commons controversy,
1–2, 244–45

interracial groups as national symbol,
107–12. *See also* Oito Batutas; racial
democracy

interracial relationships: apprehensions
about, 90–91; murder-suicide as cautionary tale about, 86–90, *87, 88;*
Neves's pursuit of, 82, 84; Oliveira's play
about, 68–69; song about, 219–20; whitening via, 85–86

Getúlio Vargas law on authors (1928), 170, 179–81; under military rule, 227; music organization established (Law 3.857), 229–30; radio as "national interest," 171–72; on work requirements, 38. *See also* anti-vagrancy measures; Bern Convention; Decrees; intellectual property law; Penal Code; Penal Code; *and leis and decretos listed in bibliography*

League of Nations, 163–64

Le Bon, Gustave, 109

Lei Áurea (Golden Law, 1888), 4

Lei (Law) Getúlio Vargas (1928), 170, 179–81

"Lenço no pescoço" (Hankerchief around the neck), 139–40

Lima, José Alves de, 104

Lindley, Thomas, 28

Linhares, José, 211, 293n52

Lins, Paulo, 255n21

Lira, José Pereira, 211

Lobo, Fernando, 218–21, 294n72

local government: samba school funding from, 195–96; UBC connections in, 205–6

Lopes, Luiz Simões, 173, 225

"Luar do sertão" (Sertão moonlight), 113–14

lundu: Casa Edison recordings of, 78; characteristics and sounds of, 19–21, 95; stereotypes associated with, 22–23; term of, 257n14; varieties of, 21–22, 258n17; whites singing, 90–91

Luso-Brazilians, 21

Macaco É Outro (Monkey is the other one, group), 98, 122

Machado, Pinheiro, 59, 250

macumba, 156, 158, 163. *See also* candomblé practices

Macunaíma (M. Andrade), 152–53

Madame Satã (João Francisco dos Santos), 235–36

maestros de assobio (whistling maestros), 159, 161

Magalhães, Paulo de, 143

malandragem (art of being a malandro): authentic vs. professional, 240; of Batista, 222–23; brazen displays of, 249; capadócios as precursors to, 251–52; of Donga, 243; of João da Baiana, *35*; of Madame Satã, 235–36; of Marçal, *142*; meaning of, 260n7; of Moreno, 86–87, 141, 143, 144; as natural tendency, 240; of Neves, 80, 82–83, 139, 140, 143, 144; predicament in, 222; as resistance, 82; sambistas linked to, 34; songs about, 139–40, 143; as thing of the past, 220–21; violence linked to, 62–63

O Malho (newspaper): contributor to, 200; on Moreno and murder-suicide, 86, *87*, 87–89, *88*; status of, 270n72

mambembes, use of term, 189

Mangione, Vicente, 202, 222

Mangue (red-light district): maxixe (dance music) in, 91, 271nn81–82; preferred actor of, 68; religious ceremony in, 152; underworld of, 97

Mangueira (favela): characteristics of, 133; musicians from, 119; samba school named for, 127; song tribute to happy lifestyle in, 139

Mano Décio da Viola (Décio Antônio Carlos), 118, 119, 120, 122, 128

Manual de namorados (*Sweethearts' Handbook*, Neves), 84

Marçal, Armando, *142*, 201

marche aux flambeaux (torchlight march): description of, 170–71; hopes in, 180–81, 226; media coverage of, 173; support for, 172, 176–77

Marrom ("Brown"; Luís Correia de Barros), 126, 127

Martins, Herivelto, 218

Martins, Lindaura, 63–64

Martins, Roberto, 139

masculinity: behavior and celebration of, 139, 143–44; Black Power and, 238; brazen and unabashed displays of, 84, 249; challenges to definitions of, 245–46;

música cafona, 227, 229, 230

música de barbeiros (barber music), use of term, 28. *See also* barber-musicians

Música Popular Brasileira (Brazilian popular music): "authenticity" deployed against, 238–41; differences in, 230–31; genres included in, 229; thought in, 235

music genres: Casa Edison preferences in, 77, *78*; fluidity of, 11; hierarchies of, 60–61; tresillo form in, 95, 96, 271n2; *specific*: barber-music, 26-2729, 32, 259nn45–46; batuque, 18, 34, *78*; cançonetas, 78; fandango, 31–32; jazz, 105, 107, 273n38, 296n41; maxixe, 91, 271nn81–82; modinhas, 78; música cafona, 227, 229, 230; nossa música, 95, 105, 114–15; rock 'n' roll, 227; tango, 95; tropicália, 227, 229. *See also* bossa nova; *choro*; *lundu*; *Música Popular Brasileira*; samba; soul music; traditional music

musicians: call for financial support for serious, 161, 163; postcolonial blues of, 174–77; Vargas and appeal of, 169–71, 172, 176–77. *See also specific organizations and individuals*

musicians, African-descendant: approach to studying, 9–11; backgrounds and connections of, 118–20; Carnival clubs and, 58–59; community milieu of, 4–8, *5*; co-workers as, 264n51; freedom of, 1–3; informal interactions with police, 49, 64; liminal spaces of, 249; musical diversity of, 11, 76–77; popular names of, 253n1; power brokers vs., 77; racial and cultural challenges for, 164–67, 283n75; religion and music linked for, 120–21; Rio's diatribe against, 83–84; SBAT's implications for, 192–93; self-identification of, 45–48; work and occupations of, 26–29, 43–48, 77, 214–17, 251–52, 298n5. *See also* authorship; definitional projects; Direitos Autorais; discursive project; historical context; ownership; punishment paradigm; reinventions; socioeconomic

context; *and specific organizations and individuals*

music market: approach to studying, 13–14; controversies in, 1–2, 244–45; good vs. bad music in, 159–61, 163–64; growth of, 71, 171–72, 178–79, 202, 205, 229; as "infected" with samba, 158; mediators in, 136–44, 248; Oliveira and popular entertainment as, 66–69; pistolão (letter of recommendation) vs. concursos (competitive exams) in, 278n77; race, authorship, and success in, 77–79; "rich blacks" in, 80–85; strategies in, summarized, 91–93; Tio Faustino's claim to instrument designs in context of, 138, 155–57, 247; Vagalume on theft of music and lyrics in, 128–29. *See also* advertisements and marketing; Casa Edison; commercialization and commodification; Figner, Fred (Frederico); historical context; professionalization; recordings and record industry; socioeconomic context

músicos ambulantes (street musicians), 83–84

music venues: author's rights payments withheld by, 200; censorship and policing of, 183–85; challenges of collecting from, 210, 213–14; fiscalizadores' attempts to monitor, 204. *See also* Carnival; circuses; festivals; religious activities, African-derived; theater

Mussolini, Benito, 174

A Nação (newspaper), 134–35, 278n67

Na prisão (Barbosa), 50

Na roda do samba (In the samba circle, Vagalume): on Alves, 129–30, 132; dedication of, 120, 131; on Donga, 128, 131, 132; on music industry problems, 128–29, 189; predictions in, 169; on *real* samba (and race), 130–32; on samba's origins, 128; on societal inequality, 132–34; structure of, 127; on Tio Faustino's instruments, 138

reconstitutions of, 123; tours of, 105–6, 107, 111–13; tuxedos of, 141. *See also* Donga; Pixinguinha

Old Guard (Grupo da Guarda Velha), 123–24, 156, 231, 281n36

"Olha ele, cuidado" (Careful, keep an eye on him), 122

Oliveira, Angenor (or Agenor) de (Cartola), 119, 139

Oliveira, Aristides Júlio de, 123

Oliveira, Benjamin de: alleged son of, 277n64; background of, 66–67; on destiny "to flee," 67, 85; entertainment career of, 67–69, 134, 193; marginalization of, 247; media connections of, 125; as mediator, 136, 137; as SBAT member, 185; writings of, 68–69

Oliveira, Bonfíglio de, 117, 118, 120

Oliveira, Florinda Grandino de (Linda Batista), 220–21

Oliveira, Luís de, 104, 272n33

Oliveira, Mário Benjamin de, 277n64

Oliveira, Milton de (King of the Caititus), 205

Oliveira, Paulo Benjamin de. *See* Paulo da Portela

omelê (friction drum), 138, 155–57, 169

Onze, Oxunã da Praça (Henrique Assumano Mina do Brasil), 120, 131

"O pé de anjo" (The angel's foot), 122

Ópera do malandro (musical), 240

"Ora vejam só" (Hey, just look at that), 122

Ordem dos Músicos do Brasil (Order of Brazilian Musicians), 229–30, 233

Orquestra Afro-Brasileira, 255n21

orthography, explained, x

Oswaldo Cruz (neighborhood), 134

"Our Music" (*nossa música*), 95, 105, 114–15

ownership: meanings of, 95; of rights to instrument designs, 138, 155–57, 247; struggles over, 114–15; women's difficulties in claiming, 124–25. *See also* authorship; Direitos Autorais; intellectual property rights

O Paiz (newspaper): on Almeida, 97; on Moreno and murder-suicide, 86–87, 88, 89; musician's feting of, 125; status of, 270n72

Palmié, Stephan, 281n34

Palmieri, Jacó, 104

Palmieri, Raul, 104

pan-Africanism, 154–55

Pan American Union, 164–65

Pandeirista Infernal. See Alfredo (Alfredo José de Alcântara)

pandeiros (hand percussion instruments): alleged police confiscation of, 32, *33*, 59; later narratives of, 249–51, *250*; prohibitions on, 32, 34

Paranhos, José Maria da Silva, Jr. (Baron of Rio Branco), 53–54

Parés, Luis, 281n39

Paris (France), Batutas in, 107, 111–13

Partido Trabalhista Nacional (National Labor Party, PTN), 136

Pasquim (periodical), 235–36

A Pátria (newspaper), 135

patronage: Afro-Brazilian musicians' role in, 118; as component of "civilizing missions," 24–26; connections via informal, 59–61; continued importance of, 3; letters of recommendation and individual, 278n77; leveraging tactic for state, 184–85; by Portuguese royal court, 23–24, 258n28

Paulo da Portela (Paulo Benjamin de Oliveira): action plans and nationalism of, 135–36; arrest of, 47; on author's rights, 144–45; death of, 144; malandro style of, 135, 141, *142*, 143; as mediator, 138; name and parentage of, 277n64; press interactions of, 134–35; samba composition contests won by, 135; samba school of, 134, 166, 197; uplift project of, 166

pau para toda obra (jacks-of-all-trades), 29. *See also* barber-musicians

"Pé de mulata" (*Mulata*'s foot), 143

Oliveira as, 67–68; censorship and, 184; competitions for, 185; De Chocolat as, 124; popular press and, 7; in SBAT, 14, 173–74, 183, 193; Vagalume as, 126. *See also* theater

police: anti-vice campaigns of, 34–35; call for action against uncivilized, 161, 163; Carnival involvement of, 54–59, 197–98, 266n90, 284n89; clerk's records of (folha obscura), 40, 48; daily record books (livros de ocorrência) of, 49; discretionary powers in prostitution cases, 45; Donga on repression by, 242–43; gendered silences in records of, 61–62; informal interactions with musicians, 49, 64; informal patronage and, 59–60; jogo do bicho ticket sellers' relations with, 50–51; monetary transactions as focus of, 52–53; "Pelo telefone" lyrics on, 98–100, 99; show houses monitored by, 183. *See also* anti-vagrancy measures; Arquivo Nacional; Casa de Detenção; censorship; punishment paradigm

policing and social control: attempt to postpone Carnival, 53–54; censorship linked to policing of author's rights, 183–85; of drum circles, 18–19; as everywhere and nowhere, 246–47; mechanisms of, 37–38; motives underlying, 13; *Reagir!* campaign and, 165; SBAT's role in, 183–85, 192–93; UBC's role in, 210–14. *See also* anti-vagrancy measures; censorship; Direitos Autorais; police

politics: binary of culture vs., 256n28; changes summarized (1888–1960s), 12; music commercialization linked to, 239; parties abolished under Vargas, 197, 199–200; samba as separate from, 231, 238–41; shift from monarchy to republic, 2–3. *See also* corporatist state structure; racial democracy; Vargas, Getúlio

poor people: anti-vagrancy measures deployed against, 39; appeal to state for help, 170; musicians' clothing as distinction from, 141; workers' organizing

to distinguish themselves from, 42. See also *gente da roda*

popular entertainment: "art music" vs., 112–13; derided but appropriated, 160–61, 163; misogynist song lyrics in, 90; Neves's success in, 80–85; Oliveira's role in transforming, 67–69; struggles around, 13–14. *See also* Carnival; circuses; recordings and record industry; theater

popular music. See *Música Popular Brasileira*

Portela Recreational Union and Samba School (Grêmio Recreativo Escola de Samba Portela), 134, 166, 197

Porto Alegre, Manuel de Araújo, 25–26, 29

Portugal, law against theater renovation into movie houses, 176

Portugal, Marcos, 25

postcolonial blues, 174–77

Praça Onze (Rio), 37, 152–53

Praça Tiradentes (Rio), 217

Prazeres, Heitor dos: authorship dispute with Sinhô, 121–22; background of, 119; on Cidade Nova area, 254n13; malandro style of, 142; as SBAT-DC member, 201; Vagalume's view of, 131

Prazeres, Primitivo Rimus Rodrigues (K. Peta), 126

Prescott, Frederick M., 70–71

Pretinho, Príncipe (José Luiz da Costa; Little Black Prince), 199

prior censorship, 184, 203, 246

professionalization: authenticity vs., 240; behavior expected in, 142–43; clothing as reflecting, 140–41, 142; divisive projects in, 192–93; meaning of process of, 8–9; musical style as reflecting, 141–43; musician-barbers as baseline in, 26–29; reflections on process of, 244–45; state organization and, 228–29; studies of, 8–9, 256n29; UBC's depiction of, 214–17. *See also* commercialization and commodification; music market; *and specific organizations* prostitutes: defense against vagrancy, 44–45, 47; labels for, 48; rights claimed by, 264n49; terminology for, 89

PTN (Partido Trabalhista Nacional; National Labor Party), 136

punishment paradigm: allegations and narratives of, 31–36, *33*, 49, 64–65, 249–52, *250*; approach to studying, 13; arrest records contradicting, 167–68; authorship of "Pelo telefone" in context of, 242–43; definition of, 13, 32; function of, 261n14; questions about, 32–34, *33*, 48; silences fostered by narratives based in, 61–65

"quasi-author" concept, 92–93, 271n84

Queiróz, Geraldo, 224

Querosene (morro), 133

race: in ABCA vs. SBAT-DC, 201; amalgamation of, 232, 296n22; apprehensions about, 90–91; authenticity linked to, 163; authorship, marketing strategy, and, 77–79; Batutas as pretos, 107; defloramento cases and, 62–64; high vs. low art marked by, 189–90; Le Bon's ideas about, 109; in M. Andrade's music history, 149–53; mediation function of, 138; murder-suicide as highlighting, 86–90, *87*, *88*; public identity vs., 85; restructuring of patriarchy in context of, 279–80n101; reversal of assumptions, 139; role in authorship disputes, 123; São Paulo "exceptionalism" and, 188–89; translating terminology of, ix; tropes of, 20; tropes of music and, 235–36, 238–41; Vagalume's *Na roda do samba* and, 127–34; in Villa-Lobos's map, *147*, 148. *See also* whitening projects

racial democracy: concept of, 12, 256–57n36; defense of, 238–39; hierarchies and differences mapped in, 163–64; paradox underlying, 151–52; "proof" of, 234–35

"racial soul" concept, 108, 109

racism: authorship of "Pelo telefone" in context of, 242–43; black workers' struggles against, 41–43; of foreigners in Brazil, 25; reinforced notion of lack of, 234–35; segregation crystallized in Rio, 227; soul music's challenge to, 230–31; story of samba's repression and, 36

O Radical (newspaper), 134

radio broadcasts and stations: Batutas and, 108; choro revival in, 231–32; commercial phase for, 171–72; music decline linked to, 159, 161, 163; payment of author's rights disputes of, 286n32; SBAT's demands of, 185; white dominance in, 129, 172

Rádio Nacional, 129

radios, 66, 161, *162*, 172

Ramos, Artur, 156

Rancho Paladinos Japoneses, 103

ranchos. See Carnival *ranchos*

Rangel, Lúcio, 144

"Rapaz folgado" (Idle boy), 140

"Rato! Rato!" (Rat! Rat!), 73, *75*, 76

Raulino, Otto, 55

RCA Victor label, 69, 156, 205, 232

Reagir! campaign: ideas underlying, 158–61, 163–64; surveillance projects and, 165

Rebouças, André, 85, 270n68

recordings and record industry: author's rights societies and, 223; Brazilian factory for manufacturing, 70, 267n15; circus background of early performers on, 67; contracts and earnings in, 73, *74*, *75*, 76–77, 268n28; emergence of, 66, 69–70; first Brazilian sound recording, 69, 71; good vs. bad in, 159; growth of, 229; higher fidelity in, 171–72; inequities in relationships in, 70–73, 136–37, 172, 202–3; Law 496 on, 182; organization focused on collecting payments from, 224; patent rights to two-sided records, 70–72. *See also* Casa Edison; gramophones and phonographs; music market

record players, 229

"Rei dos meus sambas" (King of my sambas), 122

reinventions (post–golden age era): of Donga, 241–43; identities in, 15; legal context of, 228–29; musical ideas and, 229–31; of Pixinguinha, 231–35; political context of, 227–28; tropes of race and music in, 235–36, 238–41

Reis, Antônio Rufino dos, 134

Reis, Mário, 165

"Rei vagabundo" (Vagabond king), 139

religious activities, African-derived: acceptable forms of, 51–52; barber bands and, 27; disputes and competition over, 120; feitiçaria, 19, 51–52, 153, 190–91; in M. Andrade's novel, 152–53; at musical gatherings, 60–61; music and journalism linked to, 118–21; police postures toward, 51; white fascination with and fear of, 19–20. *See also* candomblé practices; *lundu*

Renan (cronista), 111

Revista Civilização Brasileira (periodical), 229

Revista Policial (periodical), 183

Revolta da Armada (1893), 126

rhythm: "cerebral," 235; emergence of new types, 227–28; expected disappearance of African, 164; origins of, *147*, 148; primitive people linked to, 150–51; syncopated, 12, 22–23, 95–96, 233, 258n22

Ribeiro, Alberto, 199, 215

Ribeiro, Iveta, 187

rights. *See* Direitos Autorais; intellectual property rights

rights, black workers' struggles for, 41–43

Rio Branco, Baron of (José Maria da Silva Paranhos Júnior), 53–54

Rio de Janeiro: Bahia distinguished from, 121, 275n16; barber-musicians of, 26–29; batuque banned in, 34; circuses in, 67–68; cost of living in, 42, 55, 76, 269n32; diversity of sights and sounds in, 17–20; Frank's "middling groups" in, 260n61; map of, *16*; "missing middle" of, 5–8, 248; most successful black performers in, 80; movie vs. theater audi-

ences in, 176; population of, 4–5, *5*, 121; prices and salaries compared in, *75*; racial segregation crystallized in, 227; radios per household in, 172; slavery's earlier decline in, 3–4. *See also* historical context; labor market; socioeconomic context

Rio Novo (now Avaré), 31–32

Robertson, J. P., 19–20

Rocha, Casemiro Gonçalves da, 73, *75*

rock 'n' roll, 227

Rodrigues, Esther Maria, 134

Rodrigues, Raimundo Nina, 51–52, 148–49, 164

Roldán, Amadeo, 112

Romero, Silvio, 164

Rosa, Abadie Farias: Hitler's laws praised by, 173–74; on intellectual property rights, 176; marche aux flambeaux and, 177; UBC's honoring of, 201–2; in Vagalume's roda, 131

Rosa, Noel: on Aracy Almeida's performance, 139; arrested on deflowering charges, 47, 63–64; excluded from Vagalume's roda, 130; as SBAT member, 179; songs composed by, 139–40

Rosas, Alexandrino, 210

Royal Chapel (Capela Real), 23, 25–26, 29

A Rua (newspaper), 135

Rugendas, Johann Mortiz, 258n17

Rui, Evaldo, 219–20

Said, Edward, 138–39

Saludos Amigos (film), 116

Salvador: barber-musicians of, 26, 28; batuque banned in, 34; candomblé association in, 51; race- and ethnic-based organizations in, 5; radios per household in, 172

samba: as apolitical, 231, 238–41; caixa de fósforos (box of matches) symbol of, 221, 294n75; changing musical context of, 227–28; definitions of, 108; emergence of, 1, 11–12; first national conference on, 233–34, 235; influences on

literacy of, 166–67, 168; mediator for, 137, 231, 246; race of, 129; samba school founded by, 166–67; as SBAT member, 179

Silva, João Batista da, 60–61

Silva, José Barbosa da. *See* Sinhô

Silva, Marília T. Barboza da, 272n24

Silva, Orlando, 141

Silva, Patápio, 255n21

Sinhô (José Barbosa da Silva; "King of Samba"): authorship disputes of, 121–23; favela song of, 133, 139; media connections of, 125; "Pelo telefone" lyrics and, 102; religious beliefs of, 120; as SBAT member, 179; Vagalume and, 126, 131; *Weco*'s dismissal of work by, 160–61

Sinzig, Pedro, 160

slavery: abolition of (1888), 2–4, 37–38; "anomie" as legacy of, 238–39, 297n42; legal vestiges after, 37–38, 149, 262n16; Neves's terminology as referencing, 84–85; paradox of, 13; in punishment paradigm narrative, 36

slaves: activities and music of, 17–20, 151, 153–54; clothing of, 220–21; earnings from music of, 26–27; as "escrava de estimação," 67; Free Womb Law and, 4, 38; musical instruction for, 23; number of, 4, 5; origins of, 21; white expectations for, 164

slaves, former: anti-vagrancy measures deployed against, 36–41; band members belonging to, 28; labor struggles of, 41–43. *See also* Afro-Brazilians

Sociedade Brasileira de Autores, Compositores e Editores/Escritores de Música (Brazilian Society of Musical Authors, Composers, and Label Owners/Writers, SBACEM): author's rights collection and distribution by, 222–23; Carnival income of, 292n35; competition of, 202; ECAD's relation to, 244; name change of, 291n25; origins of, 201, 225; pensions from, 241; UBC's cooperation with, 212. See also *Boletim* (SBACEM periodical)

Sociedade Brasileira de Autores Teatrais (Society of Brazilian Theater Authors, SBAT): approach to studying, 14; author's rights collection and distribution by, 171, *178*, 178–79, *206*; author's rights pamphlet of, 203–5; Chiquinha Gonzaga honored by, 185–87; Composers' Department of, 198, 201; criticisms against, 198–200; gendered rhetoric of, 187; hierarchy of, 177–78, 198, 201, 217; high vs. low art marked by, 189–90; intellectual property rights concerns of, 175–76; membership of, 173, 179, 185, 187; name of, 257n37; nationalism of, 174–75; origins narrative of, 174; police censors' relation to, 179–81; policing of author's rights and censorship role of, 183–85, 192–93; São Paulo branch of, 188–89; sócio filiado category of, 179; theater as focus of, 176–77, 194; UBC agreement with, 202; utilidade pública designation for, 182–83. See also *Boletim* (SBAT periodical)

Sociedade de Resistência dos Trabalhadores em Trapiche e Café (Warehouse Workers and Coffee Porters' Resistance Society), 42

Società Italiana di Fonotipia (La Scala opera label), 70, 71

socioeconomic context (nineteenth century): acceptable practices in, 52–53; ambiguous place of musicians in, 43, 45–48; black labor struggles in, 41–43; Carnival's role in, 53–59; gendered silences in, 61–65; importance of, 12–13; story of samba's repression in, 32–36; vice and witchcraft in, 48–53. *See also* anti-vagrancy measures; historical context; patronage

sonic technology: advances in, 13–14; electromagnetic recordings, 171–72; transformations in, 66, 69–70. *See also* gramophones and phonographs; radio broadcasts and stations; recordings and record industry soul music: audiences and politics of, 230–31; commercialization and politics of, 239; emergence of, 227; popularity and influence of, 229; as "too black," 238

sound reproduction. *See* recordings and record industry; sonic technology

Sousa, Joaquim Luiz de, 142

Souto, Israel, 201, 202, 203, 211, 225

spalla, of Oito Batutas, 104, 272n34

Spinelli Circus, 67–68

stereotypes and caricatures: of Africa and rhythm, *147*, 148; in "anomie" of blacks notion, 238–39, 297n42; Batutas' use of, 110–11; of black artists, 116–17; in blackface performances, 23, 90–91, 220–21, 258n25; of blackness and syncopation, 22–23; black workers' struggles against, 41–43; in Carnival costumes, 220, 225–26; cartoons of, *88*, 270–71n80; effects of embracing, 245–47; of favelados and blackness, 139; of idleness and irresponsibility, 37–38, 244–45; of natural happiness and music, 28; in origins narrative, 24; of Pixinguinha's flute playing, 157–58; of resigned and happy type, 109–10; of "samba," 60. *See also* anti-vagrancy measures

Stokowski, Leopold, 136–37

Stowe, Harriet Beecher, 220, 294n72

street musicians (*músicos ambulantes*), 83–84

submundo (underworld): gambling in, 50–51, 53, 265n67; invention of, 49–50; maxixe (dance music) in, 91, 271nn81–82; music associated with, 45

surveillance. *See* anti-vagrancy measures; censorship; policing and social control

Sweet, James, 257n14

Sweethearts' Handbook (Manual de namorados, Neves), 84

Syncopated Band (U.S.), 111

syncopation, 12, 22–23, 95–96, 233, 258n22

Tabarin (French performer), 68

tango, 95

Teatro Casino, 184

teatro de revista, 67–68, 129, 176

Teatro Lyrico, 108

Teatro Municipal, 105, 191–92

Teatro Rio Branco, 104

technological advances: warnings about impact of, 102, 128, 172. *See also* movie houses; sonic technology

Teixeira, Humberto, 205

Teixeira, Patrício, 143, 144

Telefunken radios, 161, *162*

television, emergence of, 240

Tenentes do Diabo (organization), 104

Terceira Pretoria Criminal, 262n27. *See also* Santana and Santo Antônio (Rio police districts)

"Teu cabelo não nega" (Your hair doesn't lie), 182

theater: artistas and managers' relations in, 179–80; censorship and policing of, 183–85; decline of, 176–77; difficulties in claiming ownership of performance in, 124–25; increased state oversight of, 181; lack of state support for, 174; music's disparity with, 177–78; proceeds from performances at, *178*, 178–79; samba distinguished from, 185; as synthesis, 187–88. *See also* playwrights

theater companies: artistas defined in, 179–80; censorship and policing of, 184; increased state oversight of, 181; taxes paid by, 176; traveling, 189–90

Thompson, Daniella, 278nn73–74

Tia Ciata. *See* Almeida, Hilária Batista de

Tia Perciliana (Perciliana Maria Constança), 59, 62

Timponi, Miguel, 201–2

Tinhorão, José Ramos: on barber-musicians, 259n45; on bossa nova, 229–30, 235; on jazz, 296n41; on samba as apolitical, 239; samba conference role of, 233; on "social promiscuity," 238

Tio Faustino. *See* Conceição, Faustino Pedro da

Todámerica Música (label), 207

Todd, Ralph, 207
Tomás, João, 104
totalitarianism, 173–74
trademarks, 123–24, 138
traditional music: appropriations of, 160–61, 164–65; authorship questions and, 94–95; collecting recordings of, 149; derision of, 229–30; Figner's acquisition of rights to, 72; "Pelo telefone" origins in, 98–100; Pixinguinha and Donga's hopes to protect, 281n36
tresillo (musical paradigm), 95, 96, 271n2. *See also* syncopation
A Tribuna (newspaper), 126
tropicália, 227, 229
Trota, Frederico, 197, 290n13
Tute (Artur de Souza Nascimento), 104, 272n30

UBC, See União Brasileira de Compositores
UES (União das Escolas de Sambas; Union of Samba Schools), 196–98
ufanismo (hyperpatriotic love), 227
umbanda practice, 51
umbigadas (belly blows), 21, 258n16
Uncle Tom's Cabin (Stowe), 220, 294n72
underworld. See *submundo*
União Brasileira de Compositores (Union of Brazilian Composers, UBC): administrative and Community Chest costs of, 207–9, 216, 247; Afro-Brazilian strategies deployed against, 222–25; author's rights collection and distribution by, 205, *206*, 207, *208–9*, *210–11*, *212–13*, 222–23; author's rights laws and, 202–3; author's rights pamphlet of, 203–5; Creative Commons controversy and, 1–2, 244–45; early success and goals of, 199–201; ECAD's relation to, 244; expansion and connections fostered by, 205–7, 210–11; hierarchies and difference in, 217–22, 246; international expansion of, 207, *208–9*; limits of, 14–15, 241, 247; men honored by, 201–2; policing role

of, 210–14; SBAT agreement with, 202; state organization as trumping, 228–29; summary of, 225–26; utilidade pública designation for, 202; white dominance in, 215–17. See also *Boletim Social* (UBC periodical)
União das Escolas de Sambas (Union of Samba Schools, UES), 196–98
União dos Empregados do Comércio, 42–43
United States: black musician of, in Brazil, 207; black orchestra from, 111; commercial radio in, 171; Copyright Act of (1909), 72; Jim Crow policies in, 152; stereotypes of African Americans in, 297n42; Zoot Suiters of, 298n7
University of São Paulo, 227, 238–39, 295n2
utilidades públicas (public utilities or entities): ABCA as, 200; law to circumscribe powers of, 291n27; SBAT as, 182–83; state connection to, 9, 14; UBC as, 202; white dominance in, 9, 215–17

Vagalume (Firefly; Francisco Guimarães): appeal to SBAT, 198, 217; on authorship dispute, 121; on Donga, 3, 128, 131, 132, 243, 248; on Neves, 82; nickname of, 126; on Pedro Ernesto, 196; on "Pelo telefone," 98, 101–3, 115, 132; on people of the circle (of samba), 127, 130–34, 160. See also *Na roda do samba*
"Vagando" (Wander), 141–42
vagrants: definitions of, 37, 52–53; flâneur as romantic version of, 50; jogo linked to, 265n67; songs about, 140. See also anti-vagrancy measures
Vai Como Pode (Come as You Can). See Grêmio Recreativo Escola de Samba Portela
valorizations: of Afro-Brazilian culture, 49–50, 149; of authentic blackness, 235–36; of Batutas' pastoral style, 132; of racial identity, 26; of samba's diversity, 234; of syncopation, 233; of "traditional" cultural values, 229; of work, 211